OCEANS LAW AND POLICY DEPARTMENT
CENTER FOR NAVAL WARFARE STUDIES
NAVAL WAR COLLEGE
NEWPORT, RI 02841-5010

WAR, AGGRESSION AND
SELF-DEFENCE

This new edition is fully revised and updated following the Gulf War, the fighting in the former Yugoslavia and the political changes that have occurred with the ending of the Cold War. The book re-examines the topics of war, aggression and self-defence, and includes discussion on the legal nature of war, peace treaties, neutrality, the contemporary prohibition on the use of force, crimes against peace, war crimes and state-sponsored terrorism. Related issues, such as collective security and the use of force short of war, are also addressed. Reflecting the recent increase in the use of force and counterforce at a regional level, special attention is given to the respective roles of the Security Council, the General Assembly and the International Court of Justice in the developing 'New World Order'.

WAR, AGGRESSION AND SELF-DEFENCE

by

YORAM DINSTEIN

Professor of International Law,
Tel-Aviv University

Member, Institut de Droit International

SECOND EDITION

GROTIUS PUBLICATIONS

CAMBRIDGE
UNIVERSITY PRESS

Published by the Press Syndicate of the University of Cambridge
The Pitt Building, Trumpington Street, Cambridge CB2 1RP
40 West 20th Street, New York, NY 10011-4211, USA
10 Stamford Road, Oakleigh, Melbourne 3166, Australia

First published 1988
Second edition 1994
Reprinted 1995

Transferred to digital printing 1999

Printed in the United Kingdom by Biddles Short Run Books

A catalogue record for this book is available from the British Library

Library of Congress cataloguing in publication data applied for

ISBN 0 521 46526 5 hardback, second edition
(ISBN 0 949009 15 6 hardback, first edition)

CN

to

MY MOTHER AND FATHER

CONTENTS

SUMMARY

CONTENTS

OUTLINE

INTRODUCTION TO THE
SECOND EDITION

This is a completely revised and updated edition of a book originally published in 1988. In the few years that have elapsed since then, the world has changed dramatically. To mention only some of the highlights: the "cold war" has ended, the USSR has collapsed, the map of Europe has been redrawn time and again, and the Gulf War has been waged (*sans* termination at the time of writing). Yet, it is hyperbolic to maintain that a "New World Order" has already been established. Whereas the fears of a global cataclysm have considerably abated, the level of force and counterforce used regionally - in the Gulf, in the Balkans, in the former Soviet Union, and in other trouble spots - has reached new heights.

The outbreak of the Gulf War could not fail to have left its marks on international law. Each time that the community of nations has to contend with flagrant aggression, the *de facto* response leaves normative (*de jure*) footprints in its wake. In broader terms, every major war becomes a crucible in which the *jus ad bellum* (just like the *jus in bello*) is tested and forged. In the particular circumstances of the Gulf War, the most striking outcome has been the partial rejuvenation of the Security Council.

This edition reflects the far from negligible legal literature sprouted by recent developments. Account has also been taken of the latest studies of the International Law Commission, as well as some additional comments about the 1986 Judgment of the International Court of Justice in the *Nicaragua* case (which remains the most significant judicial pronouncement on the subject of self-defence). It is all too clear that the issues of war, aggression and self-defence command growing attention by international lawyers and laymen alike.

Tel Aviv, 1 March 1993

FROM THE INTRODUCTION TO THE FIRST EDITION

War has plagued *homo sapiens* since the dawn of recorded history and, at almost any particular moment in the annals of the species, it appears to be raging in at least a portion of the globe (frequently, in many places at one and the same time).

War has consistently been a, perhaps the, most brutal human endeavour. If for no other reason, the subject of war should be examined and reexamined continuously. There is a tendency today to avoid the use of the term "war", regarding it as arcane and largely superseded by the phrase "international armed conflict". However, apart from the fact that the expression "war" - appearing as it does in many international instruments and constituting an integral part of a host of customary international legal norms - is far from outdated, a general reference to international armed conflicts ignores the important theoretical as well as practical distinctions existing between wars and others uses of inter-State force (short of war).

This book is divided into three parts. The first part deals with questions like: What is war? When does it commence and terminate? Is there a twilight zone between war and peace? What is the difference between peace treaties, armistice agreements and cease-fires? Where can war be waged and what is the meaning of neutrality? These problems, with their numerous ramifications, seriously impact on the substance of international law.

The focus of the discussion in the second part is the contemporary prohibition of the use of force in international relations. The current state of the law is put in relief against the background of the past. The meaning of aggression, as defined by a consensus Resolution of the United Nations General Assembly in 1974, is explored. The construct of crimes against peace, which is part of the *Nuremberg* legacy, is set out. Some controversial implications of the illegality and criminality of wars of aggression are fathomed, with a view to establishing the true dimensions of the transformation undergone by modern international law in this domain.

The third part wrestles with the complex topics of self-defence and collective security. In the practice of States, most legal disputes concerning the use of force hinge on the alleged exercise of the individual or collective right of self-defence. In fact, more often than not, self-defence is invoked by both antagonists simultaneously. The question when, and under what conditions, self-defence may legitimately take place is crucial. In this context, the scope of an armed attack – giving rise to self-defence – is investigated, and a differentiation is made between armed attacks from and by a State. The functions discharged by the Security Council in the evaluation of self-defence are probed. Other pertinent matters relate to the modality of self-defence, e.g., can armed reprisals or forcible measures for the protection of nationals abroad be harmonized with the law of the UN Charter? Collective self-defence comes under a special scrutiny, and the infrastructure of the various types of treaties in which it is usually embedded is analyzed.

Collective security, as an institutionalized use of force by the international community, is still an elusive concept in reality. The original mechanism devised by the Charter has yet to be activated, although some imperfect substitutes (principally, peacekeeping forces) have evolved. An important subject of discourse is the relative powers – actual and potential – of the Security Council, the General Assembly and (in the light of the *Nicaragua* Judgment) even the International Court of Justice.

TABLE OF CASES

TABLE OF TREATIES

ABBREVIATIONS

A.C.	Appeal Cases
A.D.	Annual Digest and Reports of Public International Law Cases
A.F.D.I.	Annuaire Français de Droit International
A.I.D.I.	Annuaire de l'Institut de Droit International
A.J.I.L.	American Journal of International Law
A.L.R.	Alberta Law Review
A.P.S.R.	American Political Science Review
A.S.J.G.	Acta Scandinavica Juris Gentium
A.U.J.I.L.P.	American University Journal of International Law and Policy
A.Y.B.I.L.	Australian Year Book of International Law
Amer.U.L.R.	American University Law Review
Ar.V.	Archiv des Völkerrechts
Auck.U.L.R.	Auckland University Law Review
B.C.I.C.L.R.	Boston College International Comparative Law Review
B.F.S.P.	British and Foreign State Papers
B.J.I.L.	Brooklyn Journal of International Law
B.Y.B.I.L.	British Year Book of International Law
C.J.T.L.	Columbia Journal of Transnational Law
C.T.S.	Consolidated Treaty Series
C.W.I.L.J.	California Western International Law Journal
C.W.R.J.I.L.	Case Western Reserve Journal of International Law
C.Y.I.L.	Canadian Yearbook of International Law
Cam.L.J.	Cambridge Law Journal
Col.L.R.	Columbia Law Review
Cor.L.R.	Cornell Law Review
D.J.C.I.L.	Duke Journal of Comparative and International Law

D.J.I.L.P.	Denver Journal of International Law and Policy
D.L.J.	Denver Law Journal
D.S.B.	Department of State Bulletin
E.J.I.L.	European Journal of International Law
E.P.I.L.	Encyclopedia of Public International Law
F.	Federal
G.J.I.C.L.	Georgia Journal of International and Comparative Law
G.Y.I.L.	German Yearbook of International Law
H.I.C.L.R.	Hastings International and Comparative Law Review
H.I.L.J.	Harvard International Law Journal
H.J.I.L.	Houston Journal of International Law
Hague Conventions	*The Hague Conventions and Declarations of 1899 and 1907* (3rd ed., by J. B. Scott, 1918)
Har.L.R.	Harvard Law Review
Hof.L.R.	Hofstra Law Review
I.C.J. Rep.	Reports of the International Court of Justice
I.C.L.Q.	International and Comparative Law Quarterly
I.J.I.L.	Indian Journal of International Law
I.L.C. Ybk	Yearbook of the International Law Commission
I.L.M.	International Legal Materials
I.L.Q.	International Law Quarterly
I.L.R.	International Law Reports
I.M.T.	Trial of Major War Criminals before the International Militry Tribunal ("Blue Series")
I.R.R.C.	International Review of the Red Cross
I.Y.H.R.	Israel Yearbook on Human Rights
Int.Aff.	International Affairs
Int.Con.	International Conciliation
Int.Law.	International Lawyer

Int.Leg.	*International Legislation* (M. O. Hudson ed., 1931-50)
Int.Rel.	International Relations
Io.L.R.	Iowa Law Review
Is.L.R.	Israel Law Review
J.I.L.E.	Journal of International Law and Economics
J.Y.I.L.	Jewish Yearbook of International Law
Jur.R.	Juridical Review
Ken.L.J.	Kentucky Law Journal
L.C.P.	Law and Contemporary Problems
L.J.I.L.	Leiden Journal of International Law
L.N.T.S.	League of Nations Treaty Series
L.Q.R.	Law Quarterly Review
L.R.T.W.C.	Law Reports of Trials of War Criminals
Mar.J.I.L.T.	Maryland Journal of International Law and Trade
Mer.L.R.	Mercer Law Review
Mich.J.I.L.	Michigan Journal of International Law
Mich.L.R.	Michigan Law Review
Mil.L.R.	Military Law Review
Mod.L.R.	Modern Law Review
N.M.T.	Trials of War Criminals before the Nuremberg Military Tribunals under Control Council Law No. 10 ("Green Series")
N.T.I.R.	Nederlands Tijdschrift voor International Recht
N.Y.I.L.	Netherlands Yearbook of International Law
N.Y.U.J.I.L.P.	New York University Journal of International Law and Politics
P.A.S.I.L.	Proceedings of the American Society of International Law
P.S.Q.	Political Science Quarterly

P.Y.I.L.	Pace Yearbook of International Law
Peace Treaties	*Major Peace Treaties of Modern History 1648-1967* (F. L. Israel ed., 1967)
R.B.D.I.	Revue Belge de Droit International
R.C.A.D.I.	Recueil des Cours de l'Académie de Droit International
R.D.S.C.	Resolutions and Decisions of the Security Council
R.E.D.I.	Revue Egyptienne de Droit International
R.G.A.	Resolutions Adopted by the General Assembly
R.G.D.I.P.	Revue Générale de Droit International Public
R.I.A.A.	Reports of International Arbitral Awards
R.I.D.P.	Revue Internationale de Droit Pénal
S.D.L.R.	San Diego Law Review
S.I.U.L.J.	Southern Illinois University Law Journal
S.J.I.L.	Stanford Journal of International Law
S.J.I.L.C.	Syracuse Journal of International Law and Commerce
S.J.L.R.	St. John's Law Review
Sp.	Special
Supp.	Supplement
T.G.S.	Transactions of the Grotius Society
T.I.L.J.	Texas International Law Journal
Tul.L.R.	Tulane Law Review
U.C.L.R.	University of Chicago Law Review
U.L.R.	Utah Law Review
U.N.J.Y.	United Nations Juridical Yearbook
U.N.T.S.	United Nations Treaty Series
U.T.L.R.	University of Toledo Law Review
V.J.I.L.	Virginia Journal of International Law
V.J.T.L.	Vanderbilt Journal of Transnational Law
Vill.L.R.	Villanova Law Review
Vir.L.R.	Virginia Law Review

W.C.R.	*World Court Reports* (M. O. Hudson ed., 1934-43)
W.L.L.R.	Washington and Lee Law Review
W.U.L.Q.	Washington University Law Quarterly
W.V.L.R.	West Virginia Law Review
Y.B.W.A.	Year Book of World Affairs
Y.J.I.L.	Yale Journal of International Law
Y.L.J.	Yale Law Journal
Z.A.O.R.V.	Zeitschrift für Ausländisches Öffentliches Recht und Völkerrecht

PART I

THE LEGAL NATURE OF WAR

CHAPTER 1

WHAT IS WAR?

A. *The Definition of War*

(a) *The Numerous Meanings of War*

The phrase "war" lends itself to manifold uses. It is necessary, at the outset, to differentiate between "war" as a figure of speech heightening the effect of an oral argument or a news story in the media, and "war" as a legal term of art. In ordinary conversation, press reports or even literary publications, "war" may appear to be a flexible expression suitable for an allusion to any serious strife, struggle or campaign. Thus, references are frequently made to "war against the traffic in narcotic drugs", "class war" or "war of nerves". This is a matter of poetic licence. But in legal parlance, the term "war" is invested with a special meaning.

In pursuing that meaning, a distinction must be drawn between what war signifies in the domestic law of this or that State and what it denotes in international law. War, especially a lengthy one, is likely to have a tremendous impact on the internal legal systems of the belligerents. A decision whether war has commenced at all, is going on, or has ended, has far-ranging repercussions in many branches of private law, exemplified by frustration of contracts or recovery of insurance. Similarly, there are multiple relevant issues arising in public law, such as war powers used to requisition property, tax exemptions allowed to those engaged in military service in wartime, and criminal prosecutions for violations of wartime regulations.[1] In consequence, domestic judicial decisions pertaining to war are legion. All the same, one must not rush to adduce them as precedents on the international plane. If a municipal tribunal merely construes the term "war" in the context of the legal system within which it operates, the outcome may not be germane to international law. Even should a judgment rendered by a national court

---

[1] See W. L. Roberts, "Litigation Involving 'Termination of War'", 43 *Ken.L.J.* 195–214 (1954–5).

purport to set out the gist of war in international law, this need not be regarded as conclusive (except within the ambit of the domestic legal system concerned).

Occasionally, internal courts - dealing, for instance, with insurance litigations - address the question whether war is in progress not from the perspective of the legal system (national or international) as a whole, but simply in order to ascertain what the parties to a specific transaction had in mind.[2] When insurance policies exclude or reduce the liability of the insurer if death results from war, the parties are free to give the term "war" whatever definition they desire.[3] The definition may be arbitrary and incompatible with international law. Nevertheless, there is no reason why it should not govern the contractual relations between the parties.

At times, the parties mistakenly believe that a wrong definition actually comports with international law. If a domestic court applies that definition, one must be exceedingly careful in the interpretation of the court's judgment. The dilemma is whether the contours of war, as traced by the court, represent its considered (albeit misconceived) opinion of the substance of international law, or merely reflect the intent of the parties.

When we get to international law, we find that there is no binding definition of war stamped with the *imprimatur* of a multilateral convention in force. What we have is quite a few scholarly attempts to depict the practice of States and to articulate, in a few choice words, an immensely complex idea. Instead of seeking to compare multitudinous definitions, all abounding with variable pitfalls, we shall take as our point of departure one prominent effort to encapsulate the essence of war. This is the often-quoted definition, which appears in L. Oppenheim's treatise on International Law:

> War is a contention between two or more States through their armed forces, for the purpose of overpowering each other and imposing such conditions of peace as the victor pleases.[4]

---

[2] *Cf.* L. Breckenridge, "War Risks", 16 *H.I.L.J.* 440, 455 (1975).
[3] See R. W. Young, "Note", 42 *Mich.L.R.* 884, 890 (1953-4).
[4] L. Oppenheim, 2 *International Law* 202 (7th ed., by H. Lauterpacht, 1952).

(b) An Analysis of Oppenheim's Definition of War

There are four major constituent elements in Oppenheim's view of war: (i) there has to be a contention between at least two States; (ii) the use of the armed forces of those States is required; (iii) the purpose must be overpowering the enemy (as well as the imposition of peace on the victor's terms); and it may be implied, particularly from the words "each other", that (iv) both parties are expected to have symmetrical, although diametrically opposed, goals.

We shall proceed to examine in turn each of these strands of the definition of war. As we do so, it must be borne in mind that when references are made to the prerequisites of war, we shall not - as yet - come to grips with the central issue of the *jus ad bellum*, viz. the legality of war. Questions of legality will be raised in subsequent chapters of this study. In the meantime, we ask only what conditions have to be fulfilled so that a certain course of action may be properly labelled as "war".

i. Inter-State and Intra-State Wars

Of the four ingredients in Oppenheim's definition of war, only the first can be accepted with no demur. "One element seems common to all definitions of war. In all definitions it is clearly affirmed that war is a contest between states".[5]

Some qualifying words should nevertheless be appended. International law recognizes two disparate types of wars: inter-State wars (waged between two or more States) and intra-State wars (civil wars conducted between two or more parties within a single State). Internal armed conflicts have international legal implications for foreign States.[6] To a limited extent, these conflicts are even regulated by international law.[7] However, the rules applicable to and in

---

[5] C. Eagleton, "An Attempt to Define War", 291 *Int.Con.* 237, 281 (1933).

[6] See, e.g., Institut de Droit International, Resolution, "The Principle of Non-Intervention in Civil Wars", 56 *A.I.D.I.* 545 (Wiesbaden, 1975).

[7] See common Article 3 to the four Geneva Conventions of 1949 for the Protection of War Victims: (First) Convention for the Amelioration of the Condition of the Wounded and Sick in Armed Forces in the Field, 75 *U.N.T.S.* 31, 32-4; (Second) Convention for the Amelioration of the Condition of Wounded, Sick and Shipwrecked Members of Armed Forces at Sea, *ibid.*, 85, 86-8; (Third) Convention Relative to

(Continued on p. 6)

an intra-State strife are fundamentally different from those relating to an inter-State war.[8] Hence, Oppenheim was entirely right in excluding civil wars from his definition. In the present study, inter-State armed conflicts will constitute the sole object of our inquiry.

It is immaterial whether each belligerent party recognizes the adversary's statehood. War may actually be the device through which one challenges the sovereignty of the other. As long as both satisfy objective criteria of statehood under international law,[9] any war between them should be characterized as inter-State. Still, the States involved in an inter-State war must be aligned on opposing sides. If a civil war is raging in Ruritania, and Numidia assists the legitimate Government of Ruritania (legitimate, that is, in the eyes of the domestic constitutional law) in combating those who rise in revolt against the central authority,[10] the domestic upheaval does not turn into an inter-State war. In such a case, two States (Ruritania and Numidia) are entangled in military operations, but since they stand together against rebels, the internal nature of the conflict is retained. By contrast, if Numidia joins forces with the insurgents, supporting them against the incumbent Government of Ruritania, this is no longer a civil war.

Admittedly, in practice, the dividing line between inter-State and intra-State wars cannot always be delineated with a few easy strokes.

the Treatment of Prisoners of War, *ibid.*, 135, 136-8; (Fourth) Convention Relative to the Protection of Civilian Persons in Time of War, *ibid.*, 287, 288-90. The International Court of Justice held that this common Article expresses general international law. *Case Concerning Military and Paramilitary Activities in and against Nicaragua* (Merits), [1986] *I.C.J. Rep.* 14, 114. See also Protocol Additional to the Geneva Conventions of 12 August 1949, and Relating to the Protection of Victims of Non-International Armed Conflicts (Protocol II), 1977, [1977] *U.N.J.Y.* 135.

[8] See J. Pictet, *Development and Principles of International Humanitarian Law* 47-8 (1985).

[9] For these criteria, see J. Crawford, *The Creation of States in International Law* 36 ff. (1979).

[10] According to Article 2 of the 1975 Resolution of the *Institut de Droit International* (*supra*, note 6, at 547), it is prohibited to extend foreign assistance to any party in a civil war. Under traditional international law, however, such aid was forbidden only if rendered to the rebels (as distinct from the legitimate Government). See J. W. Garner, "Questions of International Law in the Spanish Civil War", 31 *A.J.I.L.* 66, 67-9 (1937). For an analysis of the modern practice of States, see L. Doswald-Beck, "The Legal Validity of Military Intervention by Invitation of the Government", 56 *B.Y.B.I.L.* 189-252 (1985).

When Ruritania is in a state of turmoil, and Numidia intervenes at the request of one of the feuding parties, identifying the legitimate Government and determining who is rebelling against whom may not be facile undertakings.[11]

Notwithstanding this caveat, the transition from a civil war to an inter-State war may be relatively easy to pinpoint if and when foreign States join the fray. Thus, Israel's War of Independence started on 30 November 1947 as a civil war between the Arab and Jewish populations of the British Mandate in Palestine.[12] But on 15 May 1948, upon the Declaration of Israel's Independence and its invasion by the armies of five sovereign Arab countries, the war became inter-State in character.[13]

The disintegration of Yugoslavia has exposed to light a more complex situation in which a civil war between diverse ethnic, religious or linguistic groups inside the territory of a single country is converted into an inter-State war once the fragmentation into several sovereign States is effected. As long as Serbs were fighting Bosnians within Yugoslavia, the hostilities clearly amounted to a civil war. However, when Serbia and Bosnia-Herzegovina emerged from the political ruins of Yugoslavia as independent countries, the conflict transmuted into an inter-State war by dint of the cross-border involvement of Serbian armed forces in military operations conducted by Bosnian Serbs rebelling against the Bosnian Government (in an effort to wrest control over large tracts of Bosnian land and merge them into a Greater Serbia). This is the legal position despite the fact that, from the outlook of the participants in the actual combat, very little seemed to have changed. The juridical distinction is embedded in the realignment of sovereignties in the Balkans and the substitution of old administrative boundaries by new international frontiers.

The same country may simultaneously be embroiled in both a civil war and an inter-State war, without any built-in linkage between

---

[11] See R. R. Baxter, "Ius in Bello Interno: The Present and Future Law", *Law and Civil War in the Modern World* 518, 525 (J. N. Moore ed., 1974).

[12] For the facts, see N. Lorch, *The Edge of the Sword. Israel's War of Independence 1947-1949* 46 ff. (2nd ed., 1968).

[13] For the facts, see *ibid*, 166 ff.

the external and internal foes. Yet, it is only natural for a spill-over to occur from one conflict into the other. In the Gulf War, at the outset, there was no nexus between the international coalition which came to the aid of Kuwait and Kurdish or Shiite rebels against the Baghdad regime. Eventually, Iraqi repression of the civilian population drove the Security Council to determine the existence of a threat to international peace and security in the region.[14] The outcome was that American and other troops entered the north of Iraq, creating a secure enclave for the Kurds. At a later stage, an air exclusion ("no-fly") zone was imposed over the south of the country, in order to protect the Shiite centres of population (see *infra*, Chapter 4, B, (b)).

ii. War in the Technical and in the Material Sense

The second element in Oppenheim's definition is fraught with problems. According to Oppenheim, a clash of arms between the parties to the conflict is of the essence of war. He even underlined that war is a *"contention,* i.e. *a violent struggle through the application of armed force"*.[15] But this is not uniformly in harmony with the practice of States. Experience demonstrates that, in reality, there are two different sorts of war: there is war in the material sense, but there is also war in the technical sense.

War in the technical sense commences with a declaration of war and is terminated with a peace treaty or some other formal step indicating that the war is over (see *infra*, Chapter 2, A–B). The crux of the matter is the taking of formal measures, which signify that war is about to begin (or has begun) and that it has ended. *De facto*, the armed forces of the parties may not engage in fighting even once in the interval. As an illustration, not a single shot was exchanged in anger between a number of Allied States (particularly in Latin America) and Germany in either World War.[16] Nevertheless, *de jure*, by virtue of the issuance of declarations of war, those countries were in a state of war in the technical sense.

---

[14] Security Council Resolution No. 688, 30 *I.L.M.* 858, 859 (1991).
[15] L. Oppenheim, *supra*, note 4, at 202.
[16] See J. Stone, *Legal Controls of International Conflict* 306 (1954).

Until a formal step is taken to bring it to a close, a state of war may produce certain legal and practical effects as regards, e.g., the internment of nationals of the enemy State and the sequestration of their property, irrespective of the total absence of hostilities.[17] It can scarcely be denied, either in theory or in practice, that "[a] state of war may exist without active hostilities" (just as "active hostilities may exist without a state of war", a point that will be expounded *infra*, iii).[18] Oppenheim's narrow definition must be broadened to accommodate a state of war which is not combined with actual fighting.

War in the material sense unfolds regardless of any formal steps. Its occurrence is contingent only on the outbreak of hostilities between the parties, even in the absence of a declaration of war. This is where Oppenheim's reference to a violent struggle is completely apposite. The decisive factor here is deeds rather than declarations. What counts is not a *de jure* state of war, but *de facto* combat. Granted, even in the course of war in the material sense, hostilities do not have to go on incessantly and they may be interspersed by periods of cease-fire (see *infra*, Chapter 2, C). But there is no war in the material sense without some acts of warfare.

Warfare means the use of armed force, namely, violence. Breaking off diplomatic relations with a State, or withdrawing recognition from it, does not suffice. An economic boycott or a psychological pressure is not enough. A "cold war", threats to use force, or even a declaration of war (unaccompanied by acts of violence), do not warrant the conclusion that war in the material sense exists. It is indispensable that actual armed force be employed.

The setting of an intervention in support of rebels in a civil war in another country raises some perplexing questions. What degree of intervention brings about a state of war in the material sense? It appears that the mere supply of arms to the rebels (epitomized by American support of Moslem insurgents against the Soviet-backed Government in Afghanistan in the 1980s) does not qualify as an actual use of armed force (see *infra*, Chapter 7, B, (b), v). But there

---

[17] See L. Kotzsch, *The Concept of War in Contemporary History and International Law* 248-9 (1956).

[18] See Q. Wright, "When Does War Exist?", 26 *A.J.I.L.* 362, 363 (1932).

comes a point - for instance, when the weapons are accompanied by instructors training the rebels - at which the foreign country is deemed to be waging warfare.[19]

The laws of warfare (constituting the nucleus of the international *jus in bello*) are brought into operation as soon as war in the material sense is embarked upon, despite the absence of a technical state of war. This principle is pronounced in Article 2 common to the 1949 Geneva Conventions for the Protection of War Victims:

> the present Convention shall apply to all cases of declared war or of any other armed conflict which may arise between two or more of the High Contracting Parties, even if the state of war is not recognized by one of them.[20]

Of course, if a state of war exists in the technical sense only, without any actual fighting, the issue of the application of the laws of warfare rarely emerges in practice.[21]

iii. Total Wars, Limited Wars and Incidents Short of War

The third component in Oppenheim's definition is that the purpose of war must be the overpowering of the enemy and the imposition of peace terms. His intention, no doubt, was to distinguish between a large-scale use of force (tantamount to war) and a clash of lower intensity (constituting measures short of war). Indeed, when armed units of two countries are locked in combat, the

---

[19] It is noteworthy that a breach of neutrality occurs when military advisers are assigned to the armed forces of one of the belligerents in an on-going inter-State war (see *infra*, D, (b), ii).

[20] *Supra*, note 7, at 32 (First Convention), 86 (Second Convention), 136 (Third Convention), 288 (Fourth Convention).

[21] In some extreme instances, even when the state of war exists only in a technical sense, a belligerent may still be in breach of the *jus in bello*. Thus, the mere issuance of a threat to an adversary that hostilities would be conducted on the basis of a "no quarter" policy constitutes a violation of Article 40 of the 1977 Protocol Additional to the Geneva Conventions of 12 August 1949, and Relating to the Protection of Victims of International Armed Conflicts (Protocol I), 1977, [1977] *U.N.J.Y.* 95, 110. *Cf.* Article 23(d) of the Regulations Respecting the Laws and Customs of War on Land (Annexed to Hague Convention No. II of 1899 and No. IV of 1907), *Hague Conventions* 100, 107, 116.

preliminary question is whether the use of force is comprehensive enough for the fighting to qualify as war.

Incidents involving the use of force, without reaching the threshold of war, occur quite often in the relations between States. Border patrols of neighbouring countries may exchange fire; naval units may torpedo vessels flying another flag; interceptor planes may shoot down aircraft belonging to another State; and so forth. The reasons for such incidents vary. They may happen accidentally or be caused by trigger-happy junior officers acting on their own initiative; they may be engendered by simmering tensions between the two countries; they may be the fallout of an open dispute revolving around control over a strategically or economically important area (like oil lands, a major road, a ridge of mountains or a waterway); and other motives may be at play.

In great measure, the classification of a military action as either war or a closed incident (short of war) depends on the way in which the two antagonists appraise the situation. As long as both parties choose to consider what has transpired as a mere incident, and provided that the incident is rapidly closed, it is hard to gainsay that view. Once, however, one of the parties elects to engage in war, the other side is incapable of preventing that development. The country opting for war may simply issue a declaration of war. Although the declaration is unilateral, it "brings about a state of war irrespective of the attitude of the state to which it is addressed".[22] Additionally, the State desirous of war may escalate the use of force, so that war in the material sense will take shape.

There is a marked difference between war and peace: whereas it requires two States to conclude and to preserve peace (see *infra,* Chapter 2, B, (a), i), it takes a single State to embroil itself as well as its selected enemy in war. When comprehensive force is used by Arcadia against Utopia, war in the material sense ensues and it is irrelevant that Utopia confines itself to responding with non-comprehensive force. Utopia, remaining completely passive, may offer no resistance; nevertheless, war in the material sense can result from the measures taken by the advancing Arcadian

---

[22] M. Greenspan, *The Modern Law of Land Warfare* 38 (1959).

armies.[23] If Arcadia proceeds to "devastate the territory of another with fire and sword", the invasion would be categorized as war in the material sense, discounting what the Utopian armed forces do or fail to do.[24] Hence, the invasion by the Iraqi army and the rapid takeover of Kuwait within a few hours on 2 August 1990 brought about war in the material sense. It would be erroneous to assume that the Gulf War commenced only when extensive hostilities flared up in January 1991.

Since war in the material sense is derived from deeds rather than words, third parties sometimes feel compelled to investigate the legal position on their own. This may come to pass because either the adversaries keep silent, while their armies are in constant battle, or what they say does not match what they do. "There is ... room for the view that the opinions entertained by the belligerents need not be given conclusive effect. War may be too important a matter to be left either to the generals or to the contending parties".[25]

A legal analysis of the true state of affairs, carried out objectively, hinges on a perception of the use of force as comprehensive. Force is comprehensive if it is employed (i) spatially, across sizeable tracts of land or far-flung corners of the ocean; (ii) temporally, over a prolonged period of time; (iii) quantitatively, entailing massive military operations or a high level of firepower; (iv) qualitatively, inflicting much destruction. Reliance on any one of the four criteria may prove adequate in certain instances, but generally only a combination of all four will paint a clear picture of the nature of the hostilities.

The use of force need not be unlimited for it to be comprehensive. Oppenheim's definition postulates what is termed nowadays a "total" war. Many a war is unquestionably "total" in that it is conducted with total victory in mind. Total victory consists of the capitulation of the enemy, following the overall defeat of its armed forces and/or the conquest of its territory, and if this is accomplished the victor is capable of dictating peace terms to the vanquished. When carried to extremity, a total victory may bring about

---

[23] See P. Guggenheim, "Les Principes de Droit International Public", 80 *R.C.A.D.I.* 1, 171 (1952).
[24] T. Baty, "Abuse of Terms: 'Recognition': 'War'", 30 *A.J.I.L.* 377, 381, 398 (1936).
[25] R. R. Baxter, "The Definition of War", 16 *R.E.D.I.* 1, 4 (1960).

the complete disintegration of the enemy State (see *infra,* Chapter 2, B, (c), ii). Thus, in unleashing the Gulf War, the Iraqi aim was to extinguish the political life of Kuwait as a sovereign State.

Yet, not every war is aimed at total victory. Oppenheim completely overlooked the feasibility of limited wars. Such wars are, in fact, of considerable frequency and import. In a limited war, the goal may be confined to the defeat of some segments of the opposing armed forces, the conquest of certain portions of the opponent's territory, the coercion of the enemy Government to alter a given policy, etc., without striving for total victory. Now and then, it is not easy to tell a limited war (in the material sense) apart from a grave incident short of war. The difference between the two is relative: more force, employed over a longer period of time, within a larger theatre of operations, is required in a war setting as compared to a situation short of war.

A war may be deemed "total" not only when its goal is the complete subjugation of the enemy. A war is total also when the means, used to attain a limited objective, are total. That is to say, war may be catalogued as total when the totality of the resources (human and material) of a belligerent State is mobilized, so as to secure victory at any cost. Victory at any cost should not be confused with total victory. Surely, more often than not, a State will mobilize its full resources only when the end for which it exerts itself is total victory. But a State may conduct war *à outrance* for a limited reward, like a border rectification, if the issue carries an emotional load of great weight. One must distinguish between the military war aims and the ulterior motives of war. The latter can be strategic, political, economic, and even religious, ideological or cultural. War may have a hidden agenda that transcends the tangible or ostensible gains contemplated.

The counterpart of a limited war fought with unlimited means is a total war waged with less than the total of the means available. Occasionally, a belligerent - while fighting a war that is total in terms of its objective - refrains from resorting to some destructive (conventional or unconventional) weapon systems, although they are at its disposal and their use is legally permissible. There is a broad array of causes for such self-restraint: lofty moral impulses; a concession to public opinion at home or abroad; fear of retaliation;

or purely military considerations. Either way, hostilities do not lose their legal classification as war only because some weapons remain on the shelf.

For these reasons, it is better to attenuate the rigidity of Oppenheim's definition. War need not be total to be war. At the same time, not every episodic case of use of force by States amounts to war. Only a comprehensive use of force does. The key to the definition of war should lie in the adjective "comprehensive".

iv. War as an Asymmetrical Phenomenon

The last factor in Oppenheim's definition is the implicit symmetry in the positions of the contending parties, as if both necessarily have corresponding objectives. However, the war aims of one adversary are not always a mirror image of the other's. Sometimes, only the attacking State aims at total victory, whereas the other side has a more limited objective (like driving the enemy off its territory). This is what happened in the Gulf War. Although Iraq attempted to eliminate Kuwait, the American-led coalition which came to the aid of the latter spurned exhortations to march all the way to Baghdad. Hostilities were therefore suspended (and a large international expeditionary force was dispersed) upon the liberation of Kuwait. The opposite scenario is equally conceivable. An attacking State may desire solely to gain control over a piece of territory of a neighbouring country, but the victim can respond fiercely in an effort to crush its adversary once and for all.

This brings us to another core issue. Ordinarily, hostilities are launched with a specific intention to wage war; an *animus belligerendi.* There are those who look upon such an intention as an essential component in the definition of war.[26] Yet, even if that were the case, it is clear that the intention to embark upon war "must be openly manifested" and it has to be "recognizable" by all the parties concerned (i.e. not only by whoever is harbouring the intention).[27] If a declaration of war is issued, the intention is obvious. In the

---

[26] For a synopsis of these views, see M. S. McDougal and F. P. Feliciano, *Law and Minimum World Public Order* 97-9, 104-5 (1961).

[27] W.J. Ronan, "English and American Courts and the Definition of War", 31 *A.J.I.L.* 642, 656 (1937).

absence of such a declaration, the position may be less self-evident. When all is said and done, the intention is deduced from the fact of war, and not *vice versa*.

The thesis that an *animus belligerendi* is an integral part of the definition of war is enticing, but it is insupportable. Just as war can be imposed by Arcadia (the attacking State) on Utopia against the latter's will, war can also develop contrary to the original Arcadian intentions. When it mounts a military incursion into Utopian territory, Arcadia may have in sight a brief armed encounter short of war. However, inasmuch as it is incapable of controlling the Utopian response, Arcadia may stumble into war. Arcadia acts "at its peril", since the measures of force to which it resorts can be treated by Utopia as the initiation of war.[28] Thus, the decision whether a seminal use of force will culminate in a state of war may be taken by the target State.[29] Moreover, "if acts of force are sufficiently serious and long continued", war exists "even if both sides disclaim any *animus belligerendi* and refuse to admit that a state of war has arisen between them".[30] Differently phrased, an objective inquiry (conducted, e.g., by Patagonia) may prompt the conclusion that Arcadia and Utopia are in the midst of war although, from the subjective standpoint of its intentions (*animus belligerendi*), neither country desires war.

(c) *A Proposed Definition of War*

As the foregoing discussion should indicate, the term "war" gives rise to more than a handful of definitional problems. No wonder that the assertion is made that no definition, serviceable for all purposes, can be provided.[31] Still, in the context of the present study, "war" will have the following meaning:

War is a hostile interaction between two or more States, either in a technical or in a material sense. War in the technical sense is a formal status produced by a declaration of war. War in the

[28] See A. D. McNair, "The Legal Meaning of War, and the Relation of War to Reprisals", 11 *T.G.S.* 29, 38 (1925).
[29] See E. M. Borchard, "'War' and 'Peace'", 27 *A.J.I.L.* 114, 114-15 (1933).
[30] See J. L. Brierly, "International Law and Resort to Armed Force", 4 *Cam.L.J.* 308, 313 (1930-2).
[31] See F. Grob, *The Relativity of War and Peace* 189 (1949).

material sense is generated by actual use of armed force, which must be comprehensive on the part of at least one party to the conflict.

B. *Status Mixtus*

In the past, the dominant opinion, as expressed by Grotius[32] following Cicero,[33] was that no intermediate state exists between war and peace (*inter bellum et pacem nihil est medium*). But in the last half-century, a number of scholars have strongly advocated a reconsideration of the traditional dichotomy in the light of the modern practice of States. In particular, G. Schwarzenberger called for recognition of a "*status mixtus*",[34] and P. C. Jessup urged acceptance of a state of "intermediacy" between war and peace.[35] Other commentators deny that the notion of an intermediate status between war and peace is consonant with contemporary international law.[36]

To the degree that proponents of the *status mixtus* school of thought recognize an independent third rubric, lying outside the bounds of war and peace, and subject to the application of a different set of rules,[37] there is nothing in the current practice of States to provide support for it. Nor is it justified to speak loosely of a *status mixtus* in the sense of a twilight zone between war and peace. Legally speaking, there are only two states of affairs in the relations between States - war and peace - with no undistributed middle ground.

Whenever States disagree about the application or interpretation of international law, it is necessary and possible to establish first whether a state of war or of peace is in progress. But this is not to say that the concept of a *status mixtus* is without merit in international

---

[32] Grotius, *De Jure Belli ac Pacis*, Book III, § XXI, I (1 Classics of International Law ed. (text) 592 (1913)).

[33] Cicero, *Philippics*, § VIII, I, 4 (Loeb Classical ed. 366 (1926)).

[34] G. Schwarzenberger, "Jus Pacis ac Belli?", 37 *A.J.I.L.* 460, 470 (1943).

[35] P. C. Jessup, "Intermediacy", 23 *A.S.J.G.* 16, 17 (1953); P. C. Jessup, "Should International Law Recognize an Intermediate Status between Peace and War?", 48 *A.J.I.L.* 98, 100 (1954).

[36] See G. I. Tunkin, *Theory of International Law* 265-70 (1974).

[37] See, e.g., A. N. Salpeter and J. C. Waller, "Armed Reprisals during Intermediacy - A New Framework for Analysis in International Law", 17 *Vill.L.R.* 270, 271-2 (1972).

law. One must acknowledge, as an observable phenomenon, the applicability of some laws of peace in specific war situations and of some laws of war in certain peace settings. A *status mixtus* is characterized by the simultaneous operation of the laws of war (for some purposes) and the laws of peace (for others).[38]

(a) *Peacetime Status Mixtus*

In peacetime, a *status mixtus* exists when States resort to a limited use of force. Because a state of peace continues to prevail, (i) most of the relations between the parties are still governed by the laws of peace, and (ii) the laws of neutrality are not activated between the antagonists and third parties. Nevertheless, the actual fighting will be regulated by the basic rules of warfare (*jus in bello*).

It is generally conceded nowadays that international humanitarian law (pertaining in the main to the protection of the wounded, the sick, prisoners of war and civilians) must be implemented in the course of international armed conflicts of whatever type, and not only when a state of war is in effect. This is reflected in the very title of Protocol I of 1977, Additional to the four Geneva Conventions, which relates to the Protection of Victims of International Armed Conflicts,[39] viz. not only wars. Common Article 2 of the 1949 Geneva Conventions for the Protection of War Victims (quoted *supra*, A, (b), ii) prescribes that these instruments (wherein the term "war" figures prominently) shall apply to all cases of armed conflict between contracting States, "even if the state of war is not recognized by one of them". It may be inferred from the last words that, if both adversaries jointly refuse to recognize the existence of a state of war, the Conventions are not operational.[40] Still, the correct legal position appears to be that whenever force is employed in international relations, States are obligated to carry out the

---

[38] See G. Schwarzenberger and E. D. Brown, *A Manual of International Law* 151 (6th ed., 1976).

[39] *Supra*, note 21, at 95.

[40] See A. P. Rubin, "The Status of Rebels under the Geneva Conventions of 1949", 21 *I.C.L.Q.* 472, 477 (1972).

humanitarian norms affecting the wounded and sick, prisoners of war and other protected persons.[41]

The provisions of the Geneva Conventions have gained the appellation "international humanitarian law", but they are not the only rules of warfare that must be respected at any time inter-State force is resorted to. It is submitted that other portions of the *jus in bello* (enshrined, for the most part, in the Hague Conventions) - such as those prohibiting the use of "dum-dum" bullets[42] - must similarly be applied in all international armed conflicts, whether or not a state of war exists.

(b) *Wartime Status Mixtus*

In some circumstances, widespread hostilities (entailing a large number of casualties and incalculable damage) are raging between States over a long period of time, yet the parties behave as if nothing out of the ordinary has happened.[43] They continue to maintain full diplomatic relations,[44] go on trading with each other, and otherwise assume a "business as usual" posture. As pointed out (see *supra*, A, (b), iii), third countries may be driven to probe independently the nature of the hostilities. An impartial examination may lead to the conclusion that in reality war is going on, official protests to the contrary notwithstanding.

This pattern of hostilities is liable to be highly confusing. It seems to be the other side of the coin of a state of war without warfare: here, ostensibly, warfare occurs without a state of war. In actuality, that is not so. If States use comprehensive force against one another, war in the material sense exists.

Once war is going on, the laws of war are supposed to be brought into operation in their amplitude. Can the parties to the conflict, acting in concert, suspend the application of the *jus in bello* (in whole

---

[41] See *Commentary, I Geneva Convention* 32 (J. S. Pictet ed., 1952).

[42] The prohibition is based on Hague Declaration (No. IV, 3, of 1899) Concerning Expanding Bullets, *Hague Conventions* 227.

[43] The Soviet-Japanese armed conflict of 1939 may serve as a good example. See I. Brownlie, *International Law and the Use of Force by States* 389 (1963).

[44] As a rule, war is considered "incompatible with the maintenance of diplomatic relations". G. E. do Nascimento e Silva, *Diplomacy in International Law* 172 (1972).

or in part)? To answer the question, a distinction must be drawn between the duties that the *jus in bello* imposes and the rights that it bestows. Belligerents are obligated to discharge in full the duties devolving on them under the laws of warfare. These duties cannot be evaded even if the parties to the conflict grant a dispensation to one another. But States engaged in war are not compelled by international law to make use of the full gamut of the rights accorded to them. If it so desires, each of the opposing sides is generally empowered not to insist on its rights. Subject to exceptions spelt out by international humanitarian law,[45] a belligerent is entitled to renounce its rights or to leave them in abeyance. Surely, international law does not impede warring States from continuing reciprocal trade, or retaining diplomatic relations, even when their armies are pitted in combat.

In a 1976 International Chamber of Commerce Arbitration, in the *Dalmia Cement* case, P. Lalive pronounced that war must entail "a *complete rupture* of international relations" between the belligerents, and "the continued existence of treaties as well as of diplomatic relations between the parties cannot be reconciled with a 'state of war'".[46] As for treaties, this statement is not consonant with the modern trend denying their *ipso facto* termination – and, according to the *Institut de Droit International*, even suspension – upon the outbreak of war.[47] While breaking off diplomatic relations at the commencement of hostilities is still the rule, it can no longer be viewed as an essential aspect of war.[48]

What a wartime *status mixtus* requires is some finesse in estimating the conduct of the belligerents. On the one hand, it ought to be

---

[45] The four Geneva Conventions expressly rule out the conclusion of special agreements between belligerents, which affect adversely or restrict the rights of protected persons. *Supra*, note 7, at 34 (First Convention, Article 6), 88 (Second Convention, Article 6), 142 (Third Convention, Article 6), 292 (Fourth Convention, Article 7).

[46] *Dalmia Cement Ltd. v. National Bank of Pakistan* (1976), 67 *I.L.R.* 611, 624.

[47] Institut de Droit International, Resolution, "The Effects of Armed Conflicts on Treaties", 61 (II) *A.I.D.I.* 278, 280 (Helsinki, 1985) (Article 2). *Cf.* comments by the present writer drawing attention to the contrast with the Lalive arbitral award and other sources, *ibid.*, 215.

[48] The Arbitrator himself conceded that the position was not free of doubt. See *supra*, note 46, at 623.

remembered that a state of war exists. Consequently, all wartime obligations must be complied with scrupulously. On the other hand, if the parties wish to preserve a modicum of peace in the middle of war, they are entitled to do so. The only condition is that their behaviour must not run counter to the overriding obligations of the *jus in bello*.

C. *The Region of War*

War can be waged over large portions of the planet and beyond. The space subject to the potential spread of hostilities is known as the region of war. Actual hostilities may be restricted by the belligerents to a fairly narrow theatre of operations, but the potential is always there. The combat zone on land is likely to be quite limited in geographic scope, yet naval and air units may attack targets in distant areas.

The region of war consists of the following:

(a) *The Territories of the Parties to the Conflict*

In principle, all the territories of the belligerent States, anywhere under their sovereign sway, are inside the region of war. As a corollary, the region of war does not overstep the boundaries of neutral States, and no hostilities are permitted within their respective domains.

Since the region of war comprises the territories subject to the sovereignty of the belligerent States, it includes (i) land areas; (ii) internal waters; (iii) archipelagic waters;[49] (iv) the territorial sea; (v) subsoil and submarine areas underneath these expanses of land and water; as well as (vi) the superjacent airspace above them. However, the extension of the region of war to the entire territories of the belligerent States is not immutable. An international (multilateral or bilateral) treaty may exclude from the region of any present or future war a waterway, an island or any other well-defined zone

---

[49] On the status of archipelagic waters, see E. Rauch, *The Protocol Additional to the Geneva Conventions for the Protection of Victims of International Armed Conflicts and the United Nations Convention on the Law of the Sea: Repercussions on the Law of Naval Warfare* 32 (1984).

located within the territory of an actual or prospective belligerent. Such a treaty gives rise to the "neutralization" of the specific zone.[50] Neutralization assimilates the status of an area controlled by a belligerent to that of a neutral territory.

A typical neutralization arrangement is embodied in Article 4 of the 1888 Constantinople Convention on the Suez Canal, where the contracting parties agreed that "no right of war" or "act of hostility" will be allowed in the Canal and its ports of access, or within a radius of 3 nautical miles from those ports.[51] A parallel provision, explicitly referring to neutralization, appeared in Article 3 of the 1901 Anglo-American Hay-Pauncefote Treaty (in anticipation of the construction of a canal connecting the Atlantic and Pacific oceans).[52]

In 1977, the United States and the Republic of Panama concluded a Treaty Concerning the Permanent Neutrality and Operation of the Panama Canal.[53] In general, the phrase "permanent neutrality" is to be differentiated from the term "neutralization".[54] The concept of permanent neutrality applies to the whole territory of a country, with Switzerland as the model. A country placed under a permanent neutrality regime undertakes to remain neutral in all future wars (unless attacked), to conclude no military alliances, and to allow no foreign military bases on its soil.[55] No such obligation is imposed on the Republic of Panama in the 1977 Treaty. The permanent neutrality declared therein relates only to the Panama Canal.[56] Respect for the permanent neutrality of the Canal is also a theme of a special Protocol, annexed to the Treaty and open to accession by all the States of the world.[57] In correct legal terminology, the 1977 Treaty and Protocol ensure not the permanent neutrality, but the neutralization, of the Panama Canal.

---

[50] See L. Oppenheim, *supra*, note 4, at 244.
[51] Constantinople Convention Respecting the Free Navigation of the Suez Maritime Canal, 1888, 3 *A.J.I.L.*, Supp., 123, 124 (1909).
[52] Great Britain-United States, Treaty to Facilitate the Construction of a Ship Canal (Hay-Pauncefote Treaty), 1901, 3 *A.J.I.L.*, Supp., 127, 128 (1909).
[53] United States-Panama, Treaty Concerning the Permanent Neutrality and Operation of the Panama Canal, 1977, 72 *A.J.I.L.* 238 (1978).
[54] See S. Verosta, "Neutralization", 4 *E.P.I.L.* 31, *id.* (1982).
[55] See J. L. Kunz, "Austria's Permanent Neutrality", 50 *A.J.I.L.* 418, 418-19 (1956).
[56] *Supra*, note 53, at 238-41.
[57] *Ibid.*, 241-2.

Neutralization is not restricted to international waterways. Article 6 of the 1921 Geneva Convention on the Non-Fortification and Neutralisation of the Aaland Islands lays down that, in time of war, these islands are to be considered a neutral zone and they are not to be used for any purpose connected with military operations.[58]

Protocol I Additional to the Geneva Conventions incorporates, in Article 60, a detailed stipulation relating to "demilitarized zones".[59] Parties to a conflict are forbidden to extend their military operations to zones on which they have conferred by agreement (concluded either in writing or verbally, either in peacetime or after the outbreak of hostilities) the status of a demilitarized zone. Although Article 60 refers to "demilitarized zones", the exclusion of wartime military operations signifies that the zones have been neutralized.

The two institutions of neutralization and demilitarization "must be sharply distinguished".[60] Demilitarization means that a State accepts limitations on (or waives altogether) its right to maintain armed forces and weapon systems, as well as to construct fortifications and military installations, in a certain region.[61] Demilitarization can be a component of neutralization. Conversely, demilitarization may exist without neutralization, just as neutralization may exist without demilitarization. In both instances, a well-defined zone is involved (whereas a permanent neutrality regime affects an entire State). But demilitarization is designed for periods of peace or at least cease-fire, while neutralization acquires a practical significance only in time of actual warfare. Demilitarization, particularly of a border buffer zone, places the emphasis on the prevention of incidents liable to trigger hostilities. Neutralization is premised on the assumption that hostilities do begin or have begun: the goal is to prevent the neutralized zone from being engulfed in the fighting. In demilitarization, the demilitarized zone serves only as a means to the end of the maintenance of peace, or the

---

[58] Geneva Convention Relating to the Non-Fortification and Neutralisation of the Aaland Islands, 1921, 9 *L.N.T.S.* 211, 219.

[59] *Supra*, note 21, at 118-19.

[60] J. H. W. Verzijl, 3 *International Law in Historical Perspective* 500 (1970).

[61] See J. Delbrück, "Demilitarization", 3 *E.P.I.L.* 150, *id.* (1982).

observance of a cease-fire, everywhere. In neutralization, the neutralized zone itself is the end: the objective is safeguarding the zone from the spread of warfare carried on elsewhere.

The 1959 Antarctic Treaty promulgates, in Article I, that "Antarctica shall be used for peaceful purposes only".[62] There is no lucid definition of the term "peaceful purposes".[63] However, a plain reading of the text would suggest that it eliminates the possibility of warlike activities ("warlike" being the antonym of "peaceful"). If so, a regime of neutralization has been imposed on the entire continent. Article I also provides, in greater detail, for the demilitarization of Antarctica.

(b) *The Open Seas and the Exclusive Economic Zone*

There has never been any doubt that the high seas "fall within the region of war".[64] Surprisingly, Article 88 of the 1982 United Nations Convention on the Law of the Sea, echoing the language of the Antarctic Treaty, proclaims:

The high seas shall be reserved for peaceful purposes.[65]

Under Article 58(2), this clause applies also to the exclusive economic zone.[66] A literal construction of the words used in the Convention would connote that the waging of war as such is banned throughout the high seas and the exclusive economic zone.[67]

If taken seriously, the laconic stipulation of Article 88 would bring about a veritable revolution in maritime warfare. "This is the shortest Article in the Convention, but in spirit it is the most far-reaching: ostensibly it challenges the historic role of the oceans as battlegrounds".[68] It is hard to believe that "a one-sentence reference

---

[62] Washington Antarctic Treaty, 1959, 402 *U.N.T.S.* 71, 73.
[63] See J. Hanessian, "The Antarctic Treaty 1959", 9 *I.C.L.Q.* 436, 468 (1960).
[64] L. Oppenheim, *supra,* note 4, at 239.
[65] United Nations Convention on the Law of the Sea, 1982, 21 *I.L.M.* 1261, 1287 (1982).
[66] *Ibid.,* 1280.
[67] See F. Francioni, "Use of Force, Military Activities, and the New Law of the Sea", *The Current Legal Regulation of the Use of Force* 361, 375-6 (A. Cassese ed., 1986).
[68] K. Booth, *Law, Force and Diplomacy at Sea* 82 (1985).

to peaceful purposes", in an inordinately verbose and complex instrument, was intended to produce the momentous results that seem to flow from the text.[69] The provision "is widely regarded as prohibiting only acts of aggression on the high seas".[70] Such an interpretation, which allows naval military operations on the high seas only "if undertaken as an exercise of the right of self-defense",[71] renders article 88 redundant in the light of Article 301 of the Convention[72] (quoted *infra*, Chapter 4, D). No wonder that some commentators suggest that Article 88 should not be overemphasized.[73] In any event, the practice of States in maritime hostilities conducted since the formulation of the Convention is in stark contrast to the text of Article 88 (if accepted at face value).

As for the exclusive economic zone and the continental shelf of neutral countries, it is clear that they are not excluded from the region of war.[74] All the same, due regard must be given to installations constructed by the (neutral) coastal State for the exploitation of its economic resources in these areas.

(c) *Outer Space*

Pursuant to Article IV of the 1967 Treaty on Outer Space, the moon and other celestial bodies are to be used "exclusively for peaceful purposes"[75] (once more, in substance, the Antarctic Treaty formula). The precise effect of this phrase in the 1967 Treaty proved controversial.[76] But Article 3 of a further Agreement, concluded in 1979, reiterates the same general principle and elaborates

---

[69] B. H. Oxman, "The Regime of Warships under the United Nations Convention on the Law of the Sea", 24 *V.J.I.L.* 809, 831 (1983-4).

[70] R. R. Churchill and A. V. Lowe, *The Law of the Sea* 176 n. 1 (2nd ed., 1988).

[71] R. J. Zedalis, "'Peaceful Purposes' and Other Relevant Provisions of the Revised Composite Negotiating Text: A Comparative Analysis of the Existing and the Proposed Military Regime for the High Seas", 7 *S.J.I.L.C.* 1, 18 n. 72 (1979-80).

[72] *Supra*, note 65, at 1326.

[73] See R. Wolfrum, "Restricting the Use of the Sea to Peaceful Purposes: Demilitarization in Being?", 24 *G.Y.I.L.* 200, 213 (1981).

[74] See E. Rauch, *supra*, note 49, at 38.

[75] Treaty on Principles Governing the Activities of States in the Exploration and Use of Outer Space, Including the Moon and Other Celestial Bodies, 1967, [1966] *U.N.J.Y.* 166, 167.

[76] See O. O. Ogunbanwo, *International Law and Outer Space Activities* 28-33 (1975).

upon it.[77] The 1979 provision specifically prohibits the use of force either (i) on the moon (and other celestial bodies within the solar system, except Earth); or (ii) from the Moon (and the other bodies) in relation to Earth or man-made spacecraft. It is still not forbidden to fire missiles (i) from one point on Earth against another through outer space; and (ii) from Earth against a military satellite in orbit or an incoming missile.

D. *Neutrality*

(a) *The Basic Principles*

Neutrality "presupposes war between some Powers": it is "the position of a State which does not participate in that war".[78] The laws of neutrality stem from a realization that, in an interdependent world, neutrals cannot simply ignore a war conducted by other countries. "The very nature of war causes its effects to extend also to non-participating States and their nationals whether they wish it or not".[79]

A State may be neutral at the outbreak of hostilities, turning into a belligerent at a later stage; that was the case with the United States in both World Wars. A State starting a multipartite war as a belligerent may also withdraw from the hostilities (provided that the enemy will let it do so), and become a neutral. In fact, a State may be associated with certain other countries in a war against one enemy, staying neutral in another war conducted by the same countries concurrently against another enemy. Accordingly, in the Grand Alliance of the Second World War, the Soviet Union - while bearing for several years the brunt of the fighting against Germany - remained neutral, until almost the very last moment, insofar as Japan was concerned.

The laws of neutrality are operative only as long as the neutral State retains its neutral status. Once that State becomes immersed

---

[77] Agreement Governing the Activities of States on the Moon and Other Celestial Bodies, 1979, [1979] *U.N.J.Y.* 109, 110. See also Article 1(1), *ibid.*, 109. The treaty is not widely ratified.
[78] E. Castrén, *The Present Law of War and Neutrality* 422-3 (1951).
[79] *Ibid.*, 425.

in the hostilities, the laws of neutrality cease being applicable, and the laws of warfare take their place. However, if the neutral State does not embroil itself in war, the laws of neutrality are activated from the onset of the war until its conclusion.

The laws of neutrality are predicated on two fundamental, closely interlinked, rationales: (i) the desire to guarantee to the neutral State that it will sustain minimal injury by reason of the war; (ii) the desire to guarantee to the belligerents that the neutral State will be neutral not only in name but also in deed (that is to say, it will not assist one of the belligerents against the opposing side). The two pillars of the laws of neutrality are non-participation and non-discrimination.[80]

(b) *Some Concrete Rules*

Without seeking to lay out the broad sweep of the laws of neutrality, we shall trace several characteristic rules – concretizing the basic principles of non-participation and non-discrimination – which will have some bearing on the discussion in other chapters of this study.

i. Passage of Belligerent Military Units and War Materials

As already noticed (*supra*, C, (a)), the region of war does not include the territories of neutral States, and no hostilities are permissible within neutral boundaries. A question of singular practical importance arises, however, in regard to non-violent passage of troops, weapons and supplies through neutral territory. Different legal norms have evolved in land and air warfare, as compared to maritime warfare. The general rule of land warfare, enunciated in Articles 2 and 5 of Hague Convention (No. V of 1907) Respecting the Rights and Duties of Neutral Powers and Persons in Case of War on Land, is that the movement of troops or convoys of either munitions of war or supplies, across the territory of a neutral State, is

---

[80] See T. Komarnicki, "The Place of Neutrality in the Modern System of International Law", 80 *R.C.A.D.I.* 395, 406 (1952). *Cf.* Harvard Research in International Law, Draft Convention on Rights and Duties of Neutral States in Naval and Aerial War (P. C. Jessup, Reporter), 33 *A.J.I.L.*, Sp. Supp., 167, 176 (1939) (Articles 4-5).

forbidden.[81] The entry of belligerent military aircraft into the air-space of a neutral country is equally proscribed by Article 40 of the Rules of Aerial Warfare, formulated in 1923 by a Commission of Jurists at The Hague.[82] Contrarily, under Article 10 of Hague Convention (No. XIII of 1907) Concerning the Rights and Duties of Neutral Powers in Naval War, the neutrality of a State is not impaired by the mere passage through its territorial waters of belligerent warships or prizes.[83] Subject to conditions enumerated in the Convention, belligerent warships and prizes may even enter neutral ports.[84]

The obligations outlined in Hague Convention No. V are incurred jointly by the belligerents and the neutral State. Each of the belligerents is enjoined from moving its land forces across the neutral territory (Article 2 of the Convention), and, correspondingly, the neutral State must not tolerate such movement within its territory (Article 5). If Arcadia (a belligerent) transports troops through the territory of Ruritania (a neutral) against the latter's will, Arcadia contravenes its duty towards both Ruritania and Utopia (the enemy). Should Arcadia act in complicity with Ruritania, they would both be in breach of their obligations *vis-à-vis* Utopia.

ii. Enrollment in Belligerent Armed Forces

Articles 4 and 5 of Hague Convention No. V do not permit the formation on neutral soil of corps of combatants, or the opening of recruiting agencies, to assist the belligerents.[85] In the same vein, the neutral State must not assign military advisers to the armed forces of one of the adversaries, and, if it has sent such advisers in peacetime, it is bound to recall them once hostilities commence.[86]

---

[81] Hague Convention (No. V of 1907) Respecting the Rights and Duties of Neutral Powers and Persons in Case of War on Land, *Hague Conventions* 133, 133-4.

[82] Commission of Jurists to Consider and Report upon the Revision of the Rules of Warfare, Rules of Aerial Warfare (The Hague, 1923), 32 *A.J.I.L.*, Supp., 1, 12, 34 (1938).

[83] Hague Convention (No. XIII of 1907) Concerning the Rights and Duties of Neutral Powers in Naval War, *Hague Conventions* 209, 211.

[84] *Ibid.*, 211-13.

[85] *Supra*, note 81, at 134.

[86] See L. Oppenheim, *supra*, note 4, at 687.

Yet, as stipulated in Article 6 of Convention No. V, the neutral State bears no responsibility when individuals cross its frontiers offering their services to one of the belligerents.[87]

The upshot of the laws of neutrality on this point is that they countenance individual initiatives, by nationals and residents of a neutral State, to serve in the armed forces of one of the parties to the conflict.[88] The domestic legislation of the neutral State may penalize such service in a foreign army in wartime, but international law only interdicts the dispatch of organized expeditions.[89] As long as the volunteering proceeds on a purely individual basis, it is not hindered by international law (even if the overall number of volunteers is considerable).[90] Evidently, genuine volunteers must not be confused with so-called "volunteers", who are regular troops in disguise.[91]

iii. Military Supplies to Belligerents

The Government of a neutral State must not (directly or indirectly) furnish military supplies of whatever type to a belligerent: Article 6 of Hague Convention No. XIII[92] and Article 44 of the Hague Rules of Aerial Warfare[93] are categorical about it with respect to naval and air warfare, and incontestably this is also the rule in land warfare. As for non-governmental supplies, Article 7 of both Hague Conventions Nos. V and XIII prescribes that a neutral State is not obligated to prevent private individuals from selling and exporting arms, ammunition and war materials to belligerents.[94] The only condition, set forth in Article 9 of Convention No. V, is that any prohibition or limitation decided upon by the neutral State will be applied impartially to both adversaries.[95]

---

[87] *Supra,* note 81, at 134.

[88] Under Article 47 of Protocol I of 1977, mercenaries (as defined therein) do not have the right to be combatants or prisoners of war. *Supra,* note 21, at 112-13. But the activities of mercenaries do not compromise the neutrality of their State of origin.

[89] See I. Brownlie, "Volunteers and the Law of War and Neutrality", 5 *I.C.L.Q.* 570, 571 (1956).

[90] See *ibid.,* 572.

[91] See *ibid.,* 578.

[92] *Supra,* note 83, at 210.

[93] *Supra,* note 82, at 37.

[94] *Supra,* note 81, at 134; *supra,* note 83, at 211.

[95] *Supra,* note 81, at 134.

It follows that the neutral State is at liberty to adopt one of two contradictory policies concerning sales and exports of war materials, by private individuals, to belligerents. The neutral State is entitled to impose a total embargo on such sales and exports, abolishing them altogether. Alternatively, the neutral State may erase any barrier to private trade, and afford an opportunity for the purchase of military goods by all comers in the open market. Whether the neutral State favours the one policy or the other, what is imperative is that it will apply the same yardsticks to all parties to the conflict. What the neutral State is barred from doing is establishing an embargo on individual sales of military supplies to one side, while giving a free hand to its opponent.

The neutral State may switch from one course of action to another during the war. This is what the United States did in the early days of the Second World War (prior to becoming a belligerent). When hostilities broke out in Europe in September 1939, the law in force in the United States was the Neutrality Act of 1935, which endorsed the embargo concept and unequivocally hamstrung the export of arms, ammunition and implements of war to belligerent countries.[96] In November 1939, Congress enacted a new Neutrality Act repealing the arms embargo.[97] The revised statute placed all trade with belligerents on a "cash and carry" basis.[98] It allowed the export to belligerents of any articles or materials, provided that title would be transferred to a foreign Government or a foreign national in advance of the export, and that the transport would be effected in non-American vessels.[99]

Long before its entry into the war, the United States abandoned the semblance of traditional neutrality and openly supported the United Kingdom against Nazi Germany (see *infra*, Chapter 6, D). But we must not gloss over the fact that, even in the period preceding the transition, although in theory the United States was dealing with belligerents on an equal footing, the "cash and carry" policy latently

---

[96] United States, Joint Resolution (Neutrality Act, 1935), 30 *A.J.I.L.*, Supp., 58 (1936). The term "embargo" features *ibid.*, 59.
[97] See P. C. Jessup, "The 'Neutrality Act of 1939'", 34 *A.J.I.L.* 95, 96 (1940).
[98] See H. R. Wellman, "The Neutrality Act of 1939", 25 *Cor.L.R.* 255, *id.* (1939-40).
[99] United States, Neutrality Act of 1939, 34 *A.J.I.L.*, Supp., 44, 45 (1940).

discriminated between them. The concept gravitated towards a preferential treatment of the belligerent (Great Britain) that ruled the waves and was actually able to pay cash and to carry, as opposed to the party (Germany) that could not avail itself of the open door owing to insurmountable obstacles in the way of transportation.

When the neutral State permits sales and exports of weapons, ammunition and war materials by private individuals to belligerents, it must be on the alert not to become a base of military operations against one of them.[100] This is primarily true of ships and aircraft. If a belligerent purchases a vessel or a plane from private individuals in a neutral country, and having obtained the craft adapts it thereafter to military purposes, no violation of neutrality occurs. However, if the craft bought by a warring party leaves the neutral territory armed and ready for action against the enemy, a breach of the laws of neutrality is committed.

Article 8 of Hague Convention No. XIII[101] and Article 46 of the Hague Rules of Aerial Warfare[102] instruct the neutral State to employ the means at its disposal to prevent within its jurisdiction the fitting out for use in war, the arming or the departure of a vessel or an aircraft, intended to engage in hostile operations against a belligerent. The progenitor of these provisions was the 1871 Washington Treaty,[103] concluded by the United States and Great Britain for the purposes of the famous Arbitration in the Alabama case. The "Alabama Rules", as formulated in the Treaty, used the idiom "due diligence" to describe the duty of prevention that has to be discharged by the neutral State.[104] Since the interpretation of the expression by the Arbitrators[105] turned out to be controversial,[106] the two clauses cited circumvent the problem by concentrating on the means at the disposal of the neutral State.

[100] *Supra*, note 82, at 37–8 (explanatory note).
[101] *Supra*, note 83, at 211.
[102] *Supra*, note 82, at 38.
[103] Great Britain–United States, Washington Treaty for the Amicable Settlement of All Causes of Difference between the Two Countries, 1871, 143 *C.T.S.* 145, 149.
[104] *Ibid.*, 149.
[105] *Alabama Claims* Award (1872), 1 *History and Digest of the International Arbitrations to Which the United States Has Been a Party* 653, 654 (J. B. Moore ed., 1898).
[106] See L. Oppenheim, *supra*, note 4, at 757–8.

CHAPTER 2

THE COURSE OF WAR

A. *The Beginning of War*

(a) *War in the Technical Sense*

War in the technical sense starts with a declaration of war. According to Article 1 of Hague Convention (No. III of 1907) Relative to the Commencement of Hostilities:

> hostilities ... must not commence without previous and explicit warning, in the form either of a declaration of war, giving reasons, or of an ultimatum with a conditional declaration of war.[1]

A declaration of war is a unilateral and formal announcement, issued by a Government (or any other competent authority), setting the exact point at which war begins between a given State and its designated enemy (or enemies). Article 1 explicitly mentions that reasons for such a step have to be given. But the causes of wars cannot be seriously established on the basis of a self-serving declaration. The main value of a declaration of war is derived from the fact that it pinpoints the precise time when a state of war enters into force.

An ultimatum may take one of two forms: (i) a threat that, if certain demands are not met, hostilities will be initiated; (ii) a warning that, if specific conditions are not fulfilled within a fixed time, war will commence *ipso facto*.[2] Article 1 requires an ultimatum of the second type (incorporating a conditional declaration of war). By itself, an ultimatum of the first category is not deemed sufficient under the Article, and it must be followed by a declaration of war. Only that subsequent declaration, rather

---

[1] Hague Convention (No. III of 1907) Relative to the Opening of Hostilities, *Hague Conventions* 96, *id.*

[2] See N. Hill, "Was There an Ultimatum before Pearl Harbor?", 42 *A.J.I.L.* 355, 357–8 (1948).

than the preliminary threat, would be in conformity with Hague Convention No. III.[3]

An ultimatum, almost by definition, entails a lapse of time (brief as it may be) providing an opportunity for compliance with its demands. Hostilities are not supposed to begin unless that period has expired and the response is considered unsatisfactory.

Insofar as an outright declaration of war is concerned, Hague Convention No. III does not insist on any meaningful interval before fighting starts.[4] Article 1 does prescribe that the declaration must be made "previous" to the commencement of hostilities, and even refers to it (on a par with an ultimatum) as a warning. However, it is significant that a proposed amendment of the Article, to the effect that 24 hours must pass between the issuance of the declaration and the outbreak of hostilities, was defeated in the course of the Hague Conference.[5] The upshot is that fire may be opened almost immediately after the announcement has been made.[6] A declaration of war under the Convention constitutes merely a formal measure, and it does not necessarily withhold the advantage of surprise from the attacking State.

Hague Convention No. III cannot be considered a reflection of customary international law.[7] Before the Convention, most wars were precipitated without a prelude in the form of a declaration of war.[8] The practice of States has not changed substantially since the conclusion of the Convention. Some hostilities are preceded by declarations of war, but this is the exception rather than the rule. Paradoxically, the paucity of such declarations at the present time may be linked, at least in part, to the illegality and criminality of wars of

---

[3] See *ibid.*, 358-9. Security Council Resolution No. 678 of November 1990 (45 *R.D.S.C.* 27 (1990)) is referred to by some commentators as an ultimatum to Iraq. M. Voelckel, "Faut-il Encore Déclarer la Guerre?", 37 *A.F.D.I.* 7, 21 (1991). But this is not the case, inasmuch as the Gulf War had already been in progress since the Iraqi invasion of Kuwait in August 1990 (see *supra*, Chapter 1, A, (b), iii).

[4] See E. C. Stowell, "Convention Relative to the Opening of Hostilities", 2 *A.J.I.L.* 50, 53-4 (1908).

[5] See A. P. Higgins, *The Hague Peace Conferences* 204 (1909).

[6] See T. J. Lawrence, *The Principles of International Law* 326 (7th ed., by P. H. Winfield, 1923).

[7] See G. Schwarzenberger, *The Law of Armed Conflict* 65-7 (1968).

[8] See P. M. Brown, "Undeclared Wars", 33 *A.J.I.L.* 538, 539 (1939).

aggression (see *infra*, Chapters 4-5). The contemporary injunction against war has not yet eliminated its incidence. Nevertheless, the prohibition has definitely created an atmosphere in which belligerents try to avoid the use of the expression "war". Consequently, they are indisposed to engage in declarations of "war".

Even when a declaration of war is published, in many instances this is done after the first strike, so that the act constitutes no more than a recognition of a state of war already in progress; occasionally, the declaration is issued by the State under attack, and it merely records that the enemy has launched war.[9] Of course, a post-attack declaration of war (by either party) is not in accordance with Hague Convention No. III.

When made, a declaration of war does not require "any particular *form*", although it must be authorized by a competent organ of the State.[10] This is understandable since, as a legal system, international law is singularly bereft of formalism.[11] How far the lack of formalism can go in the context of declarations of war is debatable. In the *Dalmia Cement* International Chamber of Commerce Arbitration of 1976, P. Lalive held that a broadcast delivered by the President of Pakistan in 1965 had not amounted to a declaration of war against India (pursuant to international law), inasmuch as it had not been a communication by one State to another.[12] On the other hand, a United States Federal District Court held in 1958, in the *Ulysses* case, that Egypt had declared war (consonant with international law) against Britain and France, in November 1956, in a public speech delivered by President Nasser before a large crowd in Cairo.[13] That speech, misunderstood or disregarded at the time, was later confirmed as a declaration of war in an official Egyptian statement.[14] The decision in the *Ulysses* case has been criticized on the ground

---

[9] See C. Eagleton, "The Form and Function of the Declaration of War", 32 *A.J.I.L.* 19, 32-3 (1938).

[10] E. Castrén, *The Present Law of War and Neutrality* 98 (1954).

[11] See Y. Dinstein, "International Law as a Primitive Legal System", 19 *N.Y.U.J.I.L.P.* 1, 27-9 (1986-7).

[12] *Dalmia Cement Ltd. v. National Bank of Pakistan* (1976), 67 *I.L.R.* 611, 616.

[13] *Navios Corporation v. The Ulysses II et al.* (1958), 161 *F. Supp.* 932, 942-3. The Judgment, and the reasons given therein, were affirmed by the U.S. Court of Appeals (4th Circuit) (260 *F. 2d* 959).

[14] *Ibid., id.*

that President Nasser's speech was "neither definite nor unequivocal" enough as a declaration of war.[15]

(b) *War in the Material Sense*

War in the material sense starts with actual hostilities, namely, an invasion, an assault, an artillery bombardment or, increasingly, an air raid. Hostilities may begin (i) without a declaration of war ever being made; (ii) prior to a declaration of war, which follows afterwards; (iii) simultaneously with a declaration of war; or (iv) subsequent to a declaration of war. Moreover, war in the material sense (viz. hostilities) may not commence at all, notwithstanding the delivery of a declaration of war (see *supra*, Chapter 1, A, (b), ii).

When the outbreak of hostilities does not coincide with a declaration of war (especially when the declaration lags behind the inception of the actual fighting and, more particularly, when it is emitted by the State under attack), there is likely to be some doubt as to whether war was triggered by the action or by the declaration.[16] In such a setting, it is quite possible that different dates for the outbreak of the war will be used for disparate purposes; for instance, the status of enemy nationals and the application of neutrality laws.[17]

Article 2 of Hague Convention No. III stipulates that the existence of a state of war must be notified to neutral States without delay, and it shall not affect them as long as the notification has not been received.[18] All the same, the Article lays down that, if a neutral country is in fact aware of the state of war, it cannot rely on the absence of notification. Under modern conditions, since a state of war habitually gets wide coverage in the news media, any special notification to neutrals may well be redundant.

---

[15] G. O. Fuller, "Note", 57 *Mich.L.R.* 610, 612 (1958-9).
[16] *Cf.* E. Borchard, "When Did the War Begin?", 47 *Col.L.R.* 742-8 (1947); C. Eagleton, "'Acts of War' ", 35 *A.J.I.L.* 321, 325 (1941).
[17] See M. O. Hudson, "The Duration of the War between the United States and Germany", 39 *Har.L.R.* 1020, 1021 (1925-6).
[18] *Supra*, note 1, at 96.

B. *The Termination of War*

(a) *Peace Treaties*

i. *The Significance of a Peace Treaty*

The classical and ideal method for the termination of war is the conclusion of a peace treaty between the belligerents. Traditionally, peace treaties have had an extraordinary impact on the evolution of international law, from Westphalia (1648) to Versailles (1919). The series of peace treaties signed at the close of the First World War even encompassed, in their first part (Articles 1-26), the Covenant of the League of Nations[19] (that is to say, the constitution of a comprehensive international organization, the predecessor of the United Nations). Despite their unique political standing, peace treaties are no different juridically from other types of inter-State agreements, and they are governed by the general law of treaties.[20]

After the Second World War, and as a direct consequence of the "cold war", no peace treaty could be reached with the principal vanquished country (Germany) which was divided for 45 years. It was only in 1990, following a sea change in world politics, that a Treaty on the Final Settlement with Respect to Germany could be formulated.[21] The Preamble of this instrument records the fact that the peoples of the contracting parties (the United States, the USSR, the United Kingdom, France and the two Germanies) "have been living together in peace since 1945".[22] In Article 1, a united Germany (comprising the territories of the Federal Republic of Germany, the German Democratic Republic and the whole of Berlin) is established, and "the definitive nature" of its borders - especially with Poland - is confirmed.[23] The 1990 Treaty may be deemed a final peace settlement for Germany.[24]

---

[19] Covenant of the League of Nations, 1919, 1 *Int.Leg.* 1, *id.*
[20] See G. Schwarzenberger, "Peace Treaties before International Courts and Tribunals", 8 *I.J.I.L.* 1, *id.* (1968).
[21] Treaty on the Final Settlement with Respect to Germany, 1990, 29 *I.L.M.* 1186, 1187 (1990).
[22] *Ibid., id.*
[23] *Ibid.*, 1186-9.
[24] See J. A. Frowein, "The Reunification of Germany", 86 *A.J.I.L.* 152, 157 (1992).

Peace treaties with five minor Axis countries - Italy, Bulgaria, Hungary, Romania and Finland - were concluded already in 1947 at Paris.[25] With Japan the Western Allied Powers arrived at a peace treaty, in San Francisco, in 1951.[26] The USSR was not a contracting party to the latter instrument. Instead, a Joint Declaration was adopted by the USSR and Japan, in 1956, whereby the state of war between the two parties was brought to an end.[27] The Joint Declaration sets forth that negotiations aimed at a peace treaty will continue.[28] However, since it proclaims that the state of war is ended, and that peace, friendship and good neighbourly relations are restored,[29] including diplomatic and consular relations,[30] the Declaration already attains most of the objectives of an ordinary peace treaty.

In the international armed conflicts of the post Second World War era, States commonly try to avoid not only the term "war" but also its corollary "peace treaty". An outstanding exception is the Treaty of Peace concluded, in 1979, between Egypt and Israel.[31]

The hallmark of a peace treaty is that it both (i) puts an end to a preexisting state of war, and (ii) initiates or reinstates amicable relations between the parties. The two steps need not be synchronized: under Article I of the Egyptian-Israeli Treaty of Peace, the state of war between the parties is to be terminated upon ratification, while "normal and friendly relations" are to be introduced after an interim period of three years.[32] The gradual time-table is a marginal matter. The decisive element is that a peace treaty is not just a negative instrument (in the sense of the negation of war); it is also a positive document (regulating the normalization of friendly

---

[25] Paris Peace Treaty with Italy, 1947, 4 *Peace Treaties* 2421; Paris Peace Treaty with Bulgaria, 1947, *ibid.*, 2525; Paris Peace Treaty with Hungary, 1947, *ibid.*, 2553; Paris Peace Treaty with Roumania, 1947, *ibid.*, 2585; Paris Peace Treaty with Finland, 1947, *ibid.*, 2615.

[26] San Francisco Peace Treaty with Japan, 1951, 4 *Peace Treaties* 2641.

[27] USSR-Japan, Joint Declaration, 1956, 263 *U.N.T.S.* 112, *id.* (Article 1).

[28] *Ibid.*, 116 (Article 9).

[29] *Ibid.*, 112 (Article 1).

[30] *Ibid.*, 114 (Article 2).

[31] Egypt-Israel, Treaty of Peace, 1979, 18 *I.L.M.* 362 (1979).

[32] *Ibid.*, 363. See also *ibid.*, 364 (Article III (3)), 367 (Annex I, Article I).

relations between the former belligerents).[33] Normalization produces effects in diverse areas, ranging from diplomatic to cultural exchanges, from navigation to aviation, and from trade to scientific cooperation. The quintessence of a peace treaty is writing *finis* not only to the armed phase of the conflict between the parties, but to the conflict as a whole. Hence, the conclusion of a peace treaty constitutes, in appropriate circumstances, an implied recognition of a contracting party as a State.[34]

Patently, a peace treaty is no guarantee of peace. If the root causes of the war are not eradicated, another armed conflict may erupt in time. In addition, new bones of contention, not foreseen when the peace treaty is signed, may become catalysts to another war. It even happens that the same peace treaty which closes one war lays the foundation for the next one: the Treaty of Versailles is a prime example of this deplorable state of affairs. When a peace treaty is acclaimed as a "final" settlement, and statesmen indulge in high-sounding prognostications as to its lasting power, it is advisable to recall that most wars commence between parties that have earlier concluded peace treaties. The life expectancy of an average peace treaty does not necessarily exceed the span of a generation or two. Each generation must work out for itself a fresh formula for peaceful coexistence.

Prior to the entry into force of a definitive peace treaty, the parties may agree on preliminaries of peace. Such a procedure generates the following results:

a. In the past, the peace preliminaries themselves might have brought hostilities to an end,[35] whereas the ultimate peace treaty would focus on the process of normalizing relations between the former belligerents. Nowadays, the function of peace preliminaries

---

[33] On the distinction between positive and negative peace, see H. Rumpf, "The Concepts of Peace and War in International Law", 27 *G.Y.I.L.* 429, 431-3 (1984).

[34] Express recognition is specifically agreed upon in Article III of the Egyptian-Israeli Peace Treaty, *supra*, note 31, at 363-4. But there is every reason to believe that recognition would have been implied from the treaty in any event. *Cf.* H. Lauterpacht, *Recognition in International Law* 378 (1947).

[35] See L. Oppenheim, 2 *International Law* 607 (7th ed., by H. Lauterpacht, 1952).

of this type will usually be served by an armistice agreement (see *infra*, (b)).

b. At the present time, peace preliminaries generally represent a mere "*pactum de contrahendo* on the outline of a prospective peace treaty".[36] Unless and until the projected peace treaty actually materializes, the final curtain is not drawn on the war. As an illustration, one can point to the two Camp David Framework Agreements of 1978 for Peace in the Middle East and for the Conclusion of a Peace Treaty between Egypt and Israel.[37] Here the parties agreed on certain principles and some specifics, designed to serve as guidelines for a peace settlement. However, as mentioned, the war between Egypt and Israel was terminated only by dint of the Treaty of Peace (concluded, after further negotiations, in 1979).

ii. The Legal Validity of a Peace Treaty

As long as war was regarded as a lawful course of action in international affairs (see *infra*, Chapter 3, D), peace treaties were considered perfectly valid, even when imposed by the victor on the defeated party as an outcome of the use of force.[38] As soon as the use of inter-State force was forbidden by international law (see *infra*, Chapter 4), some scholars began to argue that a peace treaty dictated by an aggressor ought to be vitiated by duress.[39] This doctrinal approach has been endorsed in Article 52 of the 1969 Vienna Convention on the Law of Treaties:

> A treaty is void if its conclusion has been procured by the threat or use of force in violation of the principles of international law embodied in the Charter of the United Nations.[40]

It can be stated with confidence that Article 52 reflects customary international law as it stands today. In 1973, the International Court

---

[36] W. G. Grewe, "Peace Treaties", 4 *E.P.I.L.* 102, 105 (1982).

[37] Egypt-Israel, Camp David Agreements, 1978: A Framework for Peace in the Middle East, 17 *I.L.M.* 1466 (1978); Framework for the Conclusion of a Peace Treaty between Egypt and Israel, *ibid.*, 1470.

[38] See Lord McNair, *The Law of Treaties* 207, 209 (1961).

[39] See H. Lauterpacht, 1 *International Law* 354 (E. Lauterpacht ed., 1979).

[40] Vienna Convention on the Law of Treaties, 1969, [1969] *U.N.J.Y.* 140, 153.

of Justice held, in a dispute between the United Kingdom and Iceland, in the *Fisheries Jurisdiction* case:

There can be little doubt, as is implied in the Charter of the United Nations and recognized in Article 52 of the Vienna Convention on the Law of Treaties, that under contemporary international law an agreement concluded under the threat or use of force is void.[41]

The International Law Commission, in its commentary on the draft of Article 52, explained that the clause does not operate retroactively by invalidating peace treaties procured by coercion prior to the development of the modern law banning the use of force by States.[42] The Commission expressed the opinion that the provision is applicable to all treaties concluded at least since 1945 (the entry into force of the Charter of the United Nations).[43]

Article 52 does not affect all peace treaties equally. The text makes it plain that "only the *unlawful* use of force ... can bring about the nullity of a treaty".[44] It follows that Article 52 invalidates solely those peace treaties which are imposed by an aggressor State on the target of aggression. As regards the reverse situation, Article 75 of the Convention proclaims:

The provisions of the present Convention are without prejudice to any obligation in relation to a treaty which may arise for an aggressor State in consequence of measures taken in conformity with the Charter of the United Nations with reference to that State's aggression.[45]

The invalidity of a peace treaty concluded under duress does not result from "vitiated consent": it is a sanction against an internationally unlawful and even a criminal act[46] (see *infra*, Chapter 5, A).

---

[41] *Fisheries Jurisdiction* Case (Jurisdiction of the Court), [1973] *I.C.J. Rep.* 3, 14.
[42] Report of the International Law Commission, 18th Session, [1966] II *I.L.C. Ybk* 172, 247.
[43] *Ibid., id.*
[44] I. Sinclair, *The Vienna Convention on the Law of Treaties* 180 (2nd ed., 1984).
[45] *Supra*, note 40, at 159.
[46] P. Reuter, *Introduction to the Law of Treaties* 140 (J. Mico and P. Haggenmacher trans., 1989).

Hence, there is nothing legally wrong in a peace treaty leaning in favour of a State victimized by aggression (assuming that it has prevailed militarily). In the words of Sir Humphrey Waldock, "[c]learly, there is all the difference in the world between coercion used by an aggressor to consolidate the fruits of his aggression in a treaty and coercion used to impose a peace settlement upon an aggressor".[47] Only "unlawful coercion" invalidates a treaty.[48]

Article 44(5) of the Vienna Convention does not permit any separation of the provisions of a treaty falling under Article 52.[49] This means that a treaty procured by coercion is void in its entirety: none of its parts may be severed from the remainder of the instrument, with a view to being saved from abrogation. The general rule would apply, *inter alia*, to a peace treaty accepted under duress by the victim of aggression. But we must be mindful of the fact that such a treaty is not always confined to undertakings advantageous to the aggressor. Indeed, the most momentous clause in the text will presumably be the one terminating the war. If the whole juridical slate is swept clean by nullity, the section devoted to ending the war would also be wiped off. Is it to be understood that the former belligerents are put again on a war footing? The answer, as furnished by Article 43 of the Vienna Convention, is that the invalidity of a treaty does not impair duties embodied therein, if these are independently binding on the parties by virtue of general international law.[50] All States must comply with the contemporary prohibition of the use of inter-State force, and the abrogation of a particular peace treaty does not alter this basic position.

Article 52 refers to a treaty procured by unlawful use or threat of force as "void". The expression is expounded by Article 69(1), which states that the "provisions of a void treaty have no legal force".[51] The concept underlying Article 52 is one of "absolute nullity".[52] It is true that a party invoking a ground for impeaching the validity of a treaty must take certain steps enumerated in

[47] H. Waldock, "Second Report on the Law of Treaties", [1963] II *I.L.C. Ybk* 36, 52.
[48] H. G. de Jong, "Coercion in the Conclusion of Treaties", 15 *N.Y.I.L.* 209, 227 (1984).
[49] *Supra*, note 40, at 152.
[50] *Ibid., id.*
[51] *Ibid.*, 158.
[52] See I. Sinclair, *supra*, note 44, at 160-1.

Article 65.[53] The obligation to observe the procedure set out in Article 65 might suggest that, should the aggrieved party (for reasons of its own) refrain from contesting the validity of the treaty, nullification would not take place.[54] However, if that were the case, the instrument would really be voidable rather than void. If a peace treaty dictated by an aggressor is genuinely void, it must be tainted by nullity automatically and *ab initio*. Therefore, any competent forum should be authorized to recognize the treaty as void, even if no attempt has been made by the State concerned to invoke invalidity.[55]

(b) *Armistice Agreements*

Under orthodox international law, an armistice was construed as an interlude in the fighting, interchangeable in substance with a truce or a cease-fire (see *infra*, C). It is characteristic that Articles 36 to 41 of the Hague Regulations, annexed to Hague Convention (No. II of 1899 and No. IV of 1907) Respecting the Laws and Customs of War on Land, employ the expression "armistice" when the subject under discussion is the suspension of hostilities.[56] By contrast, in the current practice of States, an armistice chiefly denotes a cessation of hostilities, completely divesting the parties of the right to renew military operations under any circumstances whatever. An armistice of this nature puts an end to the war, and does not merely suspend the combat.

The transformation undergone by "armistice" as a legal term of art had its origins in the armistices of November 1918, which brought about a cessation of hostilities in the First World War.[57] The innovative trend continued in a number of armistices of the Second World War resembling peace preliminaries (of the first

---

[53] *Supra*, note 40, at 157.
[54] See C. L. Rozakis, "The Law on Invalidity of Treaties", 16 *A r. V.* 150, 168-9 (1973-5).
[55] See E. Jiménez de Aréchaga, "International Law in the Past Third of a Century" 159 *R.C.A.D.I.* 1, 68 (1978).
[56] Regulations Respecting the Laws and Customs of War on Land (Annexed to Hague Conventions No. II of 1899 and No. IV of 1907), *Hague Conventions* 100, 107, 121-2.
[57] Protocol of the Conditions of an Armistice with Austria-Hungary, 1918, 13 *A.J.I.L.*, Supp., 80 (1919); Conditions of an Armistice with Germany, 1918, *ibid.*, 97.

category).[58] Significantly, in the armistices with Romania and Hungary, these two countries declared that they had "withdrawn from the war".[59] The most extreme case was the Italian armistice of September 1943,[60] leading to a declaration of war by Italy against Germany. The Preamble to the 1947 Paris Peace Treaty with Italy directs attention to the fact that Italy "thereby became a co-belligerent against Germany".[61] For a traditionalist, adhering to the notion of an armistice as a mere suspension of hostilities, "Italy's co-belligerency created a highly anomalous situation juridically, and one which to some extent defies legal analysis and classification".[62] After all, if the war between the Allied Powers and Italy did not end until the Peace Treaty of 1947, Italy – the armed forces of which were fighting, after 1943, alongside of Allied formations against a common foe (Germany) – was the co-belligerent of its enemies![63] The co-belligerency status of Italy is much easier to explain if the legal effects of the 1943 armistice are put in a new light.

The evolution in the perception of armistice reached its zenith at a later stage, with a series of General Armistice Agreements signed in 1949 between Israel, on the one hand, and Egypt, Lebanon, Jordan and Syria, on the other,[64] followed by the 1953 Panmunjom Agreement Concerning a Military Armistice in Korea.[65] These Armistice Agreements terminated the Israeli War of Independence and the Korean War, respectively, although they did not produce peace in the full meaning of the term. Typically, the Panmunjom

---

[58] See A. Klafkowski, "Les Formes de Cessation de l'Etat de Guerre en Droit International", 149 *R.C.A.D.I.* 217, 249-50 (1976).

[59] Armistice Agreement with Rumania, 1944, 9 *Int.Leg.* 139, 140 (Article I); Armistice Agreement with Hungary, 1945, *ibid.,* 276, 277 (Article I(a)).

[60] Conditions of an Armistice with Italy, 1943, 9 *Int.Leg.* 50.

[61] *Supra,* note 25, at 2421-2 (Italy).

[62] G. G. Fitzmaurice, "The Juridical Clauses of the Peace Treaties", 73 *R.C.A.D.I.* 259, 270-2 (1948).

[63] See Department of State, Commentary on the Additional Conditions of the Armistice with Italy, 1945, 40 *A.J.I.L.,* Supp., 18, *id.* (1946).

[64] Israel-Egypt, General Armistice Agreement, 1949, 42 *U.N.T.S.* 251; Israel-Lebanon, General Armistice Agreement, 1949, *ibid.,* 287; Israel-Jordan, General Armistice Agreement, 1949, *ibid.,* 303; Israel-Syria, General Armistice Agreement, 1949, *ibid.,* 327.

[65] Panmunjom Agreement Concerning a Military Armistice in Korea, 1953, 47 *A.J.I.L.,* Supp., 186 (1953).

Agreement states as its objective the establishment of an armistice ensuring "a complete cessation of hostilities and of all acts of armed force in Korea until a final peace settlement is achieved".[66] The thesis (advanced in 1992) that "the Korean War is still legally in effect",[67] is untenable.

A closer look at the Israeli Armistice Agreements may illuminate the special features and the problematics of armistice as a mechanism for ending wars. The first Article of all four Agreements prescribes that, with a view to promoting the return to permanent peace in Palestine, the parties affirm a number of principles, including a prohibition of resort to military force and aggressive action.[68] In keeping with these principles, the parties are forbidden to commit any warlike or hostile act against one another.[69] The Agreements clarify that they are concluded without prejudice to the "rights, claims and positions"[70] of the parties in the ultimate peaceful settlement of the Palestine Question.[71] The purpose of the armistice is described in terms of a transition from truce to a permanent peace.[72] Above all, the Agreements set forth that they will remain in force until a peaceful settlement between the parties is achieved.[73]

The "without prejudice" formula (so popular among lawyers) was introduced to forestall future claims of estoppel in the course of peace negotiations. The formula must not obscure the salient point that the parties reserve only their right to reopen all outstanding issues when they eventually get to negotiate an amicable settlement of the conflict. During the intervening time, the conflict continues,

---

[66] *Ibid.*, 186-7 (Preamble).

[67] G. von Glahn, *Law among Nations* 727 (6th ed., 1992).

[68] *Supra*, note 64, at 252-4 (Egypt), 288-90 (Lebanon), 304-6 (Jordan), 328-30 (Syria).

[69] *Ibid.*, 254 (Egypt, Article II), 290 (Lebanon, Article III), 306 (Jordan, Article III), 330 (Syria, Article III).

[70] For the origin of this formula, *cf.* Article 40 of the UN Charter (regarding provisional measures taken by the Security Council; see *infra*, Chapter 10, A). Charter of the United Nations, 1945, 9 *Int.Leg.* 327, 343.

[71] *Supra*, note 64, at 268 (Egypt, Article XI), 290 (Lebanon, Article II), 306 (Jordan, Article II), 330 (Syria, Article II).

[72] *Ibid.*, 268 (Egypt, Article XII), 296-8 (Lebanon, Article VIII), 318 (Jordan, Article XII), 340 (Syria, Article VIII).

[73] *Ibid.*, *id.*

but it is no longer an armed conflict. The thrust of each Agreement is that both parties waive in an unqualified manner any legal option that either of them may have had to resume hostilities and to resolve the conflict by force. The Agreements can be considered transitional, inasmuch as they were intended to be ultimately replaced by definitive peace treaties; yet, there is nothing temporary about them.[74]

Article v (2) of the Agreement with Egypt avers that the Armistice Demarcation Line "is not to be construed in any sense as a political or territorial boundary" and, again, that the line is drawn "without prejudice".[75] This clause is not replicated in the other Agreements, although a more diluted version has been inserted into Article VI (9) of the Agreement with Jordan[76] and Article V (l) of the Agreement with Syria[77] (there is no counterpart in the Agreement with Lebanon). Once more, the disclaimer may be taken as lip-service. An analysis of the Agreements in all their aspects shows that "the armistice demarcation lines can be regarded as equivalent to international frontiers, with all the consequences which that entails".[78] When a line of demarcation between States is sanctioned in such a way that it can be revised only by mutual consent (and not by force), it becomes a political or territorial border.[79] The line may not be deemed "final", but the frontiers of no country in the world are impressed with a stamp of finality. All international frontiers can be altered by mutual consent, and history shows that many of them undergo kaleidoscopic modifications through agreements.[80]

It is noteworthy that when the United Nations Security Council, in 1951, had to deal with an Israeli complaint concerning restrictions imposed by Egypt on the passage of ships through the Suez Canal,

---

[74] See S. Rosenne, *Israel's Armistice Agreements with the Arab States* 82 (1951).

[75] *Supra,* note 64, at 256 (Egypt).

[76] *Ibid.,* 312 (Jordan).

[77] *Ibid.,* 332 (Syria).

[78] S. Rosenne, *supra,* note 74, at 48.

[79] A distinction between armistice demarcation lines and other international boundaries is made in the Declaration on Principles of International Law Concerning Friendly Relations and Co-operation among States in accordance with the Charter of the United Nations. General Assembly Resolution No. 2625 (xxv), 25 *R.G.A.* 121, 122 (1970). It is submitted that this distinction is no longer valid in most cases.

[80] See J. H. W. Verzijl, 6 *International Law in Historical Perspective* 459-553 (1973).

the Council adopted Resolution No. 95 pronouncing that the armistice between the two countries "is of a permanent character" and that, accordingly, "neither party can reasonably assert that it is actively a belligerent".[81] It emerges from the text of the Resolution, and the thorough discussion preceding it, that the Council totally rejected an Egyptian contention that a state of war continued to exist with Israel after the armistice.[82]

The Israeli Armistice Agreements carry in their titles the adjective "General". This was done against the backdrop of Article 37 of the Hague Regulations,[83] which sets side by side a general and a local armistice (meaning suspension of hostilities (see *infra*, C)). The Panmunjom Armistice Agreement already omits the adjective. The omission is consistent with the modern meaning of an armistice agreement as an end to war, for a local termination of war is an oxymoronic figure of speech. An authentic termination of war must be general in its scope.

No doubt, an armistice agreement is never the equivalent of a peace treaty. When it brings war to a close, an armistice is like the first category of preliminaries of peace. Whereas a peace treaty is multi-dimensional (both negating war and providing for amicable relations), an armistice agreement is restricted to the negative aspect of the demise of war. To the extent that a distinction is drawn between associative and dissociative peace (the latter amounting to "the absence of war, a peace defined negatively"),[84] an armistice has to be marked as a dissociative peace.

Comparatively speaking, the negation of war is of greater import than the introduction or restoration of, say, trade or cultural relations. Still, when such relations are non-existent, a meaningful ingredient is missing from the fabric of peace. That is why the mere conclusion of an armistice agreement does not imply recognition of a new State. Furthermore, notwithstanding an armistice, diplomatic relations need not be established or reestablished. The frontiers (the

---

[81] Security Council Resolution No. 95, 6 *R.D.S.C.* 10, 11 (1951).
[82] See N. Feinberg, *Studies in International Law* 87-92 (1979).
[83] *Supra*, note 56, at 121.
[84] B. V. A. Röling, "International Law and the Maintenance of Peace", 4 *N.Y.I.L.* 1, 7 (1973).

Armistice Demarcation Lines) may remain closed, and, in general, relations between the former belligerents will probably be strained. After all, the armed phase of the conflict is over, but the conflict itself may continue unabated.

As a result, even after an armistice agreement, the conclusion of a peace treaty remains a high priority item on the agenda. The armistice ends the war, but the consummation of a fully-fledged peace requires a lot more. When the advent of a peace treaty in the post-armistice period is delayed, as has been the case both in the Arab-Israeli conflict and in Korea, the chances of another conflagration always loom large on the political horizon. Nevertheless, should any of the former belligerents plunge again into hostilities, this would be considered the unleashing of a new war and not the resumption of fighting in an on-going armed conflict.

There is entrenched resistance in the legal literature to any re-appraisal of the role assigned to armistice in the vocabulary of war.[85] *Pace* this doctrinal conservatism, the terminology has to be adjusted to fit the modern practice of States.[86] The metamorphosis that has occurred over the years in the legal status of armistice must be acknowledged.

(c) *Other Modes of Terminating War*

A war may be brought to its conclusion not only in a peace treaty or an armistice agreement. It may also come to an end in one of the following ways:

i. *Implied Mutual Consent*

When belligerents enter into a peace treaty or an armistice agreement, war is terminated by mutual consent expressed in the instrument. It is not requisite, however, that the mutual consent to end a war be verbalized by the parties. Such consent can also be inferred

---

[85] See, e.g., H. S. Levie, "The Nature and Scope of the Armistice Agreement", 50 *A.J.I.L.* 880, 881-6 (1956). *Cf.* S. D. Bailey, "Cease-Fires, Truces, and Armistices in the Practice of the UN Security Council", 71 *A.J.I.L.* 461, 472 (1977). *Cf.* also Italian–United States Conciliation Commission, *Mergé* Case (1955), 11 *R.I.A.A.* 236, 241.

[86] See J. Stone, *Legal Controls of International Conflict* 641-2, 644 (1954). *Cf.* M. W. Graham, "Armistices - 1944 Style", 39 *A.J.I.L.* 286, 287 (1945).

by implication from their behaviour: a state of war may come to a close by virtue of a mere cessation of hostilities on both sides.[87]

An examination of the legal consequences of the absence of warfare must be conducted prudently. The fact that all is quiet along the front line is not inescapably indicative of a tacit consent to put paid to hostilities. A lull in the fighting, or a formal cease-fire, may account for the military inactivity. War cannot be regarded as over unless some supplemental evidence is discernible that neither party proposes to resume the hostilities.[88] The evidence may be distilled from the establishment or resumption of diplomatic relations.[89]

To give tangible form to the scenario of a state of war continuing despite a lengthy hiatus in the fighting, we may take the case of Israel and Iraq. Iraq is one of the Arab countries that invaded Israel in 1948. Unlike its co-belligerents (Egypt, Lebanon, Jordan and Syria), Iraq took advantage of the fact that it has no common border with Israel and refused to sign an Armistice Agreement (simply pulling its troops out of the combat zone). After prolonged periods of avoiding a military confrontation, Iraqi and Israeli armed forces clashed again in June 1967 and in October 1973.[90] In 1981, Israeli aircraft destroyed an Iraqi nuclear reactor (under construction), which apparently had the capacity of manufacturing nuclear weapons.[91] In our opinion, the only plausible legal justification for the bombing of the reactor (see *infra*, Chapter 7, B, (a)) is that the act represented another round of hostilities in an on-going armed conflict. In 1991 – in the course of the Gulf War – Iraq launched dozens of Scud missiles against Israeli objectives (mostly, centres of population), despite the fact that Israel was not a member of the American-led coalition which had engaged in combat to restore the sovereignty of Kuwait. The indiscriminate bombardment of civilians, by missiles

---

[87] See C. C. Tansill, "Termination of War by Mere Cessation of Hostilities", 38 *L.Q.R.* 26-37 (1922).

[88] See J. M. Mathews, "The Termination of War", 19 *Mich.L.R.* 819, 828 (1920-1).

[89] See L. Kotzsch, *The Concept of War in Contemporary History and International Law* 251 (1956).

[90] See U. Shoham, "The Israeli Aerial Raid upon the Iraqi Nuclear Reactor and the Right of Self-Defense", 109 *Mil.L.R.* 191, 206 n. 67 (1985).

[91] See *ibid.*, 191, 207-10.

or otherwise, is unlawful under the *jus in bello*.[92] While the *jus* is the same in every *bellum*, it is useful to single out the relevant framework of hostilities. The Iraqi missile offensive against Israel must be observed in the legal context not of the Gulf War but of the war between Iraq and Israel which started in 1948 yet continues to this very day.[93] That war is still in progress, unhindered by the inordinate lapse of time since 1948, for hostilities flare up intermittently.

ii. Debellatio

Debellatio is a situation in which one of the belligerents is utterly defeated, to the point of its total disintegration as a sovereign nation. Since the war is no longer inter-State in character, it is terminated by itself. Even though the extinction of an existing State as a result of war is not to be lightly assumed, there comes a time when it can no longer be denied.[94] We shall return to this thorny problem *infra* (Chapter 6, E).

Debellatio necessarily involves effective military occupation of the local territory by the enemy, but it goes beyond that: all organized resistance has to disappear, and the occupied State must be "reduced to impotence".[95] The three basic parameters of *debellatio* are as follows: (i) the territory of the former belligerent is occupied in its entirety, no remnant being left for the exercise of sovereignty; (ii) the armed forces of the erstwhile belligerent are no longer in the field (usually there is an unconditional surrender), and no allied forces carry on fighting by proxy; and (iii) the Government of the former belligerent has passed out of existence, and no other Government (not even a Government in exile) continues to offer effective opposition.[96] Kuwait was saved from *debellatio* in the Gulf War, notwithstanding its total occupation by the Iraqi armed forces,

---

[92] Protocol Additional to the Geneva Conventions of 12 August 1949, and Relating to the Protection of Victims of International Armed Conflicts (Protocol I), 1977, [1977] *U.N.J.Y.* 95, 114 (Article 51(4)-(5)). *Cf.* P. Bretton, "Remarques sur le *Jus in Bello* dans la Guerre du Golfe (1991)", 37 *A.F.D.I.* 139, 149 (1991).
[93] See L. R. Beres, "After the Gulf War: Israel, Pre-Emption, and Anticipatory Self-Defense", 13 *H.J.I.L.* 259, *id.* (1990-1).
[94] See J. Crawford, *The Creation of States in International Law* 418-20 (1979).
[95] C. Phillipson, *Termination of War and Treaties of Peace* 9 (1916).
[96] See M. Greenspan, *The Modern Law of Land Warfare* 600-3 (1959).

because its Government went into exile and a large American-led coalition soon came to its aid militarily.

The phenomenon of *debellatio* has been recognized in many instances in the past.[97] Some scholars contend that a *debellatio* of Germany occurred at the end of the Second World War,[98] following the unconditional surrender of the Nazi armed forces.[99] However, the legal status of Germany in the immediate post-War period was exceedingly complicated.[100] The position was so intricate that, in the same Allied country (the United Kingdom), different dates were used for different legal purposes to mark the termination of the war with Germany.[101]

iii. Unilateral Declaration

Just as war can (and, under Hague Convention No. III, must) begin with a unilateral declaration of war, it can also end with a unilateral declaration.[102] In this way the United States proclaimed, in 1951, the termination of the state of war with Germany.[103]

The technique of a unilateral declaration can be looked upon not as an independent mode for bringing war to a close, but as an offshoot of one of the two preceding methods. As indicated (*supra*, Chapter 1, A, (b)), Arcadia can impose war on Utopia by a unilateral declaration or act. Just as Utopia is unable to prevent Arcadia from submerging them both in war, Utopia cannot effectively terminate the war when Arcadia is bent on continuing it. A unilateral declaration by Utopia ending the war is an inane gesture, if Arcadia is able and willing to go on fighting. "For war can be started by one party, but its ending presupposes the consent of both parties, if the

---

[97] See J. H. W. Verzijl, 3 *International Law in Historical Perspective* 361-2 (1970).

[98] See G. Schwarzenberger, *supra*, note 7, at 467, 730. *Cf.* H. Kelsen, "The Legal Status of Germany according to the Declaration of Berlin", 39 *A.J.I.L.* 518-26 (1945).

[99] Act of Military Surrender of Germany, 1945, 9 *Int.Leg.* 312.

[100] See L. Oppenheim, 1 *International Law* 699-700 (9th ed., by R. Jennings and A. Watts., 1992).

[101] See F. A. Mann, *Foreign Affairs in English Courts* 33 (1986).

[102] See Anonymous, "Judicial Determination of the End of the War", 47 *Col.L.R.* 255, 258 (1947).

[103] This was done in a Proclamation by President Truman pursuant to a joint resolution by Congress. Termination of the State of War with Germany, 1951, 46 *A.J.I.L.*, Supp., 12 (1952).

enemy state survives as a sovereign state".[104] A unilateral Utopian declaration promulgating that the war is over has a valid effect only if Arcadia is either completely defeated (undergoing *debellatio*) or is willing to abide by the declaration.[105] If both Utopia and Arcadia exist at the end of the war, both must agree to finish it. Yet, such an agreement may consist of a formal declaration by Utopia and the tacit consent of Arcadia.[106]

C. *The Suspension of Hostilities*

(a) *Different Types of Suspension of Hostilities*

A suspension of hostilities may evolve *de facto* when no military operations take place. A respite of this nature may endure for a long period of time. But since neither belligerent is legally committed to refrain from resuming hostilities, the fighting can break out again at any moment without warning.[107]

More importantly, belligerents may assume an obligation *de jure* to abstain from combat in the course of a war (which goes on). A number of terms are used to depict a legal undertaking to suspend hostilities: (i) truce, (ii) cease-fire, and in the past also (iii) armistice. As noted (*supra*, B, (b)), the last term – armistice – has undergone a drastic change in recent years and now principally conveys a cessation, rather than a suspension, of hostilities. The current usage of the term "cease-fire", in lieu of "armistice", must be recalled when one examines Articles 36 to 41 of the Hague Regulations (of 1899 and 1907) Respecting the Laws and Customs of War on Land.[108] These clauses do not employ the phrase "cease-fire". Instead, they refer to "armistice", commensurately with the vocabulary prevalent at the turn of the century. However, since their avowed aim is to govern the suspension of hostilities, they

---

[104] J. L. Kunz, "Ending the War with Germany", 46 *A.J.I.L.* 114, 115 (1952).

[105] See D. Ottensooser, "'Termination of War by Unilateral Declaration", 29 *B.Y.B.I.L.* 435, 442 (1952).

[106] See F. C. Balling, "Unconditional Surrender and a Unilateral Declaration of Peace", 39 *A.P.S.R.* 474, 476 (1945).

[107] See M. Sibert, "L'Armistice", 40 *R.G.D.I.P.* 657, 660 (1933).

[108] *Supra*, note 56, at 121-2.

must be deemed applicable to present-day cease-fires (as opposed to modern armistices).

The expression "truce" is embedded in tradition and history. It acquired particular resonance in the Middle Ages, in the form of the Truce of God (*Treuga Dei*). This was an ecclesiastical measure by which the Catholic Church forbade war in Christendom on certain days (initially Sundays and Holy Days, and later several days every week and whole seasons every year).[109] The phrase "cease-fire" is more modern. Although some scholars ascribe to truce and cease-fire divergent implications, the present practice of States - for the most part - treats them as synonymous.[110] As examples for an indiscriminate use of the two terms, it is possible to adduce successive resolutions adopted by the UN Security Council during Israel's War of Independence in 1948.[111]

A cease-fire (or truce) may be partial or total in scope. Article 37 of the Hague Regulations differentiates between a general cease-fire (originally, "armistice") suspending all military operations everywhere, and a local cease-fire suspending such operations only between certain units at particular locations.[112]

i. Local Cease-Fire Agreement

A cease-fire (or truce) may apply to a limited sector of the front, without impinging on the continuation of combat elsewhere. The object of such a local suspension of hostilities is to enable the belligerents to evacuate the wounded, bury the dead, conduct negotiations, and so forth. A local cease-fire may be agreed upon on the spot by military commanders (who can be relatively junior in rank), without the involvement of their respective Governments. The agreement would then be informal, and it does not have to be in writing.[113]

---

[109] See L. Halphen, "Truce and Peace of God", 15 *Encyclopaedia of the Social Sciences* 107, 108 (1935).

[110] See P. Mohn, "Problems of Truce Supervision", 478 *Int.Con.* 51, 53-7 (1952).

[111] Security Council Resolutions Nos. 49, 50, 53, 54, 56, 59, 61 and 62, 3 *R.D.S.C.* 19-30 (1948).

[112] *Supra*, note 56, at 121.

[113] See L. Oppenheim, *supra*, note 35, at 550.

Article 15 of the (First) Geneva Convention of 1949 for the Amelioration of the Condition of the Wounded and Sick in Armed Forces in the Field stipulates that, whenever circumstances permit, a suspension of hostilities is to be arranged (generally or locally) so as to facilitate the removal, exchange and transport of the wounded left on the battlefield or within a besieged or encircled area.[114] The Article employs the term "armistice", but what is actually meant in current terminology is a cease-fire.

ii. General Cease-Fire Agreement

Belligerents may enter into an agreement suspending hostilities everywhere within the region of war (see *supra*, Chapter 1, C). The duration of a general cease-fire (or truce) may be predetermined in the agreement or it may be left open.

A general cease-fire agreement is normally made in writing by (or with the approval of) the Governments concerned. In that case, it has the status of a treaty under international law.[115] The agreement may include clauses transcending the details of the suspension of hostilities, and relating to such matters as the immediate release of prisoners of war. Semantically, this may sound strange. Should a belligerent extend the detention of prisoners of war, beyond the date set for their release in a general cease-fire agreement, the act would constitute a cease-fire violation although no fire has been opened.

iii. Cease-Fire Ordered by the Security Council

The Security Council, performing its functions under Chapter VII of the Charter of the United Nations,[116] may order belligerents to cease fire. Unequivocal language to that effect is contained, for example, in Resolution No. 54 (1948)[117] adopted at the time of Israel's

---

[114] (First) Geneva Convention for the Amelioration of the Condition of the Wounded and Sick in Armed Forces in the Field, 75 *U.N.T.S.* 31, 40-2.

[115] See R. R. Baxter, "Armistices and Other Forms of Suspension of Hostilities", 149 *R.C.A.D.I.* 353, 371-2 (1976). The author did not differentiate between the terms "cease-fire" and "armistice".

[116] *Supra*, note 70, at 343-6.

[117] *Supra*, note 111, at 22.

War of Independence. As we shall see (*infra*, Chapter 10, B, (a)), UN Members are legally bound to obey a mandatory decision of this kind. However, the Council does not rush to issue direct orders. Ordinarily, it shows a proclivity for milder terms: demanding a cease-fire where necessary,[118] and more often just calling upon the parties to cease fire.[119]

In the Iran-Iraq War, the Council issued a call for a cease-fire in 1982,[120] demanding it only in 1987.[121] The text and the circumstances clearly imply that "the change in the wording from *calling* for a cease-fire to *demanding* one" conveyed a shift from a recommendation to a binding decision.[122] In the Falkland Islands War of 1982, the Council only requested the Secretary-General "to enter into contact with the parties with a view to negotiating mutually acceptable terms for cease-fire".[123] By contrast, in the Gulf War – in which the American-led coalition defeated Iraq with the direct blessing of the Council (see *infra*, Chapter 9, E) – the terms of the cease-fire were dictated by the Council in the most peremptory terms.[124] Whenever the Council uses less than peremptory wording, the parties are given an opportunity to craft a cease-fire agreement of their choosing. But if they fail to reach an agreement promptly, the Council may be driven to decree a cease-fire.

The General Assembly, too, may call upon belligerents to effect an immediate cease-fire. This is what the General Assembly did in December 1971,[125] after the outbreak of war between India and Pakistan (ultimately culminating in the creation of the independent State of Bangladesh). When such a resolution is passed by the General Assembly, it can only be issued as a recommendation and can never be binding (see *infra*, Chapter 10, E, (a)). As a non-mandatory

---

[118] See, e.g., Security Council Resolutions Nos. 234 and 235, 22 *R.D.S.C.* 3, *id.* (1967).

[119] See, e.g., Security Council Resolution No. 233, 22 *R.D.S.C.* 2, *id.* (1967).

[120] Security Council Resolution No. 514, 37 *R.D.S.C.* 19, *id.* (1982).

[121] Security Council Resolution No. 598, 42 *R.D.S.C.* 5, 6 (1987).

[122] M. Weller, "Comments: The Use of Force and Collective Security", *The Gulf War of 1980-1988* 71, 85 (I. F. Dekker and H. H. G. Post eds., 1992).

[123] Security Council Resolution No. 505, 37 *R.D.S.C.* 17, *id.* (1982).

[124] Security Council Resolution No. 687, 30 *I.L.M.* 847-54 (1991).

[125] General Assembly Resolution No. 2793 (XXVI), 26 *R.G.A.* 3, *id.* (1971).

exhortation, the resolution may be ignored with impunity, just as India disregarded the resolution in question.[126]

In recent years, most cease-fires have come in the wake of Security Council resolutions: either the parties carry out a mandatory decision of the Council or they arrive at an agreement at the behest of the Council. Even during the "cold war", as long as the Council was not in disarray owing to the exercise or the threat of a veto (see *infra*, Chapter 10, C), a cease-fire resolution became almost a conditioned reflex in response to the outbreak of hostilities. Generally speaking, the Council has tended to act as a fire-brigade, viewing its paramount task as an attempt to extinguish the blaze rather than dealing with all the surrounding circumstances.

A cease-fire directive by the Council, like an agreement between the belligerents, may be limited to a fixed time-frame. A case in point is Resolution No. 50 (1948), adopted in the course of Israel's War of Independence, which called upon all the parties to cease fire for a period of four weeks.[127] When the prescribed time expired, fighting recommenced. More often, the Council avoids setting specific terminal dates for cease-fires, preferring to couch them in an open-ended manner.

(b) *The Nature of Cease-Fire*

The suspension of hostilities must not be confused with their cessation. A cessation of hostilities means that the war is over. A suspension of hostilities connotes that the state of war goes on, but temporarily there is no actual warfare. Psychologically, a protracted general cease-fire lasting indefinitely is a state of no-war and no-peace. Legally, this is a clear-cut case of war. The state of war is not terminated, despite the absence of combat in the interval.

Renewal of hostilities before a cease-fire expires would obviously contravene its provisions. Nonetheless, it must be grasped that hostilities are only continued, after an interruption, and no new war is started. For that reason, a cease-fire violation is irrelevant to the determination of armed attack and self-defence (to be discussed

---

[126] See P. Bretton, "De Quelques Problèmes du Droit de la Guerre dans le Conflit Indo-Pakistanais", *18 A.F.D.I.* 201, 211 (1972).

[127] *Supra*, note 111, at 20.

infra, Chapter 7, B). That determination is made exclusively on the basis of the beginning of a new armed conflict. The reopening of fire in an on-going war is not germane to the issue.

A cease-fire gives the belligerents a chance to negotiate peace terms without being subjected to excessive pressure, and to turn the suspension into a cessation of hostilities. But no indispensable link exists between a cease-fire and peace. On the one hand, a peace treaty may not be preceded by any cease-fire.[128] On the other hand, a cease-fire may break down, to be followed by further bloodshed.

The pause in the fighting, brought about by a cease-fire, is no more than a convenient juncture for peace negotiations. Should the parties fail to exploit the opportunity, the period of quiescence is likely to become a springboard for further (and perhaps more intense) hostilities. This is only to be anticipated. A cease-fire, in freezing the military state of affairs extant at the moment when combat is suspended, places in an advantageous position that party which gained most ground before the deadline. While the guns are silent, the opposing sides will rearm and regroup. If no peace is attained, the belligerent most interested in a return to the *status quo ante* will look for a favourable moment (militarily as well as politically) to mount an offensive, in order to dislodge the enemy from the positions acquired on the eve of the cease-fire. A cease-fire in and of itself is, consequently, no harbinger of peace. All that a cease-fire can accomplish is set the stage for negotiations or any other mode of amicable settlement of disputes. If the parties contrive to hammer out peace terms, success will be due more to the exercise of diplomatic and political skills than to the cease-fire as such.

The Arab-Israeli conflict is a classical illustration of a whole host of cease-fires, either by consensual arrangement between the parties or by fiat of the Security Council, halting hostilities without bringing them to an end. The Council, using various phrases, insisted on immediate cease-fire, e.g., in June 1967 (the "Six Days War")[129] and in October 1973 (the so-called "Yom Kippur War").[130] Israel and Egypt negotiated a cease-fire agreement, e.g., in January

---

[128] See C. Rousseau, *Le Droit des Conflits Armés* 202 (1983).
[129] Security Council Resolutions Nos. 233-5, *supra,* notes 118-19, at 2-3.
[130] Security Council Resolution No. 338, 28 *R.D.S.C.* 10 (1973).

1949[131] and in November 1973.[132] Israel and Syria agreed on a cease-fire, e.g., in May 1974.[133]

In none of these cases did the cease-fire, whether initiated by the parties or by the Council, terminate the war. Israel's War of Independence with Egypt (begun as an inter-State war in May 1948) came to a close in February 1949, when the parties signed the General Armistice Agreement (which, in Article XII (5), expressly superseded the January General Cease-Fire Agreement[134]). The "Six Days War" between these two countries (sparked in June 1967 and proceeding through several cycles of hostilities followed by cease-fires) ended only as a result of the 1979 Treaty of Peace.[135] In the relations between Israel and Syria, or Israel and Jordan, the War of Independence also came to its final point upon the entry into force of the General Armistice Agreements of 1949 (see *supra*, B, (b)). In comparison, the "Six Days War" between these parties is not over, after more than a quarter of a century, in the absence of either a peace treaty or an armistice agreement. A number of rounds of hostilities between Israel and the Arab countries (most conspicuously, the "Yom Kippur War" of October 1973) are incorrectly adverted to as "wars". Far from qualifying as separate wars, these were merely inconsecutive time-frames of combat, punctuated by extended cease-fires, in the course of a single on-going war.

(c) *Denunciation and Breach of Cease-Fire*

Under Article 36 of the Hague Regulations, if the duration of a suspension of hostilities is not defined, each belligerent may resume military operations at any time, provided that an appropriate warning is given in accordance with the terms of the cease-fire (originally, "armistice").[136] The language of Article 36 seems to us to be imprecise. We believe that a general cease-fire, if concluded

---

[131] Egypt-Israel, General Cease-Fire Agreement, 1949, 1 *Kitvei Amana* (Israel Treaty Series) (No. 1) 13.

[132] Egypt-Israel, Cease-Fire Agreement, 1973, 12 *I.L.M.* 1312 (1973).

[133] Syria-Israel, Agreement on Disengagement between Forces, 1974, 13 *I.L.M.* 880 (1974).

[134] *Supra*, note 64, at 270 (Egypt).

[135] *Supra*, note 31, at 363 (Article 1).

[136] *Supra*, note 56, at 121.

without specifying a finite date of expiry, ought to be read in good faith as if it were undertaken for a reasonable period. Within that (admittedly flexible) stretch of time, none of the parties can be allowed to denounce the cease-fire unilaterally. Hence, it is not legitimate for a belligerent (relying on Article 36) to flout the cease-fire shortly after its conclusion. Only when a reasonable period has elapsed does the continued operation of the agreement depend on the good-will of both parties, and the cease-fire can be unilaterally denounced at will.

Article 36 contains an obligation to give advance notice to the adversary when denunciation of a cease-fire agreement occurs. But the specifics depend on what the cease-fire agreement prescribes. It appears that when the agreement is silent on this issue, hostilities may be "recommenced at once after notification".[137] If fire can be opened at once, the practical value of notification becomes inconsequential.[138]

Cease-fire (originally, "armistice") violations are the theme of Articles 40 and 41 of the Hague Regulations. Article 41 pronounces that, should the violations be committed by private individuals acting on their own initiative, the injured party would be entitled to demand their punishment or compensation for any losses sustained.[139] Under Article 40, a serious violation of the cease-fire by one of the parties empowers the other side to denounce it and, in cases of urgency, even to resume hostilities immediately.[140]

Articles 40 and 41 posit in effect a three-pronged classification of cease-fire violations: (i) ordinary violations, not justifying denunciation of the cease-fire (assuming that denunciation is not anyhow permissible under Article 36); (ii) serious violations, permitting the victim to denounce the cease-fire, but requiring advance notice before the recommencement of hostilities; and (iii) serious violations pregnant with urgency, enabling the victim to denounce the

---

[137] L. Oppenheim, *supra*, note 35, at 556.
[138] The *lex specialis* of Article 36 of the Hague Regulations apparently overrides the *lex generalis* of Article 56(2) of the Vienna Convention on the Law of Treaties (*supra*, note 40, at 154), which requires a twelve months' minimum notice of the intention to denounce a treaty.
[139] *Supra*, note 56, at 122.
[140] *Ibid., id.*

cease-fire and reopen hostilities immediately (without advance notice).[141]

The three categories of cease-fire violations are not easily applicable in reality. The question whether a breach of the cease-fire is serious, or whether any urgency is involved, seldom lends itself to objective verification. It must not be overlooked that a violation considered a minor infraction by one party may assume grave proportions in the eyes of the antagonist.[142] At the same time, the emphasis placed by Article 40 on serious cease-fire violations is consistent with the reference to a "material breach" appearing in Article 60(1) of the 1969 Vienna Convention on the Law of Treaties (in the general context of termination of bilateral treaties).[143]

---

[141] See L. Oppenheim, *supra*, note 35, at 556.
[142] See R. Monaco, "Les Conventions entre Belligérants", 75 *R.C.A.D.I.* 277, 337-8 (1949).
[143] *Supra*, note 40, at 155. *Cf.* R. R. Baxter, *supra*, note 115, at 386.

PART II

THE ILLEGALITY OF WAR

CHAPTER 3

AN HISTORICAL PERSPECTIVE OF THE LEGAL STATUS OF WAR

A. *The "Just War" Doctrine in the Past*

(a) *The Roman Origins*

The distinction between "just war" (*bellum justum*) and "unjust war" (*bellum injustum*) can be traced back to the *jus fetiale.* This body of law existed in ancient Rome, from the days of the Kings until the late republican era.[1] The *fetiales* were a college of priests charged with a number of duties, some of which pertained to the inception of war.

Cicero stated that it may be gathered from the code of the *fetiales* that no war is considered just, unless it is preceded by an official demand for satisfaction or warning, and a formal declaration has been made.[2] It follows that two indispensable conditions of a procedural nature had to be met before the commencement of hostilities. The first requisite was that a demand be addressed to the opponent, insisting on satisfaction for the grievance caused to Rome (such satisfaction taking the form of restitution, withdrawal of forces, etc.), with a fixed time allowed for a proper response.[3] The second condition was that a formal declaration of war had to be issued. The declaration entailed an elaborate ceremony, culminating in a spear being hurled across the Roman frontier into the enemy's territory, and including the recital of ancient legal formulas recorded in detail by Livy.[4] It appears that, apart from the ritualistic and procedural aspects of their duties, the *fetiales* were also

---

[1] See A. Nussbaum, *A Concise History of the Law of Nations* 10-11 (1954).

[2] Cicero, *De Officiis*, Book I, § XI, 36 (Loeb Classical ed. 38-9 (W. Miller trans., 1913)). See also Cicero, *De Re Publica*, Book III, § XXIII, 35 (Loeb Classical ed. 212-13 (C. W. Keyes trans., 1928)).

[3] See C. Phillipson, 2 *The International Law and Custom of Ancient Greece and Rome* 329-39 (1911).

[4] Livy, *Ab Urbe Condita*, Book I, § XXII, 5-14 (1 Loeb Classical ed. 114-19 (B. O. Foster trans., 1919)).

empowered to pronounce whether there were sufficient substantive grounds justifying the outbreak of hostilities (e.g., violation of a treaty or the sanctity of ambassadors, infringement of territorial rights, or offences committed against allies).[5]

As a rule, the political powers in Rome were disallowed to go to war (during the relevant period) without the explicit and prior approval of the *fetiales*.[6] Yet, it is probably fair to observe that, to all intents and purposes, the *fetiales* were the servants of their political masters and "practically bound to do their bidding".[7]

(b) Christian Theology

The *bellum justum* doctrine did not disappear with the *jus fetiale*. Instead, it was espoused by Christian theology and Canon Law. As long as the Roman Emperors were pagans, the Church upheld a pacifistic posture, and even forbade Christians to enlist as soldiers.[8] But after Christianity had become the official religion of the Empire in the days of Constantine, the Church was compelled to modify its view about war: from that point onwards, Christians were expected to shed their blood for the Empire.[9] Evidently, the Church had to find theological grounds for such a radical modification of its basic concept. This was done by St. Augustine, who revived the *bellum justum* doctrine as a moral tenet. In his celebrated book *De Civitate Dei*, St. Augustine enunciated the fundamental principle that every war was a lamentable phenomenon, but the wrong suffered at the hands of the adversary imposed "the necessity of waging just wars".[10]

The theologians and canonists who followed St. Augustine accepted his approach and expatiated upon the theme of the just war. The most influential contribution was made by St. Thomas Aquinas,

---

[5] See C. Phillipson, *supra*, note 3, at 182, 328.

[6] See *ibid.*, 328.

[7] A. S. Hershey, "The History of International Relations during Antiquity and the Middle Ages", 5 *A.J.I.L.* 901, 920 (1911).

[8] See J. von Elbe, "The Evolution of the Concept of the Just War in International Law", 33 *A.J.I.L.* 665, 667 (1939).

[9] See *ibid., id.*

[10] St. Augustine, *De Civitate Dei Contra Paganos*, Book XIX, § VII (6 Loeb Classical ed. 150-1 (W. C. Greene trans., 1960)).

who propounded that for war to be just it had to fulfil three conditions: (i) the war had to be conducted not privately but under the authority of a prince (*auctoritas principis*); (ii) there had to be a "just cause" (*causa justa*) for the war; and (iii) it was not enough to have a just cause from an objective viewpoint, but it was necessary to have the right intention (*intentio recta*) to promote good and to avoid evil.[11] The Thomist analysis pushed to the fore the question of the justice of causes of war. The canonists began to wrangle over elaborate lists of such causes, which often reflected personal and political predilections.[12]

(c) *The "Fathers" of International Law*

At the close of the Middle Ages, concurrently with the growth of the nation-States, modern international law came into being. The "fathers" of international law were jurists and scholars in the 16th and 17th centuries, all Europeans - at the outset only Catholics, but at the most formative stage also Protestants - who attempted to articulate (sometimes, practically to invent) rules of conduct binding on States. Among other concepts and institutions, these eminent scholars imported into the new international legal system the well-established religious (Catholic) doctrine that only a just war is permissible. Having done that, the "fathers" of international law, emulating the canonists, deemed it necessary to set out lists of just causes for war. These lists, too, were coloured by the bias of the respective writers.

For instance, the Spanish Dominican professor, Victoria, wrestled with the subject of his country's war against the Indians in America. Victoria rejected the premise that the Indians (as pagans) were beyond the pale of the law and bereft of any rights.[13] He maintained that, to be admissible, war against the Indians (no less than war against Christians) had to be just.[14] But, ultimately, Victoria

---

[11] St. Thomas Aquinas, *Summa Theologiae*, Secunda Secundae, Quaestio 40, 1 (35 Blackfriars ed., 80-3 (1972)).

[12] See A. Vanderpol, *La Doctrine Scolastique du Droit de Guerre* 63 (1925).

[13] Victoria, *De Indis et de Jure Belli Relectiones* 125 (Classics of International Law ed., J. P. Bate trans., 1917).

[14] *Ibid.*, 151-8.

justified what was happening in the New World, asserting that the Indians had violated the fundamental rights of the Spaniards to travel freely among them, to carry on trade and to propagate Christianity.[15]

The formulation of international law, in a manner consistent with the interests of whoever was doing the formulation, was not confined to wars against infidels in the New World. A just war could also be undertaken against Christians adhering to different political or religious creeds in Europe. Thus, the Spanish jurist Ayala, who held a position resembling that of a Judge Advocate General in the armed forces of Philip II (engaged in a struggle to put down insurrection in The Netherlands), contended that "a prince has a most just cause of war when he is directing his arms against rebels and subjects who abjure his sovereignty".[16]

Not only did each of the "fathers" of international law produce his own favoured enumeration of just causes of war, but the divergent lists spread the mantle of justice over a wide variety of controversial causes. According to Suárez, "any grave injury to one's reputation or honour" was a just cause of war.[17] Textor opined that, under certain circumstances, refusal of passage of troops *en route* to wage war against a third party "gives a just cause, if not for declaring war against the refuser, at any rate for opening a way by sword and arms".[18] Other jurists identified many additional just causes of war.

The expansion of the catalogue of just causes highlighted a perplexing problem. For the medieval theologians and canonists, any dispute as to the interpretation or application of the just war doctrine (or any other doctrine) could be resolved authoritatively by the Catholic Church. But when the doctrine was secularized, and absorbed into the mainstream of international law, the absence of

---

[15] *Ibid., id.*

[16] Ayala, *De Jure et Officiis Bellicis et Disciplina Militari*, Book I, § II, 12-13 (2 Classics of International Law ed., J. P. Bate trans., 11 (1912)).

[17] Suárez, *Selections from Three Works, De Triplici Virtute Theologia: Charitate*, Disputation XIII, § IV, 3 (2 Classics of International Law ed., G. L. Williams *et al.* trans., 817 (1944)).

[18] Textor, *Synopsis Juris Gentium*, § XVII, 37 (2 Classics of International Law ed., J. P. Bate trans., 178 (1925)).

an impartial authority - empowered to sift the evidence and appraise the justice of the cause of a concrete war - became readily apparent. Under these conditions, could war qualify as just on both sides?

Victoria argued that, even though war could really be just (from an objective standpoint) only on one side, it was not impossible that the other party acted in good faith under "invincible ignorance" either of fact or of law, and in such a case war (subjectively speaking) was just from the latter's perspective as well.[19] A similar position was taken by Grotius.[20] Gentili carried this thought further by contending that, even in objective terms, war could be just on one side but still more just on the other side.[21] Indeed, if a broad roster of independent just causes of war is admitted, this conclusion is almost unavoidable. Should the honour of Arcadia be slighted by Ruritania, Arcadia would have a just cause for war (consistent with Suárez's thesis). Yet, if Arcadia were to attack, Ruritania might also invoke a just cause for war, i.e. self-defence. As a consequence, both antagonists in the same conflict would fight one another in the name of justice, and each would be entitled to do so.

The postulate that the two belligerents in war may simultaneously rely on the justice of their clashing causes, and that they will be equally right, brought the just war doctrine in international law to a *cul de sac*. In almost every armed conflict, justice is appealed to by all parties. If the competing claims are screened on a comparative basis, and on balance only one of them can emerge as validated by considerations of justice, the register of "just causes" may conceivably serve as a useful guide for States in calculating future action. However, once war qualifies as objectively just on the part of both adversaries, there is scarcely a reason why any State should feel inhibited from going to war at will. Surely, when pressed, each Government can drum up some sort of justification for any policy. If that justification need not be superior to the claims of the enemy,

---

[19] Victoria, *supra*, note 13, at 177.
[20] Grotius, *De Jure Belli ac Pacis*, Book II, § XXIII, XIII (2 Classics of International Law ed., F. W. Kelsey trans., 565-6 (1925)).
[21] Gentili, *De Jure Belli*, Book I, § VI, 48-52 (2 Classics of International Law ed., J. C. Rolfe trans., 31-3 (1933)).

the requirement of a just cause ceases in effect to be a hurdle on the path to war.

In the 19th (and early part of the 20th) century, the attempt to differentiate between just and unjust wars in positive international law was discredited and abandoned.[22] States continued to use the rhetoric of justice when they went to war,[23] but the justification produced no legal reverberations. Most international lawyers conceded openly that "[w]ith the inherent rightfulness of war international law has nothing to do".[24] Or, in the acerbic words of T. J. Lawrence, distinctions between just and unjust causes of war "belong to morality and theology, and are as much out of place in a treatise on International Law as would be a discussion on the ethics of marriage in a book on the law of personal status".[25]

B. Recent Concepts of "Just War"

(a) Kelsen's Theory

H. Kelsen (among others) developed the concept that war is lawful only when it constituted a sanction against a violation of international law by the opponent.[26] According to Kelsen, war "is permitted only as a reaction against an illegal act, a delict, and only when directed against the State responsible for this delict".[27]

One of the central features of Kelsen's theory, as originally constructed, is that it treated war as a lawful response (a sanction) in every instance of non-compliance with international law (a delict), even if that non-compliance had not involved the use of force.[28] Once the use of inter-State force was prohibited, except in specific

---

[22] See J. L. Brierly, "International Law and Resort to Armed Force", *4 Cam.L.J.* 308, *id.* (1930-2).

[23] On the difference between the rhetoric and the reality of justice in international law, see Y. Dinstein, "The Interaction of International Law and Justice", 16 *I.Y.H.R.* 9, 21-41 (1986).

[24] G. B. Davis, *The Elements of International Law* 272 (4th ed., by G. E. Sherman, 1916).

[25] T. J. Lawrence, *The Principles of International Law* 311 (7th ed., by P. H. Winfield, 1923).

[26] See H. Kelsen, *Principles of International Law* 33-4 (1st ed., 1952).

[27] H. Kelsen, *General Theory of Law and State* 331 (1945).

[28] *Ibid.*, 333.

circumstances defined by the Charter of the United Nations (see *infra*, Chapter 4, B, (a)), Kelsen adjusted the theory to the evolution of international law. He still regarded war as lawful only when constituting a sanction, but the nature of the delict had changed: legitimate war now had to be a "counterwar", waged in response to an illegal war by the other side.[29]

There is a three-fold difficulty inherent in Kelsen's theory. First, factually, war may be an inefficacious sanction. Victory in war is contingent not on right but on might, and a weak State resorting to hostilities against a strong one is apt to find it a painful and counter-productive experience. Secondly, in the absence of an impartial forum juridically competent to determine on the merits whether a specific war ought to be considered a genuine sanction, the other side can challenge the legality of the war. It can argue that the war, instead of amounting to a sanction (a legitimate counter-war), actually constitutes a delict (an unlawful war). Thirdly, as long as the original delict could consist of any conduct in violation of international law (such as a failure to repay a loan), there was a distinct possibility of a glaring disproportion between the delict and the sanction. After all, war always generates inevitable destruction and suffering, and it cannot be contemplated as a proper sanction unless warranted by the gravest provocation.

Kelsen was not unaware of the obvious inadequacy immanent in the role of war as a general sanction, but he explained it away in the light of the primitive nature of the international legal system.[30] Kelsen called his theory "the *bellum justum* doctrine",[31] although he admitted that the term "just" in the present context means "legal".[32] Basically, J. L. Kunz was right in stating that the concept of *bellum justum* has been replaced by that of *bellum legale*: what counts is a breach of the norms of existing international law, rather than "the intrinsic injustice of the cause of war".[33]

---

[29] H. Kelsen, *supra*, note 26, at 28-9.
[30] *Ibid.*, 35-6.
[31] *Ibid.*, 33; H. Kelsen, *supra*, note 27, at 331.
[32] H. Kelsen, *supra*, note 26, at 34 n. 16.
[33] J. L. Kunz, "Bellum Justum and Bellum Legale", 45 *A.J.I.L.* 528, 532 (1951).

(b) *"Wars of National Liberation"*

In recent years, persistent attempts have been made to bring into positive international law the concept that the use of force by States in support of a just cause - especially, a "war of national liberation" carried out by a people in exercise of the right of self-determination (see *infra*, Chapter 6, E) - is lawful. It is well worth emphasizing that the real issue here is not the legitimacy of the "war of national liberation" *per se*, inasmuch as an uprising unfurling the banner of self-determination does not amount to an inter-State war (liberation or statehood being the contested goal). The focal question is whether a foreign State, embracing the cause of the "national liberation movement", may actively intervene in the hostilities in order to assist in the overthrow of the "yoke of colonialism". Those answering the question in the affirmative believe that colonialism is "a purely evil state and one which it is legal and just to fight against".[34]

Usually, the rationale offered in sustaining the proposition that the use of force between States is lawful when extended in aid of "wars of national liberation" is that these are just wars.[35] The obstacle confronting the interventionist school of thought is that the Charter of the United Nations does not incorporate support of "wars of national liberation" among the legitimate exceptions to the general prohibition of recourse to inter-State force (see *infra*, Chapter 4, B, (b)).

In his Dissenting Opinion in the *Nicaragua* case of 1986, Judge Schwebel criticized the majority of the International Court of Justice because a brief dictum in its Judgment "may be understood as inferentially endorsing" the legality of forcible "intervention in the promotion of so-called 'wars of liberation'".[36] In fact, the Court's dictum[37] is no more than a faint hint in that direction, and Judge Schwebel may have overreacted.

---

[34] A. Shaw, "Revival of the Just War Doctrine?", 3 *Auck.U.L.R.* 156, 170 (1976-9).

[35] See the statement of Chairman Khrushchev: "Moral, material and other assistance must be given so that the sacred and just struggle of the peoples for their independence can be brought to its conclusion", cited by R. E. Gorelick, "Wars of National Liberation: *Jus ad Bellum*", *C.W.R.J.I.L.* 71, 81 (1979).

[36] *Case Concerning Military and Paramilitary Activities in and against Nicaragua* (Merits), [1986] *I.C.J. Rep.* 14, 350-1.

[37] "The Court is not here concerned with the process of decolonization; this question is not in issue in the present case". *Ibid.*, 108.

Nevertheless, important milestones on the path pursued by advocates of foreign intervention in "wars of national liberation" have been set in two consensus resolutions adopted by the General Assembly: the 1970 Declaration on Principles of International Law Concerning Friendly Relations and Co-operation among States in accordance with the Charter of the United Nations,[38] and Article 7 of the 1974 Definition of Aggression.[39] These texts are not free of doubt as to their exact meaning (in regard to Article 7 of the Definition of Aggression see *infra*, Chapter 5, B). But the driving force behind them cannot be dismissed lightly.

In essence, the present-day international community is faced with a curious recrudescence of the just war doctrine. The alleged licence of one State to use force against another in abetting a "war of national liberation" is predicated not on legal norms but on claims of justice (as perceived by the claimants). Because a people striving for independence from alien domination is the *soi-disant* beneficiary of a just cause, a State endorsing that cause is purportedly authorized by international law to go to war against another State. The trouble is that, as in the heyday of the *bellum justum* doctrine, just causes of war happen to coincide with the political and ideological slant of whoever is invoking them.[40] In the words of Judge Schwebel, "the lack of beauty is in the eyes of the beholder".[41] The long and short of it is that, in the name of justice, the existing legal proscription of the use of inter-State force is corroded by political motivations.[42]

C. *The Extra-Legality of War*

War occurs in human history so repetitively that there is a tendency to take it for granted. For many centuries, war was viewed

---

[38] General Assembly Resolution No. 2625 (xxv), 25 *R.G.A.* 121, 123 (1970).

[39] General Assembly Resolution No. 3314 (xxix), 29(1) *R.G.A.* 142, 144 (1974).

[40] See W. D. Verwey, "Humanitarian Intervention", *The Current Legal Regulation of the Use of Force* 57, 69-70 (A. Cassese ed., 1986).

[41] *Supra*, note 36, at 351.

[42] See D. E. Graham, "The 1974 Diplomatic Conference on the Law of War: A Victory for Political Causes and a Return to the 'Just War' Concept of the Eleventh Century", 32 *W.L.L.R.* 25, 44 (1975).

with resignation as a perennial fact of life. The popular outlook was that war is tantamount to a "providential visitation to be compared with plague or flood or fire".[43] In similarity to these and other natural disasters (such as earthquakes and volcanic eruptions), war was expected to inflict itself on mankind in cyclical frequency. Like the plague, war would appear every once in a while, leave death and devastation in its wake and temporarily pass away to return at a later date.[44]

The analogy between war and catastrophes ordained by nature influenced lawyers, who have occasionally suggested that war falls into the same "category of events, considered incapable of legal control but entailing legal consequences".[45] Just as no legal system can forbid thunderbolts or droughts, it has been assumed that international law cannot possibly interdict war. War, so it has been said, is "neither legal nor illegal":[46] it is beyond the reach of the law. As A. Nussbaum put it, "[t]he 'outbreak' of war is a metajuristic phenomenon, an event outside the range and control of the law".[47] The Italian-American Conciliation Commission, in its decision of 1953 in the *Armstrong Cork* case, also adverted to the state of war as an "extra-juridical regime".[48]

This line of approach proved particularly attractive in the 19th (and early 20th) century, although most international lawyers were not prepared to follow the thesis to its logical conclusion. J. Westlake held that "[i]nternational law did not institute war, which it found already existing, but regulates it with a view to its greater humanity".[49] In somewhat different terms, W. E. Hall commented that "[i]nternational law has ... no alternative but to accept war, independently of the justice of its origin, as a relation which the parties to it may set up if they choose, and to busy itself only in

---

[43] C. Eagleton, *International Government* 455 (3rd ed., 1957).

[44] See W. R. Harris, *Tyranny on Trial* 514 (1954).

[45] Q. Wright, "Changes in the Conception of War", 18 *A.J.I.L.* 755, 756 (1924). The author modified his position at a later date. See Q. Wright, 2 *A Study of War* 891-3 (1942).

[46] J. L. Brierly, *The Outlook for International Law* 22 (1944).

[47] A. Nussbaum, "Just War - A Legal Concept", 42 *Mich.L.R.* 453, 477 (1943-4).

[48] *Armstrong Cork Company* Case (1953), 14 *R.I.A.A.* 159, 163.

[49] J. Westlake, 2 *International Law* 3 (2nd ed., 1913).

regulating the effects of the relation".[50] The latest (seventh) edition (dated 1952) of the second volume of L. Oppenheim's *International Law*, edited by Sir Hersch Lauterpacht, still includes the statement that "[w]ar is a fact recognised, and with regard to many points regulated, but not established, by International Law".[51]

The phraseology typical of those who represent war as an extra-legal phenomenon is that international law only "finds" or "accepts" war as a *fait accompli*. It is universally acknowledged that, once war begins, international law can and does regulate the relations between belligerents (as well as between them and neutrals).[52] However, the exponents of the extra-legality of war believe that, while there is plenty of room for a *jus in bello* (governing conduct in warfare), there can be no real *jus ad bellum* (imposing normative limitations on the commencement of hostilities). "Law cannot say *when*, but only *how* war is to be waged".[53]

The proposition that war is a meta-juridical occurrence may be tempting, but it is devoid of foundation. The assimilation of war to events taking place in nature is artificial and delusive.[54] Unlike earthquakes and epidemics, war is caused by human beings. Every form of human behaviour is susceptible of regulation by law. No category of human behaviour is excluded *a priori* from the range of application of legal norms (actual or potential). At bottom, the undisputed ability of international law to control the conduct of combatants in the course of war (*jus in bello*) proves that it can also restrict the freedom of action of belligerents in the initiation of war (*jus ad bellum*). When an epidemic is raging, law is utterly unable to dictate to the virus not only when (and if) to mount an assault upon the human body, but also how to go about it. From a jurisprudential standpoint, there is no real difference between governing the "when" and the "how" of war.

---

[50] W. E. Hall, *A Treatise on International Law* 82 (8th ed., by A. P. Higgins, 1924).

[51] L. Oppenheim, 2 *International Law* 202 (7th ed., by H. Lauterpacht, 1952).

[52] See A. Nussbaum, *supra*, note 47, at 477.

[53] C. A. Pompe, *Aggressive War an International Crime* 140 (1953). This is a summation of the legal position taken by D. Anzilotti and others.

[54] See R. W. Tucker, "The Interpretation of War under Present International Law", 4 *I.L.Q.* 11, 13 (1951).

Certainly, international law does not "establish" war. For that matter, domestic law does not "establish" murder or robbery. War, as a form of human conduct, resembles murder or robbery more than flood or drought. In the same way that murder and robbery are prohibited by domestic law, war can be forbidden by international law.

For a long time international law did refrain from obtruding upon the liberty of States to go to war (see *infra*, D). Yet, this forbearance did not mean that international law had a built-in impediment depriving it of the power to ban war. In reality, by not prohibiting recourse to war, international law indicated that war was tolerated and, therefore, permitted. War can be legal or illegal, but it is misleading to suggest that it is extra-legal.[55]

Upon analysis, the theory of the extra-legality of war is of far greater potential moment than the concept of its legality. Moving from the latter to the former is a transition from bad to worse.[56] If war is lawful in a given era, it can still be proscribed afterwards. But if war is extra-legal, it can never be made unlawful. Consequently, the prohibition of aggressive war in the 20th century (see *infra*, Chapter 4) implies (i) a denial of the doctrine of its extra-legality; as well as (ii) a confirmation of the hypothesis that, prior to the interdiction, war used to be legal.

D. *The Legality of War*

Subsequent to the virtual demise of the just war doctrine, the predominant conviction in the 19th (and early 20th) century was that every State had a right – namely, an interest protected by international law – to embark upon war whenever it pleased. The discretion of States in this matter was portrayed as unfettered. States could "resort to war for a good reason, a bad reason or no reason at all".[57]

---

[55] See *ibid., id.*

[56] See J. N. Moore, "Strengthening World Order: Reversing the Slide to Anarchy", 4 *A.U.J.I.L.P.* 1, 5 (1989).

[57] H. W. Briggs, *The Law of Nations* 976 (2nd ed., 1952). It has recently been suggested that "even before the League of Nations any war in Europe had to have a justifying cause or reason". S. Verosta, "The Unlawfulness of Wars of Aggression before 1914", 1 *Essays in Honour of Judge Taslim Olawale Elias* 117, 124 (E. G. Bello and B. A. Ajibola eds., 1992). But the evidence produced (the Greek-Turkish War of 1897) is not persuasive.

Among the legitimate reasons for war would figure the desire to use it as a sanction against non-compliance with international law (as perceived by Kelsen, *supra*, B, (a)). Equally, war could be employed as a means to challenge and upset the international legal *status quo*.[58] At one and the same time, war "had a static as well as a dynamic function": to enforce existing rights and to defy them.[59]

War came to be characterized as "a right inherent in sovereignty itself".[60] Moreover, the war-making right was thought of as the paramount attribute of sovereignty.[61] When the statehood of a specific political entity was in doubt, the best litmus test comprised of checking whether the prerogative of launching war at will was vested in it. The international legal freedom to wage war for whatever reason even impacted upon the constitutions and organic laws of quite a few countries. These instruments, when spelling out to which branch of Government the war-making power was entrusted, overtly applied different procedures to the initiation of offensive, as opposed to defensive, wars.[62]

When observed through the lens of legal theory, the freedom to indulge in war without thereby violating international law seemed to create an egregious anomaly. It did not make much sense for the international legal system to be based on respect for the sovereignty of States, while each State had a sovereign right to destroy the sovereignty of others.[63] On the one hand, it was incumbent on every State to defer to a plethora of rights accorded to other States under both customary and conventional international law. On the other hand, each State was at liberty to attack any other State whenever it pleased. J. L. Brierly termed this state of affairs "a logical impossibility".[64]

---

[58] See J. L. Kunz, "The Law of Nations, Static and Dynamic", 27 *A.J.I.L.* 630, 634 (1933).

[59] *Ibid., id.*

[60] A. S. Hershey, *The Essentials of International Public Law* 349 (1912).

[61] See M. Virally, "Panorama du Droit International Contemporain", 183 *R.C.A.D.I.* 9, 99 (1983).

[62] See E. D. Dickinson, *The Equality of States in International Law* 202-4 (1920).

[63] See C. De Visscher, *Theory and Reality in Public International Law* 286 (P. E. Corbett trans., 1957).

[64] J. L. Brierly, *supra*, note 46, at 21.

The apparent incongruity may be examined from a somewhat different point of departure. In the final analysis, every legal system has to protect the vital interests of its subjects. States are the primary subjects of international law. It is, therefore, arguable that "[a] system of international law must premise the right of states to exist".[65] When international law recognized the privilege of States to engage in war at their discretion, the net result was that the right of the target State to exist could be repudiated at any moment.[66] What emerged was a deep-rooted inconsistency in the international legal order, which "both asserts and denies the right of states to exist".[67] Some scholars even reasoned that the inconsistency was fatal to international law. To their minds, a system that failed to protect the fundamental interests of its principal subjects (the States), by restraining war, was not true law.[68]

This was by no means the prevalent opinion. Many writers totally disavowed the notion that the freedom of war was not in harmony with the existence of a genuine international legal system.[69] Others simply sidestepped the issue. In any event, irrespective of any scholarly bafflement, States and statesmen in the 19th (and early 20th) century did not consider the freedom of war to be a fatal flaw in the structure of international law. Nor did they find it inconceivable that, in the name of sovereignty, each State was empowered to challenge the sovereignty of other States. The practice of States in that period was "dominated by an unrestricted right of war",[70] and conceptual criticisms were largely ignored.

E. *Exceptions to the General Liberty to Go to War*

(a) *Special Arrangements*

Precisely because the liberty to go to war was regarded by States as the general rule, there is no dearth of bilateral treaties in the 19th

---

[65] Q. Wright, "The Present Status of Neutrality", 34 *A.J.I.L.* 391, 399 (1940).
[66] *Ibid.*, 399-400.
[67] *Ibid.*, 400.
[68] See H. Kelsen, *supra*, note 27, at 340.
[69] See, e.g., L. Oppenheim, 2 *International Law* 55 (lst ed., 1906).
[70] I. Brownlie, *International Law and the Use of Force by States* 19 (1963).

(and early 20th) century, in which the contracting parties assumed an obligation not to resort to war in their particular relations. Concomitantly, the parties consented to seek an amicable settlement (e.g., mediation or arbitration) whenever a dispute might arise between them. Such a treaty was applicable, however, only *inter partes*, without diminishing from the freedom of action of signatories *vis-à-vis* third States. In addition, the treaty was usually limited to a fixed time, although it could be subject to extension. When the prescribed period expired, every contracting party had the right to terminate the treaty on notice. Once the treaty was no longer in force, all States concerned regained the option to commence hostilities against one another.

As an illustration, we may take a treaty concluded between Honduras and Nicaragua in 1878, in which these two countries agreed that "there shall in no case be war" between them and, in the event of a dispute, undertook to turn to arbitration by a friendly nation.[71] Each party was entitled to give notice after four years, so as to terminate the treaty.[72]

The trend of concluding bilateral treaties of this kind continued well into the post First World War era. But in the 1920s and 1930s, States preferred to couch their obligations in terms of "non-aggression pacts" (thereby clearly retaining the right to wage wars of self-defence). A good example is a 1926 treaty between Persia (present-day Iran) and Turkey, wherein the parties committed themselves "not to engage in any aggression against the other" and "not to participate in any hostile action whatsoever directed by one or more third Powers against the other Party".[73]

Occasionally, a non-aggression pact had more than two contracting parties. The most important non-aggression instrument of the period was the 1925 Locarno Treaty of Mutual Guarantee, in which Germany and France, and also Germany and Belgium, were mutually bound not to "resort to war against each other".[74]

[71] Honduras-Nicaragua, Tegucigalpa Treaty of Friendship, Commerce and Extradition, 1878, 152 *C.T.S.* 415, 416 (Article II).
[72] *Ibid.*, 423 (Article XXXV).
[73] Persia-Turkey, Teheran Treaty of Friendship and Security, 1926, 106 *L.N.T.S.* 261-3.
[74] Locarno Treaty of Mutual Guarantee, 1925, 54 *L.N.T.S.* 289, 293 (Article 2).

A different approach was reflected in a series of bilateral agree-ments, known as the Bryan treaties (after the American Secretary of State who initiated them), concluded between the United States and dozens of other countries on the eve of the First World War.[75] In these treaties, the contracting parties agreed to submit all dis-putes to investigation by an International Commission, and the Commission was instructed to complete its report within one year.[76] Pending the investigation and report, the parties pledged "not to declare war or begin hostilities".[77]

The Bryan treaties did not negate the right of any State to start war eventually. What the treaties sought to accomplish was the in-troduction of a "cooling-off period" of one year to enable passions to subside.[78] The underlying assumption was that delay as such (or the gaining of time) would be advantageous, since the parties were expected to become progressively more amenable to reason.[79] As a matter of fact, reliance on lapse of time as a factor allaying suspi-cions and fears is not empirically corroborated in all instances. Some international disputes are easier to tackle, and to settle, at an earlier stage. Passage of time, far from cooling off hot tempers, may only exacerbate incipient tensions.

(b) *The Hague Conventions*

The first steps, designed to curtail somewhat the freedom of war in general international law (through multilateral treaties), were taken in the two Hague Peace Conferences of 1899 and 1907. Under Article 2 of Hague Convention (No. I of both 1899 and 1907) for the Pacific Settlement of International Disputes, contracting parties agreed that, in case of a serious dispute, before making "an appeal to arms" they would resort ("as far as circumstances allow") to good offices or mediation of friendly States.[80] The liberty to go to war

[75] See Anonymous, "The Bryan Peace Treaties", 7 *A.J.I.L.* 823, 824-5 (1913).
[76] See, e.g., Guatemala-United States, Washington Treaty for the Establishment of a Permanent Commission of Enquiry, 1913, 218 *C.T.S.* 373, 373-4.
[77] *Ibid.*, 373 (Article I).
[78] See A. Zimmern, *The League of Nations and the Rule of Law 1918-1935* 129 (1939).
[79] See J. F. Williams, *Some Aspects of the Covenant of the League of Nations* 136-8 (1934).
[80] Hague Convention (No. I of 1899 and 1907) for the Pacific Settlement of Inter-national Disputes, *Hague Conventions* 41, 43.

was circumscribed here in an exceedingly cautious way, leaving to the discretion of the parties the determination whether to employ force or to search for amicable means of settling the dispute. Article 1 of Hague Convention (No. II of 1907) Respecting the Limitation of the Employment of Force for the Recovery of Contract Debts – often called the Porter Convention (after the American delegate who had proposed it) – obligated contracting parties "not to have recourse to armed force" for the recovery of contract debts (claimed from one Government by another as being due to its nationals), unless the debtor State refused an offer of arbitration, prevented agreement on a *compromis* or rejected an arbitral award.[81] Hague Convention No. II echoed the Drago Doctrine (named after an Argentinian Foreign Minister), which had denied the justification of war as a mode of compelling payment of a public debt.[82] But the scope of the limitation on the freedom of war, as formulated in the Convention, was quite narrow. First, war was still permissible if the debtor State refused to go through the process of arbitration or abide by its results. Secondly, the Convention did not apply to direct inter-Governmental loans and was confined to contractual debts to foreign nationals (whose claims were espoused by their respective Governments).[83]

(c) *The Covenant of the League of Nations*

The Covenant of the League of Nations qualified the right to go to war in a more comprehensive way. In Article 10, Members of the League pledged "to respect and preserve as against external aggression the territorial integrity and existing political independence of all Members of the League".[84] This was an abstract provision, which lent itself to more than one interpretation. Hence, Article 10 had to be read in conjunction with, and subject to, the more specific stipulations following it.[85]

---

[81] Hague Convention (No. II of 1907) Respecting the Limitation of the Employment of Force for the Recovery of Contract Debts, *Hague Conventions* 89, *id.*
[82] See A. S. Hershey, "The Calvo and Drago Doctrines", 1 *A.J.I.L.* 26, 28–30 (1907).
[83] See G. W. Scott, "Hague Convention Restricting the Use of Force to Recover on Contract Claims", 2 *A.J.I.L.* 78, 90 (1908).
[84] Covenant of the League of Nations, 1919, 1 *Int.Leg.* 1, 7.
[85] See A. V. Levontin, *The Myth of International Security* 23 (1957).

Article 11 enunciated that any war or threat of war was a matter of concern to the entire League.[86] Pursuant to Article 12, if any dispute likely to lead to rupture arose between Members of the League, they were required to submit it to arbitration, judicial settlement or inquiry by the League's Council.[87] Members were bound "in no case to resort to war until three months after the award by the arbitrators or the judicial decision, or the report of the Council". The award of the arbitrators or the judicial decision had to be rendered "within reasonable time". The Council's report had to be arrived at no later than six months after the submission of the dispute.

Article 13 specified which subject-matters were "generally suitable" for submission to either arbitration or judicial settlement.[88] Members were obligated to carry out in good faith any arbitral award or judicial decision. They agreed that they "will not resort to war" against another Member complying with the award or decision.

In accordance with Article 15, disputes between Members, when not submitted to arbitration or judicial settlement, had to be brought before the Council.[89] The Council's role was restricted to issuing recommendations, as distinct from binding decisions. However, under paragraph 6 of the Article, if the Council's report was carried unanimously (excluding the parties to the dispute), Members consented "not to go to war with any party to the dispute which complies with the recommendations of the report". If the Council failed to reach a unanimous report (apart from the parties to the dispute), paragraph 7 reserved the right of Members to take any action that they considered necessary for the maintenance of right and justice. Paragraph 8 precluded the Council from making any recommendation, if it thought that the dispute had arisen out of a matter "which by international law is solely within the domestic jurisdiction of that party". Article 15 also enabled referral of the dispute from the Council to the Assembly of the League, in which case it was the Assembly that was empowered to make recommendations. An Assembly report, if adopted by the votes of all the

---

[86] *Supra,* note 84, at 7.
[87] *Ibid.,* 7-8 (original version), 25 (amended text).
[88] *Ibid.,* 8 (original version), 26-7 (amended text).
[89] *Ibid.,* 9-10 (original version), 28-9 (amended text).

Members of the Council and a majority of the other Members (again not counting the parties to the dispute), had the same force as a unanimous report of the Council.

In all, the Covenant did not abolish the right of States to resort to war. Subject to specific prohibitions, detailed in the Articles cited, war remained lawful.[90] If looked at from a complementary angle of vision, one could easily discern a number of "gaps" in the legal fence installed by the Covenant around the right of States to resort to war. The "gaps" opened the legal road to war in the following circumstances:[91]

a. The most blatant case in which the liberty to plunge into war was kept intact resulted from Article 15(7). In the absence of unanimity in the Council or a proper majority in the Assembly, excluding the votes of parties to the dispute, the parties retained their freedom of action.

b. In the light of Article 15(8), the Council (or the Assembly) was incompetent to reach a recommendation if in its judgment the matter came within the domestic jurisdiction of a party to the dispute. Since no recommendation would be adopted, the parties preserved their freedom of action. Thus, paradoxically, an international war could be triggered by a dispute which was ostensibly non-international in character.

c. It was implied in Article 12 that, if the Council (or the Assembly) did not arrive at a recommendation within six months – or, alternatively, if either an arbitral award or a judicial decision was not delivered within reasonable time – the parties would be free to take any action that they deemed fit.

d. Articles 13 and 15 forbade going to war against a State complying with an arbitral award, a judicial decision, a unanimous recommendation of the Council, or an Assembly recommendation based on the required majority. In conformity with Article 12, no war could be undertaken within three months of the award, decision or

---

[90] See A. Möller, 2 *International Law in Peace and War* 88 (H. M. Pratt trans., 1935).
[91] See J. B. Whitton, "La Neutralité et la Société des Nations", 17 *R.C.A.D.I.* 453, 479-90 (1927).

recommendation. The upshot was that, after three months, war could be started against a State failing to comply with the award, decision or recommendation.

e. Naturally, all the limitations on the freedom of war applied to the relations between League Members *inter se*. The Covenant did not, and could not, curtail that freedom in the relations between non-Members and Members (and *a fortiori* between non-Members among themselves). Article 17 provided that, in the event of a dispute between a Member and a non-Member or between non-Members, the non-Member(s) should be invited to accept the obligations of membership for the purposes of the dispute, and then the stipulations of Articles 12 *et seq.* would apply.[92] It goes without saying that non-Members had an option to accede to such an invitation or to decline it.

Shortly after the entry into force of the Covenant, initiatives were taken to close these "gaps". The most famous attempt was made in the Geneva Protocol on the Pacific Settlement of International Disputes, which was adopted by the Assembly of the League in 1924, but never entered into force.[93] The capstone of the Protocol was Article 2, whereby the contracting parties agreed "in no case to resort to war", except in resistance to aggression or with the consent of the League's Council or Assembly.[94] Article 2 was intended to abolish the general right to go to war.[95] Yet, since the Protocol remained abortive, war did not become illegal in principle until the Kellogg-Briand Pact of 1928.

---

[92] *Supra*, note 84, at 12.
[93] Geneva Protocol on the Pacific Settlement of International Disputes, 1924, 2 *Int.Leg.* 1378, 1379.
[94] *Ibid.*, 1381.
[95] See P. J. Noel Baker, *The Geneva Protocol* 29-30 (1925).

CHAPTER 4

THE CONTEMPORARY PROHIBITION OF THE USE OF INTER-STATE FORCE

A. *The Kellogg-Briand Pact*

1928 was a watershed date in the history of the legal regulation of the use of inter-State force. That was when the General Treaty for Renunciation of War as an Instrument of National Policy, known as the Kellogg-Briand Pact (after the American Secretary of State and the French Foreign Minister), was signed in Paris.[1] Before the outbreak of the Second World War, the Pact had 63 contracting parties,[2] a record number for that period.

The Kellogg-Briand Pact comprised only three Articles, including one of a technical nature. In Article 1, the contracting parties solemnly declared that "they condemn recourse to war for the solution of international controversies, and renounce it as an instrument of national policy in their relations with one another".[3] In Article 2, they agreed that the settlement of all disputes with each other "shall never be sought except by pacific means".[4]

With the Kellogg-Briand Pact, international law progressed from *jus ad bellum* to *jus contra bellum*.[5] But, although generally prohibited under the Pact, war remained lawful in the following circumstances:

a. A war of self-defence. No provision relating to this vitally important subject was incorporated in the text of the Pact. Nevertheless, formal notes reserving the right of self-defence were exchanged between the principal signatories prior to the conclusion of the

---

[1] General Treaty for Renunciation of War as an Instrument of National Policy (Kellogg-Briand Pact of Paris), 1928, 94 *L.N.T.S.* 57.

[2] A list of the 63 States that ratified or adhered to the Pact by the end of 1938 appears in 33 *A.J.I.L.*, Sp. Supp., 865 (1939).

[3] *Supra*, note 1, at 63.

[4] *Ibid., id.*

[5] See M. Howard, "*Temperamenta Belli*: Can War Be Controlled?", *Restraints on War* 1, 11 (M. Howard ed., 1979).

Pact,[6] and there never was any doubt that the renunciation of war had to be construed accordingly. In any event, under the Preamble of the Pact, any contracting party "which shall hereafter seek to promote its national interests by resort to war should be denied the benefits furnished by this Treaty".[7] In other words, if Arcadia went to war against Utopia in violation of the Pact, Arcadia could no longer benefit from the renunciation of war. Consequently, Utopia was allowed to mount a war of self-defence against Arcadia. It appears from the way the Preamble was phrased that permission to embark upon hostilities, in response to the violation of the Pact by Arcadia, was granted not only to Utopia (the State under attack) but also to Ruritania (any other country). This is akin to the current concept of collective self-defence in response to an armed attack (see *infra*, Chapter 9, A).

Since the topic of self-defence was not expressly regulated in the Pact, its parameters were not set out. In addition, no competent body was established to determine whether a State employing force was acting in self-defence or in breach of the Pact.

b. War as an instrument of international policy. Inasmuch as Article 1 of the Pact forbade war only as an instrument of national policy, war remained lawful as an instrument of international policy. That made recourse to war legitimate, primarily, under the aegis of the League of Nations (see *infra*, Chapter 10, A). But the "national policy" formula gave rise to the interpretation that other wars - in pursuit of religious, ideological and similar (not strictly national) goals - were also permitted.[8] J. H. W. Verzijl developed the thesis that a contracting party was entitled to resort to armed action if there was no other way to carry out an arbitral award or judicial decision, for such action did not fall under the heading of war as an instrument of national policy.[9] H. Kelsen, in keeping with the perception of war as a sanction (see *supra*, Chapter 3, B, (a)), argued that "a war which

---

[6] Identic Notes of the United States to other Governments in relation to the Pact are reproduced in 22 *A.J.I.L.*, Supp., 109-13 (1928). Replies appear in 23 *ibid*, Supp., 1-13 (1929).

[7] *Supra*, note 1, at 59-61.

[8] See H. Wehberg, *The Outlawry of War* 76 (1931).

[9] J. H. W. Verzijl, 8 *International Law in Historical Perspective* 109-10, 600 (1976).

is a reaction against a violation of international law, and that means a war waged for the maintenance of international law, is considered an instrument of international and hence not of national policy".[10] Yet, to the extent that war was undertaken in response to an ordinary violation of international law, the analysis could not be harmonized with the requirement in Article 2 of the Pact that the settlement of all disputes "shall never be sought except by pacific means".[11]

c. War outside the span of the reciprocal relations of the contracting parties. The renunciation of war in Article 1 was circumscribed to the relations between contracting parties *inter se.* Therefore, the freedom of war was preserved as between contracting and non-contracting parties (and, obviously, among non-contracting parties).

The limitation of the Pact to the renunciation of "war" elicited much criticism in the international legal literature. Apart from the fact that the term "war" seemed to some writers to be ambiguous, the disturbing implication was that the use of force short of war was left to the discretion of each State.[12]

In brief, the *jus ad bellum* engendered by the Kellogg-Briand Pact was flawed in four ways: (i) the issue of self-defence was not clearly addressed in the text; (ii) no agreed upon limits were set on the legality of war as an instrument of international policy; (iii) the prohibition of war did not embrace the entire international community; and (iv) forcible measures short of war were eliminated from consideration.

B. *The Charter of the United Nations*

(a) *The Prohibition of the Use of Inter-State Force*

When the Charter of the United Nations was drafted in San Francisco, in 1945, one of its aims was redressing the shortcomings

---

[10] H. Kelsen, *Principles of International Law* 43 (1st ed., 1952).

[11] On the import of Article 2 in the interpretation of the Pact, see J. L. Brierly, "Some Implications of the Pact of Paris", 10 *B.Y.B.I.L.* 208, *id.* (1929).

[12] See C. H. M. Waldock, "The Regulation of the Use of Force by Individual States in International Law", 81 *R.C.A.D.I.* 455, 471-4 (1952).

of the Kellogg–Briand Pact. The pivot on which the present-day *jus ad bellum* hinges is Article 2(4) of the Charter, which proclaims:

All Members shall refrain in their international relations from the threat or use of force against the territorial integrity or political independence of any state, or in any other manner inconsistent with the Purposes of the United Nations.[13]

Article 2(4) avoids the term "war". The use of force in international relations, proscribed in the Article, includes war. But the prohibition transcends war and covers also forcible measures short of war. Article 2(4) even goes beyond the actual recourse to force (whether or not reaching the level of war), and interdicts mere threats of force.[14] All the same, the use or threat of force is abolished only in the "international relations" of Member States. Intra-State clashes are out of the reach of Article 2(4).

The expression "force" in Article 2(4) is not preceded by the adjective "armed",[15] whereas the full phrase "armed force" appears elsewhere in the Charter (in Articles 41 and 46).[16] As a result, over the years, there have been many "acrimonious" debates (for example, in the context of the codification of the law of treaties) about the scope of the "force" to which Article 2(4) adverts, and, in particular, whether it extends to economic pressure.[17] However, when studied in context, the term "force" in Article 2(4) must denote armed force: psychological or economic pressure (including economic boycott) does not come within the purview of the Article.[18]

The two specific objectives of the forbidden use or threat of inter-State force, enumerated in Article 2(4), are the territorial integrity and the political independence of States. These dual idioms, when standing alone, may invite a rigid interpretation blunting the

---

[13] Charter of the United Nations, 1945, 9 *Int.Leg.* 327, 332.

[14] On the meaning of threats of force, see R. Sadurska, "Threats of Force", 82 *A.J.I.L.* 239–68 (1988).

[15] See M. Virally, "Article 2 Paragraph 4", *La Charte des Nations Unies* 113, 120 (J.-P. Cot and A. Pellet eds., 1985).

[16] *Supra*, note 13, at 343, 345.

[17] R. D. Kearney and R. E. Dalton, "The Treaty on Treaties", 64 *A.J.I.L.* 495, 534–5 (1970).

[18] See H. Wehberg, "L'Interdiction du Recours à la Force. Le Principe et les Problèmes qui se Posent", 78 *R.C.A.D.I.* 1, 69 (1951).

edge of Article 2(4). Thus, it has been suggested that the use of force within the boundaries of a foreign State does not constitute a violation of its territorial integrity, unless a portion of the State's territory is permanently lost.[19] While the argument is not exceedingly persuasive, it should highlight the consequences likely to flow from a restrictive reading of Article 2(4). If the injunction against resort to force in international relations is confined to specific situations affecting only the territorial integrity and the political independence of States, a legion of loopholes will inevitably be left open.[20]

In emphasizing the reference to the territorial integrity and the political independence of States, the restrictive construction of Article 2(4) fails to give proper account to the conjunctive phrase "or in any other manner inconsistent with the Purposes of the United Nations". In our opinion, these words form the centre of gravity of Article 2(4), because they create "a residual 'catch-all' provision".[21]

The first and foremost Purpose of the United Nations is enshrined in Article 1(1) of the Charter:

> To maintain international peace and security, and to that end: to take effective collective measures for the prevention and removal of threats to the peace, and for the suppression of acts of aggression or other breaches of the peace.[22]

Already the first paragraph of the Preamble of the Charter expounds the *raison d'être* of the Organization in enunciating the determination "to save succeeding generations from the scourge of war"[23] (interestingly, here the term "war" is not dispensed with). Moreover, Article 2(3) prescribes:

> All Members shall settle their international disputes by peaceful means in such a manner that international peace and security, and justice, are not endangered.[24]

---

[19] See A. D'Amato, *International Law: Process and Prospect* 58-9 (1987).
[20] See J. Stone, *Aggression and World Order* 43 (1958).
[21] *Cf.* M. Lachs, "The Development and General Trends of International Law in Our Time", 169 *R.C.A.D.I.* 9, 162 (1980).
[22] *Supra*, note 13, at 331.
[23] *Ibid.*, 330.
[24] *Ibid.*, 332.

Article 2(4) is "inseparable" from Article 2(3), and these two consecutive paragraphs must be perused together.[25]

The correct interpretation of Article 2(4), given such stipulations as a background, is that any use of inter-State force by Member States for whatever reason is banned, unless explicitly allowed by the Charter.[26] It is noteworthy that, in its 1986 Judgment in the *Nicaragua* case, the International Court of Justice pronounced that Article 2(4) articulates the "principle of the prohibition of the use of force" in international relations.[27] The principle was presented by the Court in a non-restrictive fashion, and a careful dissection of the Judgment will disclose that this is no accident.

The sweeping injunction against recourse to inter-State force, under Article 2(4), is subject to exceptions. But these are laid down in other provisions of the Charter. Not counting the licence to take action against the enemy States of the Second World War (Articles 53 and 107),[28] there are only two enduring settings in which the Charter permits the use of inter-State force: collective security (Article 42)[29] and self-defence (Article 51).[30] The exact range of application of these exceptional situations will be discussed in detail *infra*, Part III.

(b) *Attempts to Limit the Scope of the Prohibition*

Ever since the entry into force of the Charter, strenuous efforts have been made to portray special types of inter-State armed action, not amounting to either self-defence or collective security, as exempt from the general obligation established in Article 2(4).

One assertion along these lines is that, if a State does not comply with a judgment rendered by the International Court of Justice, the aggrieved party is entitled to seek execution through the use of

[25] M. Virally, *supra*, note 15, at 114.
[26] See J. Mrazek, "Prohibition of the Use and Threat of Force: Self-Defence and Self-Help in International Law", 27 *C.Y.I.L.* 81, 90 (1989).
[27] *Case Concerning Military and Paramilitary Activities in and against Nicaragua* (Merits), [1986] *I.C.J. Rep.* 14, 100.
[28] *Supra*, note 13, at 347-8, 362-3.
[29] *Ibid.*, 343-4.
[30] *Ibid.*, 346.

force.[31] But the claim must be rejected.[32] The aggrieved party may only turn to the Security Council which, under Article 94(2) of the Charter, is empowered to recommend or decide what measures should be taken "to give effect to the judgment".[33] The Council can determine that non-compliance with the judgment forms a threat to the peace and, by dint of this decision, activate the collective security system[34] (see *infra*, Chapter 10, A). By contrast, the Charter leaves no room for the unilateral execution of judgments by force.

It is also propounded that resort to force by Ruritania would be concordant with Article 2(4), if the purpose of the military operation is the recovery of a territory allegedly belonging to that State and "illegally occupied" by Numidia, because in such circumstances there is supposedly no infringement of Numidian territorial integrity (the Indian invasion of Goa in 1961 and the Argentine invasion of the Falkland Islands in 1982 are leading examples).[35] This position, too, cannot be sustained.[36] The argument was carried to an incongruous length when, in 1990, Iraq deigned to annex the entire territory of a sovereign neighbouring State (Kuwait) by reviving flimsy historical claims. The international community categorically rejected the transparent attempt by Iraq to circumvent Article 2(4). In Resolution No. 662, the Security Council decided that the "annexation of Kuwait by Iraq under any form and whatever pretext has no legal validity, and is considered null and void".[37]

It should be stressed that Article 2(4) introduces an overall prohibition of the use of inter-State force. Exceptions to that rule must be looked for not within Article 2(4), but in other clauses of the Charter. The only valid exceptions affirmed in the Charter are

---

[31] See C. Vulcan, "L'Exécution des Décisions de la Cour Internationale de Justice d'après la Charte des Nations Unies", 51 *R.G.D.I.P.* 187, 195 (1947).

[32] See O. Schachter, "The Enforcement of International Judicial and Arbitral Decisions", 54 *A.J.I.L.* 1, 15-16 (1960).

[33] *Supra*, note 13, at 359.

[34] *Cf.* M. E. O'Connell, "The Prospects for Enforcing Monetary Judgments of the International Court of Justice: A Study of Nicaragua's Judgment against the United States", 30 *V.J.I.L.* 891, 908-9 (1989-90).

[35] See O. Schachter, "The Right of States to Use Armed Force", 82 *Mich.L.R.* 1620, 1627 (1984).

[36] See *ibid.*, 1627-8.

[37] Security Council Resolution No. 662, 45 *R.D.S.C.* 20, *id.* (1990).

self-defence and collective security. No territorial dispute is to be resolved by force: all inter-State disputes must be settled amicably (in conformity with Article 2(3)).

Another attempt to slip through the tight net of Article 2(4) is reflected in constant endeavours to revive the just war doctrine in contemporary international law (see *supra*, Chapter 3, B, (b)). The contention, largely characteristic of the former Soviet bloc and Third World countries, is that inter-State force is excluded from the ambit of Article 2(4) if marshalled on behalf of the just cause of self-determination[38] (see *infra*, Chapter 6, E). It is averred that military support lent by Arcadia to a "war of national liberation", conducted against Utopia by a people exercising the right of self-determination, does not contradict Article 2(4). Laborious explanations have been offered, with a view to developing a legal rationale that would legitimize the use of force by Arcadia against Utopia despite Article 2(4). Foremost among them is the proposition that, since at its inception a colonial regime was installed by armed force, the continued denial of the right of self-determination amounts to "permanent" aggression.[39] Yet, this impressionistic picture is "surely a distortion".[40] Unless the condition of self-defence or collective security is satisfied, there is no way to reconcile Article 2(4) with recourse to force by one State against another, even if the target is a colonial Power.[41] In the words of Judge Schwebel (in his Dissenting Opinion in the *Nicaragua* case):

> it is lawful for a foreign State ... to give to a people struggling for self-determination moral, political and humanitarian assistance; but it is not lawful for a foreign State ... to intervene in that struggle with force.[42]

We shall return to the question in the context of the definition of aggression (*infra*, Chapter 5, B).

---

[38] See J. Zourek, "Enfin une Définition de l'Agression", 20 *A.F.D.I.* 9, 24 (1974).
[39] R. E. Gorelick, "Wars of National Liberation: *Jus ad Bellum*", 11 *C.W.R.J.I.L.* 71, 77 (1979).
[40] L. Henkin, *How Nations Behave* 144 (2nd ed., 1979).
[41] See O. Schachter, "Just War and Human Rights", 1 *P.Y.I.L.* 1, 8 (1989).
[42] *Supra*, note 27, at 351.

Notwithstanding fervent pleadings to the contrary,[43] a State using force in order to overthrow a despotic Government in another country would also run afoul of Article 2(4).[44] There is admittedly strong doctrinal support for the idea that forcible measures of "humanitarian intervention", employed by Atlantica for the sake of compelling Patagonia to cease and desist from massive violations of international human rights, are permissible.[45] In part, this approach amplifies the significance of the references in the Charter to the need to promote and encourage respect for human rights and fundamental freedoms.[46] But, once more, the underlying assumption is that, because no change is sought in the territorial integrity of Patagonia and no challenge is posed to its political independence, the use of force by Atlantica in a humanitarian intervention does not come within the bounds of the prohibition in Article 2(4).[47] We shall examine separately the cognate question whether, under the rubric of self-defence, Atlantica may protect its own nationals against an attack upon them by Patagonia (*infra*, Chapter 8, A, (a)). However, the exponents of the putative right of humanitarian intervention minimize the link of nationality and uphold the protection of all individuals or groups of individuals (even against their own Government).[48] Most commentators who favour humanitarian intervention studiously avoid the terminology of self-defence and insist that forcible measures on behalf of the victims of human rights violations are legitimate, not by virtue of compatibility with Article 51 (the exception clause) but as a result of being allowed in the first place by Article 2(4) (the general provision).[49]

---

[43] See W. M. Reisman, "Coercion and Self-Determination: Construing Charter Article 2(4)", 78 *A.J.I.L.* 642–5 (1984).
[44] See O. Schachter, "The Legality of Pro-Democratic Invasion", 78 *A.J.I.L.* 645–50 (1984).
[45] See M. S. McDougal and W. M. Reisman, "Response", 3 *Int.Law.* 438, 442–4 (1968–9).
[46] See *ibid.*, 444.
[47] See J.-P. L. Fonteyne, "The Customary International Law Doctrine of Humanitarian Intervention: Its Current Validity under the U.N. Charter", 4 *C.W.I.L.J.* 203, 253–4 (1973–4).
[48] See R. B. Lillich, "Forcible Self-Help by States to Protect Human Rights", 53 *Io.L.R.* 325, 332 (1967–8).
[49] See J. R. D'Angelo, "Resort to Force by States to Protect Nationals: The U.S. Rescue Mission to Iran and Its Legality under International Law", 21 *V.J.I.L.* 485, 496 (1980–1).

We believe that the adherents of humanitarian intervention misconstrue Article 2(4). Nothing in the Charter substantiates the right of one State to use force against another under the guise of securing the implementation of human rights.[50] In 1986, the International Court of Justice rejected the notion that the United States could employ force against Nicaragua in order to ensure respect for human rights in that country.[51] It is almost impossible to avoid the conclusion that "[t]his language unmistakably places the Court in the camp of those who claim that the doctrine of humanitarian intervention is without validity".[52] Yet, despite the conspicuously broad range of the Court's pronouncement, attempts have been made to "read [it] narrowly".[53] The *Nicaragua* Judgment has certainly not curbed the enthusiasm of commentators seeking to disencumber the preservation of human rights from the heavy weight of the general injunction against the use of force in international relations.[54]

In April 1991, in the aftermath of the hostilities in the Gulf War and against the background of Iraqi repression of the civilian population (especially, at that time, the Kurds), the Security Council - in Resolution No. 688 - insisted that Iraq "allow immediate access by international humanitarian organizations to all those in need of assistance in all parts of Iraq and to make available all necessary facilities for their operation"[55] (see *supra*, Chapter 1, A, (b), i). While Resolution No. 688 did not expressly support military intervention for humanitarian reasons, such was the actual outcome.[56] With the military help of armed forces of the United States and other coalition countries, "access" to humanitarian aid was achieved through

---

[50] See T. M. Franck and N. S. Rodley, "After Bangladesh: The Law of Humanitarian Intervention by Military Force", 67 *A.J.I.L.* 275, 299-302 (1973).

[51] *Supra*, note 27, at 134-5.

[52] N. S. Rodley, "Human Rights and Humanitarian Intervention: The Case Law of the World Court", 38 *I.C.L.Q.* 321, 332 (1989).

[53] See F. R. Tesón, *Humanitarian Intervention: An Inquiry into Law and Morality* 203-4 (1988).

[54] See, e.g., A. D'Amato, "The Invasion of Panama Was a Lawful Response to Tyranny", 84 *A.J.I.L.* 516, 520 (1990).

[55] Security Council Resolution No. 688, 30 *I.L.M.* 858, 859 (1991).

[56] See J. A. R. Nafziger, "Self-Determination and Humanitarian Intervention in a Community of Power", 20 *D.J.I.L.P.* 9, 29, 31 (1991-2).

the creation of a secure Kurdish enclave in the north of Iraq. In 1992, pursuant to the same resolution, an air exclusion ("no-fly") zone was also established over the Shiite areas in the south of the country. Iraqi defiance of the "no-fly" zone precipitated air strikes by coalition warplanes and missiles in 1993.

In analyzing these events, it must be appreciated that the circumstances were quite exceptional. First, the coalition forces acted in the course of an on-going war (in which hostilities had merely been suspended in a cease-fire). Secondly, the Security Council based its decision on the consequences of the Iraqi repression of the civilian population, held to constitute a threat to "international peace and security in the region".[57] The very fact that the coalition felt compelled to obtain from the Council a mandate for action on Iraqi territory demonstrates that there is no unilateral right of humanitarian intervention.[58]

Similar conclusions ought to be drawn from the international intervention designed to ensure the safety of humanitarian assistance within the former Yugoslavia and Somalia. In Resolution No. 781 (1992), the Council decided "to establish a ban on military flights in the airspace of Bosnia and Herzegovina" as an essential element for the delivery of humanitarian aid.[59] Likewise, in Resolution No. 794, the Council authorized the "use of all necessary means" to establish "a secure environment for humanitarian relief operations in Somalia".[60]

The Council - and the Council alone - is legally empowered to resort to such radical measures (see *infra*, Chapter 10). No individual State is authorized to act unilaterally, in the domain of human rights or in any other sphere, as if it were the policeman of the world.[61]

---

[57] *Supra*, note 55, at 859. For an analysis of the text, see P. Malanczuk, "The Kurdish Crisis and Allied Intervention in the Aftermath of the Second Gulf War", 2 *E.J.I.L.* 114, 127-9 (1991).

[58] See D. J. Scheffer, "Use of Force after the Cold War: Panama, Iraq, and the New World Order", *Right v. Might* 109, 145 (L. Henkin *et al.* eds., 2nd ed., 1991).

[59] Security Council Resolution No. 781, 31 *I.L.M.* 1477, 1478 (1992). The ban was reaffirmed in Security Council Resolution No. 786, *ibid.*, 1479, 1480.

[60] Security Council Resolution No. 794, Doc. S/RES/794 (3 December 1992).

[61] It is submitted that this is not only the law as it is, but also the law as it should be. Consequently, proposals to amend the Charter, with a view to introducing humanitarian intervention as an exception to the rule laid down in Article 2(4) (see M. J. Levitin, "The Law of Force and the Force of Law: Grenada, the Falklands, and Humanitarian Intervention", 27 *H.I.L.J.* 621, 652-5 (1986)), are not only unrealistic; they are also undesirable.

C. *Customary International Law*

(a) *The General Prohibition of the Use of Inter-State Force*

The prohibition of the use of inter-State force is not applicable only to Members of the United Nations. Article 2(4) itself forbids the use of force by UN Members against "any state", viz. either a fellow Member or a non-Member. Recourse to force by a non-Member State (against either a Member or another non-Member State) is dealt with in Article 2(6):

> The Organization shall ensure that states which are not Members of the United Nations act in accordance with these Principles so far as may be necessary for the maintenance of international peace and security.[62]

The Principles of the United Nations are enumerated in Article 2 in its entirety. Indisputably, the most pertinent Principle is the one embodied in Article 2(4).

Some scholars maintain that Article 2(6) is a "revolutionary" stipulation, in that it indirectly imposes on non-Member States the legal regime of Article 2(4).[63] If Article 2(6) purported to do that, it would indeed be revolutionary. One of the basic tenets of international law is that no treaty can bind third States without their consent. Article 35 of the 1969 Vienna Convention on the Law of Treaties promulgates that an obligation may arise for a third State from a provision of a treaty only if the third State accepts the obligation expressly and in writing.[64] Article 35 "is so worded as to make it clear that the juridical basis of the obligation for the third State is not the treaty itself but the collateral agreement whereby the third State has accepted the obligation".[65]

There is no requisite of regarding Article 2(6) as a deviation from the fundamental precept concerning treaty obligations and third States. It is quite evident from the text of Article 2(6) that the duty established therein devolves not on non-Member States, but on the

---

[62] *Supra,* note 13, at 332.
[63] H. Kelsen, *The Law of the United Nations* 106–7, 110 (1950).
[64] Vienna Convention on the Law of Treaties, 1969, [1969] *U.N.J.Y.* 140, 150.
[65] I. Sinclair, *The Vienna Convention on the Law of Treaties* 101 (2nd ed., 1984).

Organization itself.[66] What the Article says is that the Organization is obligated to take the necessary steps against non-Member States, if they undermine international peace and security. Of course, when the Organization discharges its duty *vis-à-vis* a non-Member State, any measures taken must be in keeping with general customary international law.[67] But using force against an aggressor non-Member State is not at variance with that law.

Logically, there are two possibilities here. The first is that the liberty of States to go to war has survived intact in customary international law. If that were the case, freedom of action would be a double-edged argument. Should a non-Member State unleash war invoking such freedom, the UN Organization would be equally entitled to use counter-force in the name of the self-same privilege. If lack of restraint characterizes international relations, the Organization can use the argument of the sword no less than the aggressor non-Member State.

The second logical possibility is that the unbridled prerogative of States to indulge in war has been effaced from customary international law. In that case, a breach of the peace by the aggressor (be it a Member or a non-Member) is in contravention of the new norm. If so, the UN Organization may take counter-action against a flagrant violation of international law.

In reality, the rules of the game have changed dramatically in the last half-century. The liberty to venture into war, and generally to employ inter-State force, is obsolete. Nowadays, the prohibition of the use of inter-State force, as articulated in Article 2(4) of the Charter, has become an integral part of customary international law. As such, it obligates all States, whether or not they are Members of the United Nations. The current state of customary international law in this field was authoritatively canvassed by the International Court of Justice in the *Nicaragua* case.[68]

---

[66] See R. L. Bindschedler, "La Délimitation des Compétences des Nations Unies", 108 *R.C.A.D.I.* 307, 404-5 (1963).

[67] See G. G. Fitzmaurice, "Fifth Report on Law of Treaties", [1960] II *I.L.C. Ybk* 69, 88.

[68] *Supra*, note 27, at 99-101.

Customary international law comes into being when there is "evidence of a general practice accepted as law" (to repeat the well-known formula appearing in Article 38(1)(b) of the Statute of the International Court of Justice).[69] Two elements are condensed here: the (objective) practice of States and (the subjective) *opinio juris sive necessitatis* (i.e. "a belief that this practice is rendered obligatory by the existence of a rule of law requiring it").[70]

In the *Nicaragua* proceedings, both parties were in agreement that "the principles as to the use of force incorporated in the United Nations Charter correspond, in essentials, to those found in customary international law".[71] Yet, the Court deemed it necessary to confirm the existence of a general *opinio juris* concerning the binding character of the customary prohibition of inter-State force.[72]

In determining the tenor of customary international law, the Court relied *inter alia* on the Declaration on Principles of International Law Concerning Friendly Relations and Co-operation among States in accordance with the Charter of the United Nations, unanimously adopted in 1970 by the UN General Assembly.[73] The Declaration, in its first Principle, reiterates the language of Article 2(4) of the Charter, except that the duty to refrain from the use of force is imposed on "[e]very State" instead of "[a]ll Members".[74] This was done deliberately, on the ground that all States are now subject to the same rule.[75]

While the Court in the *Nicaragua* case stressed the *opinio juris* of States, it did not strive to investigate "the ways in which governments actually behave" where the use of force is concerned.[76] The omission is not unrelated to the incontrovertible fact that the use of force continues to permeate international relations. The incidence of inter-State force is so widespread that T. M. Franck has

[69] Statute of the International Court of Justice, Annexed to the Charter of the United Nations, 1945, 9 *Int.Leg.* 510, 522.
[70] *North Sea Continental Shelf* Cases, [1969] *I.C.J. Rep.* 3, 44.
[71] *Supra*, note 27, at 99.
[72] *Ibid.*, 99-100.
[73] General Assembly Resolution No. 2625 (xxv), 25 *R.G.A.* 121 (1970).
[74] *Ibid.*, 122.
[75] See R. Rosenstock, "The Declaration of Principles of International Law Concerning Friendly Relations: A Survey", 65 *A.J.I.L.* 713, 717 (1971).
[76] F. L. Kirgis, "Custom on a Sliding Scale", 81 *A.J.I.L.* 146, 147 (1987).

argued that its proscription is totally eroded in world affairs, and that Article 2(4) "mocks us from its grave".[77]

The strident (and successful) reaction by the international community to the Iraqi invasion of Kuwait in 1990 has impelled some of those who believe in the "death" of Article 2(4) to at least tone down their "rejectionist" approach.[78] In any event, an assault upon Article 2(4), predicated on the record of multiple violations of its strictures, hardly turns this key provision of the Charter into a dead letter. As pointed out by L. Henkin, in a response to Franck, the persistence of inter-State force need not suggest the disappearance of the legal norm expressed in Article 2(4).[79] The criminal codes of all States are constantly trampled underfoot by countless criminals, yet the unimpaired legal validity of these codes is universally conceded.

To be sure, if it could be proved that Article 2(4) is generally ignored by States, no rules of customary international law might conceivably be germinated by this (supposedly barren) clause. The question whether Article 2(4) is brazenly disregarded in international relations is, therefore, of immense import. Nevertheless, in providing an answer to the question, the uppermost consideration should be that - in spite of the frequent roar of guns - States involved in armed conflicts uniformly profess their fidelity to Article 2(4).[80]

When resorting to force, States ordinarily invoke the right of self-defence (see *infra*, Chapter 7, A, (a)). Sometimes, Governments misrepresent the law or use incorrect legal terminology to label their action (see *infra*, Chapter 7, D, (c)). Infelicitous phraseology may also explain occasional abstract assertions, by senior statesmen, that "[t]he survival of states is not a matter of law".[81] In truth, the

---

[77] T. M. Franck, "Who Killed Article 2(4)? Or: Changing Norms Governing the Use of Force by States", 64 *A.J.I.L.* 809, *id.*, 835 (1970).

[78] See, e.g., A. C. Arend, "International Law and the Recourse to Force: A Shift in Paradigms", 27 *S.J.I.L.* 1, 27-8, 35-6 (1990-1).

[79] L. Henkin, "The Reports of the Death of Article 2(4) Are Greatly Exaggerated", 65 *A.J.I.L.* 544, 547 (1971).

[80] For a recent expression of this fidelity, see the consensus Declaration on the Enhancement of the Effectiveness of the Principle of Refraining from the Threat or Use of Force in International Relations, General Assembly Resolution No. 42/22, 42(1) *R.G.A.* 287, 288 (1987).

[81] D. Acheson, "Remarks", 57 *P.A.S.I.L.* 13, 14 (1963).

survival of States is very much a matter of law: it lies at the root of the right of self-defence. But the telling point is that Governments, however they understand or misunderstand the *jus ad bellum,* are not prepared – in this day and age – to uphold the proposition that there are no legal restraints whatever on the employment of inter-State force. "No state has ever suggested that violations of article 2(4) have opened the door to free use of force".[82] When Governments charge each other with infringements of Article 2(4), as happens all too frequently, such accusations are always contested. The plea that Article 2(4) is dead has never been put forward by any Government.

The Court in the *Nicaragua* case commented on the way that States behave and account for their behaviour:

> It is not to be expected that in the practice of States the application of the rules in question should have been perfect, in the sense that States should have refrained, with complete consistency, from the use of force ... The Court does not consider that, for a rule to be established as customary, the corresponding practice must be in absolutely rigorous conformity with the rule. In order to deduce the existence of customary rules, the Court deems it sufficient that the conduct of States should, in general, be consistent with such rules, and that instances of State conduct inconsistent with a given rule should generally have been treated as breaches of that rule, not as indications of the recognition of a new rule. If a State acts in a way prima facie incompatible with a recognized rule, but defends its conduct by appealing to exceptions or justifications contained within the rule itself, then whether or not the State's conduct is in fact justifiable on that basis, the significance of that attitude is to confirm rather than to weaken the rule.[83]

The discrepancy between what States say and what they do may be due to pragmatic reasons, militating in favour of a choice of the line of least exposure to censure.[84] Even so, a disinclination to challenge the validity of a legal norm has a salutary effect in that

---

[82] O. Schachter, "In Defense of International Rules on the Use of Force", 53 *U.C.L.R.* 113, 131 (1986).

[83] *Supra,* note 27, at 98.

[84] See T. Meron, "The Geneva Conventions as Customary Law", 81 *A.J.I.L.* 348, 369 (1987).

it shows that the norm is accepted, if only reluctantly, as the rule. There is a common denominator between those who try (even disingenuously) to take advantage of the refinements of the law, and those who rigorously abide by its letter and spirit. They all share a belief in the authority of the law.

(b) *The Relationship between Customary and Conventional Law*

The injunction against the use of inter-State force is the cornerstone of present-day customary international law. When inspected through an analytical prism, the current prohibition of the use of inter-State force, under customary international law, is seen to be embedded in the Kellogg-Briand Pact and in the UN Charter. As Article 38 of the Vienna Convention on the Law of Treaties sets forth, treaty norms may become binding on third States as rules of customary international law.[85] Customary and conventional international law are not kept apart in "sealed compartments",[86] and there is a lot of cross-fertilization between them. In extreme cases, the general practice and *opinio juris* of States may virtually clone norms originally created by treaty.

When conventional international law crystallizes as customary law, the norm which has its genesis in a treaty is binding on a third State *post hoc* although not *propter hoc*.[87] Historically, the duties incurred by the third State "owe their origin to the fact that the treaty supplied the basis for the growth of a customary rule of law".[88] Yet, legally, these duties are assumed by third States *qua* customary law, and the treaty (which served as a "stimulus" for that law) continues to be binding only on contracting parties.[89] It is not the conventional but the customary link that is relevant from the standpoint of non-contracting parties.[90]

---

[85] *Supra*, note 64, at 150.
[86] E. Jiménez de Aréchaga, "International Law in the Past Third of a Century", 159 *R.C.A.D.I.* 1, 13 (1978).
[87] See J. L. Brierly, "Règles Générales du Droit de la Paix", 58 *R.C.A.D.I.* 5, 223-4 (1936).
[88] R. F. Roxburgh, *International Conventions and Third States* 74 (1917).
[89] M. E. Villiger, *Customary International Law and Treaties* 192-4 (1985).
[90] It is necessary, for that reason, to pay special attention to the particular practice and *opinio juris* of non-contracting parties. See M. H. Mendelson, "The *Nicaragua Case* and Customary International Law", *The Non-Use of Force in International Law* 85, 95-6 (W. E. Butler ed., 1989).

In the *Nicaragua* proceedings, there was disagreement whether the customary and conventional (Charter) prohibitions of the use of inter-State force are identical, and whether the customary rule can still be operative in the relations between UN Member States.[91] The Court arrived at three conclusions:

a. The two sources of international law do not coincide exactly as regards the regulation of the use of force in international relations; there are variations between them on a number of points, especially insofar as the right of self-defence is concerned (see *infra*, Chapter 7, B).[92]

b. Even if the customary and conventional norms did overlap in every respect, customary law would retain its separate identity – and continue to exist alongside of conventional law – so that it might be applied between the parties when, for some reason, an adjudication could not rest on the law of the Charter (as transpired in the case before the Court).[93]

c. No conflicting standards of conduct have evolved in conventional (Charter) and customary law on the use of inter-State force.[94] Charter and customary norms in this area are not completely identical. But, fundamentally, there is no marked divergence between them, for customary international law has solidified under the influence of the Charter.[95]

There is every reason to endorse the Court's finding that a great deal of similarity, if no identity, exists between contemporary customary and conventional (Charter) *jus ad bellum.* However, the Court did not examine in detail whether any difference of degree might exist between customary international law and Article 2(4) (as distinct from Article 51 relating to self-defence). It can be taken for granted that pre-Charter customary international law was swayed by the Charter and that, in large measure, customary and Charter *jus ad bellum* have converged. But did the process of

[91] *Supra*, note 27, at 92-3, 96.
[92] *Ibid.*, 93-4.
[93] *Ibid.*, 94-6.
[94] *Ibid.*, 96-7.
[95] *Ibid.*, id.

change in customary international law come to a stop in the post-Charter era?

Even if, at the present time, customary international law can be looked upon as a replica of Article 2(4), it is hard to believe that it will "freeze" for long.[96] By its very nature, customary international law alters over the years, albeit incrementally. Will the general practice of States (accepted as law) remain steadfast in its faith in every aspect of Article 2(4)? We have noticed (*supra*, B, (b)) that efforts are frequently made to limit the scope of the overall prohibition of the use of inter-State force. Such attempts cannot override the text of Article 2(4), but they may leave their imprint on customary international law. It seems to us that an eventual dissonance between Article 2(4) and customary international law can be anticipated.

D. *Treaties Other than the Pact and the Charter*

The interdiction of the use of inter-State force has been reiterated in numerous international treaties subsequent to the Kellogg-Briand Pact and the Charter of the United Nations. Strictly speaking, there is no need to replicate the language of the Charter. Nonetheless, in some political settings, a reminder of the prohibition of recourse to force in international relations may serve a useful purpose.

Occasionally, this is done in general multilateral treaties governing a certain branch of international law. For instance, Article 301 of the 1982 United Nations Convention on the Law of the Sea stipulates that, "[i]n exercising their rights and performing their duties under this Convention, States Parties shall refrain from any threat or use of force against the territorial integrity or political independence of any State, or in any other manner inconsistent with the principles of international law embodied in the Charter of the United Nations".[97]

---

[96] See A. D'Amato, "Trashing Customary International Law", 81 *A.J.I.L.* 101, 104 (1987).

[97] United Nations Convention on the Law of the Sea, 1982, 21 *I.L.M.* 1261, 1326 (1982).

For the most part, clauses recapitulating the proscription of the use of force in international relations feature in treaties concluded either on a regional or on a bilateral basis. In the context of regional cooperation, examples may be drawn from the American continent. As early as 1933, in the Rio de Janeiro Anti-War Treaty (Non-Aggression and Conciliation) – commonly designated, after an Argentine Foreign Minister, the Saavedra Lamas Treaty – the American States, joined by several European countries, condemned wars of aggression and undertook to settle all disputes through pacific means.[98] The 1947 Rio de Janeiro Inter-American Treaty of Reciprocal Assistance also includes a formal condemnation of war, bolstered by a general undertaking not to resort to force in any manner inconsistent with the UN Charter.[99]

The American continent is not the only part of the world where recurrent commitments are made to refrain from the use of inter-State force. The language of Article 2(4) of the Charter is repeated in the 1975 Helsinki Final Act, adopted by the Conference on Security and Co-operation in Europe.[100] Although the Helsinki Final Act does not form a treaty, the International Court of Justice cited it in the *Nicaragua* case as evidence for the emergence of customary international law banning the use of inter-State force.[101] Upon the demise of the "cold war", in the 1990 Charter of Paris for a New Europe, the States participating in the Helsinki process renewed their pledge to refrain from the threat or use of force.[102]

In the bilateral relations between States, quite a few non-aggression pacts were made after the Kellogg–Briand Pact, with a view to "confirming and completing" it.[103] This is no longer common practice today. Yet, there are some bilateral or trilateral treaties of

[98] Rio de Janeiro Anti-War Treaty (Non-Aggression and Conciliation), 1933, 163 *L.N.T.S.* 393, 405 (Article 1).
[99] Rio de Janeiro Inter-American Treaty of Reciprocal Assistance, 1947, 21 *U.N.T.S.* 77, 95 (Article 1).
[100] Conference on Security and Co-operation in Europe, Helsinki Final Act, 1975, 14 *I.L.M.* 1292, 1294 (1975).
[101] *Supra*, note 27, at 100. See also *ibid.*, 133.
[102] Conference on Security and Co-operation in Europe, Charter of Paris for a New Europe, 1990, 30 *I.L.M.* 190, 196 (1991).
[103] See, e.g., Finland–USSR, Helsinki Treaty of Non-Aggression and Pacific Settlement of Disputes, 1932, 157 *L.N.T.S.* 393, 395 (Preamble).

political and military cooperation, restating the duty not to employ force in any way contrary to the UN Charter.[104] The impulse to reaffirm the essence of Article 2(4) is strongest among countries ascending from war with each other. That explains the texts of the 1966 Indian-Pakistani Tashkent Declaration,[105] and of the 1979 Egyptian-Israeli Treaty of Peace.[106]

E. *The Prohibition of the Use of Inter-State Force as Jus Cogens*

(a) *The Significance of Jus Cogens*

Article 53 of the 1969 Vienna Convention on the Law of Treaties,[107] as its title indicates, addresses the subject of *jus cogens*. Under the Article, "[a] treaty is void if, at the time of its conclusion, it conflicts with a peremptory norm of general international law". For a norm to qualify as peremptory, it has to be one "accepted and recognized by the international community of States as a whole as a norm from which no derogation is permitted and which can be modified only by a subsequent norm of general international law having the same character."

Article 53 applies to those cases in which a treaty is invalidated upon conclusion owing to a clash with a pre-existing peremptory norm. A complementary provision appears in Article 64 of the Vienna Convention, whereby "[i]f a new peremptory norm of general international law emerges, any existing treaty which is in conflict with that norm becomes void and terminates".[108] What it comes down to is that a treaty, although valid at the time of its conclusion, may be invalidated thereafter, as a result of the evolution of a conflicting *jus cogens* in the meantime.[109]

Articles 53 and 64 do not specify when a norm of general international law is to be considered peremptory in nature. But the

---

[104] See, e.g., Greece-Turkey-Yugoslavia, Bled Treaty of Alliance, Political Co-operation and Mutual Assistance, 1954, 211 *U.N.T.S.* 237, 241 (Article I).

[105] India-Pakistan, Tashkent Declaration, 1966, 5 *I.L.M.* 320, *id.* (1966).

[106] Egypt-Israel, Treaty of Peace, 1979, 18 *I.L.M.* 362, 363-4 (1979) (Article III).

[107] *Supra*, note 64, at 154.

[108] *Ibid.*, 157.

[109] Report of the International Law Commission, 18th Session, [1966] II *I.L.C. Ybk* 172, 248-9, 261.

International Law Commission, in its commentary on the draft of the Vienna Convention, identified the Charter's prohibition of the use of inter-State force as "a conspicuous example" of *jus cogens*.[110] The Commission's position was quoted by the International Court in the *Nicaragua* case.[111] In his Separate Opinion, President Singh underscored that "the principle of non-use of force belongs to the realm of *jus cogens*".[112] Judge Sette-Camara, in another Separate Opinion, also expressed the firm view that the non-use of force can be recognized as a peremptory rule.[113] Notwithstanding some lingering reservations,[114] this position seems to be unassailable at the present time.[115]

What is it that marks out peremptory norms (constituting *jus cogens*), as compared to ordinary norms of general international law (regarded as mere *jus dispositivum*)? The special standing of *jus cogens* is manifested less in enjoining States from contrary behaviour (violations), and more in aborting attempted derogations from the general norms.[116] Violations of all laws, however characterized (be they *jus cogens* or *jus dispositivum*), are forbidden. If Arcadia and Numidia were to conclude today a pact of aggression against Utopia, that instrument would palpably be in breach of general (Charter as well as customary) international law. For a breach of the Charter to be perpetrated, it does not matter whether Member States act jointly or severally. Neither Arcadia nor Numidia, when acting on its own, is permitted to wage an aggressive war against Utopia. What each is disallowed to do separately, the two of them are forbidden to do together.

When an international legal norm is classified as *jus cogens*, what is meant is not just that a particular pattern of State conduct is interdicted. The peremptory nature of the injunction signifies that

---

[110] *Ibid.*, 247.

[111] *Supra*, note 27, at 100.

[112] *Ibid.*, 153.

[113] See *ibid.*, 199.

[114] See G. A. Christenson, "The World Court and *Jus Cogens*", 81 *A.J.I.L.* 93, 101 (1987).

[115] See American Law Institute, 1 *Restatement of the Law: The Foreign Relations Law of the United States* 28 (3rd ed., 1986; L. Henkin, Chief Reporter).

[116] See J. Sztucki, *Jus Cogens and the Vienna Convention on the Law of Treaties* 67-8 (1974).

the contractual freedom of States is curtailed. Two major conclusions ensue:

a. A pact of aggression concluded between Arcadia and Numidia against Utopia will not only be stigmatized as a violation of the Charter, as well as general customary international law, but it will also be void *ab initio*[117] (on the meaning of the term "void" under the Vienna Convention, see *supra*, Chapter 2, B, (a), ii). It must be appreciated that the rule does not apply to all treaties projecting recourse to inter-State force. There is an intrinsic difference between a pact aimed at an unlawful use of force (aggression) and a treaty for the organization of legitimate measures of counter-force (collective self-defence) in the event of an armed attack[118] (see *infra*, Chapter 9, B). Only the former instrument, and not the latter, will be annulled. Should a dispute arise whether a specific treaty is invalid on the ground of conflict with *jus cogens*, the International Court of Justice would be vested with compulsory jurisdiction in the matter under Article 66(a) of the Vienna Convention.[119]

A pact of aggression ought not to be confused with a treaty, concluded between Arcadia and Numidia, clashing with ordinary rights of Utopia (i.e. rights derived from *jus dispositivum*). The validity of an ordinary treaty between Arcadia and Numidia is not affected by the infringement of Utopia's rights. Arcadia and Numidia will bear international responsibility towards Utopia, but their treaty remains in force.[120] By contrast, a pact of aggression, being in conflict with *jus cogens*, would be invalid. It is perhaps easier to understand the need for the distinction between these two categories of instruments when it is perceived that a pact of aggression is an agreement to commit a crime[121] (see *infra*, Chapter 5, A).

b. Arcadia and Numidia are not allowed to conclude a treaty derogating from *jus cogens*, even in their mutual relations *inter se*. Thus,

---

[117] See G. G. Fitzmaurice, "Third Report on Law of Treaties", [1958] II *I.L.C. Ybk* 20, 40.
[118] See I. Sinclair, *supra*, note 65, at 216.
[119] *Supra*, note 64, at 157.
[120] See *supra*, note 109, at 217.
[121] See G. Gaja, "*Jus Cogens* beyond the Vienna Convention", 172 *R.C.A.D.I.* 271, 301 (1981).

they cannot enter into a valid agreement in which they absolve each other from the prohibition of the use of inter-State force and decide to settle a dispute by war, nor will such an agreement be saved by an express pledge to safeguard the rights of non-contracting parties.[122] All States have an interest, currently protected by international law, that no war will break out in the most distant part of the globe, lest the conflagration spread to other countries far and near. A treaty initiating war by consent is abrogated, although its impact is allegedly limited to the relations *inter partes*, because of its potential deleterious effects on the international community. There is no contracting out from *jus cogens* obligations.

(b) *How Can Jus Cogens Be Modified ?*

As the International Law Commission observed, "it would clearly be wrong to regard even rules of *jus cogens* as immutable and incapable of modification in the light of future developments".[123] But any modification of a peremptory norm must be brought about (through general custom or treaty) in the same way that the original norm was established. Whereas two States cannot validly agree to release themselves from the prohibition of recourse to force in international relations, the international community as a whole is in a more advantageous position. Having constructed the peremptory norm, the international community may amend it (by narrowing or broadening its scope), supersede it with another rule, or even rescind it altogether.

A modification of an existing peremptory norm through the emergence of a conflicting general custom may prove hard to accomplish, since custom usually consists of a series of unilateral acts which in the setting of an incompatible *jus cogens* could be viewed as lacking any legal effect.[124] Arguably, a declaratory resolution, adopted by consensus by the UN General Assembly, may be of help. But can such a resolution, not supported by valid State practice, create so-called "instant custom" (an immensely controversial

---

[122] *Cf.* G. G. Fitzmaurice, *supra*, note 117, at 40.

[123] *Supra*, note 109, at 248.

[124] On this problem, see C. L. Rozakis, *The Concept of Jus Cogens in the Law of Treaties* 89-90 (1976).

concept at the best of times)[125] powerful enough to intrude upon and reshape *jus cogens?*

The modification of *jus cogens* should be easier to attain through a general (multilateral) treaty terminating or amending prior obligations. However, the process of concluding a general treaty, intended to modify a pre-existing *jus cogens*, is not free of difficulties. Sir Ian Sinclair regards the process as "enigmatic", because the modifying treaty "would, *at the time of its conclusion*, be in conflict with the very rule of *jus cogens* which it purports to modify".[126] We are inclined to think that the enigma is more apparent than real, provided that, "at the time of its conclusion", the modifying treaty has gained the backing of the international community as a whole. General support for the treaty would demonstrate that (in the words of Article 53 of the Vienna Convention) it constitutes "a subsequent norm of general international law having the same character" as the original *jus cogens.*

What is the proper manner of manifesting general support by the international community for a treaty modifying *jus cogens?* T. Meron seems to adhere to the view that the mere formulation of the modifying treaty by a large majority of States indicates the emergence of a new *jus cogens*, "even before the entry into force" of that treaty.[127] This probably goes too far. In our opinion, the required support for the novel peremptory norm is expressed only by the consent of States to be bound by the modifying treaty. Hence, the entry into force of the modifying treaty has to be conditioned on ratification or accession by the bulk of the international community. If the modifying treaty - negotiated, and perhaps signed, by almost all States - stipulates that it will enter into force following the deposit of a relatively small number of ratifications or accessions, the treaty is likely to be considered void, at the point of ostensible entry into force, due to an unequal clash with the very *jus cogens* which it tries to revise. But if the modifying treaty obtains an

---

[125] On the issue of General Assembly resolutions as evidence of customary international law, see O. Schachter, "International Law in Theory and Practice", 178 *R.C.A.D.I.* 9, 111-18 (1982). On "instant custom", see *ibid.,* 115.

[126] I. Sinclair, *supra,* note 65, at 226.

[127] T. Meron, *Human Rights Law-Making in the United Nations* 184 n. 150 (1986).

impressive number of ratifications and accessions prior to entry into force, it manages to overcome the hurdle of the pre-existing *jus cogens* and gain validity. In becoming a valid and binding instrument, it alters the obsolete peremptory norm.

The problem of modifying *jus cogens* is further complicated by the interaction of customary and conventional law. This is epitomized by a hypothetical amendment of the UN Charter. Such an amendment is permissible when a certain procedure, prescribed in Article 108,[128] is complied with. The amending power covers every single clause in the Charter, bar none. At some indefinite time in the future, Member States may theoretically avail themselves of the existing mechanism to amend even Article 2(4). Yet, it must not be forgotten that the current prohibition of the use of inter-State force derives its peremptory nature not only from Article 2(4), but also from an independently valid general customary law. The quandary is whether an amendment of Article 2(4), unaccompanied by a corresponding change in the general practice of States, may be considered a sufficient lever for modifying the existing customary *jus cogens*.

F. *State Responsibility*

(a) *Application of General Rules of State Responsibility*

Any breach of an obligation incumbent upon a State under international law, regardless of the subject-matter of the obligation, entails international responsibility.[129] In conformity with this general rule, international responsibility is generated by recourse to inter-State force in violation of the UN Charter and customary international law. We shall see *infra* (Chapter 5, C) that when an aggressive war is embarked upon, international responsibility may take the form of penal sanctions imposed on certain individuals who acted as organs of the aggressor State. But, without diminishing from such individual liability, international responsibility - whether for an

---

[128] *Supra,* note 13, at 363.
[129] See Report of the International Law Commission, 28th Session, [1976] II (2) *I.L.C. Ybk* 1, 96.

aggressive war or for any other unlawful use of inter-State force – means, first and foremost, State responsibility.

As the Permanent Court of International Justice held in 1928, in the *Chorzów Factory* case, "it is a principle of international law, and even a general conception of law, that any breach of an engagement involves an obligation to make reparation".[130] The Court went on to say that "reparation must, as far as possible, wipe out all the consequences of the illegal act and reestablish the situation which would, in all probability, have existed if that act had not been committed".[131] The aspiration to bring about a *restitutio in integrum* may be frustrated by the fact that restoring the *status quo ante* is not feasible in realistic terms. When restitution in kind is ruled out, the duty to make reparation becomes a duty to pay financial compensation "corresponding to the value which a restitution in kind would bear".[132] Where necessary, the indemnity must also include "damages for loss sustained", beyond restitution in kind or payment in its place.[133] Additionally, reparation in certain circumstances may take the shape of moral or political "satisfaction". Typical measures of satisfaction are apologies, salutes to the flag of the offended State, and punishment of the guilty persons by the offending State.[134]

When State responsibility arises for an unlawful use of inter-State force (particularly for waging war of aggression), measures of satisfaction may be offered or agreed upon, but usually they will not suffice. Restitution in kind is possible when property which has been taken away by the aggressor State is traceable[135] (a matter of the utmost importance in connection with spoliation of treasures of art). Yet, on the whole, since war causes death and irreversible destruction on a vast scale, restitution in kind cannot be considered

---

[130] *Case Concerning the Factory at Chorzów* (Claim for Indemnity) (Merits) (A/17, 1928), 1 *W.C.R.* 646, 664.

[131] *Ibid.*, 677-8.

[132] *Ibid.*, 678.

[133] *Ibid.*, *id.*

[134] See F. V. Garcia Amador, "Sixth Report on International Responsibility", [1961] II *I.L.C. Ybk* 1, 20-2.

[135] See, e.g., Article 238 of the Versailles Peace Treaty with Germany, 1919, 2 *Peace Treaties* 1265, 1394; Article 75 of the Paris Peace Treaty with Italy, 1947, 4 *ibid.*, 2421, 2452-3.

a pragmatic remedy. Payment of compensation must be looked upon as the most effective mode of reparation. In principle, the compensation should relate to all losses and injuries suffered by the victim States and their nationals as a result of the unlawful use of force.[136]

The parties to a conflict may conclude a special agreement turning over the appraisal of compensation to judges, arbitrators or assessors. But the International Court of Justice may acquire jurisdiction in the matter even without a special agreement. In the *Nicaragua* case of 1986, having rejected an American challenge to its jurisdiction and having determined that the United States employed unlawful force against Nicaragua (thus incurring an obligation to make reparation for all injuries caused), the Court decided to settle the form and amount of such reparation at a later stage.[137] Eventually, in 1991, Nicaragua renounced its right of action and the Court recorded the discontinuance of the proceedings.[138]

The obligation of an aggressor State to indemnify the victim of aggression (for the violation of the *jus ad bellum*) must not be confused with the independent liability of a belligerent party to pay compensation for a breach of the laws of warfare (the *jus in bello*). The latter duty is spelt out in Article 3 of Hague Convention (No. IV of 1907) Respecting the Laws and Customs of War on Land,[139] and in Article 91 of Protocol I of 1977 (Additional to the Geneva Conventions of 1949).[140] There is no guarantee that, if infractions of the *jus in bello* are committed, the armed forces of the aggressor will turn out to be the culpable party. It is entirely plausible that the victim of aggression will be responsible for some, if not all, such contraventions. Should this come to pass, a set-off (reducing the

---

[136] See Q. Wright, "The Outlawry of War and the Law of War", 47 *A.J.I.L.* 365, 372 (1953).

[137] *Supra*, note 27, at 142-3, 146-9.

[138] *Case Concerning Military and Paramilitary Activities in and against Nicaragua* (Order), [1991] *I.C.J. Rep.* 47, 48.

[139] Hague Convention (No. IV of 1907) Respecting the Laws and Customs of War on Land, *Hague Conventions* 100, 103.

[140] Protocol Additional to the Geneva Conventions of 12 August 1949, and Relating to the Protection of Victims of International Armed Conflicts (Protocol I), 1977, [1977] *U.N.J.Y.* 95, 132.

amount of compensation which the aggressor ought to pay to its victim) might be called for.

The pecuniary losses borne by a victim of aggression may also be fixed, in the form of a lump sum, in a peace treaty. When such a procedure is followed, much depends on policy considerations. The lump sum may reflect the principle that "the burdens of war are to be placed on the belligerents who spawn them", but it may also mirror the opposing goal of post-war reconstruction and reconciliation.[141] Another factor, not to be overlooked, is that a State emerging from a debilitating war will scarcely be in condition to carry a heavy financial load. An extended war is so devastating that any fair evaluation of the damages to be paid may end up with staggering amounts, in excess of the economic capacity of the State to which responsibility is attributed. This is especially true if remote (or indirect) losses, causally linked to the war, are to be taken into account.[142]

A good case in point is that of Germany in the First World War, i.e. even before the renunciation of war in the Kellogg-Briand Pact. In Article 231 of the 1919 Peace Treaty of Versailles, Germany accepted responsibility (shared with its allies)[143] "for causing all the loss and damage to which the Allied and Associated Governments and their nationals have been subjected as a consequence of the war imposed upon them by the aggression of Germany and her allies".[144] Article 232 recognized that the resources of Germany were not

[141] R. B. Lillich and B. H. Weston, 1 *International Claims: Their Settlement by Lump Sum Agreements* 167 (1975).

[142] The Mixed Claims Commission, United States-Germany, held (per E. B. Parker, Umpire): "It matters not whether the loss be directly or indirectly sustained as long as there is a clear, unbroken connection between Germany's act and the loss complained of. It matters not how many links there may be in the chain of causation connecting Germany's act with the loss sustained, provided there is no break in the chain and the loss can be clearly, unmistakably, and definitely traced, link by link, to Germany's act". Administrative Decision No. II (1923), 7 *R.I.A.A.* 23, 29-30. *Cf.* G. Cottereau, "De la Responsabilité de l'Iraq selon la Résolution 687 du Conseil de Sécurité", 37 *A.F.D.I.* 99, 113-14 (1991).

[143] Parallel provisions appeared in St. Germain Peace Treaty with Austria, 1919, 3 *Peace Treaties* 1535, 1598 ff. (Articles 177 *et seq.*); Neuilly Peace Treaty with Bulgaria, 1919, *ibid.*, 1727, 1769 ff. (Articles 121 *et seq.*); Trianon Peace Treaty with Hungary, 1920, *ibid.*, 1863, 1923 ff. (Articles 161 *et seq.*).

[144] *Supra*, note 135, at 1391 (Versailles).

sufficient to make complete reparation for all such loss and damage, and the compensation was limited to damage done to the civilian population of the Allied and Associated Powers and their property.[145] To determine the amount, an Inter-Allied Reparation Commission was set up in Article 233.[146] German resentment of these clauses soured international relations in the post-War era. Ultimately, the actual indemnities remitted fell far short of the levels of expectations of the architects of the Treaty of Versailles, and, according to some calculations, Germany may have paid no net reparations at all.[147] In retrospect, J. M. Keynes, the prominent economist, proved right in his admonition that a "Carthagenian peace is not *practically* right or possible".[148]

After the outbreak of the Gulf War, the Security Council - in Resolution No. 674 (1990) - reminded Iraq that "under international law it is liable for any loss, damage or injury arising in regard to Kuwait and third States, and their nationals and corporations, as a result of the invasion and illegal occupation of Kuwait by Iraq".[149] The Council further invited States "to collect relevant information regarding their claims, and those of their nationals and corporations, for restitution or financial compensation by Iraq."[150] In Resolution No. 687 (1991), laying down the terms of the cease-fire, the Council reiterated Iraq's liability under international law and decided that a fund to pay compensation for the ensuing claims would be created.[151] The Compensation Fund and a Compensation Commission were established in Resolution No. 692.[152] In Resolution No. 705, the Council decided that 30% of the Iraqi petroleum exports should be set aside for compensation.[153] Resolution No. 706 permitted Iraqi exports of petroleum up to a certain amount, provided that the proceeds go directly into an escrow account used *inter alia*

[145] *Ibid., id.*
[146] *Ibid.,* 1392.
[147] See D. Thomson, *Europe since Napoleon* 566-8 (2nd ed., 1962).
[148] J. M. Keynes, *The Economic Consequences of the Peace* 23 (2 *Collected Writings of J. M. Keynes,* 1971).
[149] Security Council Resolution No. 674, 45 *R.D.S.C.* 25, 26 (1990).
[150] *Ibid., id.*
[151] Security Council Resolution No. 687, 30 *I.L.M.* 847, 852 (1991).
[152] Security Council Resolution No. 692, 30 *I.L.M.* 864, 865 (1991).
[153] Security Council Resolution No. 705, 30 *I.L.M.* 1715, *id.* (1991).

to cover appropriate payments to the Compensation Fund.[154] Resolution No. 712 reaffirmed and specified that arrangement.[155] Since Iraq refused to cooperate in the implementation of the Council's scheme, Resolution No. 778 (1992) pronounced that all States in which there are Iraqi funds or petroleum shall transfer to the escrow account the amounts available or the proceeds of the products' sale.[156]

The Compensation Commission has already taken multiple decisions and adopted provisional rules for claims procedure.[157] In essence, Governments are given "the task of consolidating the claims of their individuals and corporations within specified categories".[158] The consolidation of claims is designed to follow a middle road between a mechanism allowing the direct submission of countless individual claims to an international tribunal, on the one hand, and the somewhat arbitrary technique of calculating lump sums, on the other.[159]

(b) Special Regime of State Responsibility

The general rules of State responsibility are not attuned to the tremendous implications of an aggressive war as a violation of *jus cogens* and a crime. It has been suggested by R. Ago (in his capacity as Special Rapporteur)[160] – and accepted by the International Law Commission[161] – that a special regime of State responsibility is required in order to cope with international crimes. At the time of writing, the practical connotations of such a regime are somewhat obscure, and the Draft Articles produced so far do not quite justify the claim to a special regime of State responsibility.

---

[154] Security Council Resolution No. 706, 30 *I.L.M.* 1719, 1720-1 (1991).
[155] Security Council Resolution No. 712, 30 *I.L.M.* 1730, 1731 (1991).
[156] Security Council Resolution No. 778, Doc. S/RES/778 (2 October 1992).
[157] United Nations Compensation Commission: Report with Decisions of the Governing Council, 1991-2, 31 *I.L.M.* 1009-70 (1992).
[158] *Ibid.,* 1010.
[159] See F. Kalshoven, "State Responsibility for Warlike Acts of the Armed Forces", 40 *I.C.L.Q.* 827, 856-7 (1991).
[160] See R. Ago, "Fifth Report on State Responsibility", [1976] II (I) *I.L.C. Ybk* 3, 32-5.
[161] See *supra,* note 129, at 95-122 (Article 19 and Commentary).

Nonetheless, three observations are apposite:

a. Ordinarily, when Patagonia (through an act of commission or omission) is in breach of an international obligation, there is a specific State (Atlantica) or group of States (Atlantica, Numidia *et al.*) vested with the right correlative to that obligation. Hence, only Atlantica, Numidia etc. will have a *jus standi* to institute an international claim against Patagonia. If Ruritania does not possess a right corresponding to the Patagonian obligation, it has no *jus standi* in the matter. In political, economic and other terms, Ruritania may have a genuine interest in any Atlantican or Numidian initiative challenging Patagonian behaviour. However, that interest is not protected by international law.

In the 1970 *Barcelona Traction* case, the International Court of Justice held that there are some obligations in contemporary international law - and the Court specifically referred, as an illustration, to those derived "from the outlawing of acts of aggression" - which arise "towards the international community as a whole": these are "obligations *erga omnes*", for all States have "a legal interest" in the protection of the rights involved.[162] In the exceptional circumstances of *erga omnes* obligations, international law protects the interests not merely of a specific State or group of States, but of all the States in the world. Each State is vested with rights corresponding to *erga omnes* obligations, thus obtaining a *jus standi* in the matter.[163]

The outcome is that when a war of aggression is let loose, every State (not just the immediate victim) may invoke the international responsibility of the aggressor.[164] The "third" State gets into a "claimant" position and may react accordingly.[165] In 1985, the International Law Commission recognized that when an internationally wrongful act constitutes an international crime, all other States are to be

---

[162] *Case Concerning the Barcelona Traction, Light and Power Company, Limited,* [1970] *I.C.J. Rep.* 3, 32.

[163] See Y. Dinstein, "The Erga Omnes Applicability of Human Rights", 30 *Ar. V.* 16, 18-19 (1992).

[164] See R. Ago, *supra,* note 160, at 29.

[165] See M. Mohr, "The ILC's Distinction between 'International Crimes' and 'International Delicts' and Its Implications", *United Nations Codification of State Responsibility* 115, 131-2 (M. Spinedi and B. Simma eds., 1987).

considered individually as "injured" parties.[166] All the same, as yet, the full range of the legal consequences of this proposition has not been outlined by the Commission.[167] It is quite obvious that only the direct victim - and not all "injured" parties - will be entitled to demand monetary compensation.[168] Still, a "non-directly injured" State has the legal right to demand, for instance, the cessation of aggression, *restitutio in integrum* (where applicable), and perhaps even guarantees against resumption of hostilities.[169]

b. We have already alluded to the existence of individual criminal responsibility for waging aggressive war (a matter that will command our attention *infra*, Chapter 5, C). Can a State, too, bear criminal responsibility for such an act? Calls for the recognition of the penal responsibility of States have been made since the 1920s.[170] Then as now, quite a few scholars,[171] as well as representatives of States,[172] have flatly denied that there is any merit in the idea. At times, writers take contradictory positions on this issue. Thus, G. I. Tunkin declares in one context that "the concept of criminal responsibility of a state is wholly unfounded".[173] Further on, in the same book, he registers the emergence in international law of a new phenomenon of "sanctions relating to the international crimes of a state", including "measures having the character of preventive punishment" (like the treatment of Germany after the Second World War).[174]

---

[166] Report of the International Law Commission, 37th Session, [1985] II (2) *I.L.C. Ybk* 1, 25 (Article 5(3)).

[167] *Ibid.*, 27 (Commentary).

[168] See B. Simma, "International Crimes: Injury and Countermeasures. Comments on Part 2 of the ILC Work on State Responsibility", *International Crimes of States* 283, 301 (J. H. H. Weiler, A. Cassese and M. Spinedi eds., 1989).

[169] See M. Spinedi, "International Crimes of States: The Legislative History", *International Crimes of States, ibid.*, 7, 132.

[170] For a brief summary, see V. V. Pella, "Towards an International Criminal Court", 44 *A.J.I.L.* 37, 50-1 (1950).

[171] See K. Marek, "Criminalizing State Responsibility", 14 *R.B.D.I.L.* 460, 483 (1978-9). See also P. M. Dupuy, "Observations sur le 'Crime International de l'Etat'", 84 *R.G.D.I.P.* 449-86 (1980).

[172] See L. Henkin, R. C. Pugh, O. Schachter and H. Smit, *International Law Cases and Materials* 534-5 (2nd ed., 1987).

[173] G. I. Tunkin, *Theory of International Law* 402 (1974).

[174] *Ibid.*, 422.

It is elementary that a State, as an artificial legal person, cannot actually be subjected to certain penal sentences (like imprisonment). However, from the outset of the debate, it has been argued that military, diplomatic and economic measures may serve as penal sanctions against States.[175] More recently, actions such as those taken against Germany and Japan after the Second World War (e.g., "the destruction of factories capable of increasing the military potential") have been offered for consideration as penal sanctions available against States.[176] G. Schwarzenberger even advocated the policy of treating States (e.g., Nazi Germany), which deliberately plan and pursue "wholesale aggression" (to be distinguished from an ordinary case of resorting to unlawful force), like "outlaws": such States should "forfeit their international personality and put themselves beyond the pale of international law".[177] These are far-fetched and not very attractive proposals. After all, when penal sanctions are inflicted on a State (an incorporeal juristic person), they are tantamount to the collective punishment of the State's population, striking at the innocent together with the guilty.[178] Modern conceptions of international human rights exclude the possibility of exposing the population of a State to indiscriminate collective punishment.[179]

The conundrum of the criminal responsibility of States is not easy to solve. Hence, in 1991, when the International Law Commission provisionally adopted a Draft Code of Crimes against the Peace and Security of Mankind, it "decided, at least at this stage, not to apply international criminal responsibility to States".[180] The Commission pointed out that, even "assuming that the criminal responsibility of the State can be codified" in the future, the "two regimes of criminal responsibility" – of the State and of the individual – would have to differ from each other.[181]

---

[175] See V. V. Pella, "Plan d'Un Code Répressif Mondial", 12 *R.I.D.P.* 348, 369 (1935).
[176] V. V. Pella, *supra*, note 170, at 52.
[177] G. Schwarzenberger, "The Judgment of Nuremberg", 21 *Tul.L.R.* 329, 351 (1946-7).
[178] See P. N. Drost, 1 *The Crime of State* 292 (1959).
[179] *Cf.* I. Brownlie, *International Law and the Use of Force by States* 153 (1963).
[180] Report of the International Law Commission, 43rd Session, 255 (mimeographed, 1991).
[181] *Ibid.*, 251.

Determining the potential consequences of the criminal culpability of an aggressor State is not enough. The imposition of veritable penal sanctions (whatever they are) should follow judicial proceedings in which guilt is impartially and authoritatively determined. On the whole, a higher priority should probably be given to the setting up of an international criminal court - the absence of which (see *infra*, Chapter 5, C, (b)) represents a structural flaw in the international legal system - than to the development of rather abstract legal norms regarding the criminal responsibility of States.[182]

c. We have seen that compensation, as a measure of reparation, is supposed to be based on the value of restitution plus damages for losses sustained. The question that presents itself is whether punitive (or exemplary) damages may be added to that computation. Opinions on the subject are divided. Some commentators assert that punitive damages do not comport with the nature of reparation, and are not countenanced by international law.[183] Others maintain that, if justified by the gravity of the unlawful act, punitive damages are consonant with diplomatic practice and the case law.[184] Even if punitive damages are generally inadmissible, their imposition in the special case of an aggressor State may be deemed proper. If punitive damages are looked at as a fine, they become a monetary punishment which may be meted out to the aggressor State.[185]

A countervailing consideration is that, if the economic burden of paying ordinary compensation for war losses may be too onerous to bear, the chances of collecting punitive damages from the responsible State is *a fortiori* slim. Should that State default, there would be no point in driving it to bankruptcy. In the first place, a bankrupt State will surely lack the capacity to discharge its war debts. Besides, ability to pay punitive damages cannot conceivably

---

[182] See F. Rigaux, "Le Crime d'Etat. Réflexions sur l'Article 19 du Projet d'Articles sur la Responsabilité des Etats", 3 *International Law at the Time of Its Codification: Essays in Honour of Roberto Ago* 301, 319 (1987).

[183] See H. E. Yntema, "The Treaties with Germany and Compensation for War Damage", 24 *Col.L.R.* 134, 138 (1924).

[184] See F. V. Garcia Amador, *supra*, note 134, at 36-7.

[185] See F. Malekian, *International Criminal Responsibility of States* 179-80, 196 (1985).

serve as an exclusive yardstick when the future of a State is at stake. A State cannot be equated with a commercial concern threatened with bankruptcy, for there are essential governmental functions which must continue to be exercised no matter what.[186]

---

[186] See J. F. Williams, "A Legal Footnote to the Story of German Reparations", 13 *B.Y.B.I.L.* 9, 31 (1932).

CHAPTER 5

THE CRIMINALITY OF WAR OF AGGRESSION

A. *War of Aggression as a Crime against Peace*

The absence of meaningful sanctions calculated to enforce respect for legal norms is a pervasive problem in every branch of international law, but nowhere is the need for such sanctions more evident than in the domain of the *jus ad bellum*. Even at the embryonic stage of the process culminating in the imposition of a legal ban on the use of inter-State force, it was generally recognized that, unless coupled with effective sanctions, the interdiction of aggressive war was liable to be chimerical. To be effective, sanctions in this context must go beyond the bounds of State responsibility (see *supra*, Chapter 4, F). Only if it dawns on the actual decision-makers that when they carry their country along the path of war in contravention of international law they expose themselves to individual criminal liability, are they likely to hesitate before taking the fateful step.

Already at the end of the First World War (prior to the proscription of war by positive international law), plans were made to prosecute the German Kaiser, Wilhelm II, on account of his personal responsibility for the War. In Article 227 of the Peace Treaty of Versailles, the Allied and Associated Powers charged the Kaiser with "a supreme offence against international morality and the sanctity of treaties".[1] As the language of the Article suggests, the Kaiser's acts were looked upon as an offence not against international law but against international morality[2] (and the sanctity of treaties, a phrase with a religious more than a legal connotation). In any event, the Kaiser found asylum in The Netherlands, not a contracting party to the Treaty of Versailles, and that country refused to extradite him on the ground that it was not obligated by international law to do so.[3]

---

[1] Versailles Peace Treaty with Germany, 1919, 2 *Peace Treaties* 1265, 1389.

[2] See L. C. Green, "Superior Orders and Command Responsibility", 27 *C.Y.I.L.* 167, 191-2 (1989).

[3] For the text of the Dutch note, see J. B. Scott, "The Trial of the Kaiser", *What Really Happened at Paris* 231, 243-4 (E. M. House and C. Seymour eds., 1921).

In the era between the two World Wars, the criminality of aggressive war was heralded in several international instruments, none of which was legally binding. Thus, the Preamble of the unratified 1924 Geneva Protocol on the Pacific Settlement of International Disputes, crafted as a device to close the "gaps" in the Covenant of the League of Nations (see *supra*, Chapter 3, E, (c)), set forth that "a war of aggression constitutes ... an international crime".[4]

The criminalization of aggressive war in a treaty in force was attained only in the aftermath of the Second World War, upon the conclusion of the Charter of the International Military Tribunal annexed to an Agreement done in London in 1945.[5] Under Article 6(a) of the Charter, the "planning, preparation, initiation or waging of a war of aggression, or a war in violation of international treaties, agreements or assurances, or participation in a common plan or conspiracy for the accomplishment of any of the foregoing" are "crimes against peace" entailing individual responsibility (and it is specifically added that "[l]eaders, organizers, instigators and accomplices participating in the formulation or execution" of the common plan or conspiracy are responsible for "all acts performed by any persons in execution of such plan").[6] The London Agreement originally had as signatories the four Big Powers – the United States, the USSR, the United Kingdom and France – but later it was adhered to by 19 additional Allied nations.[7] The Charter of the International Military Tribunal served as the fulcrum for the *Nuremberg* trial of the major German war criminals.

Article 6(a) of the London Charter represented a singular advance in the evolution of international law. The gist of the clause was soon reiterated, with some variations, in Article II (1)(a) of Control Council Law No. 10 (forming the legal foundation of the so-called Subsequent Proceedings at Nuremberg, in which other

---

[4] Geneva Protocol on the Pacific Settlement of International Disputes, 1924, 2 *Int.Leg.* 1378, 1380.

[5] Charter of the International Military Tribunal, Annexed to the London Agreement for the Establishment of an International Military Tribunal, 1945, 9 *Int.Leg.* 632, 637.

[6] *Ibid.*, 639-40.

[7] *Ibid.*, 632.

German war criminals were tried by American Military Tribunals),[8] and in Article 5(a) of the Charter of the International Military Tribunal for the Far East (issued in a Proclamation by General D. MacArthur, in his capacity as Supreme Commander of the Allied Powers in the region, and designed for the trial of the major Japanese war criminals).[9]

In its Judgment of 1946, the International Military Tribunal at *Nuremberg* held that Article 6(a) of the London Charter is declaratory of modern international law, which regards war of aggression as a grave crime.[10] Hence, the Tribunal rejected the argument that the provision of the Article amounted to *ex post facto* criminalization of the acts of the defendants, in breach of the *nullum crimen sine lege* principle.[11] The Tribunal relied heavily on the renunciation of war in the Kellogg-Briand Pact.[12] The Pact established the illegality of war as an instrument of national policy, and from that the Judgment inferred that "those who plan and wage such a war, with its inevitable and terrible consequences, are committing a crime in so doing".[13]

The Tribunal conceded that the Pact had neither expressly promulgated that war is a crime nor set up courts to try offenders.[14] But this is also true of Hague Convention (No. IV of 1907) Respecting the Laws and Customs of War on Land.[15] Hague Convention No. IV (through its Regulations) prohibits certain practices in warfare, such as the maltreatment of prisoners of war, the employment of poisoned weapons, and the improper use of flags of truce.[16] These forbidden acts have been viewed as war crimes, at least after 1907, notwithstanding the fact that the Convention does not designate them as criminal and does not introduce penal sanctions.[17] The

---

[8] Control Council Law No. 10, 1945, 1 *N.M.T.* xvi, xvii.
[9] Charter of the International Military Tribunal for the Far East, 1946, 14 *D.S.B.* 361, 362 (1946).
[10] International Military Tribunal (*Nuremberg*), Judgment (1946), 1 *I.M.T.* 171, 219-23.
[11] *Ibid.*, 219.
[12] *Ibid.*, 219-20.
[13] *Ibid.*, 220.
[14] *Ibid.*, *id.*
[15] Hague Convention (No. IV of 1907) Respecting the Laws and Customs of War on Land, *Hague Conventions* 100.
[16] *Supra*, note 10, at 220.
[17] *Ibid.*, 220-1.

Tribunal considered the criminality of war as analogous and even more compelling.[18] The Judgment adduced diverse non-binding instruments (like the Geneva Protocol of 1924), whereby aggressive war had been branded categorically as a crime, finding in them evidence for the dynamic development of customary international law.[19] The linch-pin of the Tribunal's position was that

> Crimes against international law are committed by men, not by abstract entities, and only by punishing individuals who commit such crimes can the provisions of international law be enforced.[20]

In other words, the banning of war is devoid of any practical significance, unless international law is prepared to mete out real penalties to flesh-and-blood offenders acting on behalf of the artificial legal person that is the State.

The *Nuremberg* decision concerning crimes against peace has instigated harsh criticism,[21] which cannot be pretermitted. No doubt, the weakest link in the chain constructed by the International Military Tribunal is the certitude that the illegality of war (under the Kellogg-Briand Pact) ineluctably leads to its criminality.[22] International law renders many an act of State unlawful, yet in most instances that does not mean that the interdicted conduct becomes a crime. Why is the injunction against war different from other international legal prohibitions? A reply to the question may be gleaned in another section of the Judgment:

> War is essentially an evil thing. Its consequences are not confined to the belligerent States alone, but affect the whole world.
> To initiate a war of aggression, therefore, is not only an international crime; it is the supreme international crime differing only from other war crimes in that it contains within itself the accumulated evil of the whole.[23]

---

[18] *Ibid.,* 221.

[19] *Ibid.,* 221-2.

[20] *Ibid.,* 223.

[21] See, e.g., F. B. Schick, "The Nuremberg Trial and the International Law of the Future", 41 *A.J.I.L.* 770, 783-4 (1947).

[22] See C. A. Pompe, *Aggressive War an International Crime* 245 (1953).

[23] *Supra,* note 10, at 186. This well-known dictum is based on a passage from Lord Wright, "War Crimes under International Law", 62 *L.Q.R.* 40, 47 (1946).

The decisive point is that war is a cataclysmic event. There is no way in which war can be waged as if it were a chess game. In the nature of things, blood and fire, suffering and pain, are the concomitants of war. As a result, war simply must be a crime.

The stand taken by the International Military Tribunal is not invulnerable. If wars by their very nature (because of the devastation associated with them) are viewed as *mala in se*,[24] it is incomprehensible how they could have retained their legality in the centuries preceding the Kellogg–Briand Pact. If, for most of its duration, international law managed to adapt itself to the lawfulness of war, surely the proscription of war may be deemed an achievement that is sufficient unto itself. Why are criminal sanctions, directed against the individual organs of the State, assumed to be *sine qua non* to such an extent that they have to be looked upon as implicit in the Pact?

These and other difficulties were hotly debated in the late 1940s. It seems only fair to state that when the London Charter was concluded, Article 6(a) was not really declaratory of pre-existing customary international law.[25] The *Nuremberg* Judgment was innovative when it ingested the criminality of war into general international law.[26] However, the issue is no longer of great importance. It is virtually irrefutable that present-day positive international law reflects the Judgment. War of aggression currently constitutes a crime against peace. Not just a crime, but the supreme crime under international law.

The *Nuremberg* criminalization of aggressive war was upheld, in 1948, by the International Military Tribunal for the Far East at *Tokyo*.[27] It was also endorsed in other trials against criminals of the Second World War, most conspicuously in the *Ministries* case, in 1949, the last of the Subsequent Proceedings.[28] Admittedly, no indictment for

---

[24] See Q. Wright, "The Law of the Nuremberg Trial", 41 *A.J.I.L.* 38, 63 (1947).

[25] See L. Gross, "The Criminality of Aggressive War", 41 *A.P.S.R.* 205, 218-20 (1947).

[26] See G. A. Finch, "The Nuremberg Trial and International Law", 41 *A.J.I.L.* 20, 33-4 (1947).

[27] In re *Hirota and Others* (International Military Tribunal for the Far East, Tokyo, 1948), [1948] *A.D.* 356, 362-3.

[28] *U.S.A. v. Von Weizsaecker* et al. ("The *Ministries* Case") (Nuremberg, 1949), 14 *N.M.T.* 314, 318-22.

crimes against peace (in violation of the *jus ad bellum*) has followed the multiple armed conflicts of the post Second World War era.[29] But neither have these conflicts spawned any trials of enemy personnel for traditional war crimes (in breach of the *jus in bello*), conducted on the basis of international law.[30] To the extent that penal proceedings arising out of war have been held at all, they involved either nationals of the prosecuting State charged with crimes against its domestic (civil or military) law or persons not protected by the *jus in bello* as lawful combatants.[31]

The idea of charging Saddam Hussein with a long list of international offences, above all the crime of waging a war of aggression against Kuwait, has been advanced in 1990 and thereafter by leading world statesmen as well as international lawyers.[32] But the punishment (if not the trial) of a felon presupposes his apprehension, whereas Saddam Hussein remained beyond the reach of the law. The absence of an international criminal court, however deplorable it may be (see infra, C, (d)), was not *per se* a bar to prosecution. Had Saddam Hussein been captured, an *ad hoc* international penal

---

[29] See J. F. Murphy, "Crimes against Peace at the Nuremberg Trial", *The Nuremberg Trial and International Law* 141, 153 (G. Ginsburgs and V. N. Kudriavtsev eds., 1990).

[30] In 1973, the newly established State of Bangladesh announced that it would proceed with war crimes trials of Pakistani prisoners of war held by its ally, India. But ultimately the trials did not take place. See J. J. Paust and A. P. Blaustein, "War Crimes Jurisdiction and Due Process: The Bangladesh Experience", 11 *V.J.T.L.* 1, 2-3, 34-5 (1978).

Violations of international humanitarian law in the course of the fighting in the former Yugoslavia led the Security Council to reaffirm, in Resolution No. 764 (1992), that persons who commit or order the commission of grave breaches of the 1949 Geneva Conventions are individually responsible for their acts (31 *I.L.M.* 1465, 1467 (1992)). The statement was reiterated in Resolution No. 771, which called upon States and international humanitarian organizations to collate information about such grave breaches (*ibid.*, 1470, 1471). In Resolution No. 780, the Council requested the Secretary-General to establish an impartial Commission of Experts to examine and analyze the information collated (*ibid.*, 1476, 1477). A further step was taken by the Council in Resolution No. 808, where it decided (in principle) to establish an international tribunal for the prosecution of serious offenders (Doc. S/RES/808 (22 February 1993)). See *infra*, C, (d).

[31] See Y. Dinstein, "The Distinction between Unlawful Combatants and War Criminals", *International Law at a Time of Perplexity: Essays in Honour of Shabtai Rosenne* 103, 116 (Y. Dinstein ed., 1989).

[32] See A. M. Warner, "The Case against Saddam Hussein - The Case for World Order", 43 *Mer.L.R.* 563, 598-601 (1991-2).

tribunal resembling the one functioning at *Nuremberg* could have been established. Besides, proceedings could have been carried out before domestic courts either in Kuwait or in any other country (such as the United States).[33]

The avoidance of actual trials against the perpetrators of crimes against peace is due to political constraints and other pragmatic considerations. There is no indication that States regard as anachronistic the concept that war of aggression constitutes a crime under international law. On the contrary, support for this concept has been manifested consistently in international fora. The best testimony is afforded by a string of uncontested UN General Assembly resolutions, complemented by studies undertaken by the International Law Commission.

As early as 1946, the General Assembly affirmed the principles of international law recognized by the Charter and the Judgment of the International Military Tribunal.[34] In 1947, the General Assembly instructed the International Law Commission to formulate these principles and also to prepare a Draft Code of Offences against the Peace and Security of Mankind.[35] The Commission enunciated the "Nuremberg Principles" in 1950. The text recites the Charter's definition of crimes against peace, emphasizing that offenders bear responsibility for such crimes and are liable to punishment.[36]

The first phase of the Commission's work on the Draft Code of Offences against the Peace and Security of Mankind was completed in 1954. Article 2(1) of the Draft Code enumerated as an offence of this type any act of "aggression".[37] Article 1 laid down that the offences listed "are crimes under international law, for which the responsible individuals shall be punished".[38]

---

[33] See L. R. Beres, "The United States Should Take the Lead in Preparing International Legal Machinery for Prosecution of Iraqi Crimes", 31 *V.J.I.L.* 381, 386-9 (1990-1).

[34] General Assembly Resolution No. 95 (I), 1(2) *R.G.A.* 188, *id.* (1946).

[35] General Assembly Resolution No. 177 (II), 2 *R.G.A.* 111, 112 (1947).

[36] Report of the International Law Commission, 2nd Session, [1950] II *I.L.C. Ybk* 364, 374, 376.

[37] Report of the International Law Commission, 6th Session, [1954] II *I.L.C. Ybk* 140, 151.

[38] *Ibid.*, 150.

A serious examination of the 1954 Draft Code was suspended until a definition of aggression could be agreed upon.[39] It took quite some time before the impetus favouring such a definition overcame resistance that, initially, was considerable. For two decades, the Draft Code remained dormant. Finally, in 1974, the General Assembly produced a consensus Definition of Aggression, and Article 5(2) of the text prescribes that "war of aggression is a crime against international peace".[40] Following the adoption of the Definition, a second phase in the work on the Draft Code was started.[41] In 1991, the International Law Commission, having examined nine reports submitted by a Special Rapporteur (D. Thiam), provisionally adopted - on first reading - and transmitted to Governments for comments a new Draft Code of Crimes against the Peace and Security of Mankind[42] (the governing word in this text being Crimes in lieu of Offences). Aggression - rather than war of aggression - and even the threat of aggression are defined here as crimes against the peace and security of mankind.[43]

Already in 1976, the Commission, in the course of codifying the law of State responsibility, reaffirmed that a breach of the prohibition of aggression may result in an international crime (Article 19).[44] The General Assembly, back in 1970, in the Declaration on Principles of International Law Concerning Friendly Relations and Cooperation among States in accordance with the Charter of the United Nations, proclaimed that "war of aggression constitutes a crime against peace, for which there is responsibility under international law".[45]

In all, the criminality of aggressive war has entrenched itself in an impregnable position in contemporary international law. It is true that the full consequences of this criminality are not always

---

[39] See L. Gross, "Some Observations on the Draft Code of Offences against the Peace and Security of Mankind", 13 *I.Y.H.R.* 9, 20 (1983).

[40] General Assembly Resolution No. 3314 (xxix), 29(1) *R.G.A.* 142, 144 (1974).

[41] See L. Gross, *supra*, note 39, at 26 ff.

[42] Report of the International Law Commission, 43rd Session, 238-50 (mimeographed, 1991).

[43] *Ibid*, 243-5 (Articles 15-16).

[44] Report of the International Law Commission, 28th Session, [1976] II (2) *I.L.C. Ybk* 1, 75.

[45] General Assembly Resolution No. 2625 (xxv), 25 *R.G.A.* 121, 122 (1970).

agreed upon (see *infra*, Chapter 6). But it cannot be denied that responsibility for international crimes, as distinct from responsibility for ordinary breaches of international law, entails the punishment of individuals. The criminality of war of aggression means the accountability of human beings, and not merely of abstract entities.

B. *The Definition of Aggression*

The General Assembly consensus Definition of Aggression, adopted in 1974, relates to "aggression" in a generic way. The abovementioned Article 5(2) differentiates between aggression (which "gives rise to international responsibility") and war of aggression (which is "a crime against international peace").[46] The drafters of the Definition thereby signalled clearly that not every act of aggression constitutes a crime against peace: only war of aggression does.[47] An act of aggression may trigger war. However, this is not a foregone conclusion, since aggression may also take the form of an act short of war. When an aggressive act short of war is committed, although a violation of international law occurs, no crime against peace is perpetrated.

The inseparability of crimes against peace from aggressive wars is in conformity with the definition of the crimes appearing in Article 6(a) of the London Charter of the International Military Tribunal (see *supra*, A). For its part, the International Law Commission has been trying to expand the scope of the crimes. In the 1954 Draft Code, the Commission defined "[a]ny act" of aggression as an offence against the peace and security of mankind.[48] In its 1991 Draft Code, the Commission turned all acts of aggression (as defined by the General Assembly) into crimes against the peace and security of mankind, adding the threat of aggression as well.[49] Should the Commission's present tentative formulation be confirmed in binding from, the broadening of the range of crimes

---

[46] See G. Gilbert, "The Criminal Responsibility of States", 39 *I.C.L.Q.* 345, 360 (1990).
[47] See B. Broms, "The Definition of Aggression", 154 *R.C.A.D.I.* 299, 357 (1977).
[48] *Supra*, note 37, at 151 (Article 2(1)).
[49] *Supra*, note 42, at 243-5.

against peace to acts and threats of aggression short of war would represent a striking departure from existing international law.

While Article 5(2) of the Definition of Aggression pronounces war of aggression to be a crime against international peace, the Definition as a whole is not engrossed in the criminal ramifications of aggressive war. The Resolution, to which the Definition of Aggression is annexed, makes it plain that the primary intention of the General Assembly was to recommend the text as a guide to the Security Council when the latter is called upon to determine (within its mandate under the UN Charter) the existence of an act of aggression[50] (see *infra*, Chapter 10, A). It should be borne in mind that aggression may appear in a different light when inspected by the Security Council for political purposes and when a judicial inquiry is made into criminal liability.[51]

On balance, the main value of any definition of aggression lies in the criminal field. The reason is that a tribunal vested with jurisdiction to try crimes against peace cannot possibly gloss over the theme of aggression, which is the gravamen of the charge: unless a war is aggressive in nature, no crime has been committed. By contrast, under Chapter VII of the Charter, the Security Council's powers are identical in the face of aggression, breach of the peace or any threat to the peace.[52] It is not imperative for the Council to determine specifically that aggression has been perpetrated. Irrespective of the exact classification of activities examined by the Council – as long as they can be categorized either as aggression or as breach of (or even threat to) the peace – the Council is authorized to put in effect the same measures of collective security (see *infra*, Chapter 10, A). Nevertheless, since the General Assembly largely de-emphasized the criminal aspect of its formulation, and brought to the fore the political dimension, the Definition of Aggression is less useful in its penal implications.

Having said all that, it must be acknowledged that the General Assembly's Definition of Aggression is the most recent and the most

---

[50] *Supra*, note 40, at 143.
[51] See J. I. Garvey, "The U.N. Definition of 'Aggression': Law and Illusion in the Context of Collective Security", 17 *V.J.I.L.* 177, 193-4 (1976-7).
[52] Charter of the United Nations, 1945, 9 *Int.Leg.* 327, 343-6.

widely (albeit not universally)[53] accepted. At least one paragraph of the Definition, namely, Article 3(g) (to be quoted *infra*), has been held by the International Court of Justice, in the *Nicaragua* case of 1986, to mirror customary international law.[54] Even Judge Schwebel, who cautioned in his Dissenting Opinion not to magnify the significance of the Definition, admitted that it cannot be discarded.[55] Other definitions of aggression assuredly exist, some of them in conventional form (particularly in treaties concluded by the USSR with neighbouring countries in 1933).[56] But these definitions are not applicable to non-contracting parties, and they are no more apposite to the contours of crimes against peace. *Faute de mieux*, the essence of crimes against peace has to be extracted from the General Assembly's formulation.

Au fond, the General Assembly utilized the technique of a composite definition, combining general and enumerative elements: it started with an abstract statement of what aggression means, and appended a non-exhaustive catalogue of specific illustrations.[57] The general part of the Definition is embodied in Article 1:

> Aggression is the use of armed force by a State against the sovereignty, territorial integrity or political independence of another State, or in any other manner inconsistent with the Charter of the United Nations, as set out in this Definition.[58]

In an explanatory note, the framers of the Definition commented that the term "State" includes non-UN Members, embraces a group of States and is used without prejudice to questions of recognition.[59]

Article 1 of the Definition repeats the core of the wording of Article 2(4) of the Charter (quoted *supra*, Chapter 4, B, (a)), subject

---

[53] For a scathing criticism of the Definition, see J. Stone, "Hopes and Loopholes in the 1974 Definition of Aggression", 71 *A.J.I.L.* 224–46 (1977).

[54] *Case Concerning Military and Paramilitary Activities in and against Nicaragua* (Merits), [1986] *I.C.J. Rep.* 14, 103.

[55] *Ibid.*, 345.

[56] London Conventions for the Definition of Aggression, 1933, 147 *L.N.T.S.* 67; 148 *ibid.*, 211.

[57] See S. M. Schwebel, "Aggression, Intervention and Self-Defence in Modern International Law", 136 *R.C.A.D.I.* 411, 443–4 (1972).

[58] *Supra*, note 40, at 143.

[59] *Ibid.*, *id.*

to a number of variations: (i) the mere threat of force is excluded; (ii) the adjective "armed" is interposed before the noun "force"; (iii) "sovereignty" is mentioned together with the territorial integrity and the political independence of the victim State; (iv) the victim is described as "another" (rather than "any") State; (v) the use of force is proscribed whenever it is inconsistent with the UN Charter as a whole, and not only with the Purposes of the United Nations; (vi) a linkage is created with the rest of the Definition. Some of these points are of peripheral, if not nominal, significance. Others are of greater consequence. Thus, the allusion to inconsistency with the Charter in its entirety (rather than just the Purposes of the United Nations) may imply that even technical provisions of the Charter have to be observed, so that the breach of procedures detailed in the Charter may turn the use of armed force into an unlawful aggression.[60] The cardinal divergence from Article 2(4) is, however, the first: the threat of force *per se* does not qualify as aggression, since an actual use of armed force is absolutely required.

Article 2 of the Definition stipulates that "[t]he first use of armed force by a State in contravention of the Charter shall constitute *prima facie* evidence of an act of aggression", but the Security Council may determine otherwise "in the light of other relevant circumstances, including the fact that the acts concerned or their consequences are not of sufficient gravity".[61] The "other relevant circumstances" leave a broad margin for interpretation; apparently, they include the intent and purposes of the acting State.[62] Whereas Article 2 is oriented towards the Security Council, its nucleus is equally germane to the issue of penal responsibility. First use of armed force is no conclusive evidence of the commission of a crime against peace. At most, the opening of fire creates a rebuttable presumption of culpability.[63] When all the facts are weighed, it may be the other side that will be held accountable for commencing a war of aggression.

---

[60] See B. B. Ferencz, "A Proposed Definition of Aggression: By Compromise and Consensus", 22 *I.C.L.Q.* 407, 416 (1973).

[61] *Supra*, note 40, at 143.

[62] See B. B. Ferencz, 2 *Defining International Aggression* 31 (1975).

[63] See P. Rambaud, "La Définition de l'Agression par l'Organisation des Nations Unies", 80 *R.G.D.I.P.* 835, 872 (1976).

The *de minimis* clause in Article 2 clarifies that "a few stray bullets across a boundary" cannot be invoked as an act of aggression.[64] In the same vein, slight incidents are outside the ambit of a crime against peace. Indeed, responsibility for a war of aggression may be incurred by the target State, should it resort to comprehensive force in over-reaction to trivial incidents.

The enumeration of specific acts of aggression appears in Article 3. Under the Article, the following amount to acts of aggression ("regardless of a declaration of war"):

(a) The invasion or attack by the armed forces of a State of the territory of another State, or any military occupation, however temporary, resulting from such invasion or attack, or any annexation by the use of force of the territory of another State or part thereof;

(b) Bombardment by the armed forces of a State against the territory of another State or the use of any weapons by a State against the territory of another State;

(c) The blockade of the ports or coasts of a State by the armed forces of another State;

(d) An attack by the armed forces of a State on the land, sea or air forces, or marine and air fleets of another State;

(e) The use of armed forces of one State which are within the territory of another State with the agreement of the receiving State, in contravention of the conditions provided for in the agreement or any extension of their presence in such territory beyond the termination of the agreement;

(f) The action of a State in allowing its territory, which it has placed at the disposal of another State, to be used by that other State for perpetrating an act of aggression against a third State;

(g) The sending by or on behalf of a State of armed bands, groups, irregulars or mercenaries, which carry out acts of armed force against another State of such gravity as to amount to the acts listed above, or its substantial involvement therein.[65]

---

[64] See B. Broms, *supra*, note 47, at 346.
[65] *Supra*, note 40, at 143.

These seven paragraphs identify flagrant instances of aggression, and we shall return to several of them in subsequent chapters. Obviously, in concrete settings, the acts of aggression itemized in Article 3 may consist of measures short of war. Yet, they are all branded as crimes against the peace and security of mankind in the 1991 Draft Code framed by the International Law Commission.[66]

The fact that paragraph (g) has been pronounced by the International Court of Justice to be declaratory of customary international law is possibly indicative that other portions of Article 3 may equally be subsumed under the heading of true codification. But, whatever the legal status of its sundry paragraphs, Article 3 was not intended to exhibit the entire spectrum of aggression. According to Article 4, the acts inscribed in Article 3 do not exhaust the definition of that term, and the Security Council may determine what other acts are tantamount to aggression.[67]

Under Articles 10 and 11(1) of the Charter, the General Assembly (which adopted the Definition) is authorized to make recommendations to the Security Council.[68] Although the General Assembly is incompetent to dictate a definition of aggression to the Security Council, it is empowered to offer guidelines in the form of a recommendation for the benefit of the Council. In actuality, after almost two decades of existence, the Definition of Aggression has had "no visible impact" on the deliberations of the Security Council.[69] All the same, should the Council ignore past precedents and devise novel conceptions of aggression, no criminal responsibility would necessarily ensue, since the principle *nullum crimen sine lege* is now enshrined in general international law.[70] Article 15(1) of the 1966 International Covenant on Civil and Political Rights prescribes: "No one shall be held guilty of any criminal offence on account of any act or omission which did not constitute a criminal

---

[66] *Supra*, note 42, at 244 (Article 15(4)).

[67] *Ibid., id.*

[68] *Supra*, note 52, at 334-5.

[69] M. C. Bassiouni and B. B. Ferencz, "The Crime against Peace", 1 *International Criminal Law* 167, 191 (M. C. Bassiouni ed., 1986).

[70] *Cf.* Article 10 of the 1991 Draft Code of Crimes against the Peace and Security of Mankind, *supra*, note 42, at 242.

offence, under national or international law, at the time when it was committed".[71]

Article 5(1) of the Definition of Aggression states that "[n]o consideration of whatever nature, whether political, economic, military or otherwise, may serve as a justification for aggression".[72] This clause stresses that the motive does not count: even "a good motive does not prevent an act from being illegal".[73]

Article 6 adds a proviso that "[n]othing in this Definition shall be construed as in any way enlarging or diminishing the scope of the Charter, including its provisions concerning cases in which the use of force is lawful".[74] Thus, if an act enumerated in Article 3 can legitimately be classified as either self-defence or collective security (see *infra*, Part III), it will automatically be removed from the roster of aggression.

The most controversial provision in the Definition is Article 7:

Nothing in this Definition, and in particular article 3, could in any way prejudice the right to self-determination, freedom and independence, as derived from the Charter, of peoples forcibly deprived of that right and referred to in the Declaration on Principles of International Law concerning Friendly Relations and Co-operation among States in accordance with the Charter of the United Nations, particularly peoples under colonial and racist regimes or other forms of alien domination; nor the right of these peoples to struggle to that end and to seek and receive support, in accordance with the principles of the Charter and in conformity with the above-mentioned Declaration.[75]

Textually, Article 7 reflects a compromise between irreconcilable views.[76] Politically, it gives a boost to the concept that a "war of national liberation" is a just war (see *supra*, Chapter 3, B, (b)). Legally,

---

[71] International Covenant on Civil and Political Rights, 1966, [1966] *U.N.J.Y.* 178, 183.
[72] *Supra*, note 40, at 143.
[73] A. V. W. Thomas and A. J. Thomas, *The Concept of Aggression in International Law* 52 (1972).
[74] *Supra*, note 40, at 144.
[75] *Ibid., id.*
[76] See B. B. Ferencz, "The United Nations Consensus Definition of Aggression: Sieve or Substance", 10 *J.I.L.E.* 701, 714 (1975).

the right to receive (and presumably to give) support from the out-side for a "national liberation" war is subordinated to the Principles of the Charter. Such subordination is implicit in every General As-sembly resolution (which, if clashing with the Principles of the Charter, may be deemed *ultra vires*). But, in any event, the supe-riority of the Charter is spelt out, both in general terms in Article 6 and (lest there be any misunderstanding as to how Articles 6 and 7 mesh, considering that both start with the same caveat that "[n]oth-ing in this Definition" can be construed as diminishing from the effect of either clause) specifically in Article 7 itself. The Charter does not permit the use of inter-State force, except in the exercise of self-defence or collective security (see *supra*, Chapter 4, B, (a)). If Article 7 is understood as permitting recourse to armed force by one State against another in support of the right of peoples to self-determination, in circumstances exceeding the bounds of self-defence or collective security, the dispensation would be inconsis-tent with the Charter.[77]

C. *Individual Responsibility for Crimes against Peace*

(a) *The Scope of the Crimes*

Having scanned the General Assembly's Definition of Aggres-sion, it is necessary to explore the applicability of crimes against peace *ratione materiae, ratione personae* and *ratione temporis*.

i. *Ratione Materiae*

We have already called attention to the exclusion of the threat of force from Article 1 of the General Assembly's Definition (*supra*, B). It may be argued on that basis that a threat of aggression, even one that "causes capitulation without a fight", does not amount to a crime.[78] Such a limitation would run counter to the case law of the Subsequent Proceedings at Nuremberg, where it was held that a crime against peace may be committed by mere threat of aggression, if the

---

[77] *Cf.* the Dissenting Opinion of Judge Schwebel in the *Nicaragua* case, *supra*, note 54, at 351.

[78] See B. B. Ferencz, *supra*, note 76, at 713.

weaker country "succumbs without the necessity of a 'shooting war' ".[79] However, there is no contradiction between Article 1 and the case law: the Definition simply does not come to grips with the problematics of crimes against peace. The question whether crimes against peace are restricted to certain manifestations of aggression in the context of war, or cover also related acts (such as threats), must find an answer elsewhere.

In the 1954 Draft Code, the International Law Commission defined as an offence against the peace and security of mankind, "[a]ny threat by the authorities of a State to resort to an act of aggression against another State".[80] Article 16(2) of the 1991 Draft Code not only slates the threat of aggression as a crime, but defines it as follows:

Threat of aggression consists of declarations, communications, demonstrations of force or any other measure which would give good reason to the Government of a State to believe that aggression is being seriously contemplated against that State.[81]

The use of the phrase "seriously contemplated" appears to go even beyond actual threats. Indeed, the Commission's commentary adds:

As to its concrete manifestations, the threat of aggression could take the form of intimidation, troop concentrations or military manoeuvres near another State's borders, or mobilization for the purpose of exerting pressure on a State to make it yield to demands.[82]

The potential consequences are far-reaching.

In the seminal provision of Article 6(a) of the London Charter of the International Military Tribunal (quoted *supra*, A), crimes against peace include the "planning, preparation, initiation or

---

[79] See T. Taylor, "The Nuremberg War Crimes Trials", 450 *Int.Con.* 243, 340-1 (1949).
[80] *Supra*, note 37, at 151 (Article 2(2)).
[81] *Supra*, note 42, at 245.
[82] Report of the International Law Commission, 40th Session, [1988] II (2) *I.L.C. Ybk* 1, 58.

waging" of war of aggression, "participation in a common plan or conspiracy", and complicity.[83]

A person charged with crimes against peace may be guilty cumulatively of planning, preparation, initiation and waging of war of aggression. In the event, it may not be easy to determine the exact point at which, say, planning ends and preparation begins. But the different terms used in Article 6(a) relate to separate (albeit successive) stages of the criminal course of action, each having a texture of its own. Planning consists of "the formulation of a design or scheme for a specific war of aggression", whereas preparation comprises "the various steps taken to implement the plan" before the actual outbreak of hostilities.[84] Initiation is linked to the commencement of the war, while waging continues as long as the war is not terminated.

Conspiracy is the least precise term used in Article 6(a). Had the English law definition of conspiracy been applied to crimes against peace, it would have cast a wide net.[85] The International Military Tribunal was not prepared to go that far.[86] In its Judgment, the Tribunal laid down that "the conspiracy must be clearly outlined in its criminal purpose. It must not be too far removed from the time of decision and of action".[87] To qualify as a conspirator, a person must be shown to have participated in a concrete and criminal common plan. It is not enough for this purpose that a person had supported a vague political programme, even if it ultimately led to a war of aggression.[88]

In the 1954 Draft Code, the preparation of the employment of armed force against another State constituted an offence against the peace and security of mankind.[89] Conspiracy, direct incitement, complicity and attempts to commit any act of aggression also

---

[83] See H. Donnedieu de Vabres, "Le Procès de Nuremberg devant les Principes Modernes du Droit Pénal International", 70 *R.C.A.D.I.* 481, 540-1 (1947).

[84] M. Greenspan, *The Modern Law of Land Warfare* 455 (1959).

[85] See A. L. Goodhart, "The Legality of the Nuremberg Trials", 58 *Jur.R.* 1, 10-11 (1946).

[86] See F. Biddle, "Le Procès de Nuremberg", 19 *R.I.D.P.* 1, 14 (1948).

[87] *Supra,* note 10, at 225.

[88] See H. Wechsler, "The Issues of the Nuremberg Trial", 62 *P.S.Q.* 11, 20 (1947).

[89] *Supra,* note 37, at 151 (Article 2(3)).

amounted to such offences.[90] The 1991 Draft Code encompasses the same concepts.[91]

In the *Nuremberg* trial, conspiracy, planning and preparation to wage war of aggression were all scrutinized with the advantage of hindsight, after aggression had actually been carried out and finally crushed. However, conspiracy, planning and preparation for aggression constitute crimes against peace as soon as they are committed. In theory, their perpetrators may be brought to trial and punishment even if no war materializes. In practice, of course, it is not easy to contemplate indictment and prosecution of persons accused only of conspiracy, planning and preparation for aggression, when the war is a matter of conjecture and not of historical record.[92]

ii. Ratione Personae

The waging of war of aggression forms the kernel of crimes against peace. Yet, what does "waging" mean? If the word is given a broad interpretation *ratione personae*, extending to every person who contributed to the fighting in whatever capacity, all combatants in the armed forces of the aggressor State become criminals automatically; and most civilians may be condemned, as well, on the ground of complicity. This was one of the foremost criticisms levelled at the London Charter and the *Nuremberg* trial by their detractors.[93] Indeed, the broad interpretation was subscribed to in a Separate Opinion by the President of the International Military Tribunal for the Far East (W. F. Webb) in the *Tokyo* trial.[94]

Contrarily, in the *High Command* case of 1948, an American Military Tribunal ruled that the criminality of aggressive war attaches only to "individuals at the policy-making level".[95] Another Tribunal, in the *I. G. Farben* case of the same year, declared that only those persons in the political, military or industrial spheres who bear

---

[90] *Ibid.*, 152 (Article 2(13)).
[91] *Supra*, note 42, at 239 (Article 3).
[92] See P. C. Jessup, "The Crime of Aggression and the Future of International Law", 62 *P.S.Q.* 1, 8 (1947).
[93] See Viscount Maugham, *U.N.O. and War Crimes* 18-39, 52-8 (1951).
[94] *Supra*, note 27, at 373.
[95] *U.S.A. v. Von Leeb* et al. ("The *High Command* Case") (Nuremberg, 1948), 11 *N.M.T.* 462, 486.

responsibility for the formulation and execution of policies are to be held liable for crimes against peace; a departure from this concept would lead to incongruous results: the entire population could then be charged with the crimes, including the private soldier on the battlefield, the farmer who supplied the armed forces with foodstuffs, and even the housewife who conserved essential commodities for the military industry.[96]

Notwithstanding some dicta weakening it, the general principle that can be derived from the Subsequent Proceedings at Nuremberg is that liability for crimes against peace is limited to the policy-making level.[97] The International Law Commission in 1950 arrived at the similar conclusion that only "high-ranking military personnel and high State officials" can be guilty of waging war of aggression.[98] In its 1991 Draft Code, the Commission "restricted the circle of potential perpetrators to leaders and organizers".[99]

This is not to say that responsibility for crimes against peace is reduced, even in a dictatorship, to one or two individuals at the pinnacle of power. As the Tribunal in the *High Command* case asseverated: "No matter how absolute his authority, Hitler alone could not formulate a policy of aggressive war and alone implement that policy by preparing, planning and waging such a war".[100]

The Tribunal declined to fix a distinct line, somewhere between the private soldier and the Commander-in-Chief, where liability for crimes against peace begins.[101] The Judgment did state that criminality hinges on the actual power of an individual "to shape or influence" the war policy of his country.[102] Those acting as instruments of the policy-makers "cannot be punished for the crimes of others".[103] On the whole, it is necessary to sift the evidence

---

[96] *U.S.A. v. Krauch* et al. ("The *I. G. Farben* Case") (Nuremberg, 1948), 8 *N.M.T.* 1081, 1124-5.

[97] See G. Brand, "The War Crimes Trials and the Laws of War", 26 *B.Y.B.I.L.* 414, 420-1 (1949).

[98] *Supra*, note 36, at 376.

[99] *Supra*, note 42, at 259. *Cf.* the texts of Articles 15(1) and 16(1), *ibid.*, 243, 245.

[100] *Supra*, note 95, at 486.

[101] *Ibid.*, 486-7.

[102] *Ibid.*, 488-9.

[103] *Ibid.*, 489.

concerning the personal contributions to the decision-making process by all those who belong to leadership echelons.

Relevant leadership echelons are by no means curtailed to the military. Crimes against peace may equally be committed by civilians.[104] The most obvious example relates to members of the cabinet or senior government officials whose input is apt, at times, to outweigh that of generals and admirals. But even when a civilian is not a Minister or a civil servant, he may be held accountable for crimes against peace (especially for complicity, conspiracy or preparation), if he occupies an influential position in public affairs or in the economy.[105]

iii. Ratione Temporis

The Tribunal in the *High Command* case stressed that the nature of war as aggressive or otherwise is determined by factors linked to its initiation.[106] This does not mean that persons who steer an aggressor State during an advanced stage of the war (without being involved in the outbreak of hostilities) cannot be arraigned. Waging war of aggression is a continuous offence. Periodic reviews of the changing situation are inevitable in the course of every prolonged war. Those who mould a decision to persist in the illegal use of force may be charged with waging aggressive war, although they had nothing to do with the initiation of the fighting.

The identification of the aggressor State on the basis of the commencement of war means that subsequent events do not affect the legal analysis. The aggressor, satisfied with the immediate territorial or other gains, may assume a defensive posture. The victim State, desiring to dislodge the aggressor from its positions, may be operationally on the offensive. These shifting military strategies do not remove the legal stamp of aggression, which is irreversibly attached to the opening of war by one of the parties. The relative standing of the belligerents as aggressor and victim States is not

---

[104] See M. Greenspan, *supra*, note 84, at 455-6.

[105] Yet, in the Subsequent Proceedings at Nuremberg, industrialists and financiers were acquitted from aggressive war charges. See T. Taylor, *supra*, note 79, at 309-10, 339.

[106] *Supra*, note 95, at 486.

eroded by the tide of war, nor is it altered by the means and methods of warfare. If the victim State violates a cease-fire suspending hostilities (see *supra*, Chapter 2, C), it still does not trade places with the aggressor. Even if the aggressor State conducts hostilities in perfect harmony with the *jus in bello*, while the armed forces of the victim State commit war crimes and crimes against humanity,[107] the legal position under the *jus ad bellum* remains the same as regards responsibility for crimes against peace.

A temporal issue arising after the commission of a crime is that of possible prescription. The statutory limitation of crimes is not a principle recognized by all States in their internal legislation, and it has certainly not crystallized as an international legal norm.[108] The issue is whether crimes against peace are exempt from the operation of general statutes of limitation obtaining within the domestic legal system of the prosecuting State. There are two international conventions promulgating the non-applicability of statutory limitations to war crimes and crimes against humanity: one drafted in 1968 by the General Assembly,[109] the other concluded in 1974 under the auspices of the Council of Europe.[110] Neither instrument is relevant to crimes against peace. The exemption of crimes against peace from national statutes of limitations was discussed in the context of the UN instrument, but ultimately the General Assembly decided (for political and practical reasons, without prejudging the legal question) not to deal with the matter.[111] On the other hand, Article 7 of the International Law Commission's 1991 Draft Code states unequivocally:

No statutory limitation shall apply to crimes against the peace and security of mankind.[112]

---

[107] War crimes and crimes against humanity are defined in Article 6(b)-(c) of the London Charter, *supra*, note 5, at 639-40.

[108] See F. Weiss, "Time Limits for the Prosecution of Crimes against International Law", 53 *B.Y.B.I.L.* 163, 165, 185 (1982).

[109] Convention on the Non-Applicability of Statutory Limitations to War Crimes and Crimes against Humanity, 1968, [1968] *U.N.J.Y.* 160.

[110] European Convention on the Non-Applicability of Statutory Limitation to Crimes against Humanity and War Crimes, 1974, 13 *I.L.M.* 540 (1974).

[111] See N. Lerner, "The Convention on the Non-Applicability of Statutory Limitations to War Crimes", 4 *Is.L.R.* 512, 519-20 (1969).

[112] *Supra*, note 42, at 240.

As noted, these crimes specifically include aggression and threat of aggression (see *supra*, A).

(b) *Mens Rea*

All existing international crimes have two constituent elements: the criminal act (*actus reus*), and a criminal intent or at least a criminal consciousness (*mens rea*).[113] The Definition of Aggression, adopted by the General Assembly, does not go beyond the *actus reus*.[114] However, a crime against peace is not completed unless the *actus reus* is accompanied by *mens rea*, often termed *animus agressionis*.[115]

The significance of criminal intent as an essential ingredient of crimes against peace was brought into relief by the Judgment in the *High Command* case.[116] The Tribunal noted that almost all nations, including even a traditionally neutral country like Switzerland, arm and prepare for the eventuality of war.[117] "As long as there is no aggressive intent, there is no evil inherent in a nation making itself militarily strong".[118] The International Military Tribunal at *Nuremberg*, in acquitting Schacht of the crimes with which he had been charged, emphasized that a rearmament programme by itself is not criminal: to qualify as a crime against peace, rearmament must be undertaken as part of a plan to wage aggressive war.[119]

The manufacture or purchase of armaments is not the only course of action which may appear in a different light, depending on the intention. In most countries, staff officers[120] devote a lot of time and energy to the production of contingency plans for a host of hypothetical scenarios,[121] especially war. Provided that these are

---

[113] See Y. Dinstein, "International Criminal Law", 20 *Is.L.R.* 206, 233 (1985).

[114] See R. Mushkat, "When War May Justifiably Be Waged: An Analysis of Historical and Contemporary Legal Perspectives", 15 *B.J.I.L.* 223, 235-8 (1989).

[115] See S. Glaser, "Culpabilité en Droit International Pénal", 99 *R.C.A.D.I.* 467, 504-5 (1960).

[116] *Supra*, note 95, at 486.

[117] *Ibid.*, 487-8.

[118] *Ibid.*, 488.

[119] *Supra*, note 10, at 309.

[120] On the distinction between ordinary staff officers and the Nuremberg defendants, see Lord Justice Lawrence (Lord Oaksey), "The Nuremberg Trial", 23 *Int.Aff.* 151, 157 (1947).

[121] *Cf.* H. Meyrowitz, "The Function of the Laws of War in Peacetime", 251 *I.R.R.C.* 77, 83 (1986).

genuine contingency plans, and that they are premised on the assumption of self-defence, their authors cannot be regarded as criminals. The high command may even simulate "war games", and carry out manoeuvres to test operational concepts for combat readiness. Once more, in the absence of aggressive designs, these actions are not criminal (despite the loose language used by the International Law Commission in the 1991 Draft Code (*supra*, (a), i)).

The intent to undertake war of aggression may be formed by only one or few individuals at the helm of a State. Others at the policy-making level need not be personally guided by the same intent. The acid test is whether, in assisting the preparations for war, they actually know of the aggressive schemes.[122] If they know that aggression is planned, this may suffice to establish the requisite *mens rea*.[123] The obverse side of the coin is that when a person (who actively participates in honing the military machinery) does not possess personal knowledge as to aggressive plans, he cannot be convicted of crimes against peace.

Lack of *mens rea* can be translated into assorted defences. In its 1991 Draft Code, the International Law Commission decided to leave the admissibility of defences to the discretion of the competent court.[124] But this is an unsatisfactory solution - resulting from differences of opinion on issues like error and coercion - and the Commission conceded that it would have to come up with "more appropriate provisions" at a later stage.[125] The principal defences which are relevant to crimes against peace are:

a. Mistake of fact. This defence rests on the principle of *ignorantia facti excusat*. Several judicial decisions, delivered in war crimes trials (relating to violations of the *jus in bello*), indicate that mistake of fact constitutes an admissible defence.[126] There is no reason to exclude crimes against peace from the general rule. Thus, if it can be factually determined that - when launching hostilities against Atlantica (subsequently condemned as an aggressive war) - policy-makers in

---

[122] See *supra*, note 10, at 310.
[123] *Cf. ibid.*, 282-4.
[124] See *supra*, note 42, at 243 (Article 14(1)).
[125] *Ibid.*, 258.
[126] See United Nations War Crimes Commission, 15 *L.R.T.W.C.* 184 (1949).

Patagonia mistakenly believed *bona fide* that they were acting in self-defence against an armed attack (see *infra*, Chapter 7, B),[127] this absence of *mens rea* should exonerate them from individual criminal responsibility.

b. Mistake of law. It is far less clear whether international law allows the validity of the corresponding principle of *ignorantia juris non excusat.* Many scholars are unwilling to accept as irrebuttable the presumption that every person is acquainted with international law.[128] The war crimes trials of the post Second World War period seem to disclose a tendency to recognize ignorance of international law as an excuse, particularly when the relevant norms are disputable.[129]

The allegation of mistake of law may be less potent in the context of crimes against peace than in other situations, since policy-makers are more likely than plain soldiers to be knowledgeable about international law. Even high-ranking officers and civilians may invoke *ignorantia juris* when the more subtle points of legitimate self-defence are at issue (see *infra*, Chapters 7-9). But the penumbra of uncertainty, which is characteristic of some segments of the contemporary *jus ad bellum*, should not be exaggerated. In most cases, the claim of mistake of law will not be credible when made by top-level functionaries who perpetrated a crime against peace. If the subjective knowledge of such persons with respect to specific norms of international law cannot be ascertained by direct evidence, the task can be facilitated through the use of objective criteria (such as the manifest illegality of the action taken).[130]

c. Duress. As the International Military Tribunal at *Nuremberg* phrased it, the "true test" of criminal responsibility is "whether moral choice was in fact possible".[131] Moral choice is especially impossible when the will of the accused was overpowered by duress

---

[127] The question has been posed by R. Lapidoth, "Book Review" [of the first edition of this volume], 23 *Is.L.R.* 557, 559 (1989).

[128] See Y. Dinstein, *supra*, note 113, at 236.

[129] See *supra*, note 126, at 182-3.

[130] See Y. Dinstein, *The Defence of 'Obedience to Superior Orders' in International Law* 28-9 (1965).

[131] *Supra*, note 10, at 224.

(namely, when there was a clear and present danger to himself or to those near and dear to him). In principle, duress has been expressly accepted as an admissible defence in international criminal law, subject to stringent conditions.[132] But, empirically, when the leaders of a nation deliberate the pros and cons of embarking upon an aggressive war against a foreign country, the decision is seldom (if ever) motivated by coercion in the full legal sense of the term.

(c) *Inadmissible Defence Pleas*

There are a number of spurious defence pleas, typical of war crimes trials, which must be dismissed:

a. Obedience to domestic law. When international criminal law directly imposes obligations on individuals, any provisions of national law colliding head-on with these obligations are annulled by international law. In the words of the Tribunal in the *High Command* case:

> International common law must be superior to and, where it conflicts with, take precedence over national law or directives issued by any national governmental authority. A directive to violate international criminal common law is therefore void and can afford no protection to one who violates such law in reliance on such a directive.[133]

The logic of the general rule is enhanced when the defendants are leading statesmen and military commanders who bear responsibility for crimes against peace. If the national policy-makers could seek refuge behind national enactments (often products of their own efforts), the prohibitions of international law might have an evanescent existence. Even in a dictatorship, the despot must rely on some key individuals to assist him in expounding and administering the national policy. As the International Military Tribunal at *Nuremberg* held:

> Hitler could not make aggressive war by himself. He had to have the co-operation of statesmen, military leaders, diplomats,

---

[132] See Y. Dinstein, *supra*, note 113, at 233-5.
[133] *Supra*, note 95, at 508.

and business men. ... They are not to be deemed innocent because Hitler made use of them, if they knew what they were doing.[134]

Offenders are not relieved of responsibility only because their State failed to incorporate crimes against peace (or other international crimes) in the domestic penal code. This is one of the Nuremberg Principles, as formulated by the International Law Commission.[135]

b. Obedience to superior orders. When superior orders are issued, they may be illegal from the perspective of national law as much as international law. Should that be the case, no clash between the two legal systems would be fuelled by the unlawful orders. Nevertheless, a doctrine was developed by L. Oppenheim[136] and others, whereby commanders alone incur responsibility for the war crimes of their subordinates (*respondeat superior*), so that obedience to superior orders is an admissible defence *per se*. The usual expectation is that the shield of *respondeat superior* will be raised by lower echelons. Yet, Nazi war criminals, who were in positions of immense power in the hierarchy, also tried to shift their responsibility to the dead *Führer*.

Under Article 8 of the London Charter, the fact that a defendant acted pursuant to orders does not free him from responsibility although it may be considered in mitigation of punishment.[137] The proper meaning of this provision is that the fact of obedience to superior orders must not play any part at all in the evaluation of criminal responsibility (in connection with any defence whatever), and it is only relevant in the assessment of punishment.[138] The International Military Tribunal at *Nuremberg* fully endorsed the provision of Article 8, while adding in somewhat cryptic language the "moral choice" test,[139] which is often misconstrued.[140] The Inter-

---

[134] *Supra*, note 10, at 226.
[135] *Supra*, note 36, at 374-5 (Principle II and Commentary).
[136] See L. Oppenheim, 2 *International Law* 264-5 (lst ed., 1906).
[137] *Supra*, note 5, at 640.
[138] See Y. Dinstein, *supra*, note 130, at 117.
[139] *Supra*, note 10, at 224.
[140] See Y. Dinstein, *supra*, note 130, at 147-52.

national Law Commission introduced the element of moral choice into the Nuremberg Principles,[141] whereas it employed different terminology in the 1954 Draft Code.[142] In 1991, the Commission virtually repeated the 1954 formula.[143] In the opinion of the present writer, none of these texts is satisfactory. It is submitted that the correct legal position should be set forth as follows: the fact that a defendant acted in obedience to superior orders cannot constitute a defence *per se*, but may be considered – in conjunction with other circumstances – within the compass of an admissible defence based on lack of *mens rea* (not only as an element in extenuation of punishment).[144]

c. Acts of State. According to H. Kelsen and others, the crime of aggressive war is imputed by international law to the State, and no criminal responsibility can be attached to individuals acting in their capacity as organs of that State.[145] Approval of the acts of State doctrine would have totally obstructed the goal of punishing crimes against peace, inasmuch as the perpetrators of these crimes are almost always organs of the State.

In conformity with Article 7 of the London Charter, the official position of a defendant (even as Head of State) does not free him from responsibility, nor will it mitigate his punishment.[146] The International Military Tribunal at *Nuremberg* flatly repudiated the concept underlying Kelsen's thesis:

> The principle of international law, which under certain circumstances, protects the representatives of a state, cannot be applied to acts which are condemned as criminal by international law. The

---

[141] *Supra*, note 36, at 375 (Principle IV).

[142] *Supra*, note 37, at 152. Article 4 of the Draft Code stipulates: "The fact that a person charged with an offence defined in this Code acted pursuant to an order of his Government or of a superior does not relieve him of responsibility in international law if, in the circumstances at the time, it was possible for him not to comply with that order".

[143] *Supra*, note 42, at 242. For commentary, see *ibid.*, 256-7.

[144] See Y. Dinstein, *supra*, note 130, at 252. For an analysis of the numerous texts considered by the International Law Commission until 1954, see *ibid.*, 228-51.

[145] See H. Kelsen, "Collective and Individual Responsibility for Acts of State in International Law", [1948] *J.Y.I.L.* 226, 238-9.

[146] *Supra*, note 5, at 640.

authors of these acts cannot shelter themselves behind their official position in order to be freed from punishment in appropriate proceedings.[147]

The rejection of the theory that the official position of a person can relieve him of responsibility figures prominently in the Nuremberg Principles,[148] as well as the two Draft Codes of 1954[149] and 1991.[150] There cannot be any doubt nowadays that the attribution of an act to the State, while generating State responsibility (see *supra*, Chapter 4, F), does not negate the criminal liability of individuals.

(d) *The Penal Proceedings*

How is an individual to be held responsible for crimes against peace? Rudimentary considerations of due process require that this be done only by a court of law, and not by a political body (such as the UN Security Council). One of the Nuremberg Principles is that a person charged with crimes against peace (or other offences) "has the right to a fair trial on the facts and law".[151] Detailed judicial guarantees for a fair trial are incorporated in the 1991 Draft Code.[152]

Two International Military Tribunals functioned successfully, at *Nuremberg* and at *Tokyo*, after the Second World War. However, those judicial bodies were set up by the victors in that War – for the *ad hoc* prosecution of the major enemy war criminals – and, having discharged their duties, they were dismantled.[153] At the moment, there is no international penal tribunal with jurisdiction over crimes against peace. In the absence of an international criminal court, the perpetrators of international crimes, including those committing crimes against peace, may be tried and punished only by domestic tribunals.

In the early years of the United Nations, recommendations to create an International Criminal Court were made by the International Law

---

[147] *Supra*, note 10, at 223.
[148] *Supra*, note 36, at 375 (Principle III).
[149] *Supra*, note 37, at 152 (Article 3).
[150] *Supra*, note 42, at 243 (Article 13).
[151] *Supra*, note 36, at 375 (Principle V).
[152] *Supra*, note 42, at 240-1 (Article 8).
[153] See R. K. Woetzel, *The Nuremberg Trials in International Law* 40 (1962).

Commission,[154] and by two special Committees on International Criminal Jurisdiction (appointed by the General Assembly): one in 1951,[155] the other in 1953.[156] In 1989, the General Assembly requested the International Law Commission, when considering the Draft Code, "to address the question of establishing an international criminal court or other international criminal trial mechanism".[157] Although the Commission started immediately to canvass the issue, no stand was taken when the Draft Code was provisionally adopted in 1991.[158] In 1992, following discussion of the Tenth Report of the Special Rapporteur (D. Thiam),[159] the Commission appointed a special Working Group on the subject.[160] The Working Group outlined the arguments for and against an international criminal court, and expressed its belief that "a structure for an international criminal court ... could be a workable system".[161] Broadly speaking, the Commission endorsed this proposition.[162]

At the time of writing, the International Law Commission has not yet drafted a detailed statute of the projected international criminal court. There is no shortage of recent drafts, informally produced by legal associations and individual scholars,[163] and the basic concept of creating an international penal tribunal is gaining momentum. In February 1993, the Security Council decided (in principle) to establish an international tribunal "for the prosecution of persons responsible for serious violations of international humanitarian law committed in the territory of the former Yugoslavia since 1991".[164] However, this

---

[154] *Supra,* note 36, at 378-9.

[155] Report of the [1951] Committee on International Criminal Jurisdiction, 2 *An International Criminal Law* 337, 360 (B. B. Ferencz ed., 1980).

[156] Report of the 1953 Committee on International Criminal Jurisdiction, *ibid.,* 429, 454.

[157] General Assembly Resolution No. 44/39, 44(1) *R.G.A.* 311, *id.* (1989).

[158] *Supra,* note 42, at 214-35, 240 (Article 6(3)), 241 (Article 9(3)).

[159] D. Thiam, "Tenth Report on the Draft Code of Crimes against the Peace and Security of Mankind" 5-17 (mimeographed, 1992).

[160] Report of the International Law Commission, 44th Session, 31 (mimeographed, 1992).

[161] *Ibid.,* 145.

[162] *Ibid.,* 32-3.

[163] For an illustration, see M. C. Bassiouni, *Draft Statute International Criminal Tribunal* (Association Internationale de Droit Pénal, 1992).

[164] Security Council Resolution No. 808, *supra,* note 30.

tribunal would be confined to specific crimes, locale and time. It would be irrelevant to crimes against peace.

The rationale for establishing an international criminal court for the prosecution of crimes against peace is self-evident. Trials of other international crimes (principally, war crimes and crimes against humanity) have a lot of merit even when conducted before domestic courts. But the nature of crimes against peace is such that no domestic proceedings can conceivably dispel doubts regarding the impartiality of the judges. As a matter of law, jurisdiction over crimes against peace is universal.[165] Yet, as a matter of fact, only enemy (or former enemy) States, rather than neutrals, are likely to convict and sentence offenders charged with these crimes. Any panel of judges composed exclusively of enemy (or former enemy) nationals will be suspected of irrepressible bias. There is no escape from the conclusion that the present state of affairs is lamentable, giving rise as it does to assertions of "victor's justice".[166] The flaw in the system cannot be redressed unless and until a permanent international criminal court is finally established.

---

[165] See M. Akehurst, "Reprisals by Third States", 44 B.Y.B.I.L. 1, 18 (1970).
[166] See, e.g., R. H. Minear, Victor's Justice: The Tokyo War Crimes Trial 180 (1971).

CHAPTER 6

CONTROVERSIAL CONSEQUENCES OF THE CHANGE IN THE LEGAL STATUS OF WAR

The profound change that has gripped the international legal system, as a result of the prohibition of the use of inter-State force and the criminalization of aggressive war, raises searching questions in regard to a number of concepts and institutions rooted in the obsolete axiomatic postulate that States are free to commence hostilities at will. It is true that, in some measure, the international community has already adjusted itself to the new legal environment. This is manifest, for instance, in the current invalidity of peace treaties dictated by the aggressor to the victim of aggression (see *supra*, Chapter 2, B, (a), ii). But, in many areas, modification of time-honoured doctrines encounters intractable difficulties.

The need for adaptation of the law to the present status of inter-State force is adumbrated against the silhouette of the antiquated perception of the two antagonists in war (aggressor and victim) as intrinsically equal in legal standing. It is noteworthy that, as pointed out already by Grotius, the Latin word *bellum* is derived from the more ancient term *duellum*.[1] For centuries, international law treated war in the same manner that domestic law used to deal with the duel. War, like a duel, was viewed with toleration. The parity of the contenders was taken for granted, and the sole concern was about adherence to criteria of "fair play". Yet, just as the duel is no longer permitted by national legal systems, war is now forbidden by international law.[2] The

---

[1] Grotius, *De Jure Belli ac Pacis*, Book I, § I, II (2 Classics of International Law ed., F. W. Kelsey trans., 33 (1925)).

[2] In fact, it was the prohibition of the duel that largely guided and encouraged the proponents of the outlawry of war in lobbying for the Kellogg-Briand Pact. "They were thinking in terms of generations, not of decades". It is obvious that the frequency of war has not yet been sharply reduced, despite its proscription. But there was also a lengthy interval between the formal banning of the duel and its virtual disappearance. What really counts today is that duelling has been all but eliminated. It is hoped that the fate of war will ultimately be the same. See Q. Wright, "The Outlawry of War and the Law of War", 47 *A.J.I.L.* 365, 369 (1953).

criminalization of aggressive war is incompatible with the idea of the equality of belligerents, inasmuch as by definition one of the parties is a criminal while the other is either the victim of the crime or whoever comes to the victim's rescue.

The discussion in this chapter will focus on the repercussions of the illegality and criminality of war of aggression. The problem to be confronted (in several different ways) is whether the ground has not been cut from under certain norms relevant to the status of war under international law.[3]

A. *War in the Technical Sense*

Can a formal state of war, in the technical sense, be warranted today? Evidently, full-scale hostilities may break out *de facto* in breach of international law. When that happens, the reality of conflict must be acknowledged, and the *jus in bello* will apply (subject to possible reservations as to the mode and extent of its application, to be considered *infra*, C). But do States retain the capacity to initiate *de jure* a state of war? A number of scholars deny that war can "now lawfully exist as a technical condition", maintaining that a wrong-doer should not be allowed "to assert belligerent rights arising out of his own wrong-doing".[4]

Assuming that large-scale hostilities are actually raging, and that the *jus in bello* ought to be applied in its plenitude, a negation of the existence of a state of war appears to be no more than a hollow semantic gesture. Why alter the terminology if no tangible consequences emanate from the change? The argumentation against recognition of a state of war is more compelling in those situations where the war breaks out only in the technical, and not in the material, sense (see *supra*, Chapter 1, A, (b), ii). In such circumstances, the state of war is brought about by a mere declaration. Without resorting to hostilities, conceivably without even running any risk, the country issuing the declaration is allowed to take steps seriously

---

[3] See H. Lauterpacht, "The Limits of the Operation of the Law of War", 30 *B.Y.B.I.L.* 206, 208-11 (1953).

[4] E. Lauterpacht, "The Legal Irrelevance of the 'State of War'", 62 *P.A.S.I.L.* 58, 63-5 (1968). *Cf.* Q. Wright, *supra*, note 2, at 365.

impinging on the rights of individuals (e.g., the sequestration of the property of enemy nationals).[5] The time may have come to eliminate this opportunity to use a state of war, existing essentially on paper, for what may be viewed as curtailment of domestic due process of law and even unjust enrichment by Governments at the expense of individuals.

If (as seems to be the case) a state of war in the material sense can still be triggered today, another issue comes to the fore. N. Feinberg and others ask whether the state of war can continue to exist *de jure* subsequent to the *de facto* cessation of hostilities.[6] Feinberg opines that, upon the actual cessation of hostilities, the relationship between the two opposing sides must revert from war to peace.[7] This is an attractive idea, but it is not borne out by the practice of States. Suffice it to cite Article I of the Treaty of Peace, concluded by Egypt and Israel in 1979, which provides for the termination of the state of war (and the establishment of peace) between the parties upon ratification.[8] For several years prior to the ratification of the Peace Treaty, Israel and Egypt were not engaged in hostilities. Nevertheless, the state of war continued until it was explicitly ended by consent of the parties.

B. *Inconclusive "Police Action"*

Is it possible that an international force - carrying out enforcement action by virtue of a binding decision, adopted by the Security Council under Article 42 of the Charter of the United Nations[9] (see *infra*, Chapter 10, A) - will desist from its operations before they are crowned with complete success? The question has not yet arisen in its full dimensions, since so far no enforcement action has been taken by the Security Council under Article 42. However, a comparison between the Second World War and the Korean War will make the dilemma more vivid.

---

[5] See L. Kotzsch, *The Concept of War in Contemporary History and International Law* 248-9 (1956).

[6] N. Feinberg, *Studies in International Law* 96 (1979).

[7] *Ibid.*, 97.

[8] Egypt-Israel, Treaty of Peace, 1979, 18 *I.L.M.* 362, 363 (1979).

[9] Charter of the United Nations, 1945, 9 *Int.Leg.* 327, 343-4.

During the Second World War, the Allied nations expressed their determination to continue the fighting until the Axis Powers "have laid down their arms on the basis of unconditional surrender".[10] The policy of unconditional surrender was tenaciously adhered to, and hostilities did not come to a close until the total collapse of the enemy States. All that happened in the pre-Charter era and in a War conducted by the Allies on the legal basis of collective self-defence (see *infra*, Chapter 9), rather than collective security (see *infra*, Chapter 10).

The position was remarkably different at the time of the Korean War.[11] When hostilities commenced, in June 1950, the United Nations Organization had already been functioning. The Security Council formally determined that the armed attack by North Korea against the Republic of Korea constituted a breach of the peace.[12] It further recommended that Member States render assistance to the victim State, in order to repel the armed attack and to restore the peace.[13] Such assistance was promptly extended by the United States and other nations. In July 1950, the Security Council welcomed this development, recommended to all Members providing military forces that they put their contingents under a unified command, and permitted the use of the UN flag in the course of operations against North Korea.[14] Thus, troops from 19 countries, under American command, became a United Nations force.[15]

Security Council recommendations have merely a hortatory effect, and are not legally binding (see *infra*, Chapter 10, B, (a)). Hence, the military action in Korea, pursued by UN Member States in compliance with the Council's recommendations, was voluntary in nature. The Council, having determined the existence of a breach

---

[10] Moscow Declaration on General Security, 1943, 9 *Int.Leg.* 82, 83.

[11] The Korean War is a better example than the Gulf War, inasmuch as the American-led coalition in the latter conflict did not constitute a veritable United Nations force (see *infra*, Chapter 10, C). Furthermore, if the Gulf War did not end with the unconditional surrender of Iraq, this was not due to any military reverse suffered by the coalition forces. In fact, Iraq lay prostrate when fire was ceased in February 1991.

[12] Security Council Resolution No. 82, 5 *R.D.S.C.* 4, *id.* (1950).

[13] Security Council Resolution No. 83, 5 *R.D.S.C.* 5, *id.* (1950).

[14] Security Council Resolution No. 84, 5 *R.D.S.C.* 5, 6 (1950).

[15] See D. W. Bowett, *United Nations Forces* 36-47 (1964).

of the peace, was fully authorized by the Charter to adopt a mandatory resolution ordaining enforcement measures by UN Members. In opting for a recommendation, the Council did not exploit the maximal powers which it possesses in the domain of collective security. But the critical factor is that, in Korea, a multinational force was fighting under the aegis of the United Nations.

The UN force managed to save South Korea from being crushed by the aggressor. However, the force did not contrive to achieve unadulterated victory, due to massive intervention by the People's Republic of China (through so-called "volunteers"). Ultimately, in 1953, an Armistice Agreement was concluded in Panmunjom[16] (see *supra*, Chapter 2, B, (b)). The Agreement provided for the cessation of hostilities between the United Nations Command and the North Korean/Chinese forces, along a line not radically swerving from the original 38th parallel (the springboard of the North Korean armed attack in 1950). This a far cry from what transpired in 1945. In lieu of unconditional surrender, the co-existence of the two Koreas (aggressor and victim alike) has been confirmed.

Will the Panmunjom formula serve as a satisfactory precedent if and when the Security Council activates, in a binding resolution, the full panoply of the collective security system under Article 42? As far as the text of the Charter goes, since the task assigned to the Council is that of maintaining or restoring international peace and security – rather than the punishment of aggressors – there cannot be any fault in a post-hostilities settlement which satisfies the Council. But considering the criminalization of aggressive war in international law, it is legitimate to query whether a United Nations force, charged with a mandatory enforcement mission, can limit itself to merely rebuffing an aggressor without scoring a total victory.

Several factors have to be put in balance here. On the one hand, the international functions of a United Nations force (established by the Council with a view to carrying out enforcement action against an aggressor) roughly correspond to the role played by an internal police force.[17] If the analogy is pursued to its logical

[16] Panmunjom Agreement Concerning a Military Armistice in Korea, 1953, 47 *A.J.I.L.*, Supp., 186 (1953).
[17] See F. Seyersted, *United Nations Forces in the Law of Peace and War* 208 (1966).

conclusion, always keeping in mind that an aggressor is a criminal, it appears that the goal of the United Nations force must be the unconditional surrender of the opposing side. In other words, the international "police" ought to impose law and order by suppressing the crime, and it must not make a "live and let live" type of a deal with the criminal. "The police do not negotiate with the law breaker but arrest him and subject him to judicial process".[18]

On the other hand, the analogy between a United Nations force and a modern police cannot be stretched to extreme lengths.[19] While international relations are dominated by the fundamental concept of the sovereignty of States, there is an element of wishful thinking in ascribing to any international force the authority or the sheer power of the national police. The operation of a genuine police presupposes conditions of subjection to societal restraints that are alien to the international community as presently composed.

It is also useful to remember that the domestic police is inclined to be indulgent when confronted with mass movements of law-breakers. An aggressor State constitutes a single juristic entity, but in reality – owing to the vast numbers of people who are taking up arms when a State embarks upon war – aggression is more reminiscent of a hard-to-quell domestic disturbance of the peace than of an offence committed by an individual criminal. Besides, the internal police finds it occasionally necessary to make deals even with individual criminals (such as hostage takers).

On the whole, whereas the settlement reached at the conclusion of hostilities in Korea leaves a lot to be desired, entertaining great expectations of heroic feats to be accomplished by United Nations forces is likely to prove anticlimactic. The main problem with international "police" forces is not that they fail in attaining their objectives, but that they are not established in the first place (see *infra*, Chapter 10, C). Setting unrealizable goals for UN forces will not expedite the process of their creation.

---

[18] See Q. Wright, "Law and Politics in the World Community", *Law and Politics in the World Community* 3, 9 (G. A. Lipsky ed., 1953).
[19] See F. Seyersted, *supra*, note 17, at 208-9.

C. Equal Application of the Jus in Bello

(a) Self-Defence

The most troubling problem, stemming from the drastic modification of the *jus ad bellum*, relates to the application of the *jus in
bello* on an equal footing between the opponents (the aggressor
State and the State exercising self-defence). Historically, the notion
of equality between belligerents has formed the underpinning of
the *jus in bello*. It was unchallenged as long as States were at liberty
to go to war against each other.[20] However, once war of aggression
became proscribed and criminalized, voices were raised in support
of a policy of applying the *jus in bello* in a discriminatory fashion,
adversely affecting the aggressor State.

Two main arguments are adduced against the construct of equality between the aggressor State and the victim of aggression in the
operation of the *jus in bello*:

a. The first line of approach was taken up by the prosecution in the
Nuremberg trial.[21] The contention rests on the reasoning that every
war inevitably consists of a series of acts that are criminal in nature
(murder, assault, deprivation of liberty, destruction of property, and
the like).[22] When a combatant kills an enemy soldier on the battlefield, he is immune from criminal prosecution for murder (viz. he
benefits from a "justification"), because – and to the extent that –
the war is lawful.[23] "Stripped of the mantle of such legality, the act
in question stands out starkly as an unjustifiable and inexcusable
killing of a human being".[24] That is to say, when the war loses its
legality, an umbrella protecting combatants from penal proceedings
must be folded. Their immunity is removed, and no justification for

---

[20] The principle of equality was not easily reconcilable with the just war doctrine
(discussed *supra*, Chapter 3, A). See G. I. A. D. Draper, "Wars of National Liberation
and War Criminality", *Restraints on War* 135, 136, 158 (M. Howard ed., 1979).
[21] See R. H. Jackson, "Opening Address", 2 *I.M.T.* 98, 146-7; F. De Menthon, "Opening Address", 5 *ibid.*, 368, 387; H. Shawcross, "Closing Address", 19 *ibid.*, 433, 458.
[22] See R. H. Jackson, *ibid.*, 146.
[23] See S. Glueck, "The Nuernberg Trial and Aggressive War", 59 *Har.L.R.* 396, 455
(1945-6).
[24] *Ibid.*, *id.*

premeditated homicide (or any other crime) is admissible as a defence.[25] In a sense, the killing ceases to have the juridical character of an act of war.[26] The act is indistinguishable from any other murder.[27]

All this leads up to the assertion that, inasmuch as war is lawful under contemporary international law in conditions of self-defence, but it is unlawful in case of aggression, there is no place for equality in the treatment of soldiers committing acts of war. Soldiers participating in a lawful war should be accorded the status of prisoners of war (which guarantees their lives and a humane treatment in captivity). Yet, no such privilege ought to be accessible to soldiers taking part in an unlawful war. The latter must be prosecuted and severely punished for any death or other injury that they have caused in the course of war.

b. The second train of thought is linked to the general principle *ex injuria jus non oritur*, whereby he who acts contrary to the law cannot acquire rights as a result of his transgression.[28] The thesis advocated is that no new powers (i.e. powers beyond those available in peacetime) may be gained by a State waging an unlawful war.[29] Hence, the aggressor State may not benefit from any rights bestowed by the *jus in bello*. Contrastingly, when a State is engaged in a lawful war (in response to aggression), it is entitled to the whole spectrum of belligerent rights.[30]

From a practical perspective, it is evident that acceptance of either of these two conceptual analyses would have led to a complete disintegration of the *jus in bello*. The proposition of equality between the belligerents is, first and foremost, a precept of common sense. The *jus in bello* has in the past succeeded in curbing excesses, notwithstanding the pervasive animosity towards the enemy that is characteristic of every war, only because it has generated mutual advantages for both sides. No State (least of all a State which,

[25] See B. D. Meltzer, "A Note on Some Aspects of the Nuremberg Debate", 14 *U.C.L.R.* 455, 461 (1946-7).
[26] See F. De Menthon, *supra*, note 21, at 387.
[27] See H. Shawcross, *supra*, note 21, at 458.
[28] Sec H. Lauterpacht, *supra*, note 3, at 212.
[29] See Q. Wright, *supra*, note 2, at 370-1.
[30] See *ibid.*, 371.

through its aggression, has already perpetrated the supreme crime against international law) will abide by the strictures of the *jus in bello* if it knows that it is not going to derive reciprocal benefits from the application of the norms.[31] Moreover, no aggressor is ever willing to concede that it is indeed in breach of the *jus ad bellum*. The Security Council, vested by the UN Charter with the authority to determine in a binding way who the aggressor is, rarely issues such a verdict. Each belligerent, consequently, feels free to charge that its opponent has committed aggression. If every belligerent were given a licence to deny the enemy the benefits of the *jus in bello* on the ground that it is the aggressor State, there is reason for scepticism whether any country would ever pay heed to international humanitarian law.[32] Mankind might simply slide back to the barbaric cruelty of war in the style of Genghis Khan.

Even when the position is looked at from a theoretical standpoint, it is necessary to remember that the *jus in bello* confers rights (and imposes duties) not only on the belligerent States but also on human beings.[33] A right afforded by international law to an individual, such as the right of a lawful combatant to be treated in a humane way when captured by the enemy, is not rescinded just because his State has acted in contravention of international law.[34] The individual who does not himself violate the rules of warfare is entitled to profit from these rules, irrespective of the criminal conduct of the country to which he belongs.

When considered *in abstracto*, there may be some merit in subdividing the *jus in bello* into several legal layers. Such a stratification might justify a restrictive application of the principle of equality to norms creating human rights, excluding it from operation when rights accruing for belligerent States are established. As early as 1939, the Harvard Research in International Law offered for consideration a differentiation between humanitarian rules

---

[31] See R. R. Baxter, "The Role of Law in Modern War", 47 *P.A.S.I.L.* 90, 96 (1953).
[32] See H. Lauterpacht, *supra*, note 3, at 212-13.
[33] See Y. Dinstein, "The International Law of Inter-State Wars and Human Rights", 7 *I.Y.H.R.* 139, 147-52 (1977).
[34] See Q. Wright, *supra*, note 2, at 373.

governing the conduct of hostilities and other rules (especially those concerning titles to property).[35]

Similar proposals, with somewhat diverse emphases, have been put forward since then. For instance, H. Lauterpacht - in admitting that the principle of equality must continue to prevail in the actual conduct of hostilities - suggested *de lege ferenda* that the principle be inoperative, at least after the end of the war, as regards the acquisition of title over property (so that such an acquisition, albeit consistent with the *jus in bello*, would be invalidated in the case of an aggressor State).[36]

However, any attempt to restrict the range of application of the concept of equality in the *jus in bello* is highly controversial.[37] A thorough study of the question, with all its ramifications, was conducted by the *Institut de Droit International*.[38] The study culminated, in 1963, with the *Institut* declining to endorse specific recommendations by its Rapporteur (J. P. A. François) to deviate in a meaningful way from the standard of equality.[39] The *Institut* accepted the basic premise that "there cannot be complete equality" in the operation of the rules of warfare when the competent organ of the United Nations determines that one of the belligerents has resorted to armed force unlawfully.[40] All the same, it was resolved that rules restraining the horrors of war must be equally observed by all belligerents.[41] The *Institut* did decide to explore the conditions under which "inequality must be accepted".[42] But, in the event, the sequel study was limited to United Nations forces (see *infra*, (b)).

[35] Harvard Research in International Law, Draft Convention on Rights and Duties of States in Case of Aggression (P. C. Jessup, Reporter), 33 *A.J.I.L.*, Sp. Supp., 819, 828, 830 (1939) (Articles 2-4, 14).

[36] H. Lauterpacht, *supra*, note 3, at 224-32.

[37] See H. Meyrowitz, *Le Principe de l'Egalité des Belligérants devant le Droit de la Guerre* 106-40 (1970).

[38] Institut de Droit International, 45 (I) *A.I.D.I.* 555-8 (Aix-en-Provence, 1954); 47 (I) *ibid.*, 323-606 (Amsterdam, 1957); 48 (II) *ibid.*, 178-263, 389-90 (Neuchâtel, 1959); 50 (I) *ibid.*, 5-127 (Bruxelles, 1963); 50 (II) *ibid.*, 306-56, 376 (Bruxelles, 1963); 51 (I) *ibid.*, 353-6 (Varsovie, 1965).

[39] J. P. A. François, "Rapport Définitif", 50 (I) *A.I.D.I.* 111-27 (Bruxelles, 1963).

[40] Institut de Droit International, Resolution, "Equality of Application of the Rules of the Law of War to Parties to an Armed Conflict", 50 (II) *A.I.D.I.* 376 (Bruxelles, 1963).

[41] *Ibid., id.*

[42] *Ibid., id.*

The four Geneva Conventions of 1949 for the Protection of War Victims - drafted after the Charter of the United Nations and the *Nuremberg* trial, that is, subsequent to the prohibition of the use of inter-State force and the criminalization of aggressive war - apply (under common Article 2) in "all cases" of war or any other international armed conflict[43] (see *supra*, Chapter 1, A, (b), ii). Nothing in the text may be construed as a permission to discriminate between the aggressor and its victim. Protocol I of 1977, Additional to the Geneva Conventions, states explicitly in its Preamble:

> the provisions of the Geneva Conventions of 12 August 1949 and of this Protocol must be fully applied in all circumstances to all persons who are protected by those instruments, without any adverse distinction based on the nature or origin of the armed conflict or on the causes espoused by or attributed to the Parties to the conflict.[44]

The judgments delivered in the war crimes trials of the post Second World War period demonstrate that the equal reach of the *jus in bello* to all belligerents was not lessened by the aggression of Nazi Germany (condemned as a crime against peace). There are a number of precedents for the rejection of an attempt to undermine the principle of equality. In the *Justice* case, in 1947, an American Military Tribunal responded to the argument that the criminality of the Nazi aggression taints as crimes all the acts of the defendants committed in the course of the Second World War:

> If we should adopt the view that by reason of the fact that the war was a criminal war of aggression every act which would have been legal in a defensive war was illegal in this one, we would be forced

---

[43] (First) Geneva Convention for the Amelioration of the Condition of the Wounded and Sick in Armed Forces in the Field, 1949, 75 *U.N.T.S.* 31, 32; (Second) Geneva Convention for the Amelioration of the Condition of Wounded, Sick and Shipwrecked Members of Armed Forces at Sea, 1949, *ibid.*, 85, 86; (Third) Geneva Convention Relative to the Treatment of Prisoners of War, 1949, *ibid.*, 135, 136; (Fourth) Geneva Convention Relative to the Protection of Civilian Persons in Time of War, 1949, *ibid.*, 287, 288.

[44] Protocol Additional to the Geneva Conventions of 12 August 1949, and Relating to the Protection of Victims of International Armed Conflicts (Protocol I), 1977, [1977] *U.N.J.Y.* 95, 96.

to the conclusion that every soldier who marched under orders
into occupied territory or who fought in the homeland was a
criminal and a murderer. The rules of land warfare ... would not
be the measure of conduct and the pronouncement of guilt in any
case would become a mere formality.[45]

The Tribunal refused to reach that conclusion.[46] In the *Hostage* case,
in 1948, it was held:

> international law makes no distinction between a lawful and an
> unlawful occupant in dealing with the respective duties of occu-
> pant and population in occupied territories. There is no reciprocal
> connection between the manner of the military occupation of
> territory and the rights and duties of the occupant and population
> to each other after the relationship has in fact been established.
> Whether the invasion was lawful or criminal is not an important
> factor in the consideration of this subject.[47]

Dutch courts followed the same path in several instances. Thus, in
the *Christiansen* case, a Special Court enunciated in 1948:

> The rules of international law, in so far as they regulate the meth-
> ods of warfare and the occupation of enemy territory, make no
> distinction between wars which have been started legally and
> those which have been started illegally.[48]

In the *Zuhlke* case, the Court of Cassation, also in 1948, stated (in
overruling a lower tribunal):

> it would be going too far to consider as war crimes all war-like acts,
> including those which were in accordance with the laws and cus-
> toms of war, performed against Holland or against Dutch subjects
> by Germany's military forces or other State organs on the sole
> ground of the illegality of her war of aggression.[49]

---

[45] *U.S.A. v. Altstoetter* et al. ("The *Justice* Case") (Nuremberg, 1947), 3 *N.M.T.* 954,
1027.
[46] *Ibid., id.*
[47] *U.S.A. v. List* et al. ("The *Hostage* Case") (Nuremberg, 1948), 11 *N.M.T.* 1230, 1247.
[48] Re *Christiansen* (Holland, Special Court, Arnhem, 1948), [1948] *A.D.* 412, 413.
[49] In re *Zuhlke* (Holland, Special Court of Cassation, 1948), [1948] *A.D.* 415, 416.

In short, there is not the slightest sign of a diminution in the validity of the principle of equality in the *jus in bello,* as reflected in the actual practice of States.

(b) *Collective Security*

The issue of the equal application of the *jus in bello* to both parties in wartime becomes more complex when one of the opposing sides is a United Nations force. The problem will be particularly acute once the Security Council decides, in a mandatory way, to mount an enforcement action with a view to countering an act of aggression. In such a hypothetical scenario, and even in the actual setting of the Korean War (where the UN force was set up on the basis of a mere recommendation, but a determination of the existence of an armed attack was made in a binding manner (see *supra,* B)), the element of subjectivity in identifying the aggressor disappears. Nobody can plausibly confuse a State perpetrating a crime against peace with the (semi-police) international force arrayed against it.

As for the more common "peacekeeping" UN forces (see *infra,* Chapter 10, D, (b)), although they are not established in order to combat aggressors, they too are liable to engage in hostilities with States. Should that come to pass, it would be necessary to examine whether these forces differ in their legal standing from ordinary (national) armed forces, insofar as the application of the *jus in bello* is concerned.[50]

United Nations forces consist of national contingents provided by Member States. The UN Organization as such is not a contracting party to the Geneva Conventions of 1949. But, given the almost universal acceptance of the Conventions, it is virtually certain that they are binding on Member States participating in the peacekeeping operation.[51] Are the national troops, when serving under the UN flag, absolved from the obligations assumed by their States under the Conventions?

A Committee of the American Society of International Law, having investigated the matter in 1952, maintained that a United

[50] See F. Seyersted, *supra,* note 17, at 210.
[51] See Y. Sandoz, "The Application of Humanitarian Law by the Armed Forces of the United Nations Organization", 206 *I.R.R.C.* 274, 283 (1978).

Nations force has a different status altogether from the armed forces of any State, and, when acting to check aggression, it need not feel bound by all the laws of warfare: it can "select such of the laws of war as may seem to fit its purposes (e.g., prisoners of war, belligerent occupation), adding such others as may be needed, and rejecting those which seem incompatible with its purposes".[52] A completely divergent position was taken by the *Institut de Droit International,* after an examination of the topic on the basis of a report submitted by P. De Visscher.[53] In its Resolution, dated 1971, the *Institut* affirmed that all the humanitarian rules of the law of armed conflict (an expression given a broad definition, including not only the Geneva Conventions of 1949, but all norms pertaining to the conduct of hostilities, especially those prohibiting the use of certain weapons or aiming at the protection of civilian persons and property) must be observed without fail by United Nations forces.[54] Incontestably, the predominant opinion today is that United Nations forces must comply with international humanitarian law.[55]

In 1975, the *Institut* addressed the issue of the application of other (non-humanitarian) rules of armed conflict to United Nations forces (the Rapporteur on this occasion was E. Hambro), and it was concluded that in general these rules, too, must be respected in hostilities in which United Nations forces are engaged.[56]

---

[52] Report of Committee on Study of Legal Problems of the United Nations, "Should the Laws of War Apply to United Nations Enforcement Action?" (C. Eagleton, Chairman), 46 *P.A.S.I.L.* 216, 220 (1952).

[53] Institut de Droit International, 54 (I) *A.I.D.I.* 1-228 (Zagreb, 1971); 54 (II) *ibid.,* 149-288, 465-70 (Zagreb, 1971).

[54] Institut de Droit International, Resolution, "Conditions of Application of Humanitarian Rules of Armed Conflict to Hostilities in which United Nations Forces May Be Engaged", 54 (II) *A.I.D.I.* 465, 466 (Zagreb, 1971) (Article 2).

[55] See D. Schindler, "United Nations Forces and International Humanitarian Law", *Studies and Essays on International Humanitarian Law and Red Cross Principles in Honour of J. Pictet* 521, 523 (C. Swinarski ed., 1984).

[56] Institut de Droit International, Resolution, "Conditions of Application of Rules, Other than Humanitarian Rules, of Armed Conflict to Hostilities in which United Nations Forces May Be Engaged", 56 *A.I.D.I.* 541, 543 (Wiesbaden, 1975) (Article 2).

D. *Impartial Neutrality*

Neutrality as a policy (see *supra,* Chapter 1, D) is far from *passé,* even under the law of the UN Charter. A Member State is still entitled to remain neutral in a war between other countries, as long as the Security Council does not specifically impose on it (in a binding resolution) the obligation to take part in measures of collective security.[57]

Neutrality in the traditional meaning of the term – as a concept based on the principle of impartiality and non-discrimination among belligerents – may be assimilated to the position of a spectator in a duel, who is enjoined from rendering assistance to one of the antagonists. But how can impartiality be harmonized with the criminality of war of aggression? How can a third State retain its equanimity, and remain completely above the fray, when it is witnessing a crime against peace?

At the outset, Article 2(5) of the Charter of the United Nations has to be considered:

All Members shall give the United Nations every assistance in any action it takes in accordance with the present Charter, and shall refrain from giving assistance to any state against which the United Nations is taking preventive or enforcement action.[58]

What this clause denotes is that when measures of collective security are carried out by the UN in conformity with the Charter, Member States must help one side (the UN force) and refrain from aiding and abetting the other (the aggressor State). This, to say the least, is "not neutrality in the old established sense".[59]

There are those who believe that even a non-Member of the UN must not treat a UN force (discharging collective security duties) as if it were equal to the aggressor.[60] While it is doubtful that non-

---

[57] See D. Schindler, "Aspects Contemporains de la Neutralité", 121 *R.C.A.D.I.* 221, 248-9 (1967).

[58] *Supra,* note 9, at 332.

[59] C. G. Fenwick, "Is Neutrality Still a Term of Present Law?", 63 *A.J.I.L.* 100, 101 (1969).

[60] See H. J. Taubenfeld, "International Actions and Neutrality", 47 *A.J.I.L.* 377, 395-6 (1953).

Members are subject to any obligation in the matter (an obligation that can apply to them only on the basis of customary international law), it is a safe assumption that they have a right to discriminate between a UN force and an aggressor State. The *Institut*, in its Resolution of 1975, declared that (i) every State (i.e. not only a Member State) is entitled to assist a United Nations force when requested to do so; (ii) Member States may not depart from the rules of neutrality for the benefit of the party opposing the UN force; (iii) Member States may not take advantage of the general rules of neutrality in order to evade their obligation to carry out a binding decision of the Security Council.[61]

Article 2(5) deals only with action taken by the United Nations in circumstances of collective security (see *infra*, Chapter 10), and it is not directly apposite to the case of (individual or collective) self-defence against an armed attack (see *infra*, Chapters 7-9). Yet, the rationale of Article 2(5) militates in favour of a similar solution in both situations, provided that the Security Council has determined who the aggressor is. The (duly identified) aggressor State, as a criminal, should not be treated by Member States on the basis of equality with whoever is opposing it. It may in fact be contended that, once the identity of the aggressor State has been established by the Council, all Member States must do whatever they can to foil the designs of that State and to assist the party resisting aggression.[62]

During the Gulf War, in Resolution No. 661 (1990), the Security Council called upon all States - expressly including non-Member States of the United Nations - to act strictly in accordance with the decision to impose economic sanctions on Iraq.[63] A similar call appears in Resolution No. 757 (1992), applying such sanctions to Serbia and Montenegro.[64]

In Resolution No. 678 (1990), which authorized the coalition co-operating with Kuwait to "use all necessary means" (i.e. resort to force) to secure full Iraqi compliance with its decisions, the Council

---

[61] *Supra*, note 56, at 543 (Articles 3-4).
[62] See G. Scelle, "Quelques Réflexions sur l'Abolition de la Compétence de Guerre", 58 *R.G.D.I.P.* 5, 16 (1954).
[63] Security Council Resolution No. 661, 45 *R.D.S.C.* 19, 20 (1990).
[64] Security Council Resolution No. 757, 31 *I.L.M.* 1453, 1457 (1992).

requested all States to provide appropriate support for the actions undertaken.[65] Since the Council had earlier determined in Resolution No. 660 that the Iraqi invasion of Kuwait constituted a breach of the peace,[66] an old-fashioned posture of neutrality - failing to distinguish between Iraq and the coalition - would have been beset by formidable juridical difficulties. Even non-Member States of the United Nations discontinued the policy of impartial neutrality. Thus, Switzerland fully participated in the economic sanctions against Iraq.[67] Moreover, in 1991, Switzerland apparently allowed overflights by coalition military transport aircraft (thereby facilitating logistical support for combat missions against Iraq),[68] despite the general rule prohibiting the entry of such aircraft into neutral airspace (see *supra*, Chapter 1, D, (b), i).

Strictly speaking, as long as the Council does not call on States to take specific action against an aggressor, it is arguable that no obligation is incurred by any country - not even a Member State - to abandon its neutrality.[69] But what about the situation where the Council adopts no binding decision, yet a neutral State (relying on its own judgment in the matter) desires to forsake the time-honoured principle of impartiality? A precedent for such conduct may be discerned in the policy of the United States in the early stages of the Second World War (viz. prior to the adoption of the UN Charter).

Almost from the start of hostilities in Europe, the neutrality of the United States was more benevolent towards one belligerent (Great Britain) than the other (Nazi Germany) (see *supra*, Chapter 1, D, (b), iii). As the war progressed, the balance tilted increasingly in the same direction. In September 1940, the United States transferred to the United Kingdom 50 old destroyers in consideration

---

[65] Security Council Resolution No. 678, 45 *R.D.S.C.* 27, 27-8 (1990).

[66] Security Council Resolution No. 660, 45 *R.D.S.C.* 19, *id.* (1990).

[67] See D. Schindler, "Transformations in the Law of Neutrality Since 1945", *Humanitarian Law of Armed Conflict: Challenges Ahead: Essays in Honour of Frits Kalshoven* 367, 372 (A. J. M. Delissen and G. J. Tanja eds., 1991).

[68] US Department of Defense Report to Congress on the Conduct of the Persian Gulf War, 1992, 31 *I.L.M.* 612, 640 (1992). But see D. Schindler, *supra*, note 67, at 372-3.

[69] See J. F. Lalive, "International Organization and Neutrality", 24 *B.Y.B.I.L.* 72, 82 (1947). *Cf.* M. Torrelli, "La Neutralité en Question", 96 *R.G.D.I.P.* 5, 26 (1992).

for a lease of naval and air bases in British colonies.[70] In March 1941, Congress approved the "Lend-Lease" Act, which made it possible to sell, lend or lease weapons, ammunition and supplies to a country the defence of which was deemed vital to the defence of the United States.[71] Following the new legislation, all barriers to the provision of military supplies to Britain were lifted. In May 1941, US naval forces even began to help in ensuring the delivery of the supplies to the British Isles, and, in September of that year, instructions were issued to the US fleet to open fire at sight on any German or Italian submarine or surface vessel entering a sector of the high seas the protection of which was considered necessary for American defence.[72] In December, after Pearl Harbor, the United States itself became a belligerent.

The legal philosophy underlying the far-reaching measures, taken by the United States before its entry into the Second World War, was expounded by the then Attorney-General (later Associate Justice of the Supreme Court and Chief American Prosecutor at the *Nuremberg* trial), R. H. Jackson, in an address delivered in 1941.[73] According to Jackson, the classical doctrine of impartial neutrality was founded on the assumption of the legality of war, whereas discrimination among belligerents has become permissible as a result of the prohibition of war in the Kellogg-Briand Pact.[74] Jackson traced his thesis back to Grotius,[75] who had stated that a neutral State must not hinder the party waging a just war or strengthen its adversary.[76] Lauterpacht, too, read into Grotius's words a whole concept of "qualified neutrality".[77] Support for this concept may be found in other scholarly contributions since Grotius, for example in the

---

[70] United Kingdom-United States, Exchange of Notes, 1940, 34 *A.J.I.L.*, Supp., 184-6 (1940).

[71] An Act to Promote the Defense of the United States, 1941, 35 *A.J.I.L.*, Supp., 76-9 (1941).

[72] See L. Oppenheim, 2 *International Law* 640-1 (7th ed., by H. Lauterpacht, 1952).

[73] R. H. Jackson, "Address", 35 *A.J.I.L.* 348-59 (1941).

[74] *Ibid.*, 349-50, 354.

[75] Grotius, *supra*, note 1, at Book III, § XVII, III (p. 786).

[76] R. H. Jackson, *supra*, note 73, at 351.

[77] H. Lauterpacht, "The Grotian Tradition in International Law", 23 *B.Y.B.I.L.* 1, 39-41 (1946).

Budapest Articles of Interpretation of the Kellogg-Briand Pact, adopted in 1934 by the International Law Association.[78] It has been suggested that the idea of qualified neutrality should be explained in terms of reprisals (see *infra*, Chapter 8, A, (a), iii) undertaken by third States; meaning that a neutral State may invoke an act of aggression, directed against another country, as a legitimate ground for treating the law-breaker in a manner which would normally be illegal.[79] But this rationalization is not widely shared.

Qualified neutrality is so dissociated from orthodox neutrality that some scholars prefer using the term "non-belligerency" to depict the status of a third State discriminating between the two belligerents.[80] Under whatever name, the trouble with qualified neutrality is that it is tantamount to a "'half-way house' between neutrality and belligerency".[81] The belligerent suffering from adverse treatment by a neutral State may react in kind, and relations between the two countries are liable to deteriorate to the point of open hostilities.

E. *Territorial Changes*

Can a State produce territorial changes by resorting to illegal force (or the threat of force)? We have partly addressed the issue, as it relates to the legal effect of a peace treaty ceding territory from one party to another (*supra*, Chapter 2, B, (a), ii). We have indicated that the validity of such a peace treaty depends on who the beneficiary is. If the cession is from the aggressor to the victim of aggression, there is nothing inherently wrong in the transaction; whereas if the reverse happens, the treaty is null and void.

[78] International Law Association, *Report of the Thirty-Eighth Conference* 66, 67 (Budapest, 1934) (Article 4).
[79] See M. Akehurst, "Reprisals by Third States", 44 *B.Y.B.I.L.* 1, 6 (1970).
[80] See F. R. Coudert, "Non-Belligerency in International Law", 29 *Vir.L.R.* 143, *id.* (1942-3). For a more recent presentation of the dichotomy between neutrality and so-called non-belligerency, see D. Schindler, "Neutral Powers in Naval War: Commentary", *The Law of Naval Warfare* 211, 213 (N. Ronzitti ed., 1988).
[81] See T. Komarnicki, "The Problem of Neutrality under the United Nations Charter", 38 *T.G.S.* 77, 79 (1952).

What is the legal effect of a territorial change brought about without recourse to treaty, in consequence of belligerent occupation and unilateral annexation? The rule that has emerged in international law (well before the prohibition of war and regardless of which State is the aggressor) is that belligerent occupation, by itself, cannot produce a transfer of title over territory to the occupying State.[82] As L. Oppenheim phrased it, already in 1917, "[t]here is not an atom of sovereignty in the authority of the occupant".[83] An American Military Tribunal articulated the rule, in 1948, in the *RuSHA* case:

> Any purported annexation of territories of a foreign nation, occurring during the time of war and while opposing armies were still in the field, we hold to be invalid and ineffective.[84]

Article 4 of Protocol I, Additional to the Geneva Conventions, reaffirms the principle that the occupation of a territory does not affect its legal status.[85] No territory under belligerent occupation can be validly annexed by the occupying Power acting unilaterally.

While the invalidity of a unilateral annexation subsequent to belligerent occupation is undisputed, the position is not so simple when the annexation takes place after the *debellatio* of the enemy State (see *supra*, Chapter 2, B, (c), ii). Belligerent occupation posits the existence of the enemy as a State and the continuation of the war.[86] *Debellatio* signifies the disintegration of the enemy State and the termination of the war. Under classical international law, if a process of *debellatio* occurred, the victorious State could annex unilaterally the occupied territory of the former enemy.[87] Nowadays, the legal position must be reconsidered on two grounds:

a. It is necessary to take into account the modern right of self-determination vested in the people (or peoples) inhabiting the

---

[82] See the Arbitral Award in *Affaire de la Dette Publique Ottomane* (1925), 1 *R.I.A.A.* 529, 555 (per E. Borel).

[83] L. Oppenheim, "The Legal Relations between an Occupying Power and the Inhabitants", 33 *L.Q.R.* 363, 364 (1917).

[84] *U.S.A. v. Greifelt* et al. ("The *RuSHA* Case") (Nuremberg, 1948), 5 *N.M.T.* 88, 154.

[85] *Supra*, note 44, at 97.

[86] See Y. Dinstein, "The International Law of Belligerent Occupation and Human Rights", 8 *I.Y.H.R.* 104, 105 (1978).

[87] See M. Greenspan, *The Modern Law of Land Warfare* 600-1 (1959).

conquered territory. Self-determination is referred to in many recent international instruments.[88] Preeminently, common Article 1(1) of the twin 1966 Covenants on human rights prescribes:

All peoples have the right of self-determination. By virtue of that right they freely determine their political status.[89]

If the local people is truly at liberty to determine its political status, a post-*debellatio* annexation by the victorious State must clearly be precluded. The obliteration of the sovereignty of the defeated State does not extinguish the right of self-determination conferred on the indigenous people. On the contrary, this is the most appropriate moment for that right to assert itself.

It must be appreciated, however, that the legal existence of a right is no guarantee of its implementation. The victorious country may refuse to heed the right of self-determination, annexing the conquered territory notwithstanding the wishes of the native population. This would not be the only instance in which self-determination is frustrated by the facts of life, and the Covenants do not specify how the right expressed in Article 1(1) is to be safeguarded in the absence of cooperation on the part of the State in actual control of the territory.[90]

b. Even irrespective of the issue of self-determination, a post-*debellatio* annexation of the territory of the erstwhile enemy by the victorious State may not be easily reconcilable with basic contemporary tenets. As long as the annexation is accomplished by the victim of aggression, benefiting at the expense of the former aggressor State, the process is not without its legal logic: let the

[88] The principle of self-determination is mentioned in the UN Charter in two places: Articles 1(2) and 55 (*supra*, note 9, at 331, 348). The right derived from this principle is elucidated in the Declaration on Principles of International Law Concerning Friendly Relations and Co-operation among States in accordance with the Charter of the United Nations, General Assembly Resolution No. 2625 (xxv), 25 *R.G.A.* 121, 123 (1970).

[89] International Covenant on Economic, Social and Cultural Rights, 1966, [1966] *U.N.J.Y.* 170, 171; International Covenant on Civil and Political Rights, 1966, *ibid.*, 178, 179.

[90] See Y. Dinstein, "Collective Human Rights of Peoples and Minorities", 25 *I.C.L.Q.* 102, 108 (1976).

aggressor pay for its crimes. But should the annexation expand the territory of the aggressor State, the upshot would be that might creates rights in defiance of the legal system in which these rights are embedded.[91]

We have seen that the prohibition of aggressive war constitutes *jus cogens* (see *supra,* Chapter 4, E). In the light of the principle *ex injuria jus non oritur,* many scholars subscribe to the view that a unilateral State action, no less than a treaty, can have no legal force when it is in contravention of *jus cogens.*[92] However, the notion of nullity of unilateral acts inconsistent with *jus cogens* is problematic.[93] As Sir Gerald Fitzmaurice put it, even if international law refuses to validate an act conflicting with *jus cogens,* it may be forced to recognize the situation brought about by that (illegal) act.[94]

Article 5(3) of the General Assembly's Definition of Aggression, adopted in 1974 (see *supra,* Chapter 5, B), proclaims that no territorial acquisition resulting from aggression "is or shall be recognized as lawful".[95] This clause echoes the text of the 1970 General Assembly Declaration on Principles of International Law Concerning Friendly Relations and Co-operation among States in accordance with the Charter of the United Nations.[96] There are also treaties in which contracting parties undertook not to recognize territorial acquisition brought about by armed force, such as the 1933 Saavedra Lamas Anti-War Treaty (Non-Aggression and Conciliation),[97] and the 1948 Charter of the Organization of American States.[98]

It is not entirely certain what non-recognition of territorial acquisition means in practice.[99] But probably the gist of non-recognition

---

[91] See Q. Wright, *supra,* note 2, at 366.
[92] See T. Meron, "On a Hierarchy of International Human Rights", 80 *A.J.I.L.* 1, 19-21 (1986).
[93] See *ibid.,* 21.
[94] G. Fitzmaurice, "The General Principles of International Law Considered from the Standpoint of the Rule of Law", 92 *R.C.A.D.I.* 1, 120 (1957).
[95] General Assembly Resolution No. 3314 (XXIX), 29(1) *R.G.A.* 142, 144 (1974).
[96] *Supra,* note 88, at 123.
[97] Rio de Janeiro Anti-War Treaty (Non-Aggression and Conciliation), 1933, 163 *L.N.T.S.* 405, *id.* (Article II).
[98] Bogota Charter of the Organization of American States, 1948, 119 *U.N.T.S.* 48, 56 (Article 17).
[99] See H. M. Blix, "Contemporary Aspects of Recognition", 130 *R.C.A.D.I.* 587, 662-5 (1970).

is that, despite a continuous and effective control over the annexed territory, no prescriptive rights[100] evolve in favour of the aggressor. In I. Brownlie's words, "prescription cannot purge this type of illegality".[101]

Nevertheless, if the *de facto* control of the territory annexed by the aggressor continues uninterrupted for generations, the non-prescription rule may have to give way in the end. International law must not be divorced from reality. When a post-*debellatio* annexation is solidly entrenched over many decades, there may be no escape from the conclusion that new rights (valid *de jure*) have crystallized, although they flow from a violation of international law in the remote past.[102] Even if the initial act of annexation was invalid, the prolonged (and undisturbed) exercise of sovereignty in the territory will finally create prescriptive rights, independently of the originally defective title. There comes a point at which the international legal system has "to capitulate" to facts: that stage is postponed as far as possible in the case of the extinction of States, but it cannot be completely avoided.[103] The most ardent supporters of the application of the principle *ex injuria jus non oritur* in international law concede that this maxim "often yields to the rival principle, *ex factis jus oritur*".[104] There is really "little practical alternative ... in the long term".[105]

These remarks are merely tentative and speculative, for they concern a theme that has not yet been seriously debated in a concrete setting. The criminalization of aggressive war has been a part of positive international law only since the *Nuremberg* Judgment. In the relatively short time that has elapsed, the international community has not been called upon to resolve, in a specific case of post-aggression annexation, a clash between the legal principles of

---

[100] On the concept of prescription, see L. Oppenheim, 1 *International Law* 706 (9th ed., by R. Jennings and A. Watts, 1992).

[101] I. Brownlie, *Principles of Public International Law* 514 (4th ed., 1990).

[102] See R. W. Tucker, "The Principle of Effectiveness in International Law", *Law and Politics in the World Community, supra*, note 18, at 31, 44.

[103] K. Marek, *Identity and Continuity of States in Public International Law* 579 (2nd ed., 1968)

[104] H. Lauterpacht, *supra*, note 3, at 212.

[105] L. Oppenheim, *supra*, note 100, at 186.

non-prescription and self-determination, on the one hand, and the gravitational pull of the facts, on the other. It is impossible to forecast, with any degree of confidence, what direction the future practice of States will take with respect to this subject-matter.

PART III

EXCEPTIONS TO THE PROHIBITION OF THE USE OF INTER-STATE FORCE

CHAPTER 7

THE CONCEPT OF SELF-DEFENCE

A. *The Right of Self-Defence*

(a) *The Meaning of Self-Defence*

The reliance on self-help, as a remedy available to States when their rights are violated, is and always has been one of the hallmarks of international law.[1] Self-help is a characteristic feature of all primitive legal systems, but in international law it has been honed to art form.[2]

Self-help under international law may be displayed in a variety of ways. In the first place, an aggrieved State may resort to non-forcible measures, such as severing diplomatic relations with another State or declaring a foreign diplomat *persona non grata*.[3] Additionally, legitimate self-help in the relations between States may take the shape of forcible measures, in which case these measures must nowadays meet the requirements of self-defence. Occasionally, international legal scholars regard the concepts of self-help and self-defence as related yet separate.[4] However, the proper approach is to view self-defence as a species subordinate to the genus of self-help. In other words, self-defence is a permissible form of "armed self-help".[5]

Self-defence in inter-State relations may be defined as a lawful use of force (principally, counter-force), under conditions prescribed by international law, in response to a previous unlawful use (or, at least, a threat) of force.[6] The legal term "self-defence" must not be confused with either the same or similarly sounding idioms

---

[1] See H. Kelsen, *General Theory of Law and State* 339 (1945).

[2] See Y. Dinstein, "International Law as a Primitive Legal System", 19 *N.Y.U.J.I.L.P.* 1, 12 (1986-7).

[3] See G. E. do Nascimento e Silva, *Diplomacy in International Law* 174, 177 (1972).

[4] See T. R. Krift, "Self-Defense and Self-Help: The Israeli Raid on Entebbe", 4 *B.J.I.L.* 43, 55-6 (1977-8).

[5] Report of the International Law Commission, 32nd Session, [1980] II (2) *I.L.C. Ybk* 1, 54.

[6] *Cf. ibid.*, 53.

fashionable in political rhetoric. Statesmen, in justifying the conduct of their respective countries, often claim that what has been (or is being) done is predicated on imperative requirements of self-defence, self-preservation, protection of vital interests, and the like. The juridical concept of self-defence does not necessarily coincide with such political slogans. In legal phraseology, self-defence is confined to circumstances in which a State responds with lawful force to unlawful force (or, minimally, to the threat of unlawful force).

The legal notion of self-defence has its roots in inter-personal relations, and is sanctified in domestic legal systems since time immemorial. From the dawn of international law, writers sought to apply this concept to inter-State relations, particularly in connection with the just war doctrine[7] (see *supra*, Chapter 3, A, (c)). But when the freedom to wage war was countenanced without reservation (in the 19th and early 20th centuries), concern with the issue of self-defence was largely a meta-juridical exercise. As long as recourse to war was considered free for all, against all, for any reason on earth – including territorial expansion or even motives of prestige and grandeur – States did not need a legal justification to commence hostilities. The plea of self-defence was relevant to the discussion of State responsibility for forcible measures undertaken in peacetime (see *infra*, Chapter 8, A, (a), ii - B). Still, logically as well as legally, it had no role to play in the international arena as regards the cardinal issue of war.[8] Up to the point of the prohibition of war, to most intents and purposes, "self-defence was not a legal concept but merely a political excuse for the use of force".[9] Only when the universal liberty to go to war was eliminated, could self-defence emerge as a right of signal importance in international law. Indeed, on the eve of the renunciation of war (and, subsequently, upon the proscription of all forms of inter-State force), the need for regulating the law of self-defence became manifest (see *supra*, Chapter 4,

---

[7] See M. A. Weightman, "Self-Defense in International Law", 37 *Vir.L.R.* 1095, 1099-1102 (1951).

[8] See E. Giraud, "La Théorie de la Légitime Défense", 49 *R.C.A.D.I.* 687, 715 (1934); J. L. Kunz, "Individual and Collective Self-Defense in Article 51 of the Charter of the United Nations", 41 *A.J.I.L.* 872, 876 (1947).

[9] E. Jiménez de Aréchaga, "International Law in the Past Third of a Century", 159 *R.C.A.D.I.* 1, 96 (1978).

A). The evolution of the idea of self-defence in international law goes "hand in hand" with the prohibition of aggression.[10]

The right of self-defence is enshrined in Article 51 of the Charter of the United Nations, which proclaims:

Nothing in the present Charter shall impair the inherent right of individual or collective self-defense if an armed attack occurs against a Member of the United Nations, until the Security Council has taken the measures necessary to maintain international peace and security. Measures taken by Members in the exercise of this right of self-defense shall be immediately reported to the Security Council and shall not in any way affect the authority and responsibility of the Security Council under the present Charter to take at any time such action as it deems necessary in order to maintain or restore international peace and security.[11]

The provision of Article 51 has to be read in conjunction with Article 2(4) of the Charter (see *supra*, Chapter 4, B, (a)).[12] Article 2(4) promulgates the general obligation to refrain from the use of inter-State force. Article 51 introduces an exception to this norm by allowing Member States to employ force in self-defence in the event of an armed attack.

Article 51 describes the right of self-defence as both "individual" and "collective" in nature. We shall examine *infra* (Chapter 9, A) the meaning of these two adjectives in the context of self-defence. Interestingly enough, the legislative history shows that, at its inception, the whole clause governing self-defence was inserted in the Charter with a view to confirming the legitimacy of regional security arrangements (notably, the inter-American system).[13] In actuality, Article 51 has become the main pillar of the law of self-defence in all its forms, individual as well as collective. In this chapter, we shall deal with common questions pertaining to self-defence of whatever category. The next two chapters will be devoted to specific problems relating to the two distinct types of self-defence.

---

[10] *Supra*, note 5, at 52.
[11] Charter of the United Nations, 1945, 9 *Int.Leg.* 327, 346.
[12] *Ibid.*, 332.
[13] L. M. Goodrich, E. Hambro and A. P. Simons, *Charter of the United Nations* 342-4 (3rd ed., 1969).

(b) *Self-Defence as a Right*

Article 51 explicitly refers to a "right" of self-defence. A State subjected to an armed attack is thus legally entitled to resort to force. The argument has been made that self-defence connotes only a *de facto* condition, rather than a veritable right.[14] But since it is conceded that the State exercising self-defence is "exonerated" from the duty to refrain from the use of force against the other side (the aggressor),[15] we fail to see a difference between that and a *de jure* right.

The thesis of self-defence as a legitimate recourse to force by Utopia is inextricably linked to the antithesis of the employment of unlawful force by Arcadia (its opponent). Under no circumstances can the actual use of force by both parties to a conflict be lawful simultaneously. If Utopia is properly exercising the right of self-defence, Arcadia must be in violation of the corresponding duty to abstain from an illegal resort to force. As an American Military Tribunal (following Wharton) held in the 1949 *Ministries* case, "there can be no self-defense against self-defense".[16]

In practice, when inter-State force is employed, both parties usually invoke the right of self-defence.[17] But such contradictory claims are mutually exclusive: only one of the antagonists can possibly be acting in an authentic exercise of the right of self-defence, whereas the other must be dissembling. When each persists in its posture, an authoritative determination is required to establish who is legally in the right (see *infra*, D, (a)). Even where no binding decision is made by a competent forum, it must be borne in mind that one of the parties is using force under false pretences of legality.

Self-defence, under general international law, is a right and not a duty. Vattel, like many others before and after his time, propounded that "[s]elf-defence against an unjust attack is not only a

---

[14] See R. Ago, "Addendum to Eighth Report on State Responsibility", [1980] II (1) *I.L.C. Ybk* 13, 53.

[15] *Ibid., id.*

[16] *U.S.A. v. Von Weizsaecker* et al. ("The *Ministries* Case") (Nuremberg, 1949), 14 *N.M.T.* 314, 329.

[17] See O. Schachter, "In Defense of International Rules on the Use of Force", 53 *U.C.L.R.* 113, 131 (1986).

right which every Nation has, but it is a duty, and one of its most sacred duties".[18] Although the statement may reflect morality or theology, it does not comport with international law. As a rule, international law does not lay down any obligation to exercise self-defence.[19] A State subjected to an armed attack is vested with a right, hence an option, to resort to counter-force. A prudent State may decline to exercise this right, on the ground that a political compromise is preferable to a clash of arms. The indubitable military supremacy of the adversary may have a sobering effect on the target State, inhibiting it from steps that would transmute a theoretical right into a practical disaster. The idea that a State must sacrifice realism at the altar of conceptualism, and risk defeat while prodded on by a "sacred duty", is incongruous.

The status of self-defence as a right, and not a duty, is embedded in general international law. There is no impediment to the assumption by a State of a special obligation (through a bilateral or multilateral treaty) to exercise self-defence, should an armed attack occur.[20] The duty of individual self-defence is usually incurred by a State when binding itself in a permanent neutrality regime[21] (see *supra*, Chapter 1, C, (a)). The obligation of collective self-defence is formulated in several conventional forms, such as military alliances, to be discussed in detail *infra* (Chapter 9, B).

(c) *Self-Defence as an "Inherent" Right*

Article 51 of the UN Charter pronounces self-defence to be an "inherent" right. In the French text of the Article, the phrase "inherent right" is rendered "*droit naturel*".[22] The choice of words has overtones of *jus naturale*, which appears to be the fount of the right of self-defence. However, a reference to self-defence as a "natural right", or a right generated by "natural law", is

---

[18] Vattel, *The Law of Nations or the Principles of Natural Law*, Book III, § III, 35 (3 Classics of International Law ed., C. G. Fenwick trans., 246 (1916)).

[19] See J. Zourek, "La Notion de Légitime Défense en Droit International", 56 *A.I.D.I.* 1, 51 (Wiesbaden, 1975).

[20] See *ibid., id.*

[21] See A. Verdross, "Austria's Permanent Neutrality and the United Nations Organization", 50 *A.J.I.L.* 61, 63 (1956).

[22] *Supra*, note 11, at 346.

unwarranted.[23] It may be conceived as an anachronistic residue from an era in which international law was dominated by ecclesiastical doctrines. At the present time, there is not much faith in transcendental truths professed to be derived from nature. A legal right is an interest protected by law, and it must be validated within the framework of a legal system. Self-defence, as an international legal right, must be proved to exist within the compass of positive international law.

It may be contended that the right of self-defence is inherent not in *jus naturale*, but in the sovereignty of States. This construct finds support in a series of identical notes, sent in 1928 by the Government of the United States to a number of other Governments (inviting them to become contracting parties to the Kellogg–Briand Pact), where it was stated:

> There is nothing in the American draft of an antiwar treaty which restricts or impairs in any way the right of self-defense. That right is inherent in every sovereign state and is implicit in every treaty.[24]

Yet, the principle of State sovereignty sheds no light on the theme of self-defence.[25] State sovereignty has a variable content, which depends on the stage of development of the international legal order at any given moment.[26] The best index of the altered perception of sovereignty is that, in the 19th (and early 20th) century, the liberty of every State to go to war as and when it pleased was also considered "a right inherent in sovereignty itself"[27] (see *supra*, Chapter 3, D). Notwithstanding the abolition of this liberty in the last half-century, the sovereignty of States did not crumble. The contemporary right to employ inter-State force in self-defence is no more "inherent" in sovereignty than the discredited right to resort to force at all times.

---

[23] See H. Kelsen, *The Law of the United Nations* 791-2 (1950).

[24] United States, Identic Notes, 1928, 22 *A.J.I.L.*, Supp., 109, *id.* (1928).

[25] See G. Schwarzenberger, "The Fundamental Principles of International Law", 87 *R.C.A.D.I.* 191, 339-40 (1955).

[26] See M. Virally, "Panorama du Droit International Contemporain", 183 *R.C.A.D.I.* 9, 79 (1983).

[27] See A. S. Hershey, *The Essentials of International Public Law* 349 (1912).

It is advisable to take with a grain of salt the frequently made assertion that, in the language of the Judgment of the International Military Tribunal for the Far East (delivered at *Tokyo* in 1948):

Any law, international or municipal, which prohibits recourse to force, is necessarily limited by the right of self-defence.[28]

This postulate may have always been true in regard to domestic law, and it is currently accurate also in respect of international law. But it is safer to avoid axiomatic propositions purporting to cover future eventualities for all time. Even if the right of self-defence will never be abolished in the relations between flesh-and-blood human beings, there is no guarantee of a similar immobility in international law. Self-defence exercised by States (legal entities) is not to be equated with self-defence carried out by physical persons (see *infra*, Chapter 8, A, (b), iii). It is not beyond the realm of the plausible that a day may come when States will agree to dispense completely with the use of force in self-defence, exclusively relying thenceforth on some central authority wielding an effective international police force. The allegation that the prerogative of self-defence is inherent in the sovereignty of States to such an extent that no treaty can derogate from it,[29] cannot be accepted. It is by no means clear whether the right of self-defence may be classified as *jus cogens*[30] (thus curtailing the freedom of States to contract out of it), and, in any event, even *jus cogens* is susceptible of modification (see *supra*, Chapter 4, E, (b)). Far be it from us to suggest that, at this juncture, the right of self-defence is receding or that its significance is abating. On the contrary, if anything, self-defence is gaining ground in the practice of States. Nevertheless, what is - and was - does not always equal what will be.

In its Judgment in the *Nicaragua* case, in 1986, the International Court of Justice gave a different meaning to self-defence as an "inherent right". The Court construed the expression as a reference to customary international law.[31] According to the Court, the

---

[28] In re *Hirota and Others* (International Military Tribunal for the Far East, Tokyo, 1948), [1948] *A.D.* 356, 364.

[29] See R. Ago, *supra*, note 14, at 67 n. 263.

[30] But see A. P. Rubin, "Book Review", 81 *A.J.I.L.* 254, 255-8 (1987).

[31] *Case Concerning Military and Paramilitary Activities in and against Nicaragua* (Merits), [1986] *I.C.J. Rep.* 14, 94.

framers of the Charter thereby acknowledged that self-defence was a pre-existing right of a customary nature, which they desired to preserve (at least in essence).[32] This is a sensible interpretation of Article 51, rationalizing the employment of the adjective "inherent" without ascribing to it far-fetched (and insupportable) consequences. The customary law relating to self-defence is often viewed as "best expressed" in D. Webster's formula in the *Caroline* incident[33] (*infra*, Chapter 8, B, (c)).

Article 51 addresses only the right of self-defence of UN Member States. After all, these are also the subjects of the duty, set out in Article 2(4), to refrain from the use of force (see *supra*, Chapter 4, B, (a)). The existence of the right of self-defence under general customary international law denotes that it is conferred on every State. Contemporary customary international law forbids the use of inter-State force by all States, whether or not they are UN Members (see *supra*, Chapter 4, C, (a)). In the same vein, any State (even if not a UN Member) is entitled to the right of self-defence under existing customary international law. Both the general prohibition of the use of inter-State force and the exception to it (the right of self-defence) are part and parcel of customary international law, as well as the law of the Charter.[34]

B. *Self-Defence as a Response to an Armed Attack*

(a) *Armed Attack and Preventive War*

Although the right of self-defence pursuant to the UN Charter has its origins in customary international law, there seems to be a material difference in the range of operation of the right arising from these two sources. Article 51 permits self-defence solely when an "armed attack" occurs. While some commentators believe that customary international law does the same,[35] the more common opinion is that the customary right of self-defence is also accorded

---

[32] *Ibid., id.*
[33] M. A. Rogoff and E. Collins, "The *Caroline* Incident and the Development of International Law", 16 *B.J.I.L.* 493, 506 (1990).
[34] See *supra*, note 31, at 102-3.
[35] See R. Ago, *supra*, note 14, at 65-7.

to States as a preventive measure (taken in "anticipation" of an armed attack, and not merely in response to an attack that has actually occurred).[36] The International Court of Justice, in the *Nicaragua* case, based its decision on the norms of customary international law concerning self-defence as a sequel to an armed attack.[37] However, the Court stressed that this was due to the circumstances of the case, and it passed no judgment on "the issue of the lawfulness of a response to the imminent threat of armed attack".[38]

The use of the phrase "armed attack" in Article 51 is not inadvertent. The framers of the Article preferred that expression to the term "aggression", which appears elsewhere in the Charter (in the contexts of the Purposes of the United Nations (Article 1(1)), collective security (Article 39) and regional arrangements (Article 53(1)).[39] The choice of words in Article 51 is deliberately restrictive. The exercise of the right of self-defence, in conformity with the Article, is confined to a response to an armed attack.

An armed attack is, of course, a type of aggression. We have dealt at some length with the consensus Definition of Aggression, adopted in 1974 by the General Assembly[40] (*supra*, Chapter 5, B). As observed, the Definition, while not pretending to be exhaustive, does not cover the threat of force.[41] The meaning of the term "aggression" can be stretched to include mere threats (*cf. supra*, Chapter 5, C, (a), i). But only a special form of aggression amounting to an armed attack justifies self-defence under Article 51. The French version of the Article clarifies its thrust by speaking of "*une agression armée*".[42] Under the Charter, a State is permitted to

---

[36] See N. Singh and E. McWhinney, *Nuclear Weapons and Contemporary International Law* 87 (2nd ed., 1989). It has even been erroneously maintained that the customary right of anticipatory self-defence possesses the character of *jus cogens*. See L. R. Beres, "On Assassination as Anticipatory Self-Defense: The Case of Israel", 20 *Hof.L.R.* 321, 322 n. 3 (1991-2).

[37] *Supra*, note 31, at 102-6.

[38] *Ibid.*, 103.

[39] *Supra*, note 11, at 331, 343, 347.

[40] General Assembly Resolution No. 3314 (xxix), 29(1) *R.G.A.* 142 (1974).

[41] *Ibid.*, 143 (Articles 2-4).

[42] *Supra*, note 11, at 346.

use force in self-defence only in response to aggression which is armed.

The requirement of an armed attack as a condition of legitimate self-defence, in accordance with Article 51, precludes not only threats. Recourse to self-defence under the Article is not vindicated by any violation of international law short of an armed attack. Even declarations of war, if it is evident to all that they are unaccompanied by deeds, are not enough.[43] The notion that mere mobilization or "bellicose utterances" as such may justify self-defence within the framework of Article 51,[44] has no foundation.

At bottom, self-defence consistent with Article 51 implies resort to counter-force: it comes in reaction to the use of force by the other party. When a country feels menaced by the threat of an armed attack, all that it is free to do - in keeping with the Charter - is make the necessary military preparations for repulsing the hostile action should it materialize, as well as bring the matter forthwith to the attention of the Security Council (hoping that the latter will take collective security measures in the face of a threat to the peace (see *infra*, Chapter 10, A)).[45] Either course of action may fail to inspire confidence in the successful resolution of the crisis. The military preparations can easily prove inadequate, either as a deterrence or as a shock absorber. The Council, for its part, may proceed in a nonchalant manner.[46] Regardless of the shortcomings of the system, the option of a preemptive use of force is excluded by Article 51 (although it may come within the ambit of legitimate self-defence under customary international law).

There is a strong school of thought maintaining that Article 51 only highlights one form of self-defence (viz. response to an armed attack), and that it does not negate other patterns of legitimate action in self-defence vouchsafed by customary inter-

---

[43] A declaration of war patently unaccompanied by deeds may be deemed "an overt threat of the use of force". E. Myjer, "Book Review" [of the first edition of this volume], 2 *L.J.I.L.* 278, 283 (1989). But such a threat *per se* does not constitute an armed attack.

[44] See E. Miller, "Self-Defence, International Law, and the Six Day War", 20 *Is.L.R.* 49, 58-60 (1985).

[45] See J. Zourek, *L'Interdiction de L'Emploi de la Force en Droit International* 106 (1974).

[46] For a case in point, see R. Lapidoth, "The Security Council in the May 1967 Crisis: A Study in Frustration", 4 *Is.L.R.* 534-50 (1969).

national law.[47] This approach has gained the support of Judge Schwebel who, in his Dissenting Opinion in the *Nicaragua* case, rejected a reading of the text which would imply that the right of self-defence under Article 51 exists "if, and only if, an armed attack occurs".[48]

In our opinion, however, precisely such a reading of the Article is called for. There is not the slightest suggestion in Article 51 that the occurrence of an armed attack represents only one set of circumstances (among others) in which self-defence may be exercised. In fact, if that is what the framers of the Charter had in mind, the crafting of Article 51 makes very little sense. What is the point in stating the obvious (i.e. that an armed attack gives rise to the right of self-defence), while omitting a reference to the ambiguous conditions of preventive war? Preventive war in self-defence (if legitimate under the Charter) would require regulation by *lex scripta* more acutely than a response to an armed attack, since the opportunities for abuse are incomparably greater. Not only does Article 51 fail to intimate that preventive war is allowable, but the critical tasks assigned to the Security Council are restricted to the exclusive setting of counter-force employed in response to an armed attack. Surely, if preventive war in self-defence is justified (on the basis of "probable cause" rather than an actual use of force), it ought to be exposed to no less - if possible, even closer - supervision by the Council. In all, is this not an appropriate case for the application of the maxim of interpretation *expressio unius est exclusio alterius?*

When pressed, the advocates of the legitimacy of anticipatory self-defence under the Charter are forced to frown upon Article 51 as "an inept piece of draftsmanship".[49] However, the draftsmanship appears to be quite satisfactory once it is recognized that the right of self-defence is circumscribed to counter-force stimulated by an

---

[47] See D. W. Bowett, *Self-Defence in International Law* 187-92 (1958); M. S. McDougal and F. P. Feliciano, *Law and Minimum World Public Order* 232-41 (1961); J. Stone, *Aggression and World Order* 44 (1958).

[48] *Supra*, note 31, at 347.

[49] M. S. McDougal and F. P. Feliciano, *supra*, note 47, at 234.

armed attack. The leading opinion among scholars is in harmony with the view expressed here.[50]

The proposition that UN Member States are barred by the Charter from invoking self-defence, in response to a mere threat of force, is applicable in every situation. It is sometimes put forward that "[t]he destructive potential of nuclear weapons is so enormous as to call into question any and all received rules of international law regarding the trans-boundary use of force".[51] But the inference that Article 51 is only operative under conditions of conventional warfare cannot be substantiated.

Hence, when the United States imposed a "quarantine" on Cuba in 1962, subsequent to the installation of Soviet missiles on the island, this could not be reconciled with the provision of Article 51,[52] notwithstanding valiant attempts by some writers to do so.[53] The installation of the missiles so close to American shores did pose a certain threat to the United States. Yet, in the absence of an armed attack, no recourse could be made to the exceptional right of self-defence, and the general interdiction of the use of inter-State force prevailed.

When Israeli aircraft raided an Iraqi nuclear reactor (under construction) in 1981, the legal justification of the act should have rested on the state of war which was – and still is – in progress between the two countries (see *supra*, Chapter 2, B, (c), i). Had Israel been at peace with Iraq, the bombing of the site would have been prohibited, since (when examined in itself and out of the context of an on-going war) it did not qualify as a legitimate act of self-defence consonant with Article 51. This is the position *de lege lata*, despite the understandable

---

[50] See R. Ago, *supra*, note 14, at 64-7; W. E. Beckett, *The North Atlantic Treaty, the Brussels Treaty and the Charter of the United Nations* 13 (1950); H. Kelsen, *supra*, note 23, at 797-8; J. L. Kunz, *supra*, note 8, at 877-8; L. Oppenheim, 2 *International Law* 156 (7th ed., by H. Lauterpacht, 1952); K. Skubiszewski, "Use of Force by States. Collective Security. Law of War and Neutrality", *Manual of Public International Law* 739, 767 (M. Sørensen ed., 1968); H. Wehberg, "L'Interdiction du Recours à la Force. Le Principe et les Problèmes qui se Posent", 78 *R.C.A.D.I.* 1, 81 (1951).

[51] A. D'Amato, "Israel's Air Strike upon the Iraqi Nuclear Reactor", 77 *A.J.I.L.* 584, 588 (1983).

[52] See Q. Wright, "The Cuban Quarantine", 57 *A.J.I.L.* 546, 560-2 (1963).

[53] See M. S. McDougal, "The Soviet-Cuban Quarantine and Self-Defense", 57 *A.J.I.L.* 597-604 (1963).

apprehension existing at the time – and bolstered in the wake of the hostilities during the Gulf War – that nuclear devices, if produced by Iraq, might ultimately be delivered against Israeli targets.[54]

(b) *The Scope of an Armed Attack*

i. *The Beginning of an Armed Attack*

Since self-defence (under Article 51) is linked to an armed attack, it is important to pinpoint the exact moment at which an armed attack begins to take place: this is also the moment when forcible counter-measures become legitimate as self-defence. In practice, the issue acquires another dimension as a result of the proclivity of both parties, once hostilities break out, to charge each other with the initiation of an armed attack. Verification of the precise instant at which an armed attack commences is well-nigh equivalent to an identification of the aggressor and the victim State respectively.

When confronted with contradictory claims of self-defence (and attendant charges of armed attack), the international community is generally confounded by effusions of disinformation pouring forth from dubious sources. Given that there may be meagre opportunity for impartial observers to investigate what really happened, the public tends to look for deceptively uncomplicated criteria designed to establish the starting point of the armed attack. The most simplistic touchstone is that of the "first shot", namely, finding out which State (through its armed forces) was the first to open fire.

Article 2 of the General Assembly's consensus Definition of Aggression refers to the first use of force as only *prima facie* evidence of aggression[55] (see *supra*, Chapter 5, B). This is a judicious approach that relegates the opening of fire to the level of a presumption of an armed attack. While the burden of proof shifts to the State firing the first shot, that State is not estopped from demonstrating that the

---

[54] *Per contra*, see U. Shoham, "The Israeli Aerial Raid upon the Iraqi Nuclear Reactor and the Right of Self-Defense", 109 *Mil.L.R.* 191-223 (1985); M. Silverberg, "International Law and the Use of Force: May the United States Attack the Chemical Weapons Plant at Rabta?", 13 *B.C.I.C.L.R.* 53, 60-6 (1990).

[55] *Supra*, note 40, at 143.

action came in response to steps (taken by the opponent), which were far and away more decisive as a turning point in the process leading from peace to war (or from quiescence to an armed conflict short of war).

In many instances, the opening of fire is an unreliable test of responsibility for an armed attack. The most elementary example pertains to a full-scale invasion of one country by another. An invasion constitutes the foremost case of aggression enumerated in Article 3(a) of the General Assembly's Definition.[56] It may start when Arcadian armoured or infantry divisions storm, with blazing guns, a Utopian line of fortifications. But an invasion may also be effected by Arcadian armed forces moving *en masse* across the Utopian frontier, while holding their fire. Should that come to pass, Utopian border units might shoot first, in an attempt to drive out (or not to be captured by) the advancing Arcadian echelons. When large armed formations of a foreign country cross an international frontier, without the consent of the local Government, they must be deemed to have unleashed an armed attack. The opening of fire by the Utopian border guards would amount to a legitimate measure of self-defence, in response to an Arcadian armed attack (begun at the point of overrunning the Utopian frontier posts).

Another rudimentary illustration for the need to look beyond the first shot relates to circumstances in which Arcadian military forces are stationed by permission, for a limited space of time, on Utopian soil. When the agreed upon period comes to an end, and Utopia is unwilling to prolong the stay within its territory of the Arcadian troops, Arcadia must pull them out. If Arcadia fails to do so, its refusal to withdraw from Utopia amounts to an act of aggression under Article 3(e) of the General Assembly's Definition.[57] The factual situation may be legally analyzed as a constructive armed attack.[58] When the armed forces of Utopia open fire first, with a view to compelling the evacuation of Arcadian troops from Utopian territory, they are exercising the right of self-defence.

---

[56] *Ibid., id.*

[57] *Ibid., id.*

[58] See W. Wengler, "L'Interdiction de Recourir à la Force. Problèmes et Tendances", [1971] *R.B.D.I.* 401, 408.

These are open-and-shut cases, inasmuch as the first shot fired by the Utopian armed forces is plainly provoked by an Arcadian invasion, or by an unauthorized Arcadian military presence within Utopian territory. But a State may resort to force in self-defence, even before its territory is penetrated by another State. Suppose that Numidia launches inter-continental ballistic missiles against Ruritania on the other side of the planet. The Ruritanian radar immediately detects the launching. In the few minutes left prior to impact (and before the missiles draw near the Ruritanian frontier), Ruritania activates its armed forces and a Ruritanian submarine torpedoes a Numidian warship cruising in the ocean. Although a Numidian target is the first to be hit, one can scarcely deny that Numidia (having launched its missiles previously) should be regarded as the initiator of an armed attack, whereas Ruritania ought to be able to invoke self-defence.

It may be contended that what ultimately counts in the last script is the launching of the missiles, which resembles the firing of a gun: once a button is pressed, or a trigger is pulled, the act is complete (while impact is a mere technicality). However, suppose further that the missiles launched by Numidia (rather than being ballistic) have a guidance system, so that they are capable of being diverted from their objectives at the last moment. Is the legal position really different?

Another example may attest that an armed attack need not be started by the State responsible for the opening of fire. Let us assume hypothetically that the Japanese Carrier Striking Force, *en route* to the point from which it mounted the notorious attack on Pearl Harbor in December 1941, had been intercepted and sunk by the US Pacific Fleet prior to reaching its destination and before a single Japanese naval aircraft got anywhere near Hawaii.[59] If that were to have happened, and the Americans would have succeeded in aborting an onslaught which at one fell swoop managed to change the balance of military power in the Pacific, it would have been preposterous to look upon the United States as answerable for inflicting an armed attack upon Japan.

---

[59] The Pearl Harbor example was adduced in debates in the United Nations. See M. M. Whiteman, 5 *Digest of International Law* 867-8 (1965).

All these scenarios show that an armed attack may precede the firing of the first shot. The crucial question is who embarks upon an irreversible course of action, thereby crossing the Rubicon. This, rather than the actual opening of fire, is what casts the die and forms what may be categorized as an incipient armed attack. It would be absurd to require that the defending State should sustain and absorb a devastating (perhaps a fatal) blow, only to prove an immaculate conception of self-defence. As Sir Humphrey Waldock phrased it:

> Where there is convincing evidence not merely of threats and potential danger but of an attack being actually mounted, then an armed attack may be said to have begun to occur, though it has not passed the frontier.[60]

Had the Japanese Carrier Striking Force been destroyed on its way to Pearl Harbor, this would have constituted not an act of preventive war but a miraculously early use of counter-force. To put it in another way, the self-defence exercised by the United States (in response to an incipient armed attack) would have been not anticipatory but interceptive in nature. Interceptive, unlike anticipatory, self-defence takes place after the other side has committed itself to an armed attack in an ostensibly irrevocable way. Whereas a preventive strike anticipates an armed attack which is merely "foreseeable" (or even just "conceivable"), an interceptive strike counters an armed attack which is "imminent" and practically "unavoidable".[61] It is the opinion of the present writer that interceptive, as distinct from anticipatory, self-defence is legitimate even under Article 51 of the Charter.[62]

An in-depth study of the background may be required before a decision is made regarding the classification of the first shot as anticipatory or interceptive. Thus, in the "Six Days War" of June

---

[60] C. H. M. Waldock, "The Regulation of the Use of Force by Individual States in International Law", 81 *R.C.A.D.I.* 451, 498 (1952).

[61] *Cf.* C. C. Joyner and M. A. Grimaldi, "The United States and Nicaragua: Reflections on the Lawfulness of Contemporary Intervention", 25 *V.J.I.L.* 621, 659-60 (1984-5). See also I. Pogany, "Book Review" [of the first edition of this volume], 38 *I.C.L.Q.* 435, *id.* (1989).

[62] For support of this view, see M. N. Shaw, *International Law* 695 (3rd ed., 1991).

1967, Israel was the first to open fire. Nevertheless, a careful analysis of the events surrounding the actual outbreak of the hostilities (assuming that the factual examination was conducted, in good faith, at the time of action) would lead to the conclusion that the Israeli campaign amounted to an interceptive self-defence, in response to an incipient armed attack by Egypt (joined by Jordan and Syria). True, no single Egyptian step, evaluated alone, may have qualified as an armed attack. But when all of the measures taken by Egypt (especially the peremptory ejection of the United Nations Emergency Force from the Gaza Strip and the Sinai Peninsula; the closure of the Straits of Tiran; the unprecedented build-up of Egyptian forces along Israel's borders; and constant sabre-rattling statements about the impending fighting) were assessed in the aggregate, it seemed to be crystal-clear that Egypt was bent on an armed attack, and the sole question was not whether war would materialize but when.[63]

That, at least, was the widely shared perception (not only in Israel) in June 1967. Hindsight knowledge, suggesting that - notwithstanding the well-founded contemporaneous appraisal of events - the situation may have been less desperate than it appeared, is immaterial.[64] The invocation of the right of self-defence must be weighed on the basis of the information available (and reasonably interpreted) at the moment of action, without the benefit of *post factum* wisdom.[65] In the circumstances, as perceived in June 1967, Israel did not have to wait idly by for the expected shattering blow (in the military manner of the October 1973 "Yom Kippur" offensive), but was entitled to resort to self-defence as soon as possible.

[63] See Y. Dinstein, "The Legal Issues of 'Para-War' and Peace in the Middle East", 44 *S.J.L.R.* 466, 469-70 (1970).

[64] See A. Shapira, "The Six-Day War and the Right of Self-Defence", 6 *Is.L.R.* 65, 76 (1971).

[65] This rule works both for and against the State invoking self-defence. Thus, it cannot base its recourse to forcible measures on information unavailable at the time of action and acquired only subsequently. See B. Cheng, *General Principles of Law as Applied by International Courts and Tribunals* 90 (1953).

ii. A Small Scale Armed Attack

An armed attack, justifying self-defence as a response under Article 51, need not take the shape of a massive military operation. "Low intensity" fighting, conducted on a relatively small scale, may also be deemed an armed attack. Accordingly, the International Court of Justice ruled, in the *Nicaragua* case, that the sending of armed bands into the territory of another State may count as an armed attack[66] (see *infra*, v). At the same time, the Court found it "necessary to distinguish the most grave forms of the use of force (those constituting an armed attack) from other less grave forms".[67] The Judgment mentioned "measures which do not constitute an armed attack but may nevertheless involve a use of force".[68] It also distinguished between an armed attack and "a mere frontier incident", inasmuch as an armed attack must have some "scale and effects".[69]

The Court did not elaborate upon these matters, and it is by no means clear what threshold must be reached for the use of force to qualify as an armed attack. The criteria of "scale and effects", as we shall see (*infra*, C), are of immense practical import. But they are relevant in appraising whether a counter-action taken in self-defence, in response to an armed attack, is legitimate. They do not affect the determination whether an armed attack has occurred. In reality, there is no cause to remove small-scale armed attacks from the spectrum of armed attacks. Article 51 "in no way limits itself to especially large, direct or important armed attacks".[70] The position was summed up by J. L. Kunz: "If 'armed attack' means illegal armed attack it means, on the other hand, any illegal armed attack, even a small border incident".[71]

The question of a frontier incident is particularly bothersome. It stands to reason that, if a rifle shot is fired by an Arcadian soldier

---

[66] *Supra*, note 31, at 103.
[67] *Ibid.*, 101.
[68] *Ibid.*, 110.
[69] *Ibid.*, 103.
[70] J. L. Hargrove, "The *Nicaragua* Judgment and the Future of the Law of Force and Self-Defense", 81 *A.J.I.L.* 135, 139 (1987).
[71] J. L. Kunz, *supra*, note 8, at 878.

across the border of Utopia and the bullet hits a tree or a cow, no armed attack has been perpetrated. The consensus Definiton of Aggression contains in Article 2 a *de minimis* clause[72] (see *supra*, Chapter 5, B), and what is true of aggression is all the more valid in respect of an armed attack. But it would be fallacious to dismiss automatically from consideration as an armed attack every frontier incident. As aptly put by Sir Gerald Fitzmaurice, "[t]here are frontier incidents and frontier incidents. Some are trivial, some may be extremely grave".[73] When elements of the armed forces of Arcadia open fire upon a border patrol (or some other isolated unit) of Utopia, the assault has to rank as an armed attack and some sort of self-defence must be warranted in response.[74] Many frontier incidents comprise fairly large military engagements, and an attempt to dissociate them from other forms of armed attack would be spurious.

The confusion generated by the Court's dicta is compounded by the fact that the Judgment envisaged legitimate counter-measures, "analogous" to but less grave than self-defence, in response to use of force which is less grave than an armed attack.[75] What emerges is a quadruple structure of (i) self-defence versus (ii) armed attack, and (iii) counter-measures analogous to but short of self-defence versus (iv) forcible measures short of an armed attack. The Court did not specify what counter-measures, short of self-defence, are permissible. But it carefully refrained from ruling out the possibility that such counter-measures may involve the use of force by the victim State.[76] It was "strongly suggested" in the Judgment that these counter-measures may include acts of force.[77]

While the Court did not paint a clear picture of the similarities and dissimilarities between the measures and counter-measures which it found analogous, one striking difference is emphasized in the Judgment. The Court held that when non-self-defence counter-

---

[72] *Supra*, note 40, at 143.
[73] G. G. Fitzmaurice, "The Definition of Aggression", 1 *I.C.L.Q.* 137, 139 (1952).
[74] See G. M. Badr, "The Exculpatory Effect of Self-Defense in State Responsibility", 10 *G.J.I.C.L.* 1, 17 (1980).
[75] *Supra*, note 31, at 110.
[76] *Ibid., id.*
[77] See J. L. Hargrove, *supra*, note 70, at 138.

measures are employed, there is no counterpart to collective self-defence, namely, the right of a third State to resort to force in response to the wrongful act.[78] The options of response to forcible measures short of an armed attack are, in consequence, reduced considerably.[79] Moreover, since the Court did not brand as an armed attack the supply of weapons and logistical support to rebels against a foreign State (see *infra*, (v)), a "no-man's-land" unfolds between the type of military assistance that a third State can legitimately provide and the direct exercise of collective self-defence in response to an armed attack.[80]

All this is very baffling.[81] No evidence was produced by the Court that the quadruple structure is actually reflected in customary international law. It is certainly not discernible how the whole legal edifice can be reconciled with the provisions of the Charter.

iii. The Locale of an Armed Attack

Ordinarily, an armed attack (justifying counter-measures of self-defence) is mounted across the frontier of the aggressor State into the territory of the victim country. However, the crossing of the frontier can precede the armed attack, which may commence from within the territory of the target State. We have already seen (*supra*, i) that Arcadian troops stationed by permission on Utopian soil may commit a constructive armed attack, if they refuse to withdraw upon expiry of the time allotted for their presence. In fact, the armed attack need not be constructive. An Arcadian military unit based in Utopia, under the terms of a military alliance, may – in violation of these terms – open fire on Utopian personnel or installations. An Arcadian warship admitted into a Utopian port, ostensibly for refuelling, may shell Utopian shore facilities. The use of force within Utopia by Arcadian military units, in contravention

---

[78] *Supra*, note 31, at 110, 127.

[79] See T. M. Franck, "Some Observations on the ICJ's Procedural and Substantive Innovations", 81 *A.J.I.L.* 116, 120 (1987).

[80] See L. B. Sohn, "The International Court of Justice and the Scope of the Right of Self-Defense and the Duty of Non-Intervention", *International Law at a Time of Perplexity: Essays in Honour of Shabtai Rosenne* 869, 878 (Y. Dinstein ed., 1989).

[81] See the Dissenting Opinion of Judge Schwebel, *supra*, note 31, at 349–50.

of the conditions of Utopian consent to their entry into its territory, is recognized as an act of aggression under Article 3(e) of the General Assembly's Definition[82] (see *supra*, Chapter 5, B).

An armed attack by Arcadia against Utopia can also involve (either in an active or in a passive way) the territory of a third State. For instance, Utopian targets may be bombed by Arcadian planes operating from airfields located in Ruritania (a country allied with or occupied by Arcadia). Another possibility is that Arcadian troops assault Utopian personnel stationed by consent within the territory of Numidia.

At times, an armed attack occurs beyond the boundaries of all States. This happens when an Arcadian battleship sinks a Utopian vessel on the high seas, or when missiles fired by Numidian armed forces destroy a satellite put in orbit in outer space by Ruritania.

The State subjected to an armed attack is entitled to resort to self-defence measures against the aggressor, regardless of the geographic point where the attack was delivered. An armed attack need not even be cross-border in nature: it does not have to be perpetrated beyond the frontiers of the aggressor State. If force is used by Arcadia against Utopian installations (such as a military base or an embassy) legitimately situated within Arcadian territory, this may constitute an armed attack, and Utopia would be entitled to exercise its right of self-defence against Arcadia.[83]

In the *Tehran* case of 1980, the International Court of Justice used the phrase "armed attack" when discussing the takeover by Iranian militants of the US Embassy in Tehran, and the seizure of the Embassy staff as hostages, in November 1979.[84] The allusion to an "armed attack" is particularly significant in the light of the ill-fated American attempt, in April 1980, to bring about the rescue of the hostages by military means.[85] The legality of the rescue mission was

---

[82] *Supra*, note 40, at 143.
[83] See O. Schachter, "International Law in the Hostage Crisis: Implications for Future Cases", *American Hostages in Iran* 325, 328 (W. Christopher *et al.* eds., 1985).
[84] *Case Concerning United States Diplomatic and Consular Staff in Tehran*, [1980] *I.C.J. Rep.* 3, 29, 42.
[85] See T. L. Stein, "Contempt, Crisis, and the Court: The World Court and the Hostage Rescue Attempt", 76 *A.J.I.L.* 499, 500 n. 8 (1982).

not an issue before the Court.[86] Yet, the Judgment registered the American plea that the operation had been carried out in exercise of the right of self-defence, with a view to extricating the victims of an armed attack against the US Embassy.[87] In his Dissenting Opinion in the *Nicaragua* case, Judge Schwebel called that plea "a sound legal evaluation of the rescue attempt".[88]

When inter-State force is employed inside the national boundaries of the acting State, one must not gloss over the rights of the territorial sovereign (which other States must respect). Sovereign rights allow a State to guard its borders from any unauthorized entry. There have been a number of incidents in which naval forces of coastal countries (e.g., Sweden and Norway) dropped depth charges and detonated sea-bottom mines, in order to force to the surface foreign submarines intruding into internal or territorial waters.[89] Both Article 14(6) of the 1958 Geneva Convention on the Territorial Sea and the Contiguous Zone,[90] and Article 20 of the 1982 United Nations Convention on the Law of the Sea,[91] prescribe that submarines passing through the territorial sea "are required to navigate on the surface and to show their flag". It is sometimes argued that, nevertheless, submerged passage does not give the coastal State a licence to resort to force against the foreign submarine.[92] But this assertion is unsustainable. The practice of States amply demonstrates that the use of force by the coastal State is not ruled out, if a submarine makes an unauthorized and submerged entry into the territorial or internal waters.[93] The intrusion by the submerged submarine may be regarded as an incipient armed

---

[86] *Supra,* note 84, at 43.

[87] *Ibid.,* 18.

[88] *Supra,* note 31, at 292.

[89] For the facts, see F. D. Froman, "Uncharted Waters: Non-Innocent Passage of Warships in the Territorial Sea", 21 *S.D.L.R.* 625, 680-8 (1983-4).

[90] Geneva Convention on the Territorial Sea and the Contiguous Zone, 1958, 516 *U.N.T.S.* 205, 214.

[91] United Nations Convention on the Law of the Sea, 1982, 21 *I.L.M.* 1261, 1274 (1982).

[92] See R. Sadurska, "Foreign Submarines in Swedish Waters: The Erosion of an International Norm", 10 *Y.J.I.L.* 34, 57 (1984-5).

[93] See D. P. O'Connell, 1 *The International Law of the Sea* 297 (1982).

attack (see *supra*, i), and the coastal State is allowed, therefore, to employ forcible counter-measures by way of self-defence.[94]

When war is raging between Arcadia and Utopia, Patagonia – as a neutral State – is not only entitled but is legally bound to prevent entry into its territory by belligerent land and air forces (see *supra*, Chapter 1, D, (b), i). Consequently, if Arcadian aircraft are overflying Patagonia's territory in breach of its neutrality, their intrusion into the neutral airspace may also be viewed as an incipient armed attack. Patagonian military units are accordingly allowed to open fire on the Arcadian aircraft, in the exercise of both the right to self-defence and the duties of neutrality.[95]

iv. The Target of an Armed Attack

The foremost target of an armed attack (justifying counter-measures of self-defence) is the territory of a foreign State or any section thereof – land, water or air – including persons or property (of whatever type) within the affected area. Another obvious target is a military unit belonging to the armed forces of the victim State, stationed or in transit outside the national territory. Taking forcible measures against any public (military or civilian) installation of the victim State, located outside the national territory, may also amount to an armed attack.

Does the use of force by Arcadia against a private vessel or aircraft, registered in Utopia but attacked beyond the national

---

[94] It has been suggested that the problem can be solved by excluding from the "proscribed categories of article 2(4)" of the Charter the enforcement by a State of its territorial rights against an illegal incursion. O. Schachter, "The Right of States to Use Armed Force", 82 *Mich.L.R.* 1620, 1626 (1984). But in our opinion, the span of the prohibition of the use of inter-State force, as articulated in Article 2(4), is subject to no exception other than self-defence and collective security (see *supra*, Chapter 4, B). When Arcadia uses force unilaterally against Utopia, even within Arcadian territory, this must be based on self-defence against an armed attack.

[95] M. Bothe is of the opinion that the Patagonian measures are legitimate independently of the issues of armed attack and self-defence. International Law Association, *Report of the Committee on Neutrality and Naval Warfare* 3 (Cairo, 1992; M. Bothe, Rapporteur). But the traditional laws of neutrality must be adapted to the law of the Charter, which permits a unilateral deviation from the general prohibition of inter-State use of force only in circumstances of self-defence against an armed attack.

boundaries, qualify as an armed attack against Utopia? The consensus Definition of Aggression, in Article 3(d), brings within its scope an attack on "marine and air fleets of another State"[96] (see *supra*, Chapter 5, B). The expression "fleets" was chosen advisedly, so as to exclude from the purview of the Definition the use of force by Arcadia against a single or a few commercial Utopian vessels or aircraft, especially when they enter Arcadian jurisdiction.[97] A reasonable degree of force (in the form of search and seizure) may be legitimate against foreign merchant ships even on the high seas.[98] Hence, the United States erred in 1975, when it treated the temporary seizure of the merchant ship *Mayaguez* by Cambodian naval units as an armed attack (invoking self-defence to legitimize the use of force in response).[99]

Another question is whether recourse to force by Arcadia (within its own territory) against Utopian nationals, away from any Utopian installation or vessel, may also constitute an armed attack against Utopia (thus justifying counter-force as self-defence). It is almost certain that the answer is affirmative if the Utopian victims are diplomatic envoys or visiting dignitaries.[100] A more intricate problem is whether Utopia may treat as an armed attack the use of force (within the boundaries of Arcadia) against ordinary Utopian nationals holding no official position. Is an attack against such nationals tantamount to an armed attack against Utopia itself, so that Utopia is entitled to resort to counter-force in self-defence? D. W. Bowett upholds the thesis that the protection of nationals abroad can be looked upon as protection of the State.[101] While many scholars strongly disagree,[102] others share that

---

[96] *Supra*, note 40, at 143.

[97] See B. Broms, "The Definition of Aggression", 154 *R.C.A.D.I.* 299, 351 (1977).

[98] See W. J. Fenrick, "Legal Limits on the Use of Force by Canadian Warships Engaged in Law Enforcement", 18 *C.Y.I.L.* 113, 125-45 (1980).

[99] See J. J. Paust, "The Seizure and Recovery of the *Mayaguez*", 85 *Y.L.J.* 774, 791, 800 (1975-6).

[100] *Cf.* G. Arangio-Ruiz, "The Normative Role of the General Assembly of the United Nations and the Declaration of Principles of Friendly Relations", 137 *R.C.A.D.I.* 419, 535 (1972).

[101] D. W. Bowett, *supra*, note 47, at 91-4.

[102] See J. E. S. Fawcett, "Intervention in International Law. A Study of Some Recent Cases", 103 *R.C.A.D.I.* 343, 404 (1961); T. Schweisfurth, "Operations to Rescue Nationals in Third States Involving the Use of Force in Relation to the Protection of Human Rights", 23 *G.Y.I.L.* 159, 162-5 (1980).

conception.[103] The allegation that an attack against nationals abroad can never be regarded as an attack against the State itself[104] swings away from reality: it carries the legal fiction of the State to extreme and illogical lengths.[105]

Some commentators believe that a novel rule concerning the protection of nationals abroad is currently being moulded in the crucible of customary international law.[106] The process is animated by new challenges to law and order within the international community, in particular the remarkable increase in episodes involving the taking of hostages and other incidents of transnational terrorism. If and when such a new rule becomes a part of customary international law, the protection of nationals abroad may join self-defence as another (and separate) exception to the general prohibition of the use of inter-State force. However, no such independent exception exists in the meantime.[107] At present, any forcible measures taken in a foreign territory in the interest of nationals must be based on self-defence in response to an armed attack. We shall return to this topic *infra* (Chapter 8, A, (a), iii).

v. Support of Armed Bands

In the *Nicaragua* case, the International Court of Justice held that "it may be considered to be agreed that an armed attack must be understood as including not merely action by regular armed forces across an international border", but also the dispatch of armed bands or "irregulars" into the territory of another State.[108] The Court quoted Article 3(g) of the General Assembly's Definition of

---

[103] See G. Fitzmaurice, "The General Principles of International Law Considered from the Standpoint of the Rule of Law", 92 *R.C.A.D.I.* 1, 172-3 (1957).

[104] See R. J. Zedalis, "Protection of Nationals Abroad: Is Consent the Basis of Legal Obligation?", 25 *T.I.L.J.* 209, 236-7 (1990).

[105] "[S]ince population is one of the attributes of statehood, an attack upon a state's population would seem to be just as much an attack upon that state as would an attack upon its territory". C. Greenwood, "International Law and the United States' Air Operation against Libya", 89 *W.V.L.R.* 933, 941 (1986-7).

[106] See N. Ronzitti, *Rescuing Nationals Abroad through Military Coercion and Intervention on Grounds of Humanity* 65-8 (1985).

[107] See *ibid.,* 64-5.

[108] *Supra,* note 31, at 103.

Aggression[109] (see *supra*, Chapter 5, B), which it took "to reflect customary international law".[110]

It may be added that, under the Declaration on Principles of International Law Concerning Friendly Relations and Co-operation among States in accordance with the Charter of the United Nations, adopted unanimously by the General Assembly in 1970, "every State has the duty to refrain from organizing or encouraging the organization of irregular forces or armed bands ... for incursion into the territory of another State".[111] The Draft Code of Offences against the Peace and Security of Mankind, formulated by the International Law Commission in 1954, listed among these offences the organization (or the encouragement of organization) by the authorities of a State of armed bands for incursions into the territory of another State, direct support of such incursions, and even the toleration of the use of the local territory as a base of operations by armed bands against another State.[112] The 1991 Draft Code, in enumerating the crimes against the peace and security of mankind, simply repeats the language of Article 3(g) of the Definition of Aggression.[113]

Since assaults by irregular troops, armed bands or terrorists are typically conducted by small groups, employing hit-and-run pin-prick tactics, the *de minimis* clause of the General Assembly's Definition of Aggression is clearly apposite. To qualify as an armed attack, assaults of this kind must be (in the words of the Definition) of "sufficient gravity".[114] This is not to say that every single incident, considered independently, has to meet the standard of sufficient gravity. A persuasive argument can be made that, should a distinctive pattern of behaviour emerge, a series of pin-prick assaults

---

[109] *Supra*, note 40, at 143.

[110] *Supra*, note 31, at 103.

[111] General Assembly Resolution No. 2625 (xxv), 25 *R.G.A.* 121, 123 (1970).

[112] Report of the International Law Commission, 6th Session, [1954] II *I.L.C. Ybk* 140, 151 (Article 2(4)).

[113] Report of the International Law Commission, 43rd Session, 244 (mimeographed, 1991) (Article 15(4)(g)).

[114] See V. Cassin, W. Debevoise, H. Kailes and T. W. Thompson, "The Definition of Aggression", 16 *H.I.L.J.* 589, 607-8 (1975).

might be weighed in its totality and count as an armed attack[115] (see *infra*, Chapter 8, A, (a), ii).

The Judgment in the *Nicaragua* case pronounced that "while the concept of an armed attack includes the despatch by one State of armed bands into the territory of another State, the supply of arms and other support to such bands cannot be equated with armed attack".[116] The Court did "not believe" that "assistance to rebels in the form of the provision of weapons or logistical or other support" rates as an armed attack.[117] These are sweeping statements that ought to be narrowed down. In his Dissenting Opinion, Judge Sir Robert Jennings expressed the view that, whereas "the mere provision of arms cannot be said to amount to an armed attack", it may qualify as such when coupled with "logistical or other support".[118] In another dissent, Judge Schwebel stressed the words "substantial involvement therein" (appearing in Article 3(g) of the Definition of Aggression), which are incompatible with the language used by the majority.[119]

As observed by R. Ago, in a report to the International Law Commission, when a State "encourages and even promotes" the organization of armed bands against another State (i.e. if it provides them with weapons, training or financial assistance), the bands may be considered *"de facto* organs" of the State.[120] The International Law Commission stated that whenever individuals or groups in fact act on behalf of a State, their conduct is attributed to that State and is considered an act of State under international law.[121] Arms shipments alone may not be equivalent to an armed attack.[122] But when the overall policy of the Arcadian Government discloses that it conspires with armed bands fighting against Utopia, Arcadia is definitely committing an armed attack. The armed attack is not

---

[115] See Y. Z. Blum, "State Response to Acts of Terrorism", 19 *G.Y.I.L.* 223, 233 (1976).

[116] *Supra*, note 31, at 126-7.

[117] *Ibid.*, 104.

[118] *Ibid.*, 543.

[119] *Ibid.*, 349.

[120] R. Ago, "Fourth Report on State Responsibility", [1972] II *I.L.C. Ybk* 71, 120.

[121] Report of the International Law Commission, 26th Session, [1974] II (1) *I.L.C. Ybk* 157, 277 (Article 8).

[122] See J. P. Rowles, "'Secret Wars', Self-Defense and the Charter - A Reply to Professor Moore", 80 *A.J.I.L.* 568, 579 (1986).

extenuated by the subterfuge of indirect aggression or by reliance on a surrogate.[123]

C. Conditions Precedent to the Exercise of Self-Defence

The International Court of Justice pointed out, in the *Nicaragua* case, that Article 51 "does not contain any specific rule whereby self-defence would warrant only measures which are proportional to the armed attack and necessary to respond to it, a rule well established in customary international law".[124] It is usually taken for granted that, although Article 51 is silent on this topic, the exercise of the right of self-defence is never admissible unless the two conditions precedent of necessity and proportionality - generally accompanied by a third condition of immediacy - are satisfied.[125] As we shall see *infra* (Chapter 8, B, (c)), these conditions are distilled from yardsticks set out by the American Secretary of State, D. Webster, more than a century ago.

The three conditions will be dissected, in the contexts of the different modes of self-defence, in Chapter 8. But, in broad outline, the first requirement denotes that there exists a necessity to rely on force (in response to the armed attack) because no alternative means of redress is available.[126] In other words, "force should not be considered necessary until peaceful measures have been found wanting or when they clearly would be futile".[127] When efforts to resolve the problem amicably are made, they should be carried out in good faith and not only as a matter of "ritual punctilio".[128]

The second condition is frequently depicted as "of the essence of self-defence",[129] although it is not always easy to establish what proportionality entails. Ago correctly remarked that the principle

---

[123] See M. A. Harry, "The Right of Self-Defense and the Use of Armed Force against States Aiding Insurgency", 11 *S.I.U.L.J.* 1289, 1299 (1986-7).
[124] *Supra,* note 31, at 94.
[125] See R. Ago, *supra,* note 14, at 69.
[126] See *ibid., id.*
[127] See O. Schachter, *supra,* note 94, at 1635.
[128] N. Rostow, "Nicaragua and the Law of Self-Defense Revisited", 11 *Y.J.I.L.* 437, 455 (1985-6).
[129] I. Brownlie, *International Law and the Use of Force by States* 279 n. 2 (1963).

of proportionality must be applied with some degree of flexibility.[130] We shall discuss *infra* (Chapter 8, A) the different implications of proportionality, depending on whether the measures taken in self-defence constitute war or are short of war. It is perhaps best to consider the demand for proportionality in the province of self-defence as a standard of reasonableness in the response to force by counter-force.[131]

Immediacy signifies that there must not be an undue time-lag between the armed attack and the invocation of self-defence. However, the rule is subject to certain caveats that we shall trace.

In the *Nicaragua* case, the Court rejected on other grounds a claim of (collective) self-defence by the United States. As a result, no decision in respect of necessity and proportionality (or immediacy) was required *stricto sensu*.[132] All the same, the Court commented that the condition of necessity (coupled with the condition of immediacy) was not fulfilled, inasmuch as the United States commenced its activities several months after the presumed armed attack had occurred and when the main danger could be eliminated in a different manner.[133] The condition of proportionality was not met either, according to the Judgment, in view of the relative scale of the initial measures and counter-measures.[134] It must be noted, however, that Judge Schwebel strongly disagreed with these factual findings in his Dissenting Opinion.[135]

D. *The Role of the Security Council*

(a) *The Two Phases Rule*

The excuse of self-defence has often been used by aggressors bent on scoring propaganda points. Brutal armed attacks have taken place while the attacking State sanctimoniously assured world

---

[130] R. Ago, *supra*, note 14, at 69.
[131] See K. W. Quigley, "A Framework for Evaluating the Legality of the United States Intervention in Nicaragua", 17 *N.Y.U.J.I.L.P.* 155, 180 (1984-5).
[132] *Supra*, note 31, at 122.
[133] *Ibid.*, *id.*
[134] *Ibid.*, *id.*
[135] *Ibid.*, 362-9.

public opinion that it was only responding with counter-force to the (mythical) use of force by the other side. If every State were the final arbiter of the legality of its own acts, if every State could cloak an armed attack with the disguise of self-defence, the international legal endeavour to hold force in check would have been an exercise in futility.

From another perspective, the gist of self-defence is self-help (see *supra*, A, (a)). The facts of life at present are such that a State confronted with an armed attack cannot seriously expect an effective international police force to come to its aid and repel the aggressor (see *infra*, Chapter 10, C). The State under attack has no choice but to defend itself as best it can. It must also act without undue loss of time, and, most certainly, it cannot afford the luxury of waiting for any juridical (let alone judicial) scrutiny of the situation to run its course.

The upshot is that the process of self-defence must consist of two separate stages.[136] Phase one is when the option of recourse to self-defence is left to the unfettered discretion of the victim State (and any third State ready to oppose the aggressor). The acting State determines whether the occasion calls for the use of forcible measures in self-defence, and, if so, what specific steps ought to be taken. But all this is preliminary. In the second and final phase, a competent international forum has to be empowered to review the whole flow of events and to gauge the legality of the force employed. Above all, the competent forum must be authorized to arrive at the conclusion that the banner of self-defence has been falsely brandished by an aggressor.

The Judgment of the International Military Tribunal at *Nuremberg* fully endorsed the two stages concept:

> It was further argued that Germany alone could decide, in accordance with the reservations made by many of the Signatory Powers at the time of the conclusion of the Kellogg-Briand Pact, whether preventive action was a necessity, and that in making her decision her judgment was conclusive. But whether action taken under the claim of self-defense was in fact aggressive or defensive must

---

[136] See L. Oppenheim, *supra*, note 50, at 187-8.

ultimately be subject to investigation and adjudication if international law is ever to be enforced.[137]

The International Military Tribunal for the Far East at *Tokyo* rephrased the same idea in its own words:

The right of self-defence involves the right of the State threatened with impending attack to judge for itself in the first instance whether it is justified in resorting to force. Under the most liberal interpretation of the Kellogg-Briand Pact, the right of self-defence does not confer upon the State resorting to war the authority to make a final determination upon the justification for its action.[138]

The decisive issue, of course, is whether a competent international forum has actually been assigned the task of investigating the legality of any forcible measures taken by a State in reliance on self-defence. One of the great achievements of the UN Charter is that Article 51 enables the Security Council to undertake a review of self-defence claims raised by Member States.

The Security Council is the sole international organ mentioned in Article 51. Nevertheless, as the 1986 Judgment in the *Nicaragua* case elucidated, the legitimacy of recourse to self-defence may also be explored – in appropriate circumstances – by the International Court of Justice. There is a general problem (to be discussed *infra*, Chapter 10, E, (b)) engendered by the potential concurrent jurisdictions of the Council and the Court. In any event, the Court in the *Nicaragua* case held (in 1984) that, because self-defence is a right, it has legal dimensions and judicial proceedings are not foreclosed in consequence of the authority of the Council.[139]

In his Dissenting Opinion of 1986, Judge Schwebel completely quashed the argument (advanced by some writers) that "the use of force in self-defence is a political question which no court, including the International Court of Justice, should adjudge".[140] He then grappled with a different (albeit related) view, pressed by the

---

[137] International Military Tribunal (*Nuremberg*), Judgment (1946), 1 *I.M.T.* 171, 208.
[138] *Supra,* note 28, at 364.
[139] *Case Concerning Military and Paramilitary Activities in and against Nicaragua* (Jurisdiction), [1984] *I.C.J. Rep.* 392, 436.
[140] *Supra,* note 31, at 285-7.

United States, that the capacity to determine the legality of the exercise of self-defence, especially in an on-going armed conflict, is exclusively entrusted by Article 51 to the Security Council and withheld from the Court.[141] After some deliberation, Judge Schwebel denied the validity of this contention, and yet, in his opinion – owing to the special circumstances of the case – the issue of self-defence was not justiciable at the time the Judgment was rendered.[142] The majority of the Court refused to admit the claim of injusticiability in whole or in part.[143]

Another problem connected with judicial proceedings is whether a State may resort to the use of force in self-defence after the dispute has been submitted to adjudication by the International Court of Justice. This is what the United States did, in 1980, in the unsuccessful attempt to release American hostages from Iranian captivity (see *supra*, B, (b)). The Judgment in the *Tehran* case included an *obiter dictum* to the effect that such an operation may "undermine respect for the judicial process in international relations".[144] Sir Robert Jennings admonished that "force, even lawful and justifiable force, should not be undertaken in respect of a matter which is *sub judice*, perhaps least of all by the party which itself initiated the Court proceedings".[145] However, in some exceptional situations, a litigant State may have no practical choice but to rely on forcible counter-measures *pendente lite* (for instance, when hostilities are resumed by the other side).[146]

(b) *The Options before the Security Council*

Under Article 51, a State using force in self-defence, in response to an armed attack, acts at its own discretion but also at its own risk. Measures implementing the right of self-defence must immediately be reported to the Security Council. The Council may study all the

---

[141] *Ibid.*, 287.
[142] *Ibid.*, 288-96.
[143] *Ibid.*, 26-8.
[144] *Supra*, note 84, at 43.
[145] R. Jennings, "International Force and the International Court of Justice", *The Current Legal Regulation of the Use of Force* 323, 330 (A. Cassese ed., 1986).
[146] See O. Schachter, *supra*, note 83, at 341-2.

relevant facts,[147] although it is not compelled to set in motion a thorough fact-finding process.[148] With or without a careful examination of the background, the Council is entitled to take any action it deems fit in order to maintain or restore international peace and security.

The modes of action open to the Council are manifold. *Inter alia*, the Council can (i) give its retrospective seal of approval to the exercise of self-defence; (ii) impose a general cease-fire (see *supra*, Chapter 2, C, (a), ii); (iii) demand withdrawal of forces to the original lines;[149] (iv) insist on the cessation of the unilateral action of the defending State, supplanting it with measures of collective security (see *infra*, Chapter 10); or (v) decide that the State engaged in so-called self-defence is in reality the aggressor. Either way, a mandatory decision adopted by the Council in this matter is binding on UN Members. Once a Member State is instructed in a conclusive manner to refrain from any further use of force, it must comply with the Council's directive.

Evidently, the Council is not a judicial body. It is, in the words of Judge Schwebel, "a political organ which acts for political reasons".[150] As a political body, the Council may choose to sacrifice the interests of an individual State for the sake of more general interests of international peace (as perceived by the Council).[151] The State concerned may resent such a decision and sincerely believe that the Council has been extremely unfair. But, under the Charter, the State has no remedy. If it declines to obey the Council's decision, the State may bear the brunt of measures of collective security.

---

[147] See N. Q. Dinh, "La Légitime Défense d'après la Charte des Nations Unies", 52 *R.G.D.I.P.* 223, 239 (1948).

[148] On the difficulties immanent in this process, see R. B. Bilder, "The Fact/Law Distinction in International Adjudication", *Fact-Finding before International Tribunals* 95-8 (R. B. Lillich ed., 1992).

[149] Such a step may be taken either separately or jointly with the preceding measure. For a resolution demanding both a cease-fire and a withdrawal of forces to internationally recognized boundaries, see, e.g., Security Council Resolution No. 598, 42 *R.D.S.C.* 5, 6 (1987). For two separate (albeit consecutive) resolutions making similar calls, see, e.g., Security Council Resolutions Nos. 508 and 509, 42 *ibid.*, 5-6 (1982).

[150] *Supra*, note 31, at 290.

[151] See D. W. Bowett, *supra*, note 47, at 197.

Unfortunately, in almost half a century, the Council has displayed time and again a reluctance or inability to adopt a decision identifying the aggressor in a specific armed conflict. For most of the period, the inaction of the Council was largely due to the profound rift between the blocs in the context of the "cold war". The termination of this rivalry has not brought about the millennium. Even when faced with an obvious case of an armed attack, political considerations may prevent the Council from taking a concerted stand. In the absence of an authoritative determination as to who actually attacked whom, both opposing parties can pretend that they are acting in legitimate self-defence, and the hostilities are likely to go on. To avert further carnage, the Council tends to bring about at least a cease-fire.

Article 51 sets forth that the right of self-defence may be exercised until the Council has taken the measures necessary to maintain international peace and security. Whenever the Council decrees in a binding manner a withdrawal of forces or a cease-fire, the legal position is unequivocal: every Member State is obligated to act as the Council ordains and it can no longer invoke self-defence. If the Council is paralyzed and fails to take any measure necessary to maintain international peace and security, the legal position is equally obvious: a Member State exercising the right of self-defence may persist in the use of force. But what is the legal status if the Council follows the middle of the road and refrains from issuing detailed instructions to the parties, merely calling upon them, say, to conduct negotiations aimed at settling their dispute? Does such a resolution terminate the entitlement of a Member State to rely on self-help?

Notwithstanding contrary views,[152] it is clearly not enough (under Article 51) for the Security Council to adopt just any resolution, in order to divest Member States of the right to continue to resort to force in self-defence against an armed attack.[153] Even when the

---

[152] See A. Chayes, "The Use of Force in the Persian Gulf", *Law and Force in the New International Order* 3, 5-6 (L. F. Damrosch and D. J. Scheffer eds., 1991). *Cf.* K. S. Elliott, "The New World Order and the Right of Self-Defense in the United Nations Charter", 15 *H.I.C.L.R.* 55, 68-9 (1991-2).

[153] See O. Schachter, "United Nations Law in the Gulf Conflict", 85 *A.J.I.L.* 453, 458 (1991). *Cf.* T. K. Plofchan, "Article 51: Limits on Self-Defense?", 13 *Mich.J.I.L.* 336, 372-3 (1991-2).

Council imposes economic sanctions in response to aggression, such measures by themselves cannot override the right of self-defence.[154] The only resolution that will engender that result is a legally binding decision, whereby the cessation of the (real or imagined) defensive action becomes imperative.[155] Short of such a measure, the Member State engaged in self-defence is not obligated to desist from the use of force. However, the defending State still acts at its own risk, perhaps more so than before. Continued hostilities may precipitate a decision by the Council against a self-proclaimed victim of an armed attack.[156]

(c) Failure to Report to the Security Council

The International Court of Justice, in the *Nicaragua* case, held that the reporting obligation to the Security Council pursuant to Article 51 does not constitute a part of customary international law (on which the Judgment was based).[157] Yet, the Court was of the opinion that, even "for the purpose of enquiry into the customary law position, the absence of a report may be one of the factors indicating whether the State in question was itself convinced that it was acting in self-defence".[158] The Court implied that - when the use of force is governed by the law of the Charter - a State is precluded from invoking the right of self-defence, if it fails to comply with the requirement of reporting to the Council.[159] When put in this light, the duty of reporting becomes a substantive condition and a limitation on the exercise of self-defence.[160]

Judge Schwebel disputed the majority's position, asserting that measures of self-defence may be either overt or covert (just as an armed attack may be overt or covert); covert actions - *ex hypothesi* - cannot be reported to the Council and thereby publicly

---

[154] See E. V. Rostow, "Until What? Enforcement Action or Collective Self-Defense?", 85 *A.J.I.L.* 506, 512-13 (1991).

[155] See C. H. M. Waldock, *supra*, note 60, at 495-6.

[156] See D. W. Bowett, *supra*, note 47, at 196.

[157] *Supra*, note 31, at 121.

[158] *Ibid.*, 105.

[159] *Ibid.*, 121-2.

[160] See P. S. Reichler and D. Wippman, "United States Armed Intervention in Nicaragua: A Rejoinder", 11 *Y.J.I.L.* 462, 471 (1985-6).

espoused.[161] In our view, the limitation of the reporting duty to overt operations is inconsistent with the Charter. Article 51 imposes a blanket obligation of reporting to the Council whenever the right of self-defence is exercised, and the text does not even hint at the possibility of making an exception for covert operations. Indeed, a covert military operation (supposedly undertaken in self-defence) may subvert the authority of the Council by creating a smokescreen concealing the true state of affairs.

But Judge Schwebel did not stop here. Proceeding to probe the purport of the duty under discussion, he arrived at the conclusion that the report to the Council is a procedural matter, and that, therefore, nonfeasance must not deprive a State of the substantive (and inherent) right of self-defence.[162] The nature of the reporting duty is the real issue. Should the report to the Council be regarded as a condition *sine qua non*, going to the heart of the right of self-defence, or is it a technical requirement?[163]

Article 51 does not say that non-performance of the reporting obligation carries fatal consequences for the invocation of the right of self-defence. The sequence of events envisaged by the framers of the Charter is such that initially a State takes measures in self-defence, and only thereafter does it have to transmit a report to the Council. The proposition that a failure to comport with the subsequent duty (to report) undermines the legality of the preceding measures (of self-defence) does not fit the scheme of Article 51.[164]

In practice, when States exercise the right of self-defence, they do not always respect the duty of reporting to the Council.[165] There

---

[161] *Supra*, note 31, at 374.

[162] *Ibid.*, 376–7.

[163] D. W. Greig has argued that "it hardly seems possible to have a mandatory provision in the Charter, to which there is no counterpart in customary international law, relating to the exercise of a power available under both sources". D. W. Greig, "Self-Defence and the Security Council: What Does Article 51 Require?", 40 *I.C.L.Q.* 366, 380 (1991). But this position is unsound. As the Court explicitly pronounced in the context of self-defence: "The areas governed by the two sources of law thus do not overlap exactly, and the rules do not have the same content" (*supra*, note 31, at 94).

[164] See M. Knisbacher, "The Entebbe Operation: A Legal Analysis of Israel's Rescue Action", 12 *J.I.L.E.* 57, 79 (1977–8).

[165] See J. Combacau, "The Exception of Self-Defence in U.N. Practice", *The Current Legal Regulation of the Use of Force, supra*, note 145, at 9, 15.

are numerous reasons for such an omission. Among others, Governments are apt to conjure up wrong pleas instead of relying on self-defence.[166]

It is submitted that the dispatch of a report to the Council is only one of the many factors bearing upon the legitimacy of a State's claim to self-defence. The instantaneous transmittal of a report is no guarantee that the Council will accept that claim. Conversely, the failure to file a report at an early stage should not prove an irremediable defect. If it is convinced that forcible measures were taken by a State in self-defence, the Council ought to issue a ruling to that effect, despite the absence of a report. It would be a gross misinterpretation of Article 51 for the Council to repudiate self-defence, thus condoning an armed attack, only because no report has been put on record. Certainly, if measures responsive to an armed attack are brought to the attention of the Council in an indirect manner (not earning the formal status of a report), the defending State must be absolved.[167] But even if the Council is not promptly informed of what is going on, due to lack of skill in reducing complex patterns of behaviour to Article 51 phraseology, that need not doom the entitlement to self-defence. A failure by a State resorting to force to invoke self-defence should not be fatal, provided that the substantive conditions for the exercise of this right are met.[168] Governments do not always couch their official statements in correct juridical terms. It makes no sense to allow an aggressor State to get away with an armed attack only by dint of mislabelling by the victim State of an otherwise legitimate conduct.

[166] See *ibid.*, 14.

[167] See J. N. Moore, "The Secret War in Central America and the Future of World Order", 80 *A.J.I.L..* 43, 90 n. 189 (1986).

[168] See L. C. Green, "Armed Conflict, War, and Self-Defence", 6 *Ar.V.* 387, 434 (1956-7).

CHAPTER 8

THE MODALITY OF INDIVIDUAL SELF-DEFENCE

In Chapter 7, we have dealt with several problems pertaining to the interpretation of the expression "armed attack", which constitutes the foundation of the right of self-defence under Article 51 of the Charter of the United Nations.[1] This chapter will sketch the optional modes of self-defence available to a State facing an armed attack. At the beginning of our discussion it should be pointed out that, for an armed attack to justify counter-measures of self-defence under Article 51, it need not be committed by another State. Ordinarily, the perpetrator of the armed attack is indeed a foreign State as such. Yet, in exceptional circumstances, an armed attack – although mounted *from* the territory of a foreign State – is not launched *by* that State. Whether an armed attack is initiated by or only from a foreign country, the target State is allowed to resort to self-defence by responding to unlawful force with lawful counter-force. Given, however, the different features of the two types of armed attack, we shall address them separately.

A. *Self-Defence in Response to an Armed Attack by a State*

The expression "self-defence", as used in Article 51 or in customary international law, is by no means self-explanatory. It is a tag attached to the legitimate use of counter-force. Like its corollary (armed attack), self-defence assumes more than one concrete form. The cardinal division, here as elsewhere when the use of force by States is at issue, is between war and measures short of war.

---

[1] Charter of the United Nations, 1945, 9 *Int.Leg.* 327, 346.

(a) *Measures Short of War*

i. *On-the-Spot Reaction*

The first category of self-defence relates to the case in which a small-scale armed attack elicits at once, and *in situ*, the employment of counter-force (thereby closing the incident). This is probably the most recurrent manifestation of self-defence in the world of reality. Nevertheless, as a rule, international lawyers scarcely distinguish it from other modes of self-defence. In the absence of a universally accepted appellation, the present writer offers the phrase "on-the-spot reaction", which underscores the principal characteristic of such a manner of using counter-force.

To illustrate on-the-spot reaction in practice, let us take two examples. First, suppose that a Utopian patrol, moving along the common international frontier, is subjected to intense fire by troops from Arcadian outposts. The Utopian patrol (possibly aided by other units nearby) returns fire, in order to extricate itself from the ambush, or even assaults the Arcadian position whence the attack has been delivered. It is our contention that the clash consists of an armed attack by Arcadia and self-defence by Utopia, despite dicta by the International Court of Justice in the *Nicaragua* case attempting to set an armed attack apart from "a mere frontier incident"[2] (see *supra*, Chapter 7, B, (b), ii).

Secondly, suppose that a Numidian destroyer on the high seas drops depth charges upon a Ruritanian submarine, and the submarine responds by firing torpedoes against the destroyer. Authorities agree that vessels on the high seas may use counter-force to repel an attack by other vessels or by aircraft.[3] The International Court of Justice, in the *Corfu Channel* case of 1949, seems to have taken it for granted that warships passing through international waterways are entitled to "retaliate quickly if fired upon" by coastal batteries.[4] These are clearly measures of self-defence warranted by Article 51, as well as by customary international law.

---

[2] *Case Concerning Military and Paramilitary Activities in and against Nicaragua* (Merits), [1986] *I.C.J. Rep.* 14, 103.

[3] See I. Brownlie, *International Law and the Use of Force by States* 305 (1963).

[4] *Corfu Channel* Case (Merits), [1949] *I.C.J. Rep.* 4, 31.

For on-the-spot reaction to be legitimized as self-defence, it must be in harmony with the three conditions of necessity, proportionality and immediacy (see *supra*, Chapter 7, C). Immediacy is immanent in the nature of on-the-spot reaction: the employment of counter-force must be temporally interlocked with the armed attack triggering it. Consequently, the requirement of necessity should be assessed from the vantage point of the local command. That is to say, alternative courses of action, not entailing the use of counter-force, can only be weighed as a matter of tactics rather than grand strategy. If the sequence of events includes "time out" for high-level consultations between the two Governments, in an effort to defuse the explosive situation, on-the-spot reaction is no longer a relevant mode of self-defence. As for proportionality, it means that the "scale and effects"[5] of force and counter-force must be similar. Excessive counter-force is ruled out as a permissible on-the-spot reaction.

Genuine on-the-spot reaction closes the incident. This category of self-defence does not cover actions by other units in other zones, or even future operations by the same unit which bore the brunt of the original armed attack. Admittedly, one exchange of fire can lead to another in a chain effect, so that - through gradual escalation - large military contingents will be engaged in combat. Yet, if the fighting fades away soon, the closed episode may still be reckoned as on-the-spot reaction. By contrast, should the original small incident evolve into a full-scale invasion or a prolonged campaign, the rubric of on-the-spot reaction is no longer appropriate as a legal classification of what has transpired.

ii. Defensive Armed Reprisals

Generally speaking, reprisals constitute "counter-measures that would be illegal if not for the prior illegal act of the State against which they are directed".[6] While most reprisals are non-forcible, we shall focus on armed reprisals. Apart from unarmed reprisals, the

---

[5] These are the words of the International Court of Justice used, however, in a different context. *Supra*, note 2, at 103. See *supra*, Chapter 7, B, (b), ii.

[6] O. Schachter, "International Law in Theory and Practice", 178 *R.C.A.D.I.* 9, 168 (1982).

term ought to remove from consideration "belligerent reprisals", namely, reprisals resorted to by belligerents in the midst of hostilities, after an armed conflict has begun.[7]

Armed reprisals are measures of counter-force, short of war, undertaken by one State against another in response to an earlier violation of international law. Like all other instances of unilateral use of force by States, armed reprisals are prohibited unless they qualify as an exercise of self-defence under Article 51. Only defensive armed reprisals are allowed. They must come in response to an armed attack, as opposed to other violations of international law, in circumstances satisfying all the requirements of legitimate self-defence.

A juxtaposition of defensive armed reprisals and on-the-spot reaction discloses points of resemblance as well as divergence. In both instances, the use of counter-force is limited to measures short of war. But when activating defensive armed reprisals, the responding State strikes at a time and a place different from those of the original armed attack. In the two hypothetical examples adduced above, the script must be altered as follows: (i) a few days after the Utopian patrol is fired upon by Arcadian troops, an Arcadian patrol is shelled by Utopian artillery, or Utopian commandoes raid a military base in Arcadia from which the original attack was sprung; (ii) subsequent to the depth-charging of the Ruritanian submarine by a Numidian destroyer on the high seas, a Ruritanian aircraft strafes a Numidian missile boat a thousand miles away.

The choice of the time and place for putting into operation defensive armed reprisals, like that of the object against which they are to be directed, is made by the victim State (Utopia or Ruritania). The decision obviously depends on considerations of where, when and how to deal a blow that would be most advantageous to that State. The actions taken "need not mirror offensive measures of the aggressor".[8] All the same, the rights of third States must be taken into account. This is particularly true if the defensive armed reprisals are likely to endanger international shipping at sea.[9]

---

[7] See F. Kalshoven, *Belligerent Reprisals* 33-6 (1971).

[8] *Supra*, note 2, at 379 (Dissenting Opinion of Judge Schwebel).

[9] See *ibid.*, 379-80. See also *ibid.*, 112 (Judgment of the Court); 536-7 (Dissenting Opinion of Judge Sir Robert Jennings).

When States implement defensive armed reprisals, their operations must be guided by the basic norms of the *jus in bello* (chiefly, international humanitarian law). This is true of all uses of force, even short of war (see *supra*, Chapter 1, B, (a)), and defensive armed reprisals are no exception. The interplay between international humanitarian law and defensive armed reprisals is complicated, however, by a number of treaty stipulations.

The four 1949 Geneva Conventions for the Protection of War Victims forbid certain acts of reprisals against protected persons (such as prisoners of war) and objects.[10] A parallel clause appears in Article 4(4) of the 1954 Hague Convention for the Protection of Cultural Property in the Event of Armed Conflict.[11] Protocol I of 1977, Additional to the Geneva Conventions, goes much further in banning a whole range of acts of reprisals.[12] Thus, "[a]ttacks against the civilian population or civilians by way of reprisals are prohibited" under Article 51(6) of the Protocol.[13] Article 60(5) of the 1969 Vienna Convention on the Law of Treaties makes it clear that "provisions prohibiting any form of reprisals" against protected persons, contained in treaties of a humanitarian character, are not subject to the application of the general rules enabling termination or suspension of a treaty as a consequence of its material breach by another party.[14]

In essence, the measures of reprisals interdicted in the instruments cited amount to belligerent reprisals. By their nature, the strictures of the Geneva Conventions (or the Hague Convention) are germane to defensive armed reprisals no more than they are to

---

[10] (First) Geneva Convention for the Amelioration of the Condition of the Wounded and Sick in Armed Forces in the Field, 1949, 75 *U.N.T.S.* 31, 60 (Article 46); (Second) Geneva Convention for the Amelioration of the Condition of Wounded, Sick and Shipwrecked Members of Armed Forces at Sea, 1949, *ibid.,* 85, 114 (Article 47); (Third) Geneva Convention Relative to the Treatment of Prisoners of War, 1949, *ibid.,* 135, 146 (Article 13); (Fourth) Geneva Convention Relative to the Protection of Civilian Persons in Time of War, 1949, *ibid.,* 287, 310 (Article 33).

[11] Hague Convention for the Protection of Cultural Property in the Event of Armed Conflict, 1954, 249 *U.N.T.S.* 240, 244.

[12] Protocol Additional to the Geneva Conventions of 12 August 1949, and Relating to the Protection of Victims of International Armed Conflicts (Protocol I), 1977, [1977] *U.N.J.Y.* 95, 103, 114-16 (Articles 20, 51(6), 52(1), 53(c), 54(4), 55(2) and 56(4)).

[13] *Ibid.,* 114.

[14] Vienna Convention on the Law of Treaties, 1969, [1969] *U.N.J.Y.* 140, 156.

other situations in which inter-State force is employed. If prisoners of war are captured in the course of defensive armed reprisals, they must be protected (as in all other types of hostilities), and the protection encompasses an immunity from belligerent reprisals. But even if a prisoner of war is unlawfully exposed to belligerent reprisals during a military operation characterized as a defensive armed reprisal, the legitimacy of the whole operation (as an act of counterforce in response to an armed attack) is not compromised by that breach.

A different outcome is apparently produced by the broader prohibitions of reprisals incorporated in Protocol I. Although the injunctions of the Protocol were also intended to cope with the problem of belligerent reprisals,[15] it may be inferred from their language that the discretion of a State contemplating defensive armed reprisals is curtailed where the choice of objectives for counter-strikes is concerned. If the original armed attack by Atlantica was directed against the Patagonian civilian population, Patagonia might wish (as a *quid pro quo*) to requite the wrongful action with defensive armed reprisals aimed equally at civilians. Nonetheless, under Article 51(6) of the Protocol, should Atlantican civilians be the target of Patagonian armed reprisals, the whole retaliatory operation would be illegal.[16]

Assuming that this is the correct reading of Protocol I, a considerable change is introduced in the potential application of defensive armed reprisals. Yet, it must be appreciated that the Protocol's provisions on the subject of reprisals are controversial.[17] Although the Protocol irrefutably constitutes "an authoritative text for extensive areas of international humanitarian law",[18] the sweeping proscription of reprisals against civilians is by no means declaratory of

---

[15] See S. E. Nahlik, "Belligerent Reprisals as Seen in the Light of the Diplomatic Conference on Humanitarian Law, Geneva, 1974-7", 42(2) *L.C.P.* 36-66 (1978).

[16] See F. J. Hampson, "Belligerent Reprisals and the 1977 Protocols to the Geneva Conventions of 1949", 37 *I.C.L.Q.* 818, 837 (1988).

[17] See G. B. Roberts, "The New Rules for Waging War: The Case against Ratification of Additional Protocol I", 26 *V.J.I.L.* 109, 139-46 (1985-6). *Cf.* G. H. Aldrich, "Progressive Development of the Laws of War. A Reply to Criticisms of the 1977 Geneva Protocol I", *ibid.,* 693, 710-11.

[18] H. P. Gasser, "Book Review" [of the first edition of this volume], 29 *I.R.R.C.* 256, *id.* (1989).

customary international law. Due account must be taken of the facts that the United States has formally decided not to ratify Protocol I because it "is fundamentally and irreconcilably flawed",[19] and that the instrument was not applied in the course of the Gulf War.[20] It remains to be seen whether the text will have any meaningful effect even on the practice of contracting parties to the Protocol *inter se*.[21]

As in other circumstances in which self-defence is invoked, defensive armed reprisals must meet the conditions of necessity, proportionality and immediacy. Proportionality is the quintessential factor in appraising the legitimacy of the counter-measures executed by the responding State. This was highlighted in the 1928 Arbitral Award, rendered in a dispute between Portugal and Germany, in the *Naulilaa* case.[22] The proceedings related to an incident that had taken place in 1914, shortly after the outbreak of the First World War (at a time when Portugal was still a neutral State), on the border between the German colony of South-West Africa (present-day Namibia) and the Portuguese colony of Angola. In that incident, three German nationals (one civilian official and two army officers) were shot dead. In retaliation, the German forces attacked and destroyed a number of Portuguese installations in Angola over a period of several weeks. The Arbitrators held that these measures were excessively disproportionate.[23]

It is unrealistic to expect defensive armed reprisals to conform strictly and literally to the tenet of "an eye for an eye". A precise equation of casualties and damage, caused by both sides (in the course of the armed attack and the defensive armed reprisals), is neither a necessary nor a possible condition. All the more so, since in every military operation there is an element of chance, and defensive armed reprisals can unpredictably cause more casualties

[19] Agora: The US Decision Not to Ratify Protocol I to the Geneva Conventions on the Protection of War Victims, 81 *A.J.I.L.* 910, 911 (1987).
[20] US Department of Defense Report to Congress on the Conduct of the Persian Gulf War, 1992, 31 *I.L.M.* 612, 617 (1992).
[21] See Y. Dinstein, "The New Geneva Protocols", 33 *Y.B.W.A.* 265, 277 (1979).
[22] *Naulilaa* Case (1928), 2 *R.I.A.A.* 1011, 1026.
[23] *Ibid*, 1028.

and damage than anticipated.[24] However, the responding State must adapt the magnitude of its counter-measures to the "scale and effects" of the armed attack. A calculus of force, introducing some symmetry or approximation between the dimensions of the lawful counter-force and the original (unlawful) use of force, is imperative.

As for necessity, considering that defensive armed reprisals (unlike on-the-spot reaction) anyhow post-date the initial armed attack, recourse by the victim State to counter-force is contingent on its first seeking in vain a peaceful solution to the dispute. This is another requisite condition pronounced by the Arbitrators in the *Naulilaa* case.[25] If the attacking State is ready to discharge its duty of making reparation to the target State - in conformity with the general rules of State responsibility (see *supra*, Chapter 4, F, (a)) - defensive armed reprisals would be illicit. But the need to consider alternatives to the use of counter-force does not mean that the injured State must embroil itself in prolonged and frustrating negotiations. If no redress is offered within reasonable time, a State confronted with an armed attack is entitled to put in effect measures of defensive armed reprisals.

The right of the victim State to avoid dilatory stratagems is tied in with the rule that defensive armed reprisals must also meet the requirement of immediacy. It is unlawful to engage in these measures of counter-force in response to an event that occurred in the remote past. An inordinate procrastination is liable to erode the linkage between force and counter-force, which is the matrix of the legitimacy of defensive armed reprisals.

The view expressed here, whereby armed reprisals can be a permissible form of self-defence (in response to an armed attack) under Article 51, is supported by some scholars.[26] It must be conceded, however, that most writers deny that self-defence pursuant

---

[24] *Cf.* J. H. H. Weiler, "Armed Intervention in a Dichotomized World: The Case of Grenada", *The Current Legal Regulation of the Use of Force* 241, 250 (A. Cassese ed., 1986).

[25] *Supra*, note 22, at 1026-7.

[26] See, e.g., K. Skubiszewski, "Use of Force by States. Collective Security. Law of War and Neutrality", *Manual of Public International Law* 739, 754 (M. Sørensen ed., 1968): "armed reprisals that are taken in self-defence against an armed attack are permitted". *Cf.* E. S. Colbert, *Retaliation in International Law* 202-3 (1948).

to Article 51 may ever embrace armed reprisals.[27] The International Law Commission, too, neatly separated the concepts of armed reprisals and self-defence.[28] The bifurcation is derived from the perception that armed reprisals take place "after the event and when the harm has already been inflicted", their purpose always being punitive rather than defensive.[29] In our opinion, this is a narrow approach which, to a large extent, is influenced by nomenclature. The legal analysis might benefit if the term "armed reprisals" were simply abandoned. Thus, O. Schachter comes to the conclusion that, whereas punitive armed reprisals are forbidden, "defensive retaliation" is justified when its prime motive is protective.[30]

The assertion that all armed reprisals are unlawful is incompatible with the Charter's regulation of the use of force between States. The general prohibition of recourse to inter-State force is subject to the exception of self-defence when an armed attack occurs. Both the prohibition and the exception apply to every mode of forcible action in international relations, including armed reprisals. If armed reprisals are taken in response to an ordinary breach of international law (not constituting an armed attack), they are unlawful.[31] Armed reprisals are also proscribed if they are not adapted to the demands of proportionality, necessity and immediacy. On the other hand, if armed reprisals can be subsumed under the heading of self-defence, they are admissible.[32]

Armed reprisals do not qualify as legitimate self-defence if they are impelled by purely punitive, non-defensive, motives.[33] But the

---

[27] See especially I. Brownlie, *supra*, note 3, at 281 (and authorities cited there).
[28] Report of the International Law Commission, 32nd Session, [1980] II (2) *I.L.C. Ybk* 1, 53-4.
[29] See D. Bowett, "Reprisals Involving Recourse to Armed Force", 66 *A.J.I.L.* 1, 3 (1972).
[30] O. Schachter, "The Right of States to Use Armed Force", 82 *Mich.L.R.* 1620, 1638 (1984).
[31] See H. Mosler, *The International Society as a Legal Community* 280 (1980).
[32] See G. Arangio-Ruiz, "The Normative Role of the General Assembly of the United Nations and the Declaration of Principles of Friendly Relations", 137 *R.C.A.D.I.* 419, 531 (1972). *Cf.* G. Arangio-Ruiz, "Third Report on State Responsibility" (Add. 1) 12-14 (mimeographed, 1991).
[33] It has been suggested that "[i]n considering whether an armed reprisal is consistent with article 51, the retributive or other motivation of the state is irrelevant". L. C. Green, "Book Review" [of the first edition of this volume], 27 *C.J.T.L.* 483, 503 (1988-9). However, unmodulated retribution cannot be squared with self-defence.

motives driving States to action are usually multifaceted, and a tinge of retribution can probably be traced in every instance of response to force. The question is whether armed reprisals in a concrete situation go beyond retribution. To be defensive, and therefore lawful, armed reprisals must be future-oriented, and not limited to a desire to punish past transgressions. *In fine*, the issue is whether the unlawful use of force by the other side is likely to repeat itself. The goal of defensive armed reprisals is to "induce a delinquent state to abide by the law in the future", and hence they have a deterrent function.[34] A signal that playing with fire constitutes a dangerous game is what most armed reprisals are all about. At times, armed reprisals have immediate defensive implications. To borrow an example from W. Wengler, if Arcadian troops invade the territory of Utopia, it would be "no less self-defence" for the Utopian armed forces to occupy an area belonging to Arcadia (in order to divert the military attention of the aggressor) than to resist the invading troops.[35]

There is no reason why the built-in time-lag between the original armed attack and the response of the target State, which is an inevitable feature in all armed reprisals, should divest the counter-measures of their self-defence nature.[36] The passage of time between the use of unlawful force and lawful counter-force is not unique to defensive armed reprisals. It is an attribute that defensive armed reprisals have in common with a war of self-defence undertaken in response to an armed attack short of war. Such a war, too, commences after some deliberation by policy-makers in the victim State (see *infra*, (b)). By the time that a decision is taken to employ counter-force, it is possible that the attacking military formations have already accomplished the mission assigned to them (say, the occupation of a contested mountain ridge) and they are at a standstill. Even in circumstances of on-the-spot reaction, the initial strike (for instance, an artillery barrage) may come to an end before the target

---

[34] R. W. Tucker, "Reprisals and Self-Defense: The Customary Law", 66 *A.J.I.L.* 586, 591 (1972).

[35] W. Wengler, "Public International Law. Paradoxes of a Legal Order", 158 *R.C.A.D.I.* 9, 22 (1977).

[36] See D. W. Bowett, "Book Review" [of the first edition of this volume], 59 *B.Y.B.I.L.* 263, 265 (1988).

units set in motion measures of counter-force. It is occasionally propounded that self-defence must always be undertaken while the armed attack is in progress, and that it cannot be exercised once the attacking State has consummated active military operations.[37] But this is an unacceptable thesis that would merely encourage an aggressor to adopt *Blitz* methods of combat.

In the final analysis, defensive armed reprisals are post-attack measures of self-defence short of war. The availability of such a weapon in its arsenal provides the victim State with a singularly important option. If this option were to have been eliminated from the gamut of legitimate self-defence, the State upon which an armed attack is inflicted would have been able to respond only with either on-the-spot reaction or war. On-the-spot reaction is dissatisfactory because it is predicated on employing counter-force on the spur of the moment, meaning that hostilities (i) erupt without any (or, at least, any serious) involvement of the political branch of the Government; and (ii) take place at a time as well as a place chosen by the attacking State, usually at a disadvantage for the defending State. War, for its part, requires a momentous decision that may alter irreversibly the course of history. Defensive armed reprisals enable the target State to fine-tune its response to an armed attack by relying on an intermediate means of self-defence, avoiding war but adding temporal and spatial nuances to on-the-spot reaction.

It would be incomprehensible for war to be acknowledged – as it is – as a legitimate form of self-defence in response to an isolated armed attack, if defensive armed reprisals were inadmissible. Taking into account that Article 51 allows maximal use of counter-force (war) in self-defence, there is every reason for a more calibrated form of counter-force (defensive armed reprisals) to be legitimate as well.

Evidently, international law is created in the practice of States and not in scholarly writings. Even if there existed clarity on the doctrinal level that a State "is not entitled to exercise a right of reprisal in modern international law", this would merely serve "to

---

[37] See G. M. Badr, "The Exculpatory Effect of Self-Defense in State Responsibility", 10 *G.J.I.C.L.* 1, 26 (1980).

discredit doctrinal approaches to legal analysis".[38] Since the entry
into force of the UN Charter, the record is replete with cases of
defensive armed reprisals effected by many countries (including
the Big Powers), although they frequently shy away from the expression "reprisals". Thus, in April 1986, American air strikes were
launched against several targets in Libya, in exercise of the right of
self-defence, subsequent to Libyan attacks against American citizens and installations.[39] In substance, these were acts of defensive
armed reprisals.

It is true that, on more than one occasion, the Security Council
has condemned armed reprisals "as incompatible with the purposes
and principles of the United Nations".[40] However, an examination
of its more recent decisions and deliberations seems to indicate that
the Council "may now be moving towards a partial acceptance of
'reasonable' reprisals".[41] This development "finds some support in
theory and in practice".[42]

The 1970 General Assembly Declaration on Principles of International Law Concerning Friendly Relations and Co-operation
among States in accordance with the Charter of the United Nations
proclaims that "States have a duty to refrain from acts of reprisal
involving the use of force".[43] In like manner, President Singh, in his
Separate Opinion in the Nicaragua case of 1986, stated that recourse
to armed reprisals is illegal.[44] But it is interesting to note that the
Judgment of the Court, in evaluating certain American actions in
Nicaragua (such as the laying of mines in or close to Nicaraguan
ports) which were clearly in the nature of armed reprisals - while
rejecting their justification as acts of collective self-defence[45] -

---

[38] R. A. Falk, "The Beirut Raid and the International Law of Retaliation", 63 A.J.I.L.
415, 430 (1969).
[39] See Contemporary Practice of the United States Relating to International Law,
80 A.J.I.L. 632–6 (1986).
[40] Security Council Resolution No. 188, 19 R.D.S.C. 9, 10 (1964). Cf. Security Council
Resolution No. 270, 24 ibid., 4, id. (1969).
[41] See D. Bowett, supra, note 29, at 21.
[42] D. W. Greig, International Law 889 (2nd ed., 1976).
[43] General Assembly Resolution No. 2625 (XXV), 25 R.G.A. 121, 122 (1970).
[44] Supra, note 2, at 151.
[45] Ibid., 48, 146–7.

refrained from ruling that all armed reprisals are automatically unlawful.

No country in the world seems to have adhered more consistently to a policy of defensive armed reprisals than the State of Israel. For those who negate the entire concept of defensive armed reprisals under the Charter, all acts labelled as such are lumped together in one mass of illegality. More correctly, each measure of counter-force should be put to the test whether it amounts to legitimate self-defence (in response to an armed attack), satisfying the requirements of necessity, proportionality and immediacy. When this is done, some of the Israeli armed reprisals appear to pass muster, whereas others do not. The crux of the issue in almost every instance is proportionality. The general problem is compounded in Israel's case by its predilection for a response in one extensive military operation to a cluster of pin-prick assaults taking place over a long stretch of time.[46]

When defensive armed reprisals are tailored to the measurements of an "accumulation of events", they are susceptible of charges of disproportionality.[47] But much depends on the factual background. If continuous pin-prick assaults form a distinctive pattern, a cogent argument can be made for appraising them in their totality as an armed attack[48] (see *supra*, Chapter 7, B, (b), v). It is well worth observing that R. Ago, while disavowing the legitimacy of all armed reprisals, enunciated the following rule (in the context of self-defence) in a report to the International Law Commission:

If ... a State suffers a series of successive and different acts of armed attack from another State, the requirement of proportionality will certainly not mean that the victim State is not free to undertake a single armed action on a much larger scale in order to put an end to this escalating succession of attacks.[49]

---

[46] See B. Levenfeld, "Israel Counter-*Fedayeen* Tactics in Lebanon: Self-Defense and Reprisal under Modern International Law", 21 *C.J.T.L.* 1, 40 (1982-3).

[47] See D. Bowett, *supra*, note 29, at 7.

[48] See N. M. Feder, "Reading the U.N. Charter Connotatively: Toward a New Definition of Armed Attack", 19 *N.Y.U.J.I.L.P.* 395, 415-16 (1986-7).

[49] R. Ago, "Addendum to Eighth Report on State Responsibility", [1980] II (1) *I.L.C. Ybk* 13, 69-70.

A legitimate application of what might be regarded as a book-keeping ledger to an aggregation of pin-prick attacks would only emphasize the element of elasticity, which is anyhow characteristic of the concept of proportionality.

iii. The Protection of Nationals Abroad

We have already indicated (*supra*, Chapter 7, B, (b), iv) that the use of force by Arcadia within its own territory, against Utopian nationals, is considered by many to constitute an armed attack against Utopia. If that is the case, forcible counter-measures employed by Utopia may rate as self-defence, provided that the usual conditions of necessity, proportionality and immediacy are complied with.[50] Sir Humphrey Waldock reiterated these conditions in somewhat different wording, fitting better the specific context of the protection of nationals abroad:

> There must be (1) an imminent threat of injury to nationals, (2) a failure or inability on the part of the territorial sovereign to protect them and (3) measures of protection strictly confined to the object of protecting them against injury.[51]

International practice abounds with incidents in which one country uses force within the territory of another, in order to protect or rescue nationals, while invoking self-defence.[52] Obviously, rescue missions (usually conducted against terrorists holding foreign nationals as hostages) cannot be counted as precedents if they are carried out with the consent of the Government of the local State.[53] However, from time to time, either there is a breakdown of law and order in the local State or its Government aids and abets those who put the foreign nationals in jeopardy. In such circumstances,

---

[50] See C. Greenwood, "International Law and the United States' Air Operation against Libya", 89 *W. V.L.R.* 933, 941 (1986-7).

[51] C. H. M. Waldock, "The Regulation of the Use of Force by Individual States in International Law", 81 *R.C.A.D.I.* 451, 467 (1952).

[52] See N. Ronzitti, *Rescuing Nationals Abroad through Military Coercion and Intervention on Grounds of Humanity* 30–44 (1985).

[53] See I. Brownlie, "The Principle of Non-Use of Force in Contemporary International Law", *The Non-Use of Force in International Law* 17, 23 (W. E. Butler ed., 1989).

military operations have been put in motion unilaterally by the State of nationality, with a view to securing the lives of its citizens. As an illustration, we may cite the joint Belgian-American action to rescue nationals of the two countries in the Congo in 1964.[54] A more questionable case was the landing of American troops in the Dominican Republic in 1965.[55] A particularly controversial instance was the military action taken by the United States in Grenada, in 1983, the central justification of which was the protection of approximately a thousand endangered US citizens (mainly medical students) in a chaotic situation in the island.[56] It is not easy to reconcile the operation with the three conditions enumerated by Sir Humphrey.[57] The most telling point against the American expedition is that Grenada remained occupied for months, long after the evacuation of the US nationals had been completed.[58] The principle of proportionality requires that any incursion of this nature be terminated as soon as possible, with a minimal encroachment on the sovereignty of the local State.[59] For the same reason, an attempt to predicate the legality of the United States invasion and occupation of Panama in 1989 on the need to safeguard the lives of American citizens in that country appears to be contrived.[60]

The "clearest example" of a State fulfilling the three conditions, as listed by Sir Humphrey, was the Israeli rescue mission in Entebbe

[54] See A. Gerard, "L'Opération Stanleyville-Paulis devant le Parlement Belge et les Nations Unies", [1967] *R.B.D.I.* 242, 254-6.
[55] See V. P. Nanda, "The United States' Action in the 1965 Dominican Crisis: Impact on World Order – Part I", 43 *D.L.J.* 439, 444-72 (1966).
[56] See W. C. Gilmore, *The Grenada Intervention* 31, 56 (1984).
[57] See *ibid*, 61-4.
[58] See V. P. Nanda, "The United States Armed Intervention in Grenada – Impact on World Order", 14 *C.W.I.L.J.* 395, 410-11 (1984). An intriguing question has been raised "why, in a case such as Grenada, a post hoc request by the local constitutional authorities for the US forces to remain until order was restored could not be valid". J. N. McNeill, "Book Review" [of the first edition of this volume], 84 *A.J.I.L.* 305, 306 (1990). But a *post hoc* request to stay in the local territory cannot escape suspicions concerning the genuine motives and objectives of the intervening State.
[59] See A. Abramovsky and P. L. Greene, "Unilateral Intervention on Behalf of Hijacked American Nationals Held Abroad", [1979] *U.L.R.* 231, 246.
[60] See V. P. Nanda, "The Validity of United States Intervention in Panama under International Law", 84 *A.J.I.L.* 494, 496-7 (1990). *Cf.* R. Wedgwood, "The Use of Armed Force in International Affairs: Self-Defense and the Panama Invasion", 29 *C.J.T.L.* 609, 621-2 (1991).

airport in 1976.[61] The action brought about the release of Israeli (and other Jewish) passengers of an Air France plane, hijacked by terrorists and held as hostages with the connivance of the Ugandan Government of the day headed by Idi Amin.[62] Even if the use of force on behalf of nationals abroad cannot be given open-ended approval as an exercise of self-defence, there are several exceptional features serving to legitimize the Entebbe raid:

a. Although the terrorists did not use Uganda as their regular base of operations, the Ugandan Government was directly implicated in keeping the hostages under detention. It is necessary to distinguish between cases of civil disturbances (or riots) in Arcadia, in which Utopian nationals are attacked without any complicity on the part of the Arcadian Government, and actions against Utopian nationals committed with the blessing of the Arcadian Government. A rescue mission of the Entebbe type – aimed at releasing hostages held by terrorists in another country – is justifiable as self-defence when the powers-that-be collaborate with the terrorists, whereas, in the absence of official wrongdoing, the prior consent of the local Government would usually be required before any forcible action is mobilized from the outside.[63]

b. "[T]he hostages were seized and held as part of a political action against the state of their nationality. The attack on the individuals was clearly meant as an attack on their government".[64] This is an immensely important factor at a time when international terrorists display a growing tendency to strike at innocent bystanders in Arcadia only because of their link of nationality to Utopia. If the victims are pre-selected as targets owing to their Utopian nationality, the equation between the use of force against them and an armed attack against Utopia (an equation which is the key to the exercise of the right of self-defence by Utopia) becomes unmistakable.

---

[61] O. Schachter, *supra*, note 30, at 1630.

[62] For the facts, see L. C. Green, "Rescue at Entebbe – Legal Aspects", 6. *I.Y.H.R.* 312, 313-15 (1976).

[63] See F. C. Pedersen, "Controlling International Terrorism: An Analysis of Unilateral Force and Proposals for Multilateral Cooperation", 8 *U.T.L.R.* 209, 222 (1976-7).

[64] O. Schachter, "In Defense of International Rules on the Use of Force", 53 *U.C.L.R.* 113, 139 n. 107 (1986).

c. The Israeli nationals did not go to Uganda volitionally: they were brought there against their will, in violation of international law.[65] The exceptional circumstances of their entry into the territory of the local State affect the exceptional remedy (of recourse to force) made accessible to the State of nationality.

d. The Entebbe raid was the epitome of a "surgical" military sortie. It compares well with the massive intervention in some other instances, e.g., Grenada, because it was "an in-out operation".[66] Nobody could claim that Israel took the action "as a pretext" to remain in Uganda.[67]

For all these reasons, Israel was entitled under Article 51 to use counter-force in self-defence, securing the release of its captive nationals in Uganda. Since the Entebbe raid was not in breach of the Charter, its legality is not affected by Article 14 of the 1979 International Convention against the Taking of Hostages,[68] which reads:

Nothing in this Convention shall be construed as justifying the violation of the territorial integrity or political independence of a State in contravention of the Charter of the United Nations.[69]

The fact that some non-Israeli hostages were also saved cannot diminish from the legality of the operation.[70] But it must be noted that the deliverance of the non-Israeli hostages was merely a by-product of the successful rescue of Israeli nationals. As an exercise of the right of self-defence, the protection of nationals abroad must not be confused with humanitarian intervention (see *supra*, Chapter

[65] See M. Akehurst, "The Use of Force to Protect Nationals Abroad", 5 *Int.Rel.* 3, 21 (1977).

[66] L. C. Green, "The Rule of Law and the Use of Force - The Falklands and Grenada", 24 *Ar.V.* 173, 189 (1986).

[67] O. Schachter, "International Law in the Hostage Crisis: Implications for Future Cases", *American Hostages in Iran* 325, 331 (W. Christopher *et al.* eds., 1985).

[68] See J. L. Lambert, *Terrorism and Hostages in International Law - A Commentary on the Hostages Convention 1979* 322-3 (1990).

[69] International Convention against the Taking of Hostages, 1979, [1979] *U.N.J.Y.* 124, 127.

[70] See D. W. Bowett, "The Use of Force for the Protection of Nationals Abroad", *The Current Legal Regulation of the Use of Force, supra*, note 24, at 39, 44.

4, B, (b)).[71] The rationale of self-defence, exercised in response to an armed attack against individuals abroad, is founded on the nexus of nationality; it is inapplicable when the human rights of non-nationals are deprived.[72]

(b) War

War as an act of self-defence denotes comprehensive use of counter-force in response to an armed attack. It is sometimes hard to perceive that war can be a legitimate measure. But there is no doubt that, in some situations, "[t]he right of self-defense is ... a right to resort to war".[73] In other words, "[a] forcible act of self-defense may amount to or may result in war".[74] To lower the psychological barrier, H. Kelsen contrasted war (a delict) with counter-war (a sanction), saying: "[w]ar and counterwar are in the same reciprocal relation as murder and capital punishment".[75] While the distinction is useful in many circumstances, it is not infallible. Utopia (the defending State) does not always respond with counter-war to war. Actually, Utopia may be the one initiating war, in response to an Arcadian armed attack short of war. In such a case, what we are facing is not war (started by Arcadia) and counter-war (waged by Utopia), but an isolated armed attack (commenced by Arcadia) and war (conducted in response by Utopia).

The salient questions arising in the context of a war of self-defence relate to the operation of the three conditions of necessity, proportionality and immediacy.

---

[71] We cannot accept the proposition (advocated, e.g., by L. Henkin, "The Invasion of Panama under International Law: A Gross Violation", 29 *C.J.T.L.* 293, 296-7 (1991)) that a so-called Entebbe principle – as a legitimate form of humanitarian intervention – constitutes an exception to the general prohibition of the use of inter-State force pursuant to Article 2(4) of the Charter, irrespective of the provision of Article 51.

[72] See A. Jeffery, "The American Hostages in Tehran: The I.C.J. and the Legality of Rescue Missions", 30 *I.C.L.Q.* 717, 725 (1981).

[73] J. L. Kunz, "Individual and Collective Self-Defense in Article 51 of the Charter of the United Nations", 41 *A.J.I.L.* 872, 877 (1947). *Cf.* R. R. Baxter, "The Legal Consequences of the Unlawful Use of Force under the Charter", [1968] *P.A.S.I.L.* 68, 74.

[74] P. C. Jessup, *A Modern Law of Nations* 163 (1948).

[75] H. Kelsen, *Principles of International Law* 28 (1st ed., 1952).

i. Necessity

When a war of self-defence is triggered by an all-out invasion, the issue of necessity usually becomes moot. The target State is by no means expected "to allow an invasion to proceed without resistance on the ground that peaceful settlement should be sought first".[76] Necessity comes to the fore when war is begun following an isolated armed attack. Before the defending State opens the floodgates to full-scale hostilities, it is obligated to verify that a reasonable settlement of the conflict in an amicable way is not attainable.

ii. Proportionality

The condition of proportionality has a special meaning in the context of a war of self-defence. When on-the-spot reaction or defensive armed reprisals are involved, proportionality points at a symmetry or an approximation in "scale and effects" between the unlawful force and the lawful counter-force (see *supra*, (a)). To gauge proportionality in these settings, a comparison must be made between the quantum of force and counter-force used, as well as the casualties and damage sustained.[77] Such a comparison can only be drawn *a posteriori*, weighing in the balance the acts of force and counter-force in their totality (from the first to the last moment of fighting).

Proportionality in this sense, albeit appropriate for the purposes of on-the-spot reaction and defensive armed reprisals, is unsuited for an investigation of the legitimacy of a war of self-defence. Once war is raging, the exercise of self-defence may bring about "the destruction of the enemy's army", notwithstanding the condition of proportionality.[78] The absence of correspondence between the original injury and the ensuing conflagration is conspicuous when war is waged in response to an isolated armed attack. By its nature, war (as a comprehensive use of force) is virtually bound to be

[76] O. Schachter, *supra*, note 30, at 1635.
[77] See *ibid.*, 1637.
[78] D. Alland, "International Responsibility and Sanctions: Self-Defence and Countermeasures in the ILC Codification of Rules Governing International Responsibility", *United Nations Codification of State Responsibility* 143, 183 (M. Spinedi and B. Simma eds., 1987).

disproportionate to any measure short of war. The scale of counter-force used by the victim State in a war of self-defence will be far in excess of the magnitude of the original force employed in an armed attack short of war, and the devastation caused by the war will surpass the destructive effects of the initial use of unlawful force. Proportionality, as an approximation of the overall force employed (or damage caused) by the two opposing sides, cannot be the yardstick for determining the legality of a war of self-defence caused by an isolated armed attack.

At the same time, it would be utterly incongruous to permit an all-out war whenever a State absorbs an isolated armed attack, however marginal. A war of self-defence is the most extreme and lethal course of action open to a State, and it must not be allowed to happen on a flimsy excuse. Proportionality has to be a major consideration in pondering the legitimacy of a defensive war, only the criteria for its application ought to be different from what they are in settings short of war. When war is on the agenda, the comparative evaluation of force and counter-force has to take place not at the termination of the exercise of self-defence but at its inception. The decision has to be predicated on the gravity of the isolated armed attack and the degree to which the target State is jeopardized.

War as a measure of self-defence is legitimate, in response to an armed attack short of war, only if vindicated by the critical character of the attack. There is no similarity between a minor skirmish and an artillery duel in which hundreds of cannons are thundering. It is possible to say that, in certain situations, quantity turns into quality. Only when it is established (upon sifting the factual evidence) that the original armed attack was serious enough, is the victim State free to launch war.

Whether a war of self-defence is conducted as a counter-war or in response to an isolated armed attack, once it is legitimately started, it can be fought to the finish (despite any ultimate lack of proportionality). As Ago commented, in a report to the International Law Commission:

> It would be mistaken ... to think that there must be proportionality between the conduct constituting the armed attack and the opposing conduct. The action needed to halt and repulse the

attack may well have to assume dimensions disproportionate to those of the attack suffered. What matters in this respect is the result to be achieved by the "defensive" action, and not the forms, substance and strength of the action itself.[79]

A better understanding of the applicability of the principle of proportionality to a war of self-defence may facilitate the legal analysis of the controversial "first use" of nuclear weapons. Because of the intrinsic nature and the immeasurable destructive consequences of nuclear devices, some scholars argue that their use is generally proscribed (if only by analogy and implication) by contemporary international law.[80] Although the contention is upheld by a Declaration adopted (by majority vote) in 1961 by the General Assembly,[81] it has been rejected by many commentators and – more significantly – by the leading members of the nuclear club.[82] If it is postulated that the explosion of nuclear weapons is not automatically forbidden, the argument is made that, for reasons of disproportionality, a defending State is disentitled to introduce their use when the aggressor resorts only to conventional weapons.[83] However, the prevalent opinion is that a State, legitimately engaged in a war of self-defence, may marshal against the aggressor all weapons not explicitly banned by the laws of warfare.[84] Of course, the choice of targets for nuclear (as well as other) weapons must be made consonant with the rules of the *jus in bello*.[85]

An aggressor State may lose its appetite for continuing with the hostilities, but the defending State need not be accommodating. It is occasionally maintained that, as soon as an armed attack is permanently repelled, the exercise of self-defence "must cease".[86]

---

[79] R. Ago, *supra*, note 49, at 69.
[80] See E. L. Meyrowitz, "The Laws of War and Nuclear Weapons", 9 *B.J.I.L.* 227-58 (1983).
[81] General Assembly Resolution No. 1653 (XVI), 16(1) *R.G.A.* 4, 5 (1961).
[82] See J. N. Moore, "Nuclear Weapons and the Law: Enhancing Strategic Stability", 9 *B.J.I.L.* 263, 265 (1983).
[83] See N. Singh and E. McWhinney, *Nuclear Weapons and Contemporary International Law* 100 (2nd ed., 1989).
[84] See I. Brownlie, *supra*, note 3, at 263.
[85] See Y. Dinstein, "Existing Legal Constraints on Nuclear Proliferation", *Lawyers and the Nuclear Debate* 61, 62 (M. Cohen and M. E. Gouin eds., 1988).
[86] N. Singh and E. McWhinney, *supra*, note 83, at 102.

A similar argument is that, owing to the requirement of proportionality, recourse to counter-force in self-defence has to be confined to the space where the armed attack was launched and should not be extended to remote areas.[87] But these are misconceptions. As illustrated in the Gulf War, self-defence operations can legitimately take place throughout the region of war (see *supra*, Chapter 1, C), and there is no need to adjust to artificial geographic limitations conveniencing the aggressor. In general, post-Charter State practice shows that "self-defence, individual and collective, may carry the combat to the source of the aggression".[88] War, if waged legitimately as a response to an armed attack, need not be terminated at the point when the aggressor is driven back, and it may be carried on by the defending State until final victory.[89] Particularly when engaged in a successful response to a large-scale invasion, the defending State – far from being bound to stop at the frontier – may pursue the retreating enemy forces, hammering at them up to the time of their total defeat.[90]

Thus, following Pearl Harbor, the United States could – and did – seek unconditional surrender of Japan (see *supra*, Chapter 6, B), and hostilities were not confined to stemming the tide of aggression. After the outbreak of hostilities, "no moral or legal duty exists for a belligerent to stop the war when his opponent is ready to concede the object for which war was made".[91] In the Iran-Iraq war, once the Iraqi invasion (launched in 1980) failed to crush Iran and degenerated into military stalemate, Iraq was more than willing to call off the fighting while Iran insisted on proceeding with the war to the point of completely defeating the enemy.[92] Iran was fully empowered to take that stand, as long as it did not defy a legally binding Security Council resolution decreeing cease-fire (see *infra*,

---

[87] See C. Greenwood, "Self-Defence and the Conduct of International Armed Conflict", *International Law at a Time of Perplexity: Essays in Honour of Shabtai Rosenne* 273, 277 (Y. Dinstein ed., 1989).

[88] *Supra*, note 2, at 371 (Dissenting Opinion of Judge Schwebel).

[89] See J. L. Kunz, *supra*, note 73, at 876.

[90] See J. Zourek, "La Notion de Légitime Défense en Droit International", 56 *A.I.D.I.* 1, 49-50 (Wiesbaden, 1975).

[91] L. Oppenheim, 2 *International Law* 225 (7th ed., by H. Lauterpacht, 1952).

[92] See S. H. Amin, "The Iran-Iraq Conflict: Legal Implications", 31 *I.C.L.Q.* 167, 186 (1982).

Chapter 10, A). After several resolutions of a recommendatory nature, the Council issued a mandatory demand for cease-fire in 1987.[93] This was Resolution No. 598,[94] actually complied with by Iran only in 1988.[95]

In the Gulf War, had it desired to do so, Kuwait (supported by the international coalition which came to its rescue) could have chased the beaten Iraqi forces all the way to the last bunker in Baghdad. The allegation that - under Resolution No. 678 (1990)[96] - the Security Council "authorized force only to liberate Kuwait",[97] is groundless. Since the Council confirmed the entitlement of Kuwait and those cooperating with it to exercise self-defence (see *infra*, Chapter 9, E), there was no legal impediment to extending the hostilities across Iraq's border. In fact, the Gulf War displays the hazards of using sparingly counter-force in self-defence. As soon as Saddam Hussein realized that his regime was safe, Iraq reiterated its territorial claims against Kuwait and reverted to a policy of harassing the latter's border. Violations of the terms of the cease-fire, imposed on Iraq in Resolution No. 687 (1991),[98] leave the Council discredited. Not surprisingly, the American-led coalition had to launch several air strikes at Iraq, in January 1993, hoping that these would impel the Government in Baghdad to refrain from further provocations.

iii. Immediacy

War may not be undertaken in self-defence long after an isolated armed attack. Yet, there are two notable provisos. First, a war of self-defence does not have to commence within a few minutes, or even a few days, from the original armed attack. A State under attack cannot be expected to shift gear from peace to war instantaneously.

---

[93] See M. J. Ferretti, "The Iran-Iraq War: United Nations Resolution of Armed Conflict", 35 *Vill.L.R.* 197, 204-28 (1990).

[94] Security Council Resolution No. 598, 42 *R.D.S.C.* 5, 6 (1987).

[95] See K. H. Kaikobad, "'*Ius ad Bellum*': Legal Implications of the Iran-Iraq War", *The Gulf War of 1980-1988* 51, 70 (I. F. Dekker and H. H. G. Post eds., 1992).

[96] Security Council Resolution No. 678, 45 *R.D.S.C.* 27-8 (1990).

[97] M. E. O'Connell, "Enforcing the Prohibition on the Use of Force: The UN's Response to Iraq's Invasion of Kuwait", 15 *S.I.U.L.J.* 453, 479 (1990-1).

[98] Security Council Resolution No. 687, 31 *I.L.M.* 847, 849 (1991).

A description of a human being under attack as having "no moment for deliberation" would be accurate. But when such an expression is applied to a State confronted with an armed attack (see *infra*, B, (b)), it is a hyperbolic statement. Front-line officers in the target country must report to, and receive instructions from, headquarters. The high command is not inclined to embark upon full-scale hostilities, in response to an isolated armed attack, without some deliberation. When there is no military junta in power, the civilian Government will have to give a green light to the armed forces. In all, moving forward to a war of self-defence is a time-consuming process, especially in a democracy where the wheels of government grind slowly. P. C. Jessup remarked that "[t]elegraphic or radio communication between the officer and his superiors can be taken as a counterpart of the impulses in the nervous system of the individual whose brain instructs his arm to strike".[99] This is true only in a metaphorical sense. Despite the means of modern communication available in the electronic age, States respond to pressure more tardily than individuals.

Secondly, even when the interval between an armed attack and a recourse to war of self-defence is longer than usual, the war may still be legitimate if the delay is warranted by circumstances. Suppose that Numidian troops forcibly occupy a part of the territory of Ruritania. Instead of promptly employing counter-force, Ruritania elects to give amicable negotiations a try (thus meeting the aforementioned condition of necessity). If the negotiations fail, and Ruritania then resorts to war, the action ought to be regarded as self-defence notwithstanding the lapse of time.[100] The Gulf War shows that the use of counter-force in self-defence can begin almost half a year after the armed attack. The condition of immediacy was not transgressed, inasmuch as persistent attempts to resolve the conflict amicably were foiled by Iraqi obduracy. Claims that the option of self-defence existed in early August 1990 but expired a few months later[101] are simply fallacious.

---

[99] P. C. Jessup, *supra*, note 74, at 164.

[100] J. Barboza, "Necessity (Revisited) in International Law", *Essays in International Law in Honour of Judge M. Lachs* 27, 41 (J. Makarczyk ed., 1984).

[101] See T. Yoxall, "Iraq and Article 51: A Correct Use of Limited Authority", 25 *Int.Law.* 967, 985 (1991).

A justifiable delay in the response of Ruritania may also occur when the region forcibly occupied by Numidia is distant from the centre of Government, and lengthy preparations are required before the military machinery can function smoothly. The Falkland Islands War of 1982 concretizes this state of affairs.[102]

B. Self-Defence in Response to an Armed Attack from a State

(a) Extra-Territorial Law Enforcement

We have discussed the issue of armed bands operating against Utopia under conditions in which they may be deemed "de facto organs" of Arcadia[103] (see supra, Chapter 7, B, (b), v). The position is different when armed bands strike at Utopia, from a base of operations located within the territory of Arcadia, without being inspired or prodded by the Arcadian Government. One possibility is that the armed bands merely find a haven in the territory of Arcadia, and, while taking evasive action against the Arcadian security forces, emerge (when the opportunity presents itself) for hit-and-run attacks against Utopia. Alternatively, Arcadia may tolerate the presence of the armed bands on its soil without being linked to them so closely that they may be considered its "de facto organs".[104]

Clearly, Utopia is entitled to employ force within its own territory, so as to extirpate all hostile armed bands (wherever they come from). The question is whether, when the armed bands operate from within Arcadian territory but there is no complicity between them and the Arcadian Government, Utopia may take forcible counter-measures inside Arcadia.

The International Court of Justice pronounced, in the *Corfu Channel* case of 1949, that every State is under an obligation "not to allow knowingly its territory to be used for acts contrary to the rights of other States".[105] Accordingly, a State must not permit its

---

[102] See A. Cassese, "Article 51", *La Charte des Nations Unies* 769, 773 (J.-P. Cot and A. Pellet eds., 1985).

[103] R. Ago, "Fourth Report on State Responsibility", [1972] II *I.L.C. Ybk* 71, 120.

[104] See P. L. Zanardi, "Indirect Military Aggression", *The Current Legal Regulation of the Use of Force, supra,* note 24, at 111, 112-13.

[105] *Supra,* note 4, at 22.

territory to be used as a sanctuary for armed bands bent on attacking military or civilian objects in another country. It is irrefutable that the toleration by a State of activities by armed bands, directed against another country, is unlawful.[106] Under the 1954 Draft Code of Offences against the Peace and Security of Mankind, as formulated by the International Law Commission, such toleration even constitutes a crime under international law[107] (see *supra,* Chapter 7, B, (b), v).

In its Judgment of 1980, in the *Tehran* case, the International Court of Justice held that, if the authorities of one State are required under international law to take appropriate acts in order to protect the interests of another State, and – while they have the means at their disposal to do so – completely fail to comply with their obligations, the inactive State bears international responsibility towards the other State.[108] Indeed, a State which does not fulfil its international obligation of "vigilance", and fails "in its specific duty not to tolerate the preparation in its territory of actions which are directed against a foreign Government or which might endanger the latter's security", assumes international responsibility for this international wrongful act of omission[109] (see *supra,* Chapter 4, F).

Irrespective of questions of State responsibility, the assault by armed bands from Arcadian territory against objectives within the domain of Utopia may amount to an armed attack. Armed attacks by non-State armed bands are still armed attacks, even if commenced only from – and not by – another State.[110] It is no accident that, in 1967, the Security Council employed the phrase "armed attacks" several times, in a resolution condemning the failure of

---

[106] See I. Brownlie, "International Law and the Activities of Armed Bands", 7 *I.C.L.Q.* 712, 734 (1958).

[107] Report of the International Law Commission, 6th Session, [1954] II *I.L.C. Ybk* 140, 151 (Article 2(4)).

[108] *Case Concerning United States Diplomatic and Consular Staff in Tehran,* [1980] *I.C.J. Rep.* 3, 32-3, 44.

[109] R. Ago, *supra,* note 103, at 120.

[110] The crucial question is whether an armed attack actually occurred. Thus, a hypothetical military action by the United States against drug traffickers in Colombia would not be justifiable as self-defence. See J. R. Edmunds, "Nonconsensual U.S. Military Action against the Colombian Drug Lords under the U.N. Charter", 68 *W.U.L.Q.* 129, 154 (1990).

Portugal to prevent groups of mercenaries from using the territory of Angola (then under Portuguese administration) as a base of operations against Congo.[111]

Whereas Arcadia may bear international responsibility for having tolerated the activities of armed bands carrying out an armed attack from within its territory against Utopia, that does not mean that the armed attack as such is attributable to Arcadia. The conduct of Arcadia may be unlawful under international law, without constituting an armed attack on its part against Utopia.[112] For that matter, not always is Arcadia in any breach of international law. When armed bands turn a portion of Arcadian territory into a staging area for raids against Utopia, the Arcadian Government may not be aware of what is happening (especially when the armed bands organize in remote and sparsely populated areas). As long as Arcadia does not "knowingly" allow its territory to be used contrary to the rights of Utopia, Arcadia incurs no international responsibility towards Utopia under the *Corfu Channel* ruling.

Even when the Government of Arcadia is fully aware of the presence within its territory of armed bands hostile to Utopia, it may be incapable of putting an end to their activities. A Government does not always succeed in suppressing armed bands, which direct their activities against itself. *A fortiori*, the Government of Arcadia may be unable to stop the use of its territory as a springboard for attacks by armed bands against Utopia. However, it is incumbent on Arcadia, under international law, to exercise due diligence - that is, to take all reasonable measures called for by the situation - so as to prevent the armed bands from mounting attacks against Utopia, or to apprehend and punish them after an attack has been perpetrated.[113]

When the Government of Arcadia does not condone the operations of armed bands emanating from within its territory against Utopia, but it is too weak (militarily, politically or otherwise) to prevent these operations, Arcadian responsibility *vis-à-vis* Utopia (if

---

[111] Security Council Resolution No. 241, 22 *R.D.S.C.* 14, *id.* (1967).
[112] See P. L. Zanardi, *supra*, note 104, at 113.
[113] See R. B. Lillich and J. M. Paxman, "State Responsibility for Injuries to Aliens Occasioned by Terrorist Activities", 26 *Amer.U.L.R.* 217, 268-9, 275 (1976-7).

engaged at all) may be nominal. Nevertheless, it does not follow that Utopia must patiently endure painful blows, only because no sovereign State is to blame for the turn of events. All the more so, if Arcadia is in breach of international law towards Utopia, although the breach does not qualify as an inter-State armed attack. Just as Utopia is entitled to exercise self-defence against an armed attack by Arcadia, it is equally empowered to defend itself against armed bands operating from within the Arcadian territory.[114]

This is an extraordinary case demanding, and getting, an extraordinary solution in international law. Article 51 permits Utopia to resort to self-defence in response to an armed attack. Utopia may, therefore, dispatch military units into Arcadian territory, in order to destroy the bases of the hostile armed bands (provided that the destruction of the bases is the "sole object" of the expedition).[115] When Utopia takes these measures, it does what Arcadia itself should have done, "had it possessed the means and disposition to perform its duty".[116]

Like on-the-spot reaction, this category of self-defence has no generally accepted appellation. Now and then, there are references to "hot pursuit", but the phrase - borrowed from the law of the sea - is rooted in "a wholly untenable analogy".[117] The right of maritime hot pursuit forms an exception to the freedom of the high seas.[118] It is governed by Article 23 of the 1958 Geneva Convention on the High Seas,[119] and Article 111 of the 1982 United Nations Convention on the Law of the Sea.[120] In conformity with both provisions, the right of hot pursuit relates to a foreign ship that has violated the laws and regulations of the coastal State. Hot pursuit has to be uninterrupted, and it must be commenced when the offending ship

---

[114] See C. G. Fenwick, *International Law* 274 (4th ed., 1965).

[115] J. E. S. Fawcett, "Intervention in International Law. A Study of Some Recent Cases", 103 *R.C.A.D.I.* 343, 363 (1961).

[116] C. C. Hyde, 1 *International Law Chiefly as Interpreted and Applied by the United States* 240 (2nd ed., 1945).

[117] M. R. Garcia-Mora, *International Responsibility for Hostile Acts of Private Persons against Foreign States* 123 (1962).

[118] See N. M. Poulantzas, *The Right of Hot Pursuit in International Law* 39 (1969).

[119] Geneva Convention on the High Seas, 1958, 450 *U.N.T.S.* 82, 94-5.

[120] United Nations Convention on the Law of the Sea, 1982, 21 *I.L.M.* 1261, 1290 (1982).

(or one of its boats) is within the internal waters, the territorial sea or the contiguous zone of the coastal State (under the 1958 Convention), as well as the archipelagic waters (under the 1982 Convention, which also extends the right of hot pursuit *mutatis mutandis* to violations occurring in the exclusive economic zone or the continental shelf). Most significantly, the right of hot pursuit ceases as soon as the vessel being chased enters the territorial sea of its own country or of a third State. On land, the operation undertaken against hostile armed bands need not begin while they are still within the territory of the acting State; it does not have to be uninterrupted; and, far from coming to a halt at the border of a foreign State, it consists of an incursion into the territory of that State.

More often, the exercise of self-defence in the factual setting under discussion used to be called "necessity".[121] On the initiative of its Special Rapporteur on State Responsibility (Ago),[122] the International Law Commission even went so far as to deal with a situation of this kind – characterized as a state of necessity – apart from the concept of self-defence.[123] As a result of the notional disjunction between necessity and self-defence, the Commission did not really find an adequate solution to the problem of a State exposed to an armed attack from (rather than by) another State.[124] The separation between self-defence and necessity is artificial. As we shall see (*infra*, (b)), the use of cross-border counter-force against armed bands is historically tied to the subject of self-defence, and there is no reason to cut that umbilical cord. In any event, necessity has more than a few connotations in international law.[125] Within the very framework of self-defence, we have already encountered necessity (together with proportionality and immediacy) as a requisite condition for the admissibility of counter-force when an armed attack occurs.

---

[121] See L. Oppenheim, 1 *International Law* 298-9 (8th ed., by H. Lauterpacht, 1955).
[122] R. Ago, *supra*, note 49, at 39-40, 61-2.
[123] *Supra*, note 28, at 44, 57.
[124] *Cf.* P. Malanczuk, "Countermeasures and Self-Defence as Circumstances Precluding Wrongfulness in the International Law Commission's Draft Articles on State Responsibility", 43 *Z.A.O.R.V.* 705, 779-85 (1983).
[125] See *supra*, note 28, at 34-52.

In this study, we propose to use the idiom "extra-territorial law enforcement". We believe that it properly telescopes the notion of measures enforcing international law, taken by one State within the territory of another. Extra-territorial law enforcement is a form of self-defence, and it can be undertaken by Utopia against armed bands inside Arcadian territory, in response to an armed attack unleashed by them from that territory. Utopia is entitled to enforce international law extra-territorially only when Arcadia is unable or unwilling to prevent repetition of that armed attack.

(b) *The Practice of States*

Extra-territorial law enforcement as a mode of self-defence was most recently manifested in 1992, when Turkish troops crossed into Northern Iraq in an attempt to deny Kurdish armed bands a sanctuary in an enclave carved out of Iraq in the aftermath of the hostilities in the Gulf War (see *supra*, Chapter 4, B, (b)). However, the best contemporary illustration of extra-territorial law enforcement was provided by the Israeli incursion into Lebanon, in 1982, designed to destroy a vast complex of Palestinian bases from which multiple armed attacks across the international frontier had originated.[126] The Government of Lebanon was incapable of putting an end to the formidable Palestinian military presence within its territory, and Israel felt compelled to cope with the problem by sending a sizeable expeditionary force into Southern Lebanon. Israeli and Lebanese forces did not exchange fire at any point in 1982, and the Israeli operation did not amount to a war with Lebanon. Yet, Israeli and Syrian armed forces in Lebanon did clash vigorously. These hostilities formed another round in an on-going war between Israel and Syria that has been in progress (interspersed by lengthy ceasefires) since 1967 (see *supra*, Chapter 2, C, (b)).

A case of striking similarity was the American military expedition of 1916 into Mexico, provoked by attacks across the Rio Grande by Mexican armed bands headed by Francisco Villa, at a time when the central Government in Mexico City had little control over the

---

[126] For the facts, see B. A. Feinstein, "The Legality of the Use of Armed Force by Israel in Lebanon - June 1982", 20 *Is.L.R.* 362, 365-70 (1985).

outlying areas.[127] President Wilson justified the dispatch of a substantial force, pursuing the bandits deep into Mexican territory, as necessary to protect the American border from hostile attacks, since the Mexican authorities were powerless and there was no other remedy.[128]

There are other historical precedents for extra-territorial law enforcement in self-defence.[129] The most famous among them is the *Caroline* incident.[130] In 1837, during the Mackenzie Rebellion against the British rule in Upper Canada, the insurgents took over an island on the Canadian side of the Niagara River. The American population along the border largely sympathized with the cause of the rebellion, and the steamboat *Caroline* was used for transporting men and materials from the US bank of the Niagara River to the rebel-held island. When British protests failed to stop the line of supplies, a British unit crossed the border in the dark of night, boarded the vessel, set it on fire, and sent it drifting to eventual destruction upon the awesome Falls. In the course of the incident, several American citizens were killed or injured. The United States lodged a protest with the British Government for violating American sovereignty, but the British invoked self-defence. In his correspondence about the incident with British envoys (in 1841-2), Secretary of State D. Webster took the position that - for the claim of self-defence to be admitted - Britain is required to "show a necessity of self-defence, instant, overwhelming, leaving no choice of means, and no moment for deliberation".[131] The action taken must also involve "nothing unreasonable or excessive; since the act, justified by the necessity of self-defence, must be limited by that necessity, and kept clearly within it".[132] The British reply finally conciliated the United States, and the case was closed.[133]

---

[127] For the facts, see G. A. Finch, "Mexico and the United States", 11 *A.J.I.L.* 399-406 (1917).

[128] Quoted by C. C. Hyde, *supra*, note 116, at 244 n. 21.

[129] See, e.g., *ibid.*, 240 n. 7 (the case of the US incursion into West Florida in 1818).

[130] For the facts, see R. Y. Jennings, "The *Caroline* and McLeod Cases", 32 *A.J.I.L.* 82, 82-9 (1938).

[131] 29 *B.F.S.P.* 1129, 1138 (Webster to Fox) (1840-1).

[132] *Ibid., id.*

[133] 30 *B.F.S.P.* 195, 196-8 (Lord Ashburton to Webster); 201, *id.* (Webster to Lord Ashburton) (1841-2).

(c) Webster's Formula

The language used in Webster's correspondence, in the *Caroline* incident, made history. It came to be looked upon as transcending the specific legal contours of extra-territorial law enforcement, and has markedly influenced the general *materia* of self-defence. This has happened despite the lack of evidence that Webster had in mind any means of self-defence other than extra-territorial law enforcement, and notwithstanding the time-frame of the episode, which preceded the prohibition of the use of inter-State force. R. Y. Jennings called the *Caroline* incident the "*locus classicus*" of the law of self-defence.[134] More than a century after the episode, the International Military Tribunal at *Nuremberg* quoted Webster's formulation as a standard for evaluating (and rejecting) the German allegation that the invasion of Norway in 1940 - which had amounted to war and not to extra-territorial law enforcement - constituted a legitimate exercise of self-defence.[135] It is sometimes put forward that the rule emerging from the *Caroline* incident is no longer valid under the UN Charter.[136] But there is no corroboration of this view in the text of the Charter.

Although Webster's prose was inclined to overstatement, the three conditions of necessity, proportionality and immediacy can easily be detected in it. These conditions are now regarded as pertinent to all categories of self-defence (see *supra*, Chapter 7, C). We have seen in what different ways they are to be applied to on-the-spot reaction, defensive armed reprisals and war (see *supra*, A).

When Utopia resorts to extra-territorial law enforcement within the territory of Arcadia, the necessity to infringe upon Arcadian sovereignty has to be manifest. The forcible measures employed by Utopia must be reactive to an attack already committed by hostile armed bands, and not only anticipatory of what is no more than a future threat (see *supra*, Chapter 7, B, (a)). Additionally, a repetition of the attack has to be expected, so that the extra-territorial law enforcement can qualify as defensive and not purely punitive. The absence of alternative means for putting an end to the operations

---

[134] R. Y. Jennings, *supra*, note 130, at 92.
[135] International Military Tribunal (*Nuremberg*), Judgment (1946), 1 *I.M.T.* 171, 207.
[136] See M. R. Garcia-Mora, *supra*, note 117, at 119.

of the armed bands has to be demonstrated beyond reasonable doubt.

The condition of immediacy requires that the incursion by Utopia into Arcadian territory will take place soon after the assault by the armed bands, so that the cause (armed attack) and effect (self-defence) are plain for all to see. Besides, as accentuated by Webster, there has to be a perception of urgency impelling extra-territorial law enforcement before these bands strike again.

As for proportionality, when Utopia sends an expeditionary force into Arcadia, the operation is to be directed exclusively against the armed bands, and it must not be confused with defensive armed reprisals.[137] Surely, no forcible action may be taken against the Arcadian civilian population.[138] Furthermore, even the Arcadian armed forces and installations ought not to be harmed. If the Utopian expeditionary force – on its way to or from the target (viz. the bases of the armed bands) – encounters Arcadian military units, it is disallowed to open fire on them. Correspondingly, international law imposes on Arcadia a duty of "acquiescence", or non-interference, with the Utopian operation;[139] for there is no self-defence against self-defence (supra, Chapter 7, A, (b)).

If the Arcadian Government is too weak to suppress the activities of armed bands from within its territory against Utopia, Arcadia must not display unwonted prowess against the Utopian expeditionary force (which is only doing what Arcadia ought to have done in the first place). Should Arcadian troops open fire on the Utopian units, this could amount to an armed attack by Arcadia against Utopia, although the act is committed within Arcadian territory (see supra, Chapter 7, B, (b), iii). In point of fact, by demonstrating that it aids and abets the armed bands, Arcadia may now be charged with responsibility for the original armed attack perpetrated by these bands against Utopia.

---

[137] At least one writer uses the term "enforcement" in adverting to what is actually a defensive armed reprisal (directed at a Government). See A. D'Amato, *International Law: Process and Prospect* 29 (1987).

[138] See J. L. Taulbee, "Retaliation and Irregular Warfare in Contemporary International Law", 7 *Int.Law.* 195, 203 (1973).

[139] D. W. Bowett, *Self-Defence in International Law* 60 (1958).

CHAPTER 9

COLLECTIVE SELF-DEFENCE

A. *The Meaning of Collective Self-Defence*

The phrase "individual or collective self-defence", as used in Article 51 of the Charter of the United Nations[1] (see *supra*, Chapter 7, A, (a)), is not easily comprehensible. A close examination of the text, in the light of the practice of States, shows that more than a simple dichotomy is involved. It seems necessary to distinguish between no less than four categories of self-defence: (i) individual self-defence individually exercised; (ii) individual self-defence collectively exercised; (iii) collective self-defence individually exercised; and (iv) collective self-defence collectively exercised.

The first category represents the most straightforward exercise of the right of self-defence, and it has been dealt with in Chapter 8: Arcadia perpetrates an armed attack against Utopia, and in response Utopia resorts to self-defence. This is a one-on-one encounter, and the right of individual self-defence is applied individually.

The second category relates to the situation where an armed attack is launched by the same aggressor (Arcadia), either simultaneously or consecutively, against several States (Utopia, Ruritania, etc.). Both Utopia and Ruritania are entitled to resort to measures of individual self-defence against Arcadia. These measures may still be taken individually, each target State declining any suggestion of cooperation with the other. Utopia and Ruritania, while resisting armed attacks by the same aggressor (Arcadia), are not obliged to consolidate a united front. When recent relations between Utopia and Ruritania have been characterized by a deeply-felt animosity, let alone a long-standing antagonism with historical roots, either country is apt to be opposed to the idea of recasting the political landscape, and it may elect to act on its own.

However, particularly when a large-scale invasion is in progress, States trying to resist aggression tend to forget past grievances and

---

[1] Charter of the United Nations, 1945, 9 *Int.Leg.* 327, 346.

form a coalition, proceeding on the basis of the principle that "the enemy of my enemy is my friend". The essence of a coalition is that its members marshal their combined resources and act jointly in the exercise of their aggregate rights of self-defence. It is sometimes argued that such a situation was envisaged by the authors of the Charter when they referred to "collective" self-defence.[2] In actuality, rather than collective self-defence, what we have here is "nothing more than a plurality of acts of 'individual' self-defence committed collectively".[3]

A coalition in self-defence, dictated by expediency, emerged in the course of the Second World War, following the Nazi invasion of the Soviet Union in June 1941. By July of that year, an Agreement was made by Great Britain and the USSR (Powers that had not been on the best of terms prior to this date) Providing for Joint Action between the Two Countries in the War against Germany.[4] In May 1942, the same two States concluded a follow-up Treaty for an Alliance in the War against Hitlerite Germany and Her Associates in Europe, and Providing also for Collaboration and Mutual Assistance Thereafter.[5]

The 1942 Anglo-Soviet Alliance illuminates two interesting points. First, the contracting parties sought to extend the operation of the instrument into the post-War period. Future events did not bear out the optimism engendered by the constellation of the Second World War. In general, a military alliance, if welded in the course of war by otherwise polarized countries, is not likely to outlast the advent of peace. For that reason, many wartime alliances are confined to the immediate needs of combating a common foe. Secondly, the Soviet-British treaty proved that an alliance concluded in the midst of hostilities need not embrace all the belligerents positioned on the same side, nor does it have to be directed

---

[2] See D. W Bowett, *Self-Defence in International Law* 216 (1958).
[3] R. Ago, "Addendum to Eighth Report on State Responsibility", [1980] II (1) *I.L.C. Ybk* 13, 68.
[4] Great Britain–USSR, Moscow Agreement Providing for Joint Action between the Two Countries in the War against Germany, 1941, 204 *L.N.T.S.* 277.
[5] Great Britain–USSR, London Treaty for an Alliance in the War against Hitlerite Germany and Her Associates in Europe, and Providing also for Collaboration and Mutual Assistance Thereafter, 1942, 204 *L.N.T.S.* 353.

against all the enemies of the allies. Thus, (i) the United States (and other countries waging war at the time against Nazi Germany) did not accede to the treaty; (ii) the stated goal of the treaty was to fight together against Germany and its associates in Europe, thereby excluding Japan with which Britain – but not the USSR – was then at war.

Collective self-defence has a different meaning. The scenario is that Arcadia initiates an armed attack against Utopia (and only against Utopia), but Numidia – although beyond the range of the attack – decides to come to the assistance of Utopia. There is no doubt that, in principle, Article 51 permits one UN Member to help another if it has fallen prey to an armed attack.[6] When Numidia avails itself of the option, this is a case of collective self-defence, exercised individually, as per the third category listed above.

The fourth category is that of collective self-defence carried out collectively. It becomes apposite when two or more States (Numidia, Atlantica and so forth) act together in supporting the victim country (Utopia).

The question is whether, from an analytical standpoint, the aid furnished to Utopia by Numidia (acting alone or in conjunction with other countries) may properly be considered *self*-defence. Occasionally, the concept is repudiated.[7] But there is no good reason to deny the existence of a "collective" self of groupings of States.[8] If Utopian "safety and independence are deemed vital to the safety and independence" of Numidia, any assistance offered by Numidia to Utopia in repelling an armed attack by Arcadia can be viewed as a measure of Numidian self-defence.[9] The security of various States is often interwoven, so that when Numidia helps Utopia, it is truly defending itself.[10]

[6] See H. Kelsen, "Collective Security and Collective Self-Defense under the Charter of the United Nations", 42 *A.J.I.L.* 783, 792 (1948).
[7] See D. W. Bowett, "The Interrelation of Theories of Intervention and Self-Defense", *Law and Civil War in the Modern World* 38, 46-7 (J. N. Moore ed., 1974).
[8] M. S. McDougal and F. P. Feliciano, *Law and Minimum World Public Order* 248-50 (1961).
[9] L. Oppenheim, 2 *International Law* 155 (7th ed., by H. Lauterpacht, 1952).
[10] See the Dissenting Opinion of Judge Sir Robert Jennings in *Case Concerning Military and Paramilitary Activities in and against Nicaragua* (Merits), [1986] *I.C.J. Rep.* 14, 545.

The actual stake that Numidia may have in the security of Utopia is a matter of perception. Insofar as legal theory is concerned, we have already noted (*supra*, Chapter 4, F, (b)) the statement of the International Court of Justice, in the *Barcelona Traction* case of 1970, that the outlawing of aggression has created obligations applicable *erga omnes*, since all States have valid interests in the protection of the rights involved.[11] Of course, in pragmatic terms, "it is highly unlikely" that Numidia will immerse itself in an armed conflict with Arcadia, unless there is a clear and present danger to Numidian security.[12] Nevertheless, there are many utilitarian considerations that may galvanize Numidia into action against Arcadia when Utopia is attacked.

To begin with, if Numidia is a super-Power, it is apt to think of the whole world as its bailiwick. In that case, an armed attack initiated anywhere, no matter why and against whom it is unleashed, may be interpreted by Numidia as a direct challenge to its vital interests.

Additionally, from the vantage point of smaller Powers (particularly, although by no means exclusively, within a prescribed geographic region), their overall security is detrimentally affected when one of them is invaded by a potent aggressor. The repeated lesson of history (from the Second World War to the Gulf War) has been that, once an aggressor starts out on the path of territorial expansion, attaining a rapid and facile success, it develops an appetite for further conquests. When multiple States - none of which is strong enough to withstand alone the steamroller of an armed attack - face the danger of overwhelming force, the only chance of averting "piecemeal annihilation" lies in closing ranks together while there is still time.[13] Believing as they do that, in the long run, all of them are anyhow destined to become victims of aggression, each may opt to join the fray as soon as one of the others is subjected to an armed attack. In truth, it is the selfish interest of the State

---

[11] *Case Concerning the Barcelona Traction, Light and Power Company, Limited,* [1970] *I.C.J. Rep.* 3, 32.

[12] O. Schachter, "The Right of States to Use Armed Force", 82 *Mich.L.R.* 1620, 1639 (1984).

[13] L. Oppenheim, *supra*, note 9, at 156.

expecting to be next in line for an armed attack that compels it not to be indifferent to what is happening across its borders.

It may be said that an armed attack is like an infectious disease in the body politic of the family of nations. Every State has a demonstrable self-interest in the maintenance of international peace, for once the disease starts to spread there is no telling if and where it will stop. This is the fundamental concept underlying the UN Charter. As long as the system of collective security within the UN Organization is ineffective (see *infra*, Chapter 10, C), collective self-defence constitutes the sole insurance policy against an armed attack.

Collective self-defence may be exercised either spontaneously (as an unplanned response to an armed attack after it has become a reality) or premeditatedly (on the footing of a prior agreement contemplating a potential armed attack). There are those who deny one possibility or the other. It has been contended that support of a State in the grip of an armed attack is contingent on the existence of a collective self-defence treaty.[14] Conversely, it has been maintained that Article 51 precludes Member States (acting outside the pale of the UN) from elaborating strategic plans, or coordinating their military forces under a combined high command, before an armed attack takes place.[15] In reality, there is no sustenance in the text for either interpretation. The latter position has been rightly termed "astonishing",[16] and so is the former. States are entitled to exercise the right of collective self-defence either on the spur of the moment or after thorough preparation for a rainy day. The military action taken by the American-led coalition against Iraq in support of Kuwait, with the full blessing of the Security Council (see *infra*, E), shows that "any state may come to the aid of a state that has been illegally attacked".[17]

In the *Nicaragua* case of 1986, the International Court of Justice held that the right of collective self-defence is well established not

[14] See A. Martin, *Collective Security* 170 (1952).
[15] See F. B. Schick, "The North Atlantic Treaty and the Problem of Peace", 62 *Jur.R.* 26, 49 (1950).
[16] A. L. Goodhart, "The North Atlantic Treaty of 1949", 79 *R.C.A.D.I.* 183, 229 (1951).
[17] See O. Schachter, "United Nations Law in the Gulf Conflict", 85 *A.J.I.L.* 452, 457 (1991).

only in Article 51 of the UN Charter but also in customary international law.[18] Judge Oda, in his Dissenting Opinion, criticized the majority for not sufficiently probing the concept that the right of collective (as opposed to individual) self-defence is "inherent" in pre-Charter customary law.[19] There is indeed some authority for the view that, in opening the door to collective self-defence, Article 51 expanded the right of self-defence as previously understood.[20] However, whether or not the right of collective self-defence can be traced back to pre-Charter customary norms, there is hardly any doubt that it constitutes an integral part of customary international law as it stands today.

B. *Collective Self-Defence Treaties*

Article 52 of the UN Charter expressly permits the existence of "regional arrangements or agencies" for dealing with matters that relate to the maintenance of international peace and security (and are appropriate for regional action), provided that such arrangements or agencies (and their activities) are consistent with the Purposes and Principles of the United Nations.[21] A region in the sense of Article 52 should not be construed narrowly, along lines of "geographical propinquity", and it may comprise any limited community of States "joined together by ties of interests".[22] Every group of like-minded States, drawn by political, ideological or other affinity, is entitled to make such arrangements. Since the size of the group is not delineated in Article 52, a regional arrangement may apparently be limited to two States.[23]

As for the nature of regional arrangements under Article 52, while they may have manifold purposes, surely one of the most

---

[18] *Supra*, note 10, at 102-4.

[19] *Ibid.*, 256-8 (Dissenting Opinion of Judge Oda).

[20] See L. Oppenheim, *supra*, note 9, at 155. But *cf. supra*, Chapter 4, A, regarding the Preamble of the Kellogg-Briand Pact (General Treaty for Renunciation of War as an Instrument of National Policy, 1928, 94 *L.N.T.S.* 57, 59-61).

[21] *Supra*, note 1, at 346-7.

[22] A. V. W. Thomas and A. J. Thomas, *Non-Intervention* 178 (1956).

[23] See M. Akehurst, "Enforcement Action by Regional Agencies, with Special Reference to the Organization of American States", 42 *B.Y.B.I.L.* 175, 177 (1967).

important is to pave the road for collective self-defence. It has been suggested that a joint defence of a region against an external danger of an armed attack, originating from another region, exceeds the limits of a regional arrangement within the meaning of Article 52.[24] But this restrictive interpretation of Article 52 is specious.

In anticipation of a future armed attack, States can conclude several forms of treaties. The three principal categories are: (i) mutual assistance; (ii) military alliance; or (iii) guarantee. Only a State placed under a permanent neutrality regime (see *supra*, Chapter 1, C, (a)) is barred from engaging in a mutual assistance treaty or a military alliance - and, whereas it may benefit from a guarantee, it must never become a guarantor - for permanent neutrality is incompatible with any obligations liable to implicate the State concerned in war.[25]

(a) *Mutual Assistance Treaties*

A mutual assistance treaty is an instrument whereby the contracting parties proclaim that an armed attack against one of them will be regarded as an armed attack against all, pledging to help out each other in such circumstances. A treaty of mutual assistance may be either bilateral or multilateral in scope. As an example for a bilateral treaty, we may cite an agreement made by the United States and South Korea in 1953.[26]

The trouble with a mutual assistance treaty is that, as a rule, a State is ready to employ force in aid of another country only if such conduct is consonant with its vital interests as perceived at the time of action, rather than in the past (when the treaty was signed). Hence, when an armed attack occurs, Atlantica may rush to Numidia's rescue despite the absence of a mutual assistance treaty between them, yet fail to succour Utopia notwithstanding the existence of such a treaty.

---

[24] See J. Stone, *Legal Controls of International Conflict* 249 (1954).
[25] See A. Verdross, "Austria's Permanent Neutrality and the United Nations Organization", 50 *A.J.I.L.* 61, 64 (1956).
[26] United States-Republic of Korea, Washington Treaty, 1953, 48 *A.J.I.L.*, Supp., 147 (1954).

If Atlantica is disinclined to abide by its obligations under a mutual assistance treaty, it will not have to contrive to find an ingenious escape clause in the text. Even if the treaty is formulated in an unequivocal manner, and does not have legal loopholes enabling a reluctant party to refuse to take action altogether, a sufficient margin of discretion is always left to contracting parties. It is simply impossible to resolve beforehand, except in crude outlines, pragmatic issues that in the reality of an armed attack assume crucial significance, like the precise scale of the military support to be afforded, its pace, and the concrete shape that it will take.[27] There are no objective comparative benchmarks by which these matters can be assessed. Decisions have to be taken against the background of the armed attack, once it unfolds in fact, and there is no way to settle differences of opinion in advance through airtight juridical clauses.

It may be deduced that a mutual assistance treaty *per se* cannot provide assurance that meaningful aid will actually be obtained when called for. The main benefit derived from such a treaty lies in the political sphere, for publication of the text serves notice on friends and foes alike as to the cords of affiliation uniting the contracting parties. This may deter potential enemies and encourage States that are favourably disposed. Nonetheless, a mutuality of political interests must not be confused with a binding commitment for reciprocal military support.

Admittedly, contracting parties do not always seek ways to evade carrying out the stipulations of a treaty of mutual assistance. The most momentous illustration of compliance with such a treaty is that of the 1939 British–Polish Agreement of Mutual Assistance,[28] the implementation of which turned the Nazi invasion of Poland into the Second World War. But we must be mindful of the relevant

---

[27] Military supplies can be sent at once by airlift, but they can also be shipped slowly and arrive after the fighting is over. Should an expeditionary force be dispatched, its size might range from a token detachment to several army corps. The type of military units sent over (air squadrons, armoured units, paratroopers, regular infantry, etc.), their combat readiness and mastery of state-of-the-art equipment would all make a tremendous difference.

[28] Great Britain-Poland, London Agreement of Mutual Assistance, 1939, 199 *L.N.T.S.* 57.

dates: the formal agreement was signed on 25 August, the Nazi invasion of Poland began on 1 September, and the British Declaration of War was issued on 3 September. Thus, it all happened within the span of ten days. The longer the lapse af time following the conclusion of a mutual assistance treaty, the fewer the chances for its being respected in practice.

A treaty of mutual assistance may be multilateral (often regional) instead of bilateral. Here the obligation to help a contracting party, upon the outbreak of an armed attack, is imposed not on a single State but on a cluster of States. In principle, collective self-defence ought to be exercised collectively by the entire group. If any member of the group is averse to the idea of participating in an armed conflict when the need arises, it may still shirk its duty in practice. However, the assumption is that, among a whole host of parties, there will be at least one ready to honour its commitment.

The question is whether a single contracting party in a multilateral mutual assistance treaty is permitted to act on its own, offering assistance to the victim State, without waiting for an authoritative decision on behalf of the group. The treaty may require a group decision, and the process of arriving at it can be frustrated by opposition on the part of one or more countries, or at least delayed by protracted debates. All the same, a multilateral mutual assistance treaty, in creating a collective *duty* of collective self-defence, does not diminish from the individual *right* of collective self-defence under the Charter.[29] This right may be exercised by any contracting party to the mutual assistance treaty, unwilling to wait inertly while the victim of an armed attack is gradually strangulated.

An example of a multilateral treaty of mutual aid is the 1947 Rio de Janeiro Inter-American Treaty of Reciprocal Assistance.[30] The basic principle is spelt out in Article 3(1):

The High Contracting Parties agree that an armed attack by any State against an American State shall be considered as an attack

---

[29] See J. N. Moore, "The Secret War in Central America and the Future of World Order", 80 *A.J.I.L.* 43, 104-5 (1986).

[30] Rio de Janeiro Inter-American Treaty of Reciprocal Assistance, 1947, 21 *U.N.T.S.* 77, 93. (A Protocol of Amendment to the Rio Treaty was done at San José in 1975 (14 *I.L.M.* 1122 (1975)), but has not entered into force).

against all the American States and, consequently, each one of the said Contracting Parties undertakes to assist in meeting the attack in the exercise of the inherent right of individual or collective self-defense recognized by Article 51 of the Charter of the United Nations.[31]

When an armed attack occurs, Article 3(2) permits response on two levels: (i) at the request of the attacked State, each contracting party may take immediate measures individually; (ii) a central Organ of Consultation of the American States may put in motion measures of a collective character.[32] The distinction between collective self-defence exercised individually (as a first stage) and collective self-defence exercised collectively (as a second stage) is plainly discernible.[33] On both levels of response, actual recourse to collective self-defence depends on the free will of each contracting party. Under Article 17, resolutions of the Organ of Consultation are to be adopted by a two-thirds majority.[34] But the minority cannot be dragged into hostilities against its wishes. Article 20 clarifies that no contracting party is "required to use armed force without its consent".[35] The obligation of mutual assistance is in effect, yet assistance in the only form that really counts is not automatic.

(b) *Military Alliances*

An acute practical problem in the field of mutual assistance is that, in the absence of prior coordination, it is immensely difficult for separate armed forces of sovereign States (with divergent command structures, equipment, training and often languages) to act in unison against an aggressor, even if the political decision to resort to collective self-defence has been taken. This is why a peacetime military alliance becomes a natural extension of a mutual assistance arrangement. Such an alliance is motivated by the concept that "if you want peace, prepare for war (*si vis pacem, para bellum*)". A treaty

---

[31] *Ibid.,* 95.
[32] *Ibid.,* 95-7.
[33] See J. L. Kunz, "The Inter-American Treaty of Reciprocal Assistance", 42 *A.J.I.L.* 111, 120 (1948).
[34] *Supra,* note 30, at 101.
[35] *Ibid.,* 103.

of alliance goes beyond an abstract commitment for mutual assistance in the event of an armed attack. Induced by the apprehension of a future armed attack, the parties undertake to start preparing their common defence right away.

The hallmarks of a military alliance are the integration of the military high command, the amalgamation of staff planning, the unification of ordnance, the establishment of bases on foreign soil, the organization of joint manoeuvres, and the exchange of intelligence data. The political decision whether or not to use force (and especially to go to war), in support of a State subjected to an armed attack, is retained by each of the allied Governments.[36] But an integrated high command reduces considerably the freedom of action of the individual States, and the sense of solidarity is reinforced by the presence of military units belonging to other members of the alliance within the territory of a country directly threatened by an armed attack.[37] The forces of the allied nations may be so inextricably intertwined that it becomes impossible to disentangle them once hostilities begin. When armed units of Ruritania are stationed on Utopian soil, they can become hostages to fate. Should the Ruritanian troops sustain severe casualties as a result of an Arcadian armed attack against Utopia, the theoretical discretionary power of Ruritania to avoid discharging its duty towards Utopia would be eliminated in practice. In this fashion, an armed attack against one allied State may sweep the entire group into the flow of hostilities, preempting any genuine opportunity for the exercise of individual choice in the matter.

It is not always easy to tell on the face of the text of a given document whether it is only a treaty of mutual assistance or the constituent instrument of a military alliance. Nor is the nature of the undertaking invariably determined by the language of the seminal treaty. The initial instrument may be limited to enunciating the guiding principle of mutual assistance and setting up central organs, while the details of military cooperation can be worked out

---

[36] See W. E. Beckett, *The North Atlantic Treaty, the Brussels Treaty and the Charter of the United Nations* 28 (1950).

[37] See M. Virally, "Panorama du Droit International Contemporain", 183 *R.C.A.D.I.* 9, 298 (1983).

in supplementary agreements or empirically. This is epitomized by the 1949 North Atlantic Treaty.[38] Article 5 of the Treaty, which lays down the principle of mutual assistance,[39] is couched in terms similar to those used in Article 3(1) of the Rio Inter-American Treaty. Article 3 of the North Atlantic Treaty further sets forth that the parties "will maintain and develop their individual and collective capacity to resist armed attack".[40] Article 9 provides for the creation of some central organs.[41] These innocuous clauses have brought into being the North Atlantic Treaty Organization (NATO), which has evolved over the years (particularly in the aftermath of the Korean War) into a sophisticated military alliance with a vast structure.[42]

Since most States (Big Powers included) succumb to a touch of paranoia, perennially suspecting the intentions of other countries, military alliances like NATO have outlasted the "cold war". A single State, first and foremost a super-Power, may concurrently assume assorted commitments to support potential victims of aggression. The United States, for instance, is a party to a wide range of military alliances and mutual assistance treaties.

The agendas and concerns of diverse associations of States do not always mesh. But when one Big Power straddles several political groupings, a fusion effect can be generated. It may well be asked, e.g., whether the involvement of the United States in collective self-defence in Europe (under the North Atlantic Treaty) may not trigger the obligations incurred by other American countries in accordance with the Rio Treaty.[43] A similar problem can arise for smaller States when, in an elusive quest for added security, they reinsure themselves in a number of ways. A case in point is the trilateral Treaty of Alliance, Political Co-operation and Mutual Assistance, concluded in Bled in 1954 between Greece, Turkey and Yugoslavia.[44] The first

---

[38] North Atlantic Treaty, 1949, 34 *U.N.T.S.* 243.

[39] *Ibid.,* 246.

[40] *Ibid., id.*

[41] *Ibid.,* 248.

[42] See D. W. Bowett, *The Law of International Institutions* 180-5 (4th ed., 1982).

[43] *Cf.* C. G. Fenwick, "The Atlantic Pact", 43 *A.J.I.L.* 312, 314-16 (1949).

[44] Greece-Turkey-Yugoslavia, Bled Treaty of Alliance, Political Co-operation and Mutual Assistance, 1954, 211 *U.N.T.S.* 237.

two parties were members of NATO, whereas the third was not. Pressures on Yugoslavia could have produced a suction process, drawing in non-contracting parties belonging to NATO (through the pipeline of Greece and Turkey).

On the other hand, the fact that two countries are associated in the same multilateral military alliance, provides no assurance of good bilateral relations between them. Of late, because of the Cyprus issue, Greece and Turkey often behave as if they were foes, rather than allies.

Frequently, military alliances and mutual assistance treaties are aligned in fact, albeit not necessarily on paper, against each other. Thus, opposite NATO, there stood for many years the Warsaw Pact alliance.[45] Although the machinery constructed in the Warsaw Pact was the political and military antithesis of NATO, there was no legal contradiction immanent in their coexistence. The rationale is that, under either treaty of alliance, contracting parties undertook to render military assistance to one another only in response to an armed attack, if it occurred (presumably on the initiative of members of the opposite group).[46] Both treaties expressly subordinated themselves to the Charter of the United Nations.[47]

The duty of collective self-defence, under a military alliance or a mutual assistance treaty, may be restricted to the occurrence of a specifically defined armed attack (instead of being linked to any armed attack against a contracting party, wherever and whenever it takes place). The condition activating the duty of a contracting party to lend support to the victim of aggression is called casus foederis.[48] The obligation of affording military aid may be reduced to the eventuality of an armed attack mounted by a certain State (and no other) or in a given region (and no other). For example, in 1925 two treaties were concluded in Locarno between France (on one side), Poland and Czechoslovakia (respectively, on the other), whereby the parties undertook to assist each other in case of an

---

[45] Warsaw Treaty of Friendship, Co-operation and Mutual Assistance, 1955, 219 *U.N.T.S.* 3, 24.

[46] *Supra*, note 38, at 246 (Article 5); *supra*, note 45, at 28 (Article 4).

[47] *Supra*, note 38, at 246, 248 (Articles 5, 7); *supra*, note 45, at 28 (Article 4).

[48] See L. Oppenheim, 1 *International Law* 1322 (9th ed., by R. Jennings and A. Watts, 1992).

attack by Germany (and none but Germany).[49] Pursuant to the aforementioned Article 5 of the North Atlantic Treaty, an armed attack against one of the contracting parties is deemed an armed attack against all only if it takes place in Europe or North America, in contradistinction to other regions of the world.

A military alliance may rely primarily on a super-Power (like the United States in NATO) whose might constitutes the backbone of the association. An alliance may also be based on the combined strengths of many a small State. Either way, a military alliance hinges on the principle of reciprocity. A super-Power (like the USA) not only spreads a nuclear umbrella over its allies, but also benefits from their contribution to the alliance, actively (through contingents of armed forces, equipment and supplies) as well as passively (permission to station troops on their soil).

(c) *Treaties of Guarantee*

A completely different legal technique for ensuring military assistance to a State dreading an armed attack is the issuance of a guarantee. The term "guarantee" demands an explanation. When Atlantica undertakes to carry out its part of an agreement with Utopia, it may be said that Atlantica guarantees performance. A certain territory or other property belonging to a State may also be considered a guarantee. Thus, Article 428 of the 1919 Peace Treaty of Versailles prescribed that the German territory situated west of the Rhine (the Rhineland) would be occupied by Allied and Associated troops, for a period of fifteen years, as a guarantee for the execution of the Treaty by Germany.[50] However, when the expression "guarantee" is employed, this is not the type of cases which comes immediately to mind.

A guarantee is "essentially a trilateral transaction",[51] in the sense that Atlantica promises Utopia to respond in a certain way to conduct by Arcadia (which is not necessarily a party to the transaction).

---

[49] France-Poland, Locarno Treaty of Mutual Guarantee, 1925, 54 *L.N.T.S.* 353, 355 (Article I); France-Czechoslovakia, Locarno Treaty of Mutual Guarantee, 1925, *ibid.,* 359, 361 (Article I).

[50] Versailles Peace Treaty with Germany, 1919, 2 *Peace Treaties* 1265, 1524.

[51] Lord McNair, *The Law of Treaties* 240 (1961).

A guarantee may fulfil an economic function: Atlantica may guarantee to Utopia that Arcadia will honour a financial debt, so that Atlantica will secure payment if Arcadia defaults.[52] But even though this is a routine transaction among private persons, it is not common among States. An inter-State guarantee is mostly political-military in character, and it relates to the security, the sovereignty and the territorial integrity of Utopia. The thrust of the guarantee is that, should Utopia become a victim of an Arcadian armed attack, Atlantica will come to its aid.

A guarantee may be given *erga omnes* (encompassing any country in the world) or it may be linked to a well defined danger faced by Utopia from a specific source (Arcadia). The guarantee is generally granted by a Big Power (militarily capable of offering credible aid) – or by a group of States – to a small country (which is in need of it) as part of a territorial arrangement, a political settlement, a regime of permanent neutrality, and the like.

While a guarantee may be issued as a binding unilateral declaration by the guarantor, or a decision of the Security Council, it is chiefly incorporated in a treaty between the guarantor and the State benefiting from the guarantee. A treaty of guarantee is similar in form to a mutual assistance treaty, but they are dissimilar in substance. In a mutual assistance treaty, all the contracting parties are obligated to come to each other's help in the event of an armed attack. Contrarily, a treaty of guarantee is unidirectional in nature: should an armed attack occur, only the guarantor would be required to extend aid to the guaranteed State, and there is no reciprocity. A disparity in the relative positions and undertakings of the contracting parties is an intrinsic trait of a treaty of guarantee.

At times, a complex treaty is concluded embodying mixed components of guarantee and mutual assistance. A case in point is the 1925 Locarno Treaty of Mutual Guarantee between Germany, Belgium, France, Great Britain and Italy.[53] In Article 1, the contracting parties "collectively and severally" guaranteed the German–French and the German–Belgian frontiers.[54] From the viewpoint of France

---

[52] See J. H. W. Verzijl, 6 *International Law in Historical Perspective* 457 (1973).
[53] Locarno Treaty of Mutual Guarantee, 1925, 54 *L.N.T.S.* 289.
[54] *Ibid.*, 293.

and Belgium (each being both a guarantor, as far as the other's frontiers with Germany were concerned, and a guaranteed State), this was in effect a mutual assistance treaty. Insofar as Britain and Italy were concerned, it was an authentic treaty of guarantee. The phrase "mutual guarantee", appearing in the titles of the various Locarno Treaties (see also the other instruments mentioned *supra,* (b))), actually merges two separate concepts of mutual assistance and guarantee.

Whenever a guarantee is collective, it is debatable whether the obligation arises for each guarantor independently or is only enforceable in respect of all the guarantors together.[55] If the duty devolving on the guarantors is activated jointly or not at all, a single party refusing to budge can effectively frustrate the guarantee. A multilateral treaty of guarantee may expressly permit action to be taken either jointly or severally (as was done in Article 1 of the Locarno Treaty), and anyhow the right of collective self-defence remains unimpaired. Nevertheless, individual action will be a right rather than a duty: no guarantor in a collective guarantee is legally compelled to act alone.[56]

When a multilateral treaty of guarantee reserves the right of each guarantor to take the necessary measures on its own, this may ultimately prove counter-productive from the perspective of the guaranteed State. A poignant illustration is the 1960 Nicosia Treaty of Guarantee.[57] Here – in Article II – Greece, Turkey and the United Kingdom guaranteed the independence, territorial integrity and security of Cyprus, as well as the state of affairs established by its Constitution.[58] In Article IV, each of the guarantors reserved the right to take action where necessary to reestablish the state of affairs created by the Treaty.[59] Turkey relied on Article IV when it carried out, in 1974, an armed intervention on behalf of the Turkish minority in the island (leading to the nascence of the so-called Turkish Federated State of Cyprus).[60]

---

[55] See Lord McNair, *supra,* note 51, at 240-1.
[56] See J. F. Williams, "Sanctions under the Covenant", 17 *B.Y.B.I.L.* 130, 135 (1936).
[57] Nicosia Treaty of Guarantee, 1960, 382 *U.N.T.S.* 3.
[58] *Ibid.,* 4.
[59] *Ibid.,* 6.
[60] See N. Ronzitti, *Rescuing Nationals Abroad through Military Coercion and Intervention on Grounds of Humanity* 118-19 (1985).

The circumstances of the case were admittedly exceptional, bearing in mind not only the broad language of Article IV but also another instrument signed in 1960: the tripartite Nicosia Treaty of Alliance authorizing Greece and Turkey to keep military contingents in Cyprus.[61] All the same, to the extent that Article IV purports to enable a guarantor to use force other than in the legitimate exercise of collective self-defence, it does not conform to the Charter.[62] According to the Charter, an armed intervention on behalf of a persecuted minority can only take place at the behest of the Security Council (see *infra*, Chapter 10).

As a legal institution, a guarantee suffers from all the shortcomings of a mutual assistance treaty (not linked to a military alliance), for there is no certainty that actual military aid will materialize when the moment of truth arrives. In view of the guarantee's asymmetrical nature, and the fact that it lays a burden on the guarantor without spawning any direct benefit for it (unless the treaty is exploited as a lever of intervention *à la* Cyprus), the chances of implementation of a guarantee in reality are perceptibly lower than those of a mutual assistance treaty.

C. *The Legal Limitations of Collective Self-Defence*

(a) *The Primacy of the UN Charter*

In the past, States used to conclude treaties of mutual assistance and military alliances of an offensive-defensive nature.[63] Arcadia and Patagonia would undertake to render aid to one another, whenever war was waged against Utopia, regardless of the question which side started the war. At the present time, an agreement projecting complicity in aggression will be in violation of the UN Charter. Article 103 of the Charter promulgates that, in the event of a conflict between obligations assumed by UN Members under the Charter and other international agreements, their Charter obligations

---

[61] Greece-Turkey-Cyprus, Nicosia Treaty of Alliance, 1960, 397 *U.N.T.S.* 287, 289, 291 (Articles III-IV and Additional Protocol I).

[62] See R. St. J. Macdonald, "International Law and the Conflict in Cyprus", 19 *C.Y.I.L.* 3, 12-17, 25-6 (1981).

[63] See J. H. W. Verzijl, *supra*, note 52, at 444-5.

shall prevail.[64] The meaning of Article 103 is controversial.[65] Some commentators believe that any treaty conflicting with the Charter (even if concluded with a non-Member State) is abrogated.[66] Others take the position that such a treaty is legally valid, but a Member is required to breach it and, if necessary, compensation will be paid to the non-Member contracting party.[67] Be the correct interpretation of Article 103 as it may, there can be no doubt about the current nullity of treaties countenancing aggression. This is a direct outcome of the peremptory nature of the prohibition of the use of inter-State force as *jus cogens* (see *supra*, Chapter 4, E, (a)).

When a mutual assistance treaty or a military alliance is formulated, it is usually subordinated in no uncertain terms to the provisions of the Charter. The North Atlantic and the now defunct Warsaw treaties both exemplify this trend (see *supra*, B). Under Article 30(2) of the 1969 Vienna Convention on the Law of Treaties, "[w]hen a treaty specifies that it is subject to, or that it is not to be considered as incompatible with, an earlier or later treaty, the provisions of that other treaty prevail".[68] Therefore, the Charter must govern the exercise of collective self-defence by contracting parties to the North Atlantic Treaty or formerly the Warsaw Pact.

(b) *The Requirement of an Armed Attack*

As the International Court of Justice in the *Nicaragua* case emphasized, States do not have a right to employ force in collective self-defence, under either the Charter or customary international law, except in response to acts constituting an armed attack.[69] If Ruritania resorts to force against Arcadia, invoking collective self-

---

[64] *Supra*, note 1, at 361.

[65] See R. St. J. Macdonald, "Reflections on the Charter of the United Nations", *Des Menschen Recht zwischen Freiheit und Verantwortung: Festschrift für Karl Josef Partsch* 29, 37–42 (J. Jekewitz *et al.* eds., 1989).

[66] See H. Lauterpacht, "[First] Report on Law of Treaties", [1953] II *I.L.C. Ybk* 90, 157.

[67] See G. G. Fitzmaurice, "Third Report on Law of Treaties", [1958] II *I.L.C. Ybk* 20, 43.

[68] Vienna Convention on the Law of Treaties, 1969, [1969] *U.N.J.Y.* 140, 148.

[69] *Supra*, note 10, at 110.

defence, it must show that an armed attack has been initiated by Arcadia against Utopia.[70]

The insistence on an armed attack as a condition of collective self-defence sounds like a truism. But even a truism may be lost sight of in intricate situations. For instance, if Utopia conducts a legitimate operation of extra-territorial law enforcement against hostile armed bands ensconced within the territory of Arcadia, this is an act of self-defence in which Arcadia has to acquiesce (see *supra*, Chapter 8, B, (c)). Since Utopia does not commit an armed attack against Arcadia, Numidia cannot employ counter-force against Utopia in reliance on collective self-defence. To be regarded as a defending State, Numidia must first demonstrate that Utopia is an attacking State. This ties in with the principle that there is no self-defence against self-defence (see *supra*, Chapter 7, A, (b)).

The Court also ruled that a State (Ruritania) may not exercise the right of collective self-defence merely "on the basis of its own assessment of the situation".[71] The direct victim of an armed attack (Utopia) must first "form and declare the view" that it has been subjected to such an attack.[72] Moreover, a request for help has to be made by the victim State (Utopia): in the absence of such a request, collective self-defence by Ruritania is excluded.[73]

In his Dissenting Opinion, Judge Sir Robert Jennings doubted whether the prerequisite of "some sort of formal declaration and request" by the victim State (a declaration that it is under an armed attack and a request for assistance) is realistic in all instances.[74] Indisputably, military aid (especially the dispatch of Ruritanian troops to the combat zone) may not be forced on Utopia against its will. As Judge Jennings remarked, "[o]bviously the notion of collective self-defence is open to abuse and it is necessary to ensure that it is not employable as a mere cover for aggression disguised as protection".[75] However, the majority appears to have missed the kernel of collective self-defence. The Judgment referred to "the use of

---

[70] *Ibid., id.*
[71] *Ibid.,* 104.
[72] *Ibid., id.*
[73] *Ibid.,* 105.
[74] *Ibid.,* 544-5.
[75] *Ibid.,* 544.

collective self-defence by the third State for the benefit of the attacked State".[76] In fact, collective self-defence is above all the defence of self (see *supra,* A), and, when Ruritania responds to an armed attack by Arcadia against Utopia, it is not a "third State" in the strict sense. Judge Jennings rightly commented that the Court's way of looking at collective self-defence "seems to be based almost upon an idea of vicarious defence by champions", whereas, legally speaking, Ruritania (at least in some measure) should be defending itself.[77]

The issue has important practical dimensions. In certain situations, such as the notorious *Anschluss* of Austria by the German *Reich* in March 1938, the direct victim of an armed attack (Utopia) does not resist the aggressor. In general, as already observed (*supra,* Chapter 7, A, (b)), self-defence is a right and not a duty. Utopia is not obligated, therefore, to attempt to repel an invasion or any other form of an armed attack by Arcadia (unless a pledge to exercise individual self-defence is incorporated in a treaty in force, such as a permanent neutrality arrangement). Ruritania cannot coerce Utopia to accept help against its will (again, unless both parties are bound by a specific treaty regulating collective self-defence, e.g., a military alliance[78]). Yet, there is a palpable distinction between a case in which Ruritania proceeds to send its troops into the territory of Utopia (in order to fight there against the invading armed forces of Arcadia) and a setting in which Ruritania announces that, exercising its right of collective self-defence in response to an Arcadian armed attack (of which Utopia is the direct victim), it will use forcible measures against Arcadia outside Utopian territory.

In the absence of a special treaty conferring on Ruritania the right to dispatch an expeditionary force to Utopia, the unsolicited arrival of Ruritanian troops on Utopian soil - notwithstanding the avowed desire of Utopia to be left alone - amounts to an invasion

---

[76] *Ibid.,* 104.

[77] *Ibid.,* 545.

[78] The requirement of a request by the victim of an armed attack, as a condition for outside assistance, is apparently not reconcilable with many existing treaties. See F. L. Morrison, "Legal Issues in the *Nicaragua* Opinion", 81 *A.J.I.L.* 160, 163 (1987). *Cf.* D. K. Linnan, "Self-Defense, Necessity and U.N. Collective Security: United States and Other Views", 1 *D.J.C.I.L.* 57, 103 (1991).

(no different from the previous invasion by Arcadia), namely, an armed attack. Before its troops enter Utopian territory, Ruritania must await a call for help from the country which it purportedly seeks to assist (Utopia).

The legal position is completely different when the Ruritanian response to the Arcadian armed attack takes place outside the territorial boundaries of Utopia. In this factual situation, why should there be any need of a declaration or a request emanating from Utopia? Ruritania's right of collective self-defence is independent of Utopia's right of individual self-defence. Ruritania's right corresponds to the duty binding all nations (and applicable *erga omnes*) to refrain from an armed attack. When Arcadia commences an armed attack (the direct victim of which is Utopia), and Ruritania perceives that its own security is endangered, Ruritania is entitled under Article 51 of the Charter to resort to counter-force. There is no allusion in the Article to prior approval by Utopia as a condition to the exercise of the right of collective self-defence by Ruritania.

If Utopia categorically denies that it has been the target of an armed attack by Arcadia, any collective self-defence measures directed by Ruritania against Arcadia - even beyond the frontiers of Utopia - would be suspect. But this is merely one factor among many, to be weighed by the Security Council when it reviews the entire series of events at a later stage (see *supra,* Chapter 7, D, (a)). During the first phase, Ruritania should be allowed to gauge the Arcadian action by itself, irrespective of any protestations by Utopia.

(c) *Other Conditions for the Exercise of Collective Self-Defence*

The three conditions precedent to the exercise of the right of self-defence (see *supra,* Chapter 7, C) - necessity, proportionality and immediacy - are applicable to collective, no less than to individual, self-defence. This was underscored by the Court in the *Nicaragua* case.[79]

As we have seen (*supra,* Chapter 7, D, (c)), Article 51 imposes on a State exercising the right of self-defence a duty of immediately reporting to the Security Council. In establishing the reporting duty,

---

[79] *Supra,* note 10, at 122-3.

the Article does not differentiate between individual and collective self-defence. It emerges from the Judgment in the *Nicaragua* case (where the obligation was looked upon as a material rather than a technical condition) that each State resorting to measures of self-defence has to submit such a report.[80] If so, it is not enough for Utopia (the direct victim) to communicate a message to the Security Council about the Arcadian armed attack and the counter-measures taken in individual self-defence. When Ruritania invokes the right of collective self-defence, it must file a separate report. Such a report by Ruritania is particularly called for if (as just explained) it acts alone against Arcadia, whereas Utopia declines to exercise its right of individual self-defence.

In addition, Article 54 of the Charter stipulates that when activities for the maintenance of international peace and security are undertaken (or even contemplated) by regional agencies under regional arrangements, the Security Council must be kept fully informed.[81]

D. *The Modality of Collective Self-Defence*

The modality of individual self-defence (see *supra*, Chapter 8) is not available in its full range to a State invoking collective self-defence. Thus, the protection of nationals abroad (when it qualifies as legitimate self-defence) is a proper remedy only for the State directly affected. This mode of response to an armed attack is based, by definition, on a nexus of nationality. Hence, it may not be subrogated by another country in the name of collective self-defence. Otherwise, the limited right for the protection of nationals abroad (as a measure of self-defence) will spin off a general freedom of humanitarian intervention (see *supra*, Chapter 4, B, (b)).

On-the-spot reaction, too, is not usually germane to the right of collective self-defence. This is due to the limited scope of the incident and the fact that it is closed rapidly. It is conceivable that Numidian troops, stationed on Utopian soil as a result of a military alliance, will be attacked by Arcadian armed forces and return fire

---

[80] *Ibid.*, 105, 121-2.
[81] *Supra*, note 1, at 348.

(thereby closing the incident). Here is a characteristic instance of on-the-spot reaction, but it has nothing to do with collective self-defence. The exchange of fire represents a run-of-the-mill case of individual self-defence, exercised by Numidia against an Arcadian armed attack. The only extraordinary aspect of the clash is that both the Arcadian armed attack and the Numidian response occur within the territory of a third State (Utopia) (see *supra*, Chapter 7, B, (b), iii). On-the-spot reaction as a manifestation of collective self-defence takes place only if the Arcadian attack is directed at a Utopian patrol, yet a Numidian military unit deployed nearby (either within Utopia or in Numidia itself, assuming that these are allied and neighbouring countries) rushes immediately to the assistance of the Utopian patrol, and the incident is soon closed.

There are no clear-cut precedents for extra-territorial law enforcement measures, taken by Atlantica within Arcadian territory against armed bands striking at Utopian targets from bases in Arcadia (without the backing of the Arcadian Government). But since the dispatch of armed forces into a foreign territory (with a view to performing the neglected functions of the local sovereign) is an exceptional course of action, it appears that extra-territorial law enforcement should be left to the bilateral relations between Utopia and Arcadia. Unlike an armed attack by a State, which threatens to spread far and wide, assaults by armed bands are of a more insular nature. Atlantica can hardly claim that such assaults against Utopia constitute an armed attack against itself. Consequently, the theoretical underpinning of collective self-defence collapses.

The position may be different when defensive armed reprisals are at issue. There seems to be some authority for the thesis that third States are entitled to resort to unarmed reprisals, at least in special circumstances.[82] It has been argued that armed reprisals, too, may be carried out by allied nations within the framework of collective self-defence.[83] To a degree, the practice of States corroborates the argument. The United States employed armed reprisals against Nicaragua in 1984, invoking the right of collective self-

[82] See M. Akehurst, "Reprisals by Third States", 44 *B.Y.B.I.L.* 1-18 (1970).
[83] See J.-C. Venezia, "La Notion de Représailles en Droit International Public", 64 *R.G.D.I.P.* 465, 490 (1960).

defence.[84] The International Court of Justice rejected the American claim to collective self-defence, determining that the measures taken had not come in response to an armed attack.[85] At the same time, the Court passed no judgment on the specific issue of the legality of armed reprisals, either in individual or in collective self-defence (*supra*, Chapter 8, A, (a), ii).

The archetypical case of the implementation of the right of collective self-defence is war. Multipartite recourse to war, in response to an armed attack, is the primary goal of collective self-defence treaties (see *supra*, B). But irrespective of treaty obligations, when Numidia exercises in practice the theoretical right of collective self-defence against Arcadia – in response to an Arcadian armed attack against Utopia – it will usually do so by embarking upon war (although it may avoid using this term). In all likelihood, the Numidian action will be in the form of a counter-war (as opposed to war in response to an isolated armed attack short of war). To reiterate (see *supra*, A), there is little prospect of Numidia plunging into war against Arcadia when Utopia is attacked, unless what is at stake is perceived as critical to Numidia's own security. Ordinarily, nothing short of a full-scale invasion of Utopia will induce Numidia to get involved in a war of self-defence with Arcadia, considering that Numidia itself is not the direct victim of the Arcadian attack.

E. *The Gulf War and Collective Self-Defence*

The invasion of Kuwait by Iraq on 2 August 1990 triggered within a few hours Security Council Resolution No. 660, which determined the existence of "a breach of international peace and security", and demanded immediate and unconditional withdrawal of the Iraqi forces.[86] Afterwards, the Council imposed on Iraq economic sanctions (Resolution No. 661[87]) and even a blockade (Resolution No. 665[88]) (*infra*, Chapter 10, C). When Iraq did not relent, the

---

[84] *Supra*, note 10, at 22.
[85] *Ibid.*, 103-6.
[86] Security Council Resolution No. 660, 45 *R.D.S.C.* 19, *id.* (1990).
[87] Security Council Resolution No. 661, 45 *R.D.S.C.* 19, 19-20 (1990).
[88] Security Council Resolution No. 665, 45 *R.D.S.C.* 21, 21-2 (1990).

Council reached a crossroads. A vital decision had to be made whether to proceed to military enforcement measures by the United Nations – in the exercise of collective security (*infra*, Chapter 10, A) – or to recommend, and rely on, collective self-defence. Surmounting some apparent hesitation, the Council opted for the latter path.

In Resolution No. 678 of 29 November 1990, the Council authorized the "Member States co-operating with the Government [in exile] of Kuwait" – should Iraq not fully comply with previous Council resolutions by 15 January 1991 – "to use all necessary means to uphold and implement resolution 660 (1990) and all subsequent relevant resolutions and to restore international peace and security in the area".[89] Although Resolution No. 678 did not speak in a lapidary manner about the employment of force by the countries cooperating with Kuwait, nobody could fail to grasp the purport of the authorization "to use all necessary means" in order to secure full compliance with the Council's decisions. Resolution No. 678 "has to be read against the background of the earlier resolutions on Kuwait", taking into account that Iraq had impudently (and imprudently) disregarded other means falling short of comprehensive force.[90]

Pursuant to Resolution No. 678, and upon the expiry of the waiting period, the armed forces of a large American-led coalition struck at Iraq on the night of 16/17 January 1991. At the outset, the military operations were confined to air warfare (missiles, bombings and strafings). On 24 February, a massive land offensive was launched: Kuwait was liberated (and about 15% of Iraq's territory were occupied) within 100 hours. At this point, on 28 February, President G. Bush announced the suspension of hostilities. Preliminary conditions of a cease-fire were proclaimed by the Council on 2 March, in Resolution No. 686.[91] Definitive terms were dictated to Iraq only on 3 April, in Resolution No. 687.[92] All these conditions and terms were

---

[89] Security Council Resolution No. 678, 45 *R.D.S.C.* 27, 27-8 (1990).
[90] C. Greenwood, "New World Order or Old? The Invasion of Kuwait and the Rule of Law", 55 *Mod.L.R.* 153, 166 (1992).
[91] Security Council Resolution No. 686, 30 *I.L.M.* 568-9 (1991).
[92] Security Council Resolution No. 687, 30 *I.L.M.* 847-54 (1991).

reluctantly accepted (although, in the end, not fully adhered to) by Iraq.

The role that the Council played in the Gulf War deserves an intense scrutiny. Did the armed forces of the coalition constitute a United Nations force predicated on genuine collective security (see *infra*, Chapter 10, A)? The answer is emphatically negative. At no time did the Council establish a United Nations force for combat purposes against Iraq.[93] All that happened was that the Council determined conclusively (in Resolution No. 660) that there had been an Iraqi invasion - i.e. an armed attack - against Kuwait, and then (primarily in Resolution No. 678) authorized recourse to force against Iraq by the coalition cooperating with Kuwait. The use of force by the coalition against Iraq was legitimized by the Council within the purview of collective self-defence (Article 51), as opposed to collective security.[94]

Resolution No. 678 has animated diverse comments in the legal literature. One can put aside extravagant (and incongruous) allegations that the resolution "was contrary to the United Nations Charter".[95] Closer attention must be paid to the assertion that "[t]he use of force to liberate Kuwait ... involved not self-defense but, rather, the interpretation and application of a Security Council resolution".[96] Yet, an interpretation of a Council's resolution and collective self-defence, far from being mutually exclusive, are interlinked in this instance. In the words of N. Rostow, "[A]rticle 51 rights can be exercised in the context of Security Council approval".[97]

---

[93] See K. Boustany, "La Guerre du Golfe et le Système d'Intervention Armée de l'ONU", 28 *C.Y.I.L.* 379, 391-2 (1990). It may be added that, following the cease-fire, the United Nations Iraq-Kuwait Observation Mission (UNIKOM) was established to monitor a demilitarized zone. See Resolution No. 687, 30 *I.L.M.* 847, 850 (1991); and Resolution No. 689, *ibid.*, 863, *id.* Clearly, UNIKOM is not a combat force.

[94] See O. Schachter, *International Law in Theory and Practice* 402-3 (1991).

[95] Y. Le Bouthillier and M. Morin, "Réflexions sur la Validité des Opérations Entreprises contre l'Iraq en regard de la Charte des Nations Unies et du Droit Canadien", 29 *C.Y.I.L.* 142, 220 (1991).

[96] B. M. Carnahan, "Protecting Nuclear Facilities from Military Attack: Prospects after the Gulf War", 86 *A.J.I.L.* 524, 527 (1992).

[97] N. Rostow, "The International Use of Force after the Cold War", 32 *H.I.L.J.* 411, 420 (1991).

A specific affirmation of "the inherent right of individual or collective self-defence, in response to the armed attack by Iraq against Kuwait, in accordance with Article 51 of the Charter", was incorporated already in Resolution No. 661.[98] At the time, this reference to Article 51 puzzled some commentators.[99] Later events proved that it was not accidental.[100] Resolution No. 678 denotes that, while the Council abstained from deploying a veritable United Nations force as an instrument of collective security, it gave its blessing in advance to the voluntary exercise of collective self-defence by the members of the coalition (following an interval of several weeks designed for the exhaustion of the political process). The core of the resolution was the prospective approval of future action.[101] In an ordinary constellation of events, States first employ force in individual or collective self-defence and only then report to the Council about the measures that they have taken, so that the Council investigates the nature of the hostilities retrospectively. As noted (*supra*, Chapter 7, D, (c)), this is the chronological sequence envisaged by the framers of the Charter. In the particular case of Iraq, the coalition sought and obtained from the Council a green light for the exercise of collective self-defence against the perpetrator of an armed attack well before the projected military clash. Thereafter, the coalition did not have to worry about the reaction of the Council, inasmuch as that reaction had predated the actual combat.

The principal beneficiaries of the collective self-defence orientation of the operations against Iraq were the Americans who led the coalition. They, rather than the UN, were in command. Consequently, theirs - and almost theirs alone - was the decision when and in what form to strike subsequent to 15 January 1991, at what juncture (if at all) to mount a ground offensive, and under what circumstances to halt the advance. It is useful to recall that, as a Permanent

---

[98] *Supra*, note 87, at 19.

[99] See, e.g., L. C. Green, "Iraq, the U.N. and the Law", 29 *A.L.R.* 560, 565-6 (1991).

[100] Even the phrase "Member States co-operating with the Government of Kuwait" may suggest that these are "nations engaged in collective [self-]defense with Kuwait". J. N. Moore, *Crisis in the Gulf: Enforcing the Rule of Law* 151 (1992).

[101] See A. Pyrich, "United Nations: Authorizations of Use of Force", 32 *H.I.L.J.* 265, 268 (1991).

Member of the Council, the US could also veto any posterior resolution which might have obstructed the military moves of the coalition.

Considering that the operations of the coalition forces in the Gulf War were a manifestation of collective self-defence - rather than collective security - once Resolution No. 660 was adopted, there was technically no need for the specific mandate of Resolution No. 678 to legally validate the launching of the strikes against Iraq.[102] Article 51 *per se* ought to have sufficed in authorizing the coalition to resort to force in response to the Iraqi armed attack, and arguably Resolution No. 678 only tied the hands of the countries cooperating with Kuwait in that they had to hold their fire until 15 January.[103] But in political and psychological terms, Resolution No. 678 had an incalculable effect: internationally (cementing the solidarity of the coalition and swelling its ranks) as well as domestically (mobilizing public opinion to political support of the action against Iraq).

There is a resemblance between the Gulf War and the Korean War. In both instances, the Council determined the existence of a breach of the peace, yet refrained from taking legally binding decisions activating genuine collective security (see *infra*, Chapter 10, C). In both cases, an international coalition led by the United States came to the aid of the victim of an armed attack, heeding the Council's recommendation or authorization.[104] Still, there are some unmistakable dissimilarities.[105] First, whereas in Korea the fighting was continuous, in the Gulf - since Kuwait had been completely overrun by the Iraqi forces - there was a temporal interlude between the original armed attack and the military response. Secondly, in contrast to the near-unanimity that characterized relations between

---

[102] See C. Greenwood, *supra*, note 90, at 163. *Cf.* D. R. Penna, "The Right to Self-Defense in the Post-Cold War Era: The Role of the United Nations", 20 *D.J.I.L.P.* 41, 49-50 (1991-2).

[103] See C. Dominicé, "La Sécurité Collective et la Crise du Golfe", 2 *E.J.I.L.* 85, 104 (1991).

[104] The difference between authorization and recommendation (stressed by L. Henkin, "Law and War after the Cold War", 15 *Mar.J.I.L.T.* 147, 160 (1991)) appears to be more verbal than real.

[105] See S. M. De Luca, "The Gulf Crisis and Collective Security under the United Nations Charter", 3 *P.Y.I.L.* 267, 295-6 (1991).

the Permanent Members during the Gulf War,[106] the resolutions in the Korean War (which occurred in the heyday of the "cold war") were made possible only by a fortuitous albeit fleeting Soviet boycott of the Council's sessions. Thirdly, and conversely, in Korea the contingents confronting the aggressor were allowed to fly the United Nations flag and became a United Nations force (see *supra*, Chapter 6, B), whereas the coalition that came to the rescue of Kuwait had no similar status. But here as there the command was American and the financing of the operation formed no part of the United Nations budget. Legally speaking, in both wars the American-led expeditionary forces fought in exercise of collective self-defence (induced by the Council) as distinct from collective security.[107]

---

[106] China alone abstained in the vote on Resolution No. 678. It voted in favour of all the preceding resolutions against Iraq.

[107] See O. Schachter, *supra*, note 94, at 402-3.

CHAPTER 10

COLLECTIVE SECURITY

A. *The Meaning of Collective Security*

Collective security postulates the institutionalization of the lawful use of force in the international community.[1] What is required is a multilateral treaty, whereby contracting parties create an international agency vested with the power to employ force against aggressors (and perhaps other law-breakers). Such an instrument is basically "introverted" in character (designed against a potential future aggressor from among the contracting parties), unlike a collective self-defence treaty (see *supra*, Chapter 9, B) which is "extroverted" (envisaging aggression from outside the system).[2] Collective security shares with collective self-defence the fundamental premise that recourse to force against aggression can (and perhaps must) be made by those who are not the immediate and direct victims. But self-defence, either individual or collective, is exercised at the discretion of a single State or a group of States. Collective security operates on the strength of an authoritative decision made by an organ of the international community.

The system of collective security has its roots in the League of Nations. Article 10 of the Covenant empowered the League's Council to advise Member States on the means to be taken in case of aggression or threat of aggression.[3] Article 11 declared that any war or threat of war, whether or not immediately affecting any Member, was a matter of concern to the whole League, which had to take action as required to safeguard peace among nations.[4] Article 16 stipulated that, if any Member resorted to war in violation of its obligations under Articles 12, 13 or 15 of the Covenant (see *supra*, Chapter 3, E, (c)), it was *ipso facto* deemed to have committed an act

---

[1] See G. Schwarzenberger and E. D. Brown, A *Manual of International Law* 153 (6th ed., 1976).

[2] H. Rumpf, "The Concepts of Peace and War in International Law", 27 *G.Y.I.L.* 429, 440 (1984).

[3] Covenant of the League of Nations, 1919, 1 *Int.Leg.* 1, 7.

[4] *Ibid., id.*

of war against all other Members.[5] All trade or financial relations with the transgressor, including commerce between nationals, had to be severed. The Article went on to instruct the Council to recommend to the Governments concerned what effective military, naval or air contribution they should make to the armed forces which were to be used for the protection of the Covenant's obligations. Expulsion of a Member from the League for violation of any of the Covenant's obligations was also authorized. Article 17 applied the provisions of Article 16 in the event that a non-Member State embarked upon war against a Member.[6]

Article 16 of the Covenant drew a line of distinction between economic sanctions and military action. Member States were duty-bound to apply commercial and financial measures against an aggressor, but – insofar as military action was concerned – the League's Council was only entitled to make (non-binding) recommendations.[7] Economic sanctions (partial, temporary and ineffective in nature) were indeed imposed on Italy, following the latter's aggression against Ethiopia in 1935-6.[8] Yet, even mandatory economic sanctions are not likely to stop war by themselves. As long as an international organization cannot obligate Member States to impose military sanctions against an armed attack, one cannot speak of a veritable collective security system.

The main objective of the framers of the Charter of the United Nations was to introduce into international relations a genuine mechanism of collective security. The UN organ entrusted with the task of activating and supervising the mechanism is the Security Council. In Article 24, Member States "confer on the Security Council primary responsibility for the maintenance of international peace and security, and agree that in carrying out its duties under this responsibility the Security Council acts on their behalf".[9]

---

[5] *Ibid.*, 11.
[6] *Ibid.*, 12.
[7] See J. F. Williams, *Some Aspects of the Covenant of the League of Nations* 156-7 (1934).
[8] See J. H. Spencer, "The Italian-Ethiopian Dispute and the League of Nations", 31 *A.J.I.L.* 614, 624-41 (1937).
[9] Charter of the United Nations, 1945, 9 *Int.Leg.* 327, 339.

The Charter's collective security system is constructed in Chapter VII (Articles 39 to 50).[10] Article 39, in opening Chapter VII, reads:

The Security Council shall determine the existence of any threat to the peace, breach of the peace, or act of aggression and shall make recommendations, or decide what measures shall be taken in accordance with Articles 41 and 42, to maintain or restore international peace and security.[11]

The last words in the Article put in a nutshell the Security Council's mandate: it is to maintain or restore international peace and security.[12]

The notion of maintaining international peace and security has a preemptive thrust. The purpose is to ensure, before it is too late, that no breach of the peace will in fact occur. Measures taken by the Council to forestall a breach of the peace will, therefore, have deterrence and prevention as their goals. By contrast, the idea of restoring international peace and security posits that such a breach has already happened. This being the case, the Council has to employ enforcement measures calculated to reestablish international law and order.

The Charter endows the Council with a whole array of powers, enabling it to maintain or restore international peace and security. Thus, Article 41 authorizes the Council to put into operation measures not involving the use of armed force, such as complete or partial interruption of economic relations, cutting off communication (by rail, sea, air, post, telegraph, radio, etc.), and severance of diplomatic relations.[13] The list of measures enumerated in Article 41 is not exhaustive, but none of the steps taken under this provision of the Charter involves the use of armed force.[14]

---

[10] *Ibid.*, 343-6. As a matter of fact, the last clause in Chapter VII is Article 51. But this provision deals, of course, with self-defence rather than collective security.

[11] *Ibid.*, 343.

[12] On the meaning of the term "security", as used in Article 39 in combination with "international peace", see H. Vetschera, "International Law and International Security: The Case of Force Control", 24 *G.Y.I.L.* 144, 145-6 (1981).

[13] *Supra*, note 9, at 343.

[14] See B. Broms, *The United Nations* 313 (1990).

Article 50 prescribes that, if a State (whether or not a UN Member) is confronted with special economic problems arising from the carrying out by the Council of preventive or enforcement action against another State, it may consult the Council as regards the solution of these problems.[15] The provision is devised to cope with the plight of a country that – owing to geographic proximity to, or special trade with, the State against which steps are taken – suffers unduly from the imposition of the economic sanctions, and requires special assistance.[16] A telling example is that of the Kingdom of Jordan in the course of the Gulf War. This country was exceptionally affected by the economic sanctions imposed on Iraq, and it invoked Article 50 in September 1990.[17] In response to Jordanian and other requests for special assistance, the Security Council adopted Resolution No. 669, which entrusted the Sanctions Committee (established in Resolution No. 661[18]) with the task of examining requests under Article 50 and making recommendations for appropriate action.[19] In the event, regrettably, Jordan chose the course of continuing to trade with Iraq in violation of Resolution No. 661[20] (*infra*, C). It may be added that the Council also recalled Article 50 in the context of the air embargo imposed on Libya in Resolution No. 748 (1992).[21]

Conceptually, Article 41 may be viewed as an outgrowth of the League's Covenant. However, the framers of the Charter were not content with non-forcible sanctions. A far-reaching leap forward was made in Article 42, which represents the fulcrum of the UN collective security system:

Should the Security Council consider that measures provided for in Article 41 would be inadequate or have proved to be in-

---

[15] *Supra*, note 9, at 346.
[16] See L. M. Goodrich, E. Hambro and A. P. Simons, *Charter of the United Nations* 341 (3rd ed., 1969).
[17] See V. P. Nanda, "The Iraqi Invasion of Kuwait: The U.N. Response", 15 *S.I.U.L.J.* 431, 443 (1990-1).
[18] Security Council Resolution No. 661, 45 *R.D.S.C.* 19, 20 (1990).
[19] Security Council Resolution No. 669, 45 *R.D.S.C.* 24, *id.* (1990).
[20] US Department of Defense Report to Congress on the Conduct of the Persian Gulf War, 1992, 31 *I.L.M.* 612, 638-9 (1992).
[21] Security Council Resolution No. 748, 31 *I.L.M.* 750, *id.* (1992).

adequate, it may take such action by air, sea, or land forces as may be necessary to maintain or restore international peace or security. Such action may include demonstrations, blockade, and other operations by air, sea, or land forces of Members of the United Nations.[22]

In brief, under Article 42, the Council may exert force, either on a limited or on a comprehensive scale.

The scope of the discretion granted to the Council, in discharging its duties within the ambit of the Charter, is very wide. It is noteworthy that, by virtue of Article 51 of the Charter[23] (see *supra*, Chapter 7, A, (a)), individual or collective self-defence is permitted only in response to an armed attack. Conversely, collective security can be brought into action whenever the Council determines that there exists a threat to the peace, a breach of the peace, or an act of aggression. An unambiguous bifurcation ensues in respect of lawful use of inter-State force consonant with the Charter. On the one hand, every State or group of States is allowed to resort to force in international relations, although only in the exceptional circumstances of a legitimate response to an armed attack and subject to ultimate review by the Council (see *supra*, Chapters 7-9). On the other hand, the Council is empowered to employ force in the name of collective security, and the degree of latitude bestowed upon it by the Charter is well-nigh unlimited. The Council may wield force to counter any type of aggression, not necessarily amounting to an armed attack,[24] and it may even respond to a mere threat to the peace.

In exercising collective security, the Council is not just free to decide whether and how to use force, but it is also at liberty to determine when to do so and against whom. Since the Charter seems,

---

[22] *Supra*, note 9, at 343-4.

[23] *Ibid.*, 346.

[24] It has been argued, in the context of the consensus Definition of Aggression, that "it would presumably be absurd to suggest that any act that (according to the definition) the Security Council might properly find to qualify as an 'aggression' might not give rise at least to the right of self-defense". J. L. Hargrove, "The *Nicaragua* Judgment and the Future of the Law of Force and Self-Defense", 81 *A.J.I.L.* 135, 139 n. 15 (1987). But there is no absurdity in an act of aggression failing to qualify as an armed attack.

to give it a *carte blanche* in evaluating any given situation, the Council may initiate a preventive war in anticipation of a future breach of the peace (figuring only as a threat to the peace at the time of action), a privilege that the Charter withholds from any individual State or group of States acting alone (see *supra,* Chapter 7, B, (a)).

Nowhere is the Council under less strictures than in its determination that a threat to the peace exists. A "threat to the peace" (adverted to in Article 39) is not to be confused with a "threat ... of force", mentioned in Article 2(4)[25] (see *supra,* Chapter 4, B, (a)).[26] A threat of force under Article 2(4) is an illegal act, whereas a threat to the peace alluded to in Article 39 "may be the consequence of legitimate activities".[27] Realistically, "a threat to the peace is whatever the Security Council says is a threat to the peace".[28] Even an internal situation (within the boundaries of a single State) may be deemed by the Council a threat to international peace and security "because of the potential for international conflict".[29] A good illustration is Security Council Resolution No. 688 (1991) holding the consequences of Iraqi repression of the civilian population (particularly the Kurds) to be a threat to "international peace and security in the region".[30]

It is important to remember that the Council is a political and not a judicial organ (see *supra,* Chapter 7, D, (b)). It is composed of Member States, and its decisions are (and have every right to be) linked to political motivations that are not necessarily congruent with legal considerations. As a non-judicial body, the Council is not required to set out reasons for its decision.[31] It may opt to stigmatize as a threat to the peace a situation that does not appear to anyone else as disturbing the equilibrium of international security. Yet, a determination by the Council that a threat to the peace exists is

---

[25] *Supra,* note 9, at 332.
[26] See H. Kelsen, *The Law of the United Nations* 727 (1950).
[27] B. V. A. Röling, "On Aggression, on International Criminal Law, on International Criminal Jurisdiction - I", 2 *N.T.I.R.* 167, 173 (1955) .
[28] M. Akehurst, *A Modern Introduction to International Law* 219 (6th ed., 1987).
[29] D. J. Harris, *Cases and Materials on International Law* 876 (4th ed., 1991).
[30] Security Council Resolution No. 688, 30 *I.L.M.* 858, 859 (1991).
[31] See J. E. S. Fawcett, "Security Council Resolutions on Rhodesia", 41 *B.Y.B.I.L.* 103, 116-17 (1965-6).

conclusive. All Member States must accept the Council's verdict, despite any misgivings that they may entertain concerning the merits of the case.

Just as the Council may take action against a threat to the peace which is imperceptible to the public eye, it may also decline to acknowledge the existence of a manifest threat to the peace. By the time that the Council formally recognizes a threat to the peace, the state of affairs may have progressed way past the mark of mere threats. Thus, in mid-July 1948, exactly two months after an inter-State war had commenced in the area, the Council determined that the situation in Palestine constituted "a threat to the peace within the meaning of Article 39".[32] Factually, the resolution seemed unsynchronized with what was happening in the conflict region.[33] Legally, the Council was fully competent to determine what it did when it thought it appropriate.

Attempts are sometimes made to demarcate an unblurred line between the categories of a breach of the peace and aggression.[34] But the Charter (or, for that matter, the practice of the Council) does not provide any clear guidance in discriminating between the two expressions. In pragmatic terms, as long as the authority of the Council to act in a given context is unassailable under the Charter, it is of little consequence whether one stamp or the other is affixed to the measures taken.

Article 40 warrants recourse by the Council to provisional measures, without prejudice to the positions of the parties, before final decisions or recommendations are adopted.[35] The original object of this clause was to ensure that a threat to the peace does not become an actual breach. However, in the practice of the Council, it is also utilized to bring about a cease-fire after hostilities have broken out[36] (see *supra*, Chapter 2, C, (a), iii).

---

[32] Security Council Resolution No. 54, 3 *R.D.S.C.* 22, *id.* (1948).

[33] For the "discrepancy between the nature of events in Palestine and the response of the Security Council", see I. S. Pogany, *The Security Council and the Arab-Israeli Conflict* 27-44 (1984).

[34] See G. Cohen Jonathan, "Article 39", *La Charte des Nations Unies* 645, 657-9 (J.-P. Cot and A. Pellet eds., 1985).

[35] *Supra*, note 9, at 343.

[36] See L. M. Goodrich, E. Hambro and A. P. Simons, *supra*, note 16, at 303-4.

Article 42 does not require that the use of force by the Council will be directed against a State.[37] The Council is entitled to determine that the activities of a non-Governmental entity (or group of individuals) pose a threat to the peace, which must be countered by enforcement measures under Article 42.[38] For instance, hypothetically, the Council may arrive at the conclusion that a combined military operation ought to be conducted against international terrorists. Implementation of the Council's decision is likely to impinge upon the territorial sovereignty of one State or another (where the terrorists find harbour). But the broad powers conferred on the Council in the province of collective security may override, if necessary, the sovereignty of any UN Member State.

The Council can even impose domestic order within a country riven by a civil strife, without obtaining the consent of the local Government.[39] Given its broad powers under Chapter VII, the Council is free to brand an explosive internal situation as a threat to international peace, and then to move in with all the means in its possession.[40] Article 2(7) of the Charter, in precluding intervention by the United Nations "in matters which are essentially within the domestic jurisdiction of any state", expressly adds a reservation that "this principle shall not prejudice the application of enforcement measures under Chapter VII".[41]

---

[37] See J. W. Halderman, "Legal Basis for United Nations Armed Forces", 56 *A.J.I.L.* 971, 982 (1962).

[38] See G. Fischer, "Article 42", *La Charte des Nations Unies, supra,* note 34, at 705, 713.

[39] A related but separate issue is whether the Council may intervene in an internal situation, at the request of the local Government, when the action taken does not constitute an enforcement measure under Chapter VII. See G. Abi-Saab, *The United Nations Operation in the Congo 1960-1964* 39-40 (1978).

[40] See L. Gross, "Domestic Jurisdiction, Enforcement Measures and the Congo", [1965] *A.Y.B.I.L.* 137, 146.

[41] *Supra,* note 9, at 332.

B. *The Decision-Making Process*

(a) *The Duties Incumbent on UN Member States*

As noted (*supra*, A), it is the function of the Security Council, pursuant to Article 39 of the Charter, to decide or recommend what measures are to be taken in order to maintain or restore international peace and security. By definition, recommendations are not binding, and they can only urge Members to action.[42] For their part, Members can make up their own minds whether to follow or to ignore non-compulsory calls for action issued by the Council. Decisions are in a different class. Under Article 25, UN Members agree to accept and carry out the decisions of the Council in accordance with the Charter.[43] It is not altogether free of doubt which decisions are covered by Article 25. But, indisputably, decisions adopted by the Council under the aegis of Chapter VII, aimed at maintaining or restoring the peace, are legally binding.

In its Advisory Opinion of 1971, in the *Namibia* case, the International Court of Justice held that Article 25 does not apply solely to Security Council decisions under Chapter VII.[44] However, there was no question about the mandatory nature of the Council's decisions concerning enforcement action, in conformity with Articles 41 and 42 of the Charter. The Court pronounced that the binding effect of such decisions is vouchsafed not only by the general provision of Article 25, but also by the specific stipulations of Articles 48 and 49.[45]

Article 48 sets forth that the action required to carry out decisions of the Council for the maintenance of international peace and security is to be taken by all UN Members, or some of them, as determined by the Council.[46] In other words, the Council may lay the burden of implementing its decisions on a few of the Members

---

[42] See G. Schwarzenberger, *International Constitutional Law* 204-5 (1976).
[43] *Supra*, note 9, at 339.
[44] *Legal Consequences for States of the Continued Presence of South Africa in Namibia (South West Africa) notwithstanding Security Council Resolution 276 (1970)*, [1971] *I.C.J. Rep.* 16, 52-3.
[45] *Ibid.*, 53.
[46] *Supra*, note 9, at 345-6.

(such as the Big Powers), or it may apportion different assignments to all Members large and small. Either way, Article 49 enjoins all Members to assist in carrying out the measures decided upon by the Council.[47]

In Resolution No. 667 (1990), during the Gulf War, the Council - while acting under Chapter VII - stated its determination "to ensure respect for its decisions and for Article 25 of the Charter of the United Nations".[48] The Council reaffirmed that determination in Resolution No. 670, which also cited Article 48 of the Charter, proclaiming that any acts of the Government of Iraq contrary to the Council's decisions and to these two Articles are null and void.[49] Article 25 was also invoked in Resolution No. 686 (1991), which set out preliminary conditions of a cease-fire after the Iraqi defeat at the hands of the coalition.[50] In the context of the fighting in Yugoslavia, the Council adverted to Article 25 in Resolution No. 743 (1992), which established the United Nations Protection Force (UNPROFOR).[51]

Article 53 promulgates that, where appropriate, the Council shall utilize regional arrangements or agencies for enforcement action under its authority.[52] The Article emphasizes that, nevertheless, no enforcement action may be taken by regional agencies without the authorization of the Council. The existence of regional arrangements, while perfectly legitimate under the Charter, does not modify the fundamental rules pertaining to the use of force. The position of a regional group of States (for example, the countries participating in the Conference on Security and Co-operation in Europe vis-à-vis the former Yugoslavia) is not appreciably different from that of an individual State. Recourse to measures of collective security constitutes a monopoly of the Council. Unless it gets a green light from the Council to perform enforcement functions, a regional agency (like any single State) can resort to lawful force only within the purview of collective self-defence (see *supra*,

---

[47] *Ibid.*, 346.
[48] Security Council Resolution No. 667, 45 *R.D.S.C.* 23, *id.* (1990).
[49] Security Council Resolution No. 670, 45 *R.D.S.C.* 24, 24-5 (1990).
[50] Security Council Resolution No. 686, 30 *R.D.S.C.* 568, *id.* (1991).
[51] Security Council Resolution No. 743, 31 *I.L.M.* 1447, 1448 (1992).
[52] *Supra*, note 9, at 347-8.

Chapter 9). Inaction by the Council does not amount to authorization for collective security measures, even by a regional agency.[53]

(b) *The Responsibility of the Security Council*

Chapter VII obligations devolve not only on Member States, but also on the Security Council itself. As indicated (*supra*, A), the primary responsibility for the maintenance of international peace and security is conferred by the Charter on the Council. Article 39 employs the mandatory expression "shall" to describe the Council's task in the field of collective security: the Council "shall" determine the existence of a threat to the peace, a breach of the peace or an act of aggression, and "shall" either make recommendations or decide what is to be done in order to maintain or restore international peace and security.

Naturally, any action taken by the Council is contingent on the adoption of an enabling resolution. Under Article 27, as amended, resolutions of the Council can only be carried by an affirmative vote of at least nine of its fifteen Members.[54] Moreover, a resolution must obtain the concurring votes of the five Permanent Members of the Council. This is the celebrated veto power: should even 14 of the 15 Members of the Council support a draft resolution, a lone dissenter – if it is one of the Permanent Members (China, France, Russia, the United Kingdom and the United States) – may prevent adoption of the proposed text by casting a negative vote.

Article 27 has been construed in the Council's proceedings in such a way that only a negative vote by a Permanent Member signifies that it does not concur with a resolution, thus constituting a veto (which defeats the motion), whereas an abstention (or non-participation in a vote) does not count.[55] When the generally accepted interpretation of Article 27 was challenged, in the *Namibia* case, the

---

[53] See O. Schachter, "The Right of States to Use Armed Force", 82 *Mich.L.R* 1620, 1640-1 (1984).

[54] *Supra*, note 9, at 340. The numbers involved were amended as of 1965. Protocol of Entry into Force of the Amendments to Articles 23, 27 and 61 of the Charter of the United Nations, [1965] *U.N.J.Y.* 159, 160.

[55] See C. A. Stavropoulos, "The Practice of Voluntary Abstentions by Permanent Members of the Security Council under Article 27, Paragraph 3, of the Charter of the United Nations", 61 *A.J.I.L.* 737, 742-4 (1967).

International Court of Justice endorsed the consistent and uniform practice of the Council.[56]

Article 27 lays down that, in certain matters, a party to a dispute must abstain from voting in the Council. But the obligation does not apply to decisions under Chapter VII. Hence, a Permanent Member may cast the veto, in a vote on the application of Chapter VII measures, notwithstanding the fact that it is a party to the dispute. That is to say, a Permanent Member may always bar the adoption of any resolution putting into effect the provisions of Chapter VII, if the action decided upon (or recommended) is pointed at itself (or at a State with which it is closely associated). In practical terms, there is more than an element of truth in the cynical observation that the collective security system of the Charter is only geared to handle "minor disturbers of the peace".[57]

C. An Overview of the Security Council's Record

Until the Gulf war, the Security Council showed a great deal of reticence about invoking Chapter VII, or any specific Article therein, as the source of its authority. Both Articles 39 and 40 were identified by the Council when it ordered a cease-fire in Palestine, in July 1948.[58] The same two Articles were enumerated in July 1987, when the Council determined (after seven years of war) that "there exists a breach of the peace as regards the conflict between Iran and Iraq".[59] An express reference to Article 41 was made when the Council determined, in 1966, that the situation in Southern Rhodesia amounted to a threat to international peace and security, deciding that all Member States must avoid certain imports from and exports to that land.[60] In 1977, the Council, basing itself on Chapter VII in general, imposed a mandatory arms embargo oǹ South Africa.[61]

---

[56] *Supra*, note 44, at 22.

[57] I. L. Claude, "The United Nations and the Use of Force", 532 *Int.Con.* 323, 330 (1961).

[58] *Supra*, note 32, at 22.

[59] Security Council Resolution No 598, 42 *R.D.S.C.* 5, 6 (1987).

[60] Security Council Resolution No. 232, 21 *R.D.S.C.* 7, *id.* (1966).

[61] Security Council Resolution No. 418, 32 *R.D.S.C.* 5, *id.* (1977).

Since the outbreak of the Gulf War, the Council no longer feels restraint in adducing Chapter VII. A long string of resolutions openly relying on this chapter is a testimony to the new spirit characteristic of the post-"cold war" era. These resolutions are of critical importance in the evolution of the law of the Charter. It is necessary, however, to evaluate dispassionately what they include and what they exclude.

First came Resolution No. 660 of 2 August 1990 (the very day of the invasion of Kuwait by Iraq), in which the Council determined the existence of "a breach of international peace and security", and - acting specifically under Articles 39 and 40 of the Charter - condemned the invasion, demanding immediate and unconditional withdrawal of the Iraqi forces.[62] On 6 August, the Council adopted Resolution No. 661, which - citing Chapter VII - imposed on Iraq mandatory economic sanctions: the Council decided in particular that all States must prevent any imports or exports from or to Iraq or occupied Kuwait (except for medications and, in humanitarian circumstances, foodstuffs), as well as any other type of trade, supply or transfer of funds.[63] The Council also established a special Committee, consisting of all its members (generally referred to as the Sanctions Committee), with a view to supervising the implementation of the resolution.[64]

In Resolution No. 665 of 25 August, the Council recorded that Resolution No. 661 had imposed "economic sanctions under Chapter VII of the Charter of the United Nations".[65] It called upon the "Member States co-operating with the Government [in exile] of Kuwait" (which were deploying maritime forces in the area) to use such measures "as may be necessary under the authority of the Security Council to halt for inspection purposes all inward and outward maritime shipping", in order "to ensure strict implementation" of Resolution No. 661.[66] In practical terms, Iraq was subjected

[62] Security Council Resolution No. 660, 45 R.D.S.C. 19, id. (1990).
[63] Supra, note 18, at 19-20.
[64] Ibid., 20. On the mandate and work of the Sanctions Committee, see M. Koskenniemi, "Le Comité des Sanctions (Crée par la Résolution 661 (1990) du Conseil de Sécurité)", 37 A.F.D.I. 119-37 (1991).
[65] Security Council Resolution No. 665, 45 R.D.S.C. 21, id. (1990).
[66] Ibid., 21-2.

in consequence to a blockade, although Resolution No. 665 avoided that expression.[67]

While the mandatory economic sanctions imposed on Iraq in Resolution No. 661 were plainly predicated on Article 41, the blockade went beyond the scope of that provision. As noted (*supra*, A), the term "blockade" appears in the Charter in the text of Article 42 (military sanctions) rather than Article 41 (economic sanctions). Did the Council introduce and apply "Article 41 and a half"?[68] In actuality, the maritime operations intercepting imports and exports to and from Iraq were conducted by the United States, the United Kingdom and other naval Powers cooperating with Kuwait on the basis of the right of collective self-defence pursuant to Article 51.[69] Resolution No. 661, which Resolution No. 665 was designed to implement, makes an all-inclusive reference to Chapter VII. It ought to be underscored that Article 51 (just like Articles 41 and 42) figures in that chapter.

The Council acted again under Chapter VII in Resolution No. 670, deciding that - irrespective of any rights or obligations conferred or imposed by any international agreement,[70] contract or licence - all States must deny permission to any aircraft to take off from or overfly their territories when destined to land in Iraq or occupied Kuwait (unless authorized by the Sanctions Committee).[71] The Council further called upon all States to detain any ships of Iraqi registry which entered their ports in violation of Resolution No. 661, and threatened to consider measures in case of evasion of either resolution.[72]

As can be expected, Chapter VII was invoked by the Council in Resolution No. 678 authorizing the "Member States co-operating

---

[67] On the similarities and dissimilarities to blockade, see H. B. Robertson, "Specific Means and Methods of Application of Force", 1 *D.J.C.I.L.* 1, 11 (1991).

[68] The phrase was coined, in the general context of the Council's activities in the Gulf War, by P. Weckel, "Le Chapitre VII de la Charte et son Application par le Conseil de Sécurité", 37 *A.F.D.I.* 165, 202 (1991).

[69] See C. Greenwood, "New World Order or Old? The Invasion of Kuwait and the Rule of Law", 55 *Mod.L.R.* 153, 161 (1992).

[70] The Council expressly recalled in this context the provision of Article 103 of the Charter (*cf. supra*, Chapter 9, C, (a)). *Supra*, note 49, at 25.

[71] *Ibid., id.*

[72] *Ibid., id.*

with the Government of Kuwait", after a prescribed space of time, "to use all necessary means to uphold and implement resolution 660 (1990) and all subsequent relevant resolutions and to restore international peace and security in the area".[73] Yet, as indicated (*supra*, Chapter 9, E), this watershed resolution constituted a specific mandate for the exercise of collective self-defence under Article 51.[74] Claims that the resolution was based on Article 42[75] are totally unwarranted.[76]

Additionally, the Council alluded to Chapter VII in multiple resolutions both prior and subsequent to the Iraqi military defeat at the hands of the coalition. The pre-hostilities citations of Chapter VII appear in Resolution No. 664 concerning the safety of foreign nationals held as hostages by Iraq;[77] Resolution No. 666 empowering the Sanctions Committee to determine whether there was an urgent humanitarian need to supply foodstuffs to Iraq or occupied Kuwait;[78] Resolution No. 667 condemning aggressive acts perpetrated by Iraq against diplomats in Kuwait, and demanding the immediate release of all foreign nationals;[79] Resolution No. 674 demanding that Iraq cease and desist from a series of violations of international law, pointing out that it would be liable for any loss, damage or injury resulting from the invasion of Kuwait;[80] and Resolution No. 677 condemning Iraqi attempts to alter the demographic composition of the population of Kuwait.[81]

The post-hostilities references to Chapter VII are to be found in Resolution No. 686 setting out preliminary conditions for a ceasefire;[82] Resolution No. 687 laying down the definitive terms of the

---

[73] Security Council Resolution No. 678, 45 *R.D.S.C.* 27, 27-8 (1990).
[74] See O. Schachter, "United Nations Law in the Gulf Conflict", 85 *A.J.I.L.* 452, 459-60 (1991).
[75] See C. Warbrick, "The Invasion of Kuwait by Iraq - Part II", 40 *I.C.L.Q.* 965, 966 (1991).
[76] See P.-M. Dupuy, "Après la Guerre du Golfe", 95 *R.G.D.I.P.* 621, 624-5 (1991).
[77] Security Council Resolution No. 664, 45 *R.D.S.C.* 21, *id.* (1990).
[78] Security Council Resolution No. 666, 45 *R.D.S.C.* 22, *id.* (1990).
[79] *Supra*, note 48, at 23-4.
[80] Security Council Resolution No. 674, 45 *R.D.S.C.* 26, *id.* (1990).
[81] Security Council Resolution No. 677, 45 *R.D.S.C.* 27, *id.* (1990).
[82] *Supra*, note 50, at 568.

cease-fire;[83] Resolution No. 689 establishing the modalities of operation of the United Nations Iraq-Kuwait Observation Mission (UNIKOM);[84] Resolution No. 692 creating a Compensation Fund for claims against Iraq;[85] Resolution No. 705 deciding that 30% of the Iraqi petroleum exports should be set aside for compensation;[86] Resolution No. 706 permitting Iraqi exports of petroleum up to a certain amount, provided that the proceeds go directly into an escrow account used *inter alia* to cover United Nations costs and appropriate payments to the Compensation Fund;[87] Resolution No. 712 reinforcing and specifying that arrangement;[88] Resolution No. 778 deciding that, absent Iraqi cooperation, the Compensation Fund will be based on Iraqi funds and proceeds from sale of Iraqi petroleum in the hands of other countries;[89] as well as Resolution No. 806 underlining the inviolability of the international boundary between Kuwait and Iraq.[90] In Resolution No. 688 – serving as a basis for an egregious intervention in internal Iraqi affairs (see *supra*, Chapter 4, B, (b)) – the Council, without naming Chapter VII, held that the consequences of the Iraqi repression of the civilian population (particularly the Kurds) "threaten international peace and security in the region".[91]

Once the Council became inured to citing Chapter VII, it has adverted to it in a number of political contexts. Thus, specific references to Chapter VII appear in Resolution No. 748 imposing an air embargo and other sanctions against Libya, by reason of its failure to comply with a demand to surrender for trial certain officials accused of terrorist atrocities (especially the destruction of

---

[83] Security Council Resolution No. 687, 30 *I.L.M.* 847, 849 (1991). On the meaning and significance of this resolution (which is unprecedented in many respects), see S. Sur, "La Résolution 687 (3 Avril 1991) du Conseil de Sécurité dans l'Affaire du Golfe: Problèmes de Rétablissement et de Garantie de la Paix", 37 *A.F.D.I.* 25-97 (1991).

[84] Security Council Resolution No. 689, 30 *I.L.M.* 863, *id.* (1991).

[85] Security Council Resolution No. 692, 30 *I.L.M.* 864, 865 (1991).

[86] Security Council Resolution No. 705, 30 *I.L.M.* 1715, *id.* (1991).

[87] Security Council Resolution No. 706, 30 *I.L.M.* 1719, 1720 (1991).

[88] Security Council Resolution No. 712, 30 *I.L.M.* 1730, *id.* (1991).

[89] Security Council Resolution No. 778, Doc. S/RES/778 (2 October 1992).

[90] Security Council Resolution No. 806, Doc. S/RES/806 (5 February 1993).

[91] *Supra*, note 30, at 859.

Pan American flight 103 at Lockerbie in 1988);[92] Resolution No. 788 imposing an arms embargo on Liberia following civil war in that country;[93] and Resolution No. 794 authorizing the use of "all necessary means" to establish "a secure environment for humanitarian relief operations in Somalia".[94]

The fighting in Yugoslavia - before and after its disintegration - generated manifold references to Chapter VII. These include Resolution No. 713 imposing an arms embargo on Yugoslavia;[95] Resolution No. 724 reaffirming the embargo and establishing a committee to supervise it;[96] Resolution No. 757 (adopted after the dissolution of Yugoslavia) determining unequivocally[97] that the situation - especially in Bosnia and Herzegovina - constitutes a threat to international peace and security, and imposing on Serbia and Montenegro economic sanctions[98] (patterned after Resolution No. 661); Resolution No. 760 allowing for essential humanitarian products to be excepted from the sweeping prohibitions of the preceding resolution;[99] Resolution No. 770 demanding unimpeded access by the International Committee of the Red Cross and other humanitarian organizations to all camps, prisons and detention centres;[100] Resolution No. 771 condemning the policy of "ethnic cleansing" and demanding compliance with international humanitarian law;[101] Resolution No. 787 (where Chapter VII is cited three times) allowing States, acting either individually or regionally, to use "such measures commensurate with the specific circumstances as may be necessary" - a euphemism for the use of force - to inspect cargoes

---

[92] *Supra,* note 21, at 750. On the background of this resolution, see F. Beveridge, "The Lockerbie Affair", 41 *I.C.L.Q.* 907-20 (1992).

[93] Security Council Resolution No. 788, Doc. S/RES/788 (19 November 1992).

[94] Security Council Resolution No. 794, Doc. S/RES/794 (3 December 1992).

[95] Security Council Resolution No. 713 (1991), 31 *I.L.M.* 1431, 1432 (1992).

[96] Security Council Resolution No. 724 (1991), 31 *I.L.M.* 1435, 1436 (1992).

[97] Already in Resolution 713 (*supra,* note 95, at 1433), the Council expressed concern that the *continuation* of the situation in Yugoslavia constitutes a threat to international peace and security. On the ambiguity of the earlier text, see M. Weller, "The International Response to the Dissolution of the Socialist Federal Republic of Yugoslavia", 86 *A.J.I.L.* 569, 579 (1992).

[98] Security Council Resolution No. 757, 31 *I.L.M.* 1453, 1455 (1992).

[99] Security Council Resolution No. 760, 31 *I.L.M.* 1461 *id.* (1992).

[100] Security Council Resolution No. 770, 31 *I.L.M.* 1468, 1469 (1992).

[101] Security Council Resolution No. 771, 31 *I.L.M.* 1470, 1471 (1992).

and to ensure strict implementation of Resolutions Nos. 713 and 757;[102] and Resolution No. 807 determining that repeated violations of the cease-fire in Croatia constitute a threat to peace and security in the region.[103] That determination is reiterated in the context of the decision in Resolution No. 808 to establish an international tribunal for prosecuting offenders against humanitarian law in the former Yugoslavia.[104]

It is manifest from the spate of resolutions that the Council currently interprets its mandate under Chapter VII in the most liberal manner. Indeed, in January 1992, the Council held a special and unprecedented meeting at the level of Heads of States and Governments to discuss its responsibility concerning the maintenance of international peace and security. The Members of the Council reaffirmed their commitment to the collective security system of the Charter, and invited the Secretary-General to submit recommendations for strengthening the effectiveness of this commitment.[105] The Secretary-General, B. Boutros-Ghali, issued his recommendations in June 1992, in a report entitled "An Agenda for Peace".[106] He noted that the Council has not so far made use of Article 42, and suggested that action under this provision "is essential to the credibility of the United Nations as a guarantor of international security".[107] Admittedly, such a move would require concluding the special agreements envisaged in Article 43 (see *infra*, D, (a)), but the Secretary-General felt that negotiations could now be initiated.[108] In the meantime, he recommended that "peace-enforcement units" from Member States - as distinct from peacekeeping forces (see *infra*, D, (b)) - should be made available to the Council "on call".[109] It is too soon to judge whether these interesting and far-reaching proposals are likely to be carried out.

---

[102] Security Council Resolution No. 787, 31 *I.L.M.* 1481, 1483-4 (1992).
[103] Security Council Resolution No. 807, Doc. S/RES/807 (19 February 1993).
[104] Security Council Resolution No. 808, Doc. S/RES/808 (22 February 1993).
[105] Note by the President of the Security Council, 31 *I.L.M.* 759, 781 (1992).
[106] Report of the Secretary-General, "An Agenda for Peace", 31 *I.L.M.* 956 (1992).
[107] *Ibid.*, 966.
[108] *Ibid.*, *id.*
[109] *Ibid.*, *id.*

It is symptomatic that throughout the Gulf War, and equally in other settings, despite the litany of references to Chapter VII, the Council abstained from imposing mandatory military sanctions. The upshot is that, after close to half a century, the key clause in the collective security system – Article 42 – has yet to be made use of. The more recent recoil by the Council from the application of Article 42 was foreshadowed in the Korean War (see *supra*, Chapter 9, E). We have seen that in 1950, too, whereas the Council determined that the North Korean armed attack against the Republic of Korea constituted a breach of the peace, the operative resolution was confined to a mere recommendation that Member States render assistance to the victim[110] (*supra*, Chapter 6, B). Although four decades apart temporally, and light years apart psychologically, the Korean and the Gulf Wars are similar in that the coalitions which gathered to repel armed attacks acted in the exercise of collective self-defence (in conformity with the recommendation or the authorization of the Council) rather than collective security (decreed by the Council in a legally binding fashion).

On another occasion, in 1984, the Council also condemned armed attacks by South Africa against Angola, reaffirmed Angola's right to defend itself under Article 51, and requested Member States to extend assistance to the victim country.[111] Had that resolution become the catalyst for an international coalition, the ensuing use of force would have amounted once again to collective self-defence exercised with the *imprimatur* of the Council. While in Angola's case the resolution remained unheeded, there are all too many instances in which the Council avoided any recommendation. A particularly retrogressive step was taken in the Falkland Islands War of 1982, when the Council determined that there existed a breach of the peace[112] and still refrained from any concrete authorization of military action.

In the course of the "cold war", the record of the Council was replete with instances in which it was deadlocked, due to political cleavages splitting the five Permanent Members. When a breach of

[110] Security Council Resolutions Nos. 82 and 83, 5 *R.D.S.C.* 4-5 (1950).
[111] Security Council Resolution No. 546, 39 *R.D.S.C.* 1, 1-2 (1984).
[112] Security Council Resolution No. 502, 37 *R.D.S.C.* 15, *id.* (1982).

(or a threat to) the peace directly affected one of the five, or even their "client States", the veto power could be counted on to ensure that only an anodyne resolution would be adopted. To this very day, the Council often declines to take meaningful action in the face of threats to (or even breaches of) the peace, if these are entirely local in character and a policy of benign neglect appears likely to contain the conflict (so that the Permanent Members will not become involved).

On the whole, considering that the use of inter-State force is still rampant in the international community, the performance of the Council in almost half a century leaves a lot to be desired. Even in the post-Gulf War period it is deplorably obvious that, in a substantial portion of the conflicts besetting mankind, the Council does not manage to fulfil its mission of maintaining or restoring international peace and security. During the "cold war" it was easy to pin the blame on the use and abuse of the veto power in the Council for which there were abundant illustrations.[113] At present, it is clear that the Council is principally hampered by the lack of standing forces at its disposal.

D. *The Mechanism of Employing Collective Force*

(a) *Special Agreements*

The Charter does not seem to envisage the establishment of a permanent international force, with troops recruited directly by the UN Organization itself. Instead, Article 42 refers to the carrying out of military operations (as decided by the Security Council) through

---

[113] It has been calculated that, between 1946 and the end of 1986, the veto was cast 242 times as regards 203 proposals (meaning that sometimes more than one Permanent Member wielded its power to prevent the adoption of a resolution). See S. D. Bailey, *The Procedure of the UN Security Council* 201-9 (2nd ed., 1988). No doubt, in many of these instances, the item on the agenda had nothing to do with collective security. Conversely, in numerous other cases, the mere threat of a veto had a chilling effect, so that the Council did not proceed to a formal vote. In the political atmosphere prevalent in the "cold war", enforcement measures involving military action were not even contemplated by the Council when some wars broke out. See A. C. Arend, "The Falklands War and the Failure of the International Legal Order", *The Falklands War* 52, 54-5 (A. R. Coll and A. C. Arend eds., 1985).

the forces of Member States. How will these forces be accessible to the Council? Under Article 43, UN Members are obligated to make available to the Council the necessary armed forces, but the duty is subject to the condition that this will be done "in accordance with a special agreement or agreements" (governing the numbers and types of forces, their degree of readiness and general location).[114] The rationale underlying the scheme of the special agreements is plain. The Council cannot accomplish the mission assigned to it by the Charter, unless it acts swiftly once a crisis breaks out. Since no permanent international force exists, advance preparations have to be made for the rapid deployment of forces belonging to Member States. In particular, Member States must identify combat-ready units that can be drawn upon by the Council at a moment's notice.

It stands to reason that the Council is not required to conclude a special agreement with all UN Members, not even all Permanent Members of the Council.[115] But the question is whether a Member is bound to place armed forces at the disposal of the Council when no special agreement has been signed. There are two conflicting interpretations of the Charter on this issue. One approach is that the Council may insist on Members furnishing military units at its behest, although no special agreements are concluded (or in excess of the forces pledged in the agreements).[116] The other, and more common, opinion is that the duty of Members under the Charter - to do their share in a collective security operation mounted by the Council - is purely abstract, and, unless it is concretized in special agreements, the Members may evade their undertaking.[117]

Article 43 prescribes that the special agreements "shall be negotiated as soon as possible on the initiative of the Security Council". Nevertheless, almost half a century later, no special agreements have been reached, and this crucial provision is sometimes looked upon as a dead letter.[118] Article 106 enunciates that, pending the coming into force of the special agreements referred to in Article

[114] *Supra*, note 9, at 344.
[115] See L. M. Goodrich and A. P. Simons, *The United Nations and the Maintenance of International Peace and Security* 395-6 (1955).
[116] See H. Kelsen, *supra*, note 26, at 756.
[117] See C. Chaumont, "Nations Unies et Neutralité", 89 *R.C.A.D.I.* 1, 39-40 (1956).
[118] See O. Schachter, *supra*, note 74, at 464.

43, the five Permanent Members shall consult with a view to taking "such joint action on behalf of the Organization as may be necessary for the purpose of maintaining international peace and security".[119] Although Article 106 was expected to be transitional, it vests the Permanent Members with "an almost unlimited power for an indefinite period of time".[120] However, inasmuch as action must be joint, it presupposes unity among the five. "The special agreements called for in Article 43 have never been concluded because of disagreement among the permanent members, and this same inability to agree has rendered ineffective the provisions of Article 106".[121]

Article 44 stipulates that, before being called upon to provide armed forces, a UN Member not represented in the Council will be invited to participate in any decisions concerning the employment of these forces.[122] The case is exceptional, for a regular UN Member is hereby entitled not just to have its voice heard in the deliberations of the Council, but actually to take part in the Council's decision-making process by voting on any proposal (albeit only in regard to the employment of the Member's own armed forces).[123] All the same, the Member has only one vote, and it may be overruled by the majority in the Council.

To facilitate the launching of a combined UN enforcement action in urgent cases, Member States are instructed by Article 45 to keep air force contingents immediately available.[124] This clause, too, is conditional on the existence of the special agreements projected in Article 43.

Articles 46 and 47 establish a Military Staff Committee, consisting of the Chiefs of Staff of the five Permanent Members of the Council or their representatives, its mission being to advise and assist the Council on all military matters.[125] The Committee was stalemated in the early days of the UN, and, while continuing to meet periodically, it "has done no substantive work for almost forty

---

119 *Supra*, note 9, at 362.
120 H. Kelsen, *supra*, note 26, at 761.
121 L. M. Goodrich, E. Hambro and A. P. Simons, *supra*, note 16, at 631.
122 *Supra*, note 9, at 344.
123 See L. M. Goodrich, E. Hambro and A. P. Simons, *supra*, note 16, at 327.
124 *Supra*, note 9, at 344-5.
125 *Ibid.*, 345.

years".[126] Interestingly enough, in Resolution No. 665 (adopted in August 1990), the Security Council requested the States "co-operating with the Government of Kuwait" - while carrying out a blockade of Iraq - to coordinate their actions using the mechanism of the Military Staff Committee.[127] However, the American-led coalition preferred to leave the Committee dormant.[128]

(b) *Peacekeeping Forces*

As a result of the failure to conclude special agreements, under Article 43, no advance preparations have been made for prompt action in the event of a breach of the peace, and no standing military units are ready to do as the Security Council bids. Yet, the Council is not completely impotent. Over the years, a number of UN forces have been set up (not always by the Council itself) for service in Korea, the Middle East, etc.[129]

The common denominator of all UN forces created so far is that they have come into being *ad hoc*, as and when required in specific cases, and their dependence on voluntary cooperation by Member States (willing to contribute the military contingents of which the forces are composed) has been absolute.[130] The only UN force ever mobilized for the purpose of direct combat against a sovereign State was the first one, in Korea.[131] Subsequent UN forces have come to be known as "peacekeeping" operations. While peacekeeping forces may have manifold missions,[132] the principal one is to form a *cordon sanitaire*, setting opponents apart and preventing bloodshed.[133]

---

[126] S. D. Bailey, *supra*, note 113, at 253.

[127] *Supra*, note 65, at 22.

[128] See G. K. Walker, "The Crisis over Kuwait, August 1990 - February 1991", 1 *D.J.C.I.L.* 25, 49 (1991).

[129] On the different ways in which UN forces were initially set up, see F. Seyersted, *United Nations Forces* 128-43 (1966).

[130] See R. Sommereyns, "United Nations Forces", 4 *E.P.I.L.* 253, 254-6 (1982).

[131] See D. Schindler, "United Nations Forces and International Humanitarian Law", *Studies and Essays on International Humanitarian Law and Red Cross Principles in Honour of J. Pictet* 521, 522 (C. Swinarski ed., 1984).

[132] See E. Suy, "United Nations Peacekeeping System", 4 *E.P.I.L.* 258, 262 (1982).

[133] See E. Jiménez de Aréchaga, "International Law in the Past Third of a Century", 159 *R.C.A.D.I.* 1, 130 (1978).

As it has evolved over the years, a peacekeeping operation is completely different from an enforcement action. The two special attributes of a peacekeeping force are that (i) it is established and maintained with the consent of all the States concerned; and (ii) it is not authorized to take military action against any State.[134] These special features are generally conceded, yet they are not free of difficulties.

The concept of consent has stirred up a number of thorny problems in its practical application.[135] Consent may also be induced by the Security Council in circumstances where the State concerned has little or no real choice. Thus, the United Nations Iraq-Kuwait Observation Mission (UNIKOM) was set up with Iraq's reluctant consent after that country's military defeat in the Gulf War.[136] Resolution No. 689 (1991) proclaimed categorically that the deployment of UNIKOM "can only be terminated by a decision of the Council".[137]

Insofar as combat is at issue, some peacekeeping forces have been empowered to resort to force against non-State elements.[138] On top of that, the possibility cannot be ruled out that a UN force, although structured as a peacekeeping operation, will in fact become entangled in hostilities against a State.[139] However, a peacekeeping force is not intended to impose military sanctions on States.

Since all UN forces have hitherto consisted of national contingents, assembled on a purely voluntary and *ad hoc* basis, the component units are neither fully integrated nor released from national discipline. In the words of Lord Pearce in the *Nissan* case (which arose before the UK House of Lords, in 1969, and related to the United Nations Force in Cyprus):

> the commander of the United Nations force is head in the chain of command and is answerable to the United Nations. The functions of the force as a whole are international. But its individual

---

[134] See *Certain Expenses of the United Nations (Article 17, Paragraph 2, of the Charter)*, [1962] *I.C.J. Rep.* 151, 170, 177.

[135] See J. I. Garvey, "United Nations Peacekeeping and Host State Consent", 64 *A.J.I.L.* 241-69 (1970).

[136] *Supra*, note 83, at 850.

[137] *Supra*, note 84, at 863.

[138] See E. Suy, *supra*, note 132, at 262.

[139] See F. Seyersted, *supra*, note 129, at 210.

component forces have their own national duty and discipline and remain in their own national service.[140]

When an international force is put together for strictly peacekeeping (as opposed to enforcement) purposes, it does not come within the compass of Chapter VII. For that reason, it need not be set up specifically by the Security Council (or any other organ of the United Nations). Under a Protocol annexed to the Egyptian-Israeli Treaty of Peace of 1979, the parties requested the United Nations to provide forces and observers for supervising the implementation of the terms agreed upon between them.[141] When it turned out that the Security Council was unable to accede to that request, Egypt and Israel (with the active assistance of the United States) concluded in 1981 another Protocol Establishing the Sinai Multinational Force and Observers.[142] This Force operates successfully in lieu of the UN force originally visualized, without being linked to the UN Organization.[143]

E. Is There an Alternative to the Security Council?

(a) The General Assembly

The impasse reached by the Security Council during the "cold war" - as a result of frequent exercise of the veto power - became apparent shortly after the entry into force of the Charter. In 1950, the General Assembly adopted a famous Resolution - entitled "Uniting for Peace" - which was supposed to surmount the obstacles standing in the way of concerted international action in the face of aggression:

> Resolves that if the Security Council, because of lack of unanimity of the permanent members, fails to exercise its primary responsibility for the maintenance of international peace and security in any case where there appears to be a threat to the peace, breach

---

[140] Attorney-General v. Nissan (1969), [1970] A.C. 179, 223.
[141] Egypt-Israel, Treaty of Peace, 1979, 18 I.L.M. 362, 367, 372 (1979) (Article VI).
[142] Egypt-Israel, Protocol Establishing the Sinai Multinational Force and Observers, 1981, 20 I.L.M. 1190 (1981).
[143] See T. M. Franck, Nation against Nation 180 (1985).

of the peace, or act of aggression, the General Assembly shall consider the matter immediately with a view to making appropriate recommendations to Members for collective measures, including in the case of a breach of the peace or act of aggression the use of armed force when necessary, to maintain or restore international peace and security. If not in session at the time, the General Assembly may meet in emergency special session within twenty-four hours of the request therefor.[144]

When adopted, the "Uniting for Peace" Resolution was greeted as "epoch-making".[145] With the passage of time, much of the original appeal of the Resolution has vanished. The radical increase in the composition of the General Assembly has turned it into an unwieldy body, ill-suited for the task at hand.[146] Apart from its size, the overall record of the General Assembly has given rise to a lot of criticism and a sense of disenchantment. It has been aptly remarked that "members of the Non-Aligned Movement (NAM) regularly disport their numerical preponderance to heighten tensions and hinder dialogue".[147]

There is no need to dwell upon the fact that the "Uniting for Peace" Resolution did not, and could not, amend the Charter. Nowhere in the text did the General Assembly purport to arrogate powers exceeding those allotted to it in the Charter.[148] Nor does the Resolution say that the General Assembly will supplant the Security Council.

The central question concerning "Uniting for Peace" is often presented as one of defining a failure on the part of the Security Council to exercise its responsibility or, at least, ascertaining which UN organ is to decide that such a failure has occurred.[149] But, in reality, this is a side issue. The main problem is that, in all matters pertaining to international peace and security, the General

---

[144] General Assembly Resolution No. 377 (v), 5 R.G.A. 10, id. (1950).

[145] L. H. Woolsey, "The 'Uniting for Peace' Resolution of the United Nations", 45 A.J.I.L. 129, 130 (1951).

[146] P. R. Baehr and L. Gordenker, The United Nations 78 (1984).

[147] T. M. Franck, supra, note 143, at 117.

[148] See J. Andrassy, "Uniting for Peace", 50 A.J.I.L. 563, 572 (1956).

[149] See H. Reicher, "The Uniting for Peace Resolution on the Thirtieth Anniversary of Its Passage", 20 C.J.T.L. 1, 10 (1981).

Assembly is authorized (under Chapter IV)[150] to adopt only non-binding recommendations. Each Member State "remains legally free to act or not to act on such recommendation".[151] In its Advisory Opinion of 1962, in the *Certain Expenses* case, the International Court of Justice held that - although, generally speaking, the responsibility of the Security Council respecting the maintenance of international peace and security is "primary" rather than exclusive - only the Council possesses the power to impose explicit obligations of compliance under Chapter VII.[152]

From time to time, especially in the 1970s, the General Assembly appears to have "pre-empted, prejudged or usurped the role or work of the Security Council" in the realm of international peace and security.[153] As a rule, General Assembly resolutions calling for sanctions against States[154] have been ignored in practice. But even if Member States were to take coercive action against a particular country in the wake of a General Assembly recommendation - and in the absence of a legally binding decision of the Security Council - such action would not assume the nature of authentic collective security. Any forcible measures employed may be politically fortified by the resolution, but the General Assembly is incapable of placing them on a new juridical footing.[155] In that, a General Assembly resolution falls conspicuously short of a Security Council decision, which (by dint of Articles 42 and 51) can legitimize an otherwise unlawful use of force.

A General Assembly recommendation to employ force should be interpreted as an exhortation addressed to Member States, to take joint action in the exercise of their inherent right to collective

---

[150] *Supra*, note 9, at 334-8.

[151] J. Stone, *Legal Controls of International Conflict* 274-5 (1954).

[152] *Supra*, note 134, at 163.

[153] N. D. White, *The United Nations and the Maintenance of International Peace and Security* 113, 118 ff. (1990).

[154] See, e.g., General Assembly Resolution No. ES-9/1, 9th Emergency Special Session *R.G.A.* 3 (1982). Here the General Assembly called upon Member States to suspend military and economic assistance to Israel; to sever diplomatic, trade and cultural relations with it; and in general to isolate it in all fields (*ibid.*, 3-4).

[155] See C. Leben, "Les Contre-Mesures Inter-Etatiques et les Réactions a l'Illicite dans la Société Internationale", 28 *A.F.D.I.* 9, 33 (1982).

self-defence[156] (see *supra,* Chapter 9). Unlike a similar recommendation by the Security Council (see *supra,* C), the General Assembly
is unable even to stamp the action with a legal seal of approval as
self-defence. Having said that, we cannot accept the assertion that
the General Assembly lacks competence to recommend that Members resort to self-defence.[157] As long as the Security Council retains
its ultimate power to come to grips with the situation, there is no valid
reason to deny the prerogative of the General Assembly to encourage
Member States to exercise a right which is bestowed upon them under
the Charter (as well as customary international law).

Collective security differs from collective self-defence in that the
right to decide whether to fight an aggressor is accorded not to
every single State, but to a central organ of the international community. It is settled in the Charter that the organ in question is the
Security Council. When the Council fails to carry out its mandate,
no other UN organ can serve as its surrogate. Collective self-defence
may be organized on the initiative of the General Assembly. Yet, if
it is, freedom of inaction redounds on every Member State.

When the Security Council refrains from setting in motion collective security measures, any force used by States must be restricted to self-defence (individual or collective), namely, a response
to an armed attack. The "Uniting for Peace" Resolution was carefully phrased in specifying that the General Assembly may recommend recourse to armed force only when an actual breach of the
peace or aggression occurs, and not in circumstances of a threat to
the peace. Perhaps the Resolution ought to have been drafted even
more meticulously, for, under the Charter, a breach of the peace or
aggression as such is not an adequate justification for the use of
counter-force (unauthorized by the Security Council), unless it constitutes an armed attack.

(b) *The International Court of Justice*

In the *Nicaragua* case, the United States challenged the jurisdiction of the International Court of Justice (as a judicial organ) to deal

---

[156] See A. V. W. Thomas and A. J. Thomas, *Non-Intervention* 175-6 (1956).
[157] See H. Kelsen, *Recent Trends in the Law of the United Nations* 979 (1951).

with complaints concerning the unlawful use of force (including acts of aggression or other breaches af the peace), on the ground that this is a task assigned by the Charter to the political organs of the United Nations, chiefly the Security Council.[158] The Court, in 1984, rejected the argument, inasmuch as the responsibility ascribed to the Security Council in this domain is only "primary" and not exclusive.[159] The Judgment distinguished between the purely judicial role of the Court and the political duties entrusted to the Council.[160] In the Court's words, "[b]oth organs can therefore perform their separate but complementary functions with respect to the same events".[161] Judge Schwebel upheld the same line of approach in his Dissenting Opinion of 1986:

> while the Security Council is invested by the Charter with the authority to determine the existence of an act of aggression, it does not act as a court in making such a determination. It may arrive at a determination of aggression – or, as more often is the case, fail to arrive at a determination of aggression – for political rather than legal reasons. However compelling the facts which could give rise to a determination of aggression, the Security Council acts within its rights when it decides that to make such a determination will set back the cause of peace rather than advance it. In short, the Security Council is a political organ which acts for political reasons. It may take legal considerations into account but, unlike a court, it is not bound to apply them.[162]

This is a correct analysis of the powers of the Security Council. Under the Charter, the Council is put in charge of the all-important mission of maintaining or restoring international peace and security. The Council must concentrate on that task, functioning as a political rather than a judicial organ. As stressed by Sir Gerald Fitzmaurice, the Council is not supposed to settle a dispute as such,

---

[158] *Case Concerning Military and Paramilitary Activities in and against Nicaragua* (Jurisdiction), [1984] *I.C.J. Rep.* 392, 431-3.

[159] *Ibid.,* 434.

[160] *Ibid.,* 435.

[161] *Ibid., id.*

[162] *Case Concerning Military and Paramilitary Activities in and against Nicaragua* (Merits), [1986] *I.C.J. Rep.* 14, 290.

or to prevent or punish any violation of international law, although indirectly it may achieve these results as well.[163] The Council is not the most suitable body to pass judgment as to which side in an armed conflict is "guilty of violating its legal obligations"; such a determination may indeed impede it from taking the measures conducive to the safeguarding of international peace and security.[164] By contrast, the Court, not being hampered by political constraints or by motivations of expediency, is fully qualified to bring legal yardsticks to bear upon the armed conflict in a dispassionate fashion.[165]

Since the Council and the Court are both authorized to pronounce on the same events – one body applying political, and the other legal, criteria – the question that comes to mind is how to obviate the theoretical contingency of two contradictory, equally binding, decisions being reached by the two organs simultaneously. Most assuredly, such a clash is not likely to develop in reality. The Council's foremost problem is not a surfeit but a paucity of mandatory decisions adopted in matters of collective security (or even self-defence), especially when one of the parties to the dispute is a Permanent Member of the Council equipped with the veto power. The Court is not often seized with disputes of this type, either. For jurisdictional and other reasons, it is reasonable to assume that the "judicial regulation of armed conflicts will remain peripheral" in the future.[166] Besides, once the Council issues a verdict about the occurrence of an act of aggression, it is hard to believe that the Court would be inclined to contradict it. Nevertheless, as a matter of speculative inquiry, the scenario of a potential collision between the Council and the Court cannot be lightly dismissed. What happens if the Council determines that an act of aggression has been committed by Arcadia against Utopia, whereas the Court rules that Arcadia is not to blame and that it is actually the victim of

[163] G. G. Fitzmaurice, "The Foundations of the Authority of International Law and the Problem of Enforcement", 19 *Mod.L.R.* 1, 5 (1956).

[164] O. Schachter, "The Quasi-Judicial Role of the Security Council and the General Assembly", 58 *A.J.I.L.* 960, *id.* (1964).

[165] See B. S. Chimni, "The International Court and the Maintenance of Peace and Security: The Nicaragua Decision and the United States Response", 35 *I.C.L.Q.* 960, 967-9 (1986).

[166] O. Schachter, "Self-Defense and the Rule of Law", 83 *A.J.I.L.* 259, 276-7 (1989).

aggression initiated by Utopia? In the *Nicaragua* case, the Court observed that, in the context of those proceedings, it was not "asked to say that the Security Council was wrong".[167] But what would the Court do in the future, if it is requested to say precisely that?

One way to resolve the difficulty is to apportion different time-frames for the performance of the dissimilar functions of the Council and the Court. Thus, in an on-going armed conflict (as argued by the United States),[168] it would be preferable for the Security Council alone to exercise its mission of restoring international peace and security. The Council may ordain a cease-fire, insist on withdrawal of forces, and even initiate an enforcement action, without tackling the legality of the underlying issues. The measures taken by the Council need not diminish from the power of the Court to investigate the legality of the use of force – as well as other legal rights and wrongs – after the hostilities are over. In the aftermath of the fighting, the Court will be at liberty to take a fresh look at the situation from the perspective of juridical standards. It may then come to conclusions that are at variance with those previously reached by the Council. For instance, the Court may rule that a disputed territorial zone, from which Arcadia was ordered by the Council to withdraw, actually belongs to it. In that case, Arcadian troops would be allowed to reoccupy the area.

Analytically, given different time-frames and divergent criteria for decision-making, there need be no real collision between a decree by the Council and a different ruling by the Court. The Council's responsibility in an on-going conflict is to restore international peace and security. The Court's role is to settle disputes in accordance with international law. The restoration of peace is more urgent than the settlement of the dispute, and it should be given temporal priority. But the measures taken by the Council are not necessarily the last word on the subject. The final judgment is left to the Court (provided, of course, that it has jurisdiction).

There is a remote possibility that the parties to an armed conflict (acting together) may elect to submit their dispute to the Court, even in the midst of hostilities. Should that happen, there is no reason

---

[167] *Supra*, note 158, at 436.
[168] *Ibid., id.*

for the Court to decline jurisdiction.[169] "Because litigation is a way of depoliticising a dispute", a decision to go to the Court would signal a "desire to reduce tension and pursue a peaceful settlement".[170] Under these circumstances, the Council ought to allow the Court to exercise its judicial powers without undue interference, although a cease-fire order will not be out of place.

Nevertheless, if the parties to the conflict are not at one in their desire to bring their dispute before the Court, and as long as hostilities are not terminated, it is submitted that the Court ought to exercise judicial restraint. The reason is not that the "factual matrix is fluid and constantly changing",[171] but that the Court should do whatever it can to avoid an actual or potential clash with the Council. While the armed conflict continues, and in the absence of agreement between the parties as to the Court's jurisdiction, the Court ought to defer to the Council, letting it discharge its duties pursuant to the Charter. If an application instituting contentious proceedings is filed with the Court *pendente bello,* unless all the parties explicitly urge the Court to entertain the dispute without delay, it is on the whole better to regard the case as unripe - as yet - for judicial determination.

---

[169] See R. B. Bilder, "Judicial Procedures Relating to the Use of Force", 31 *V.J.I.L.* 249, 265 (1990-1).
[170] J. G. Merrills, *International Dispute Settlement* 149 (2nd ed., 1991).
[171] K. Highet, "Evidence, the Court, and the Nicaragua Case", 81 *A.J.I.L.* 1, 43 (1987).

CONCLUSION

Aggressive war is currently forbidden by both customary and conventional international law, and it even constitutes a crime against peace. The legal proscription of war forms the bedrock of the contemporary international legal system. Admittedly, to date, the prohibition has not had a profound impact on the actual conduct of States. As of now, its imprint has been more noticeable in the vocabulary of States. An international climate has been generated in which the term "war" has an unsavoury connotation. Hence, while States continue to wage war, they prefer to describe their activities in more palatable euphemisms.[1] One may say, in a combination of cynicism and realism, that so far the legal abolition of war has stamped out not wars but declarations of war. This lip-service to the cause of peace may be hypocritical. However, as pithily put by La Rochefoucauld, "*l'hypocrisie est un hommage que le vice rend à la vertu*".[2] The recognition of virtue is an indispensable first step without which no vice is likely to be eliminated.

Nevertheless, a taboo on the use of the word "war" in legal analysis makes no sense at all.[3] The fact that war is banished linguistically will not make it vanish empirically. Whether we employ this or that phrase does not alter the incontrovertible truth that comprehensive armed conflicts still permeate international relations. If the phenomenon of war is to be eradicated, it must be faced and not ignored. Otherwise, all that we are left with is hypocrisy.

For aggressive war (as well as unlawful uses of force short of war) to disappear, the international community must establish effective measures of collective security. The "harnessing" of force to international procedures of law and order is the real challenge of our day.[4]

---

[1] For the practice of States since the UN Charter, see C. Greenwood, "The Concept of War in Modern International Law", 36 *I.C.L.Q.* 283, 290-4 (1987).

[2] La Rochefoucauld, *Oeuvres Complètes* 432 (*Maxime* 218) (Gallimard ed., 1964).

[3] See R. R. Baxter, "The Law of War", U.S. Naval War College, 62 *International Law Studies* 209, *id.* (Readings in International Law, R. R. Lillich and J. N. Moore eds., 1980).

[4] R. Y. Jennings, "General Course on Principles of International Law", 121 *R.C.A.D.I.* 323, 584 (1967).

Unfortunately, the lacklustre performance of the United Nations Security Council (which has been entrusted with this task by the Charter) has instigated widespread disappointment and dissatisfaction. In its first meeting at a level of Heads of States and Governments in January 1992, the members of the Council noted that, while the end of the "cold war" produced a momentous change and raised hopes for a safer world, the search for peace is far from over.[5] Proposals for concrete action, submitted by the Secretary-General (in June 1992) in response to the Council's invitation,[6] strike a chord worldwide. But it is not patently clear at the time of writing whether the collective security mechanism of the United Nations - embedded in Article 42 of the Charter - is likely to be revitalized in a "New World Order".

As long as the Charter's scheme of collective security fails to function adequately, States are left to their own devices when confronted with an unlawful use of force. Again and again, they invoke the right of (individual or collective) self-defence in response to an armed attack. Thus, instead of being a provisional interlude pending the exercise of collective security, self-defence (individual as well as collective) has virtually taken the place of collective security.[7] The very "centre of gravity in the United Nations has swung from Article 39 to Article 51".[8]

As demonstrated by the Gulf War, even when the Security Council itself unanimously desires to repel aggression and to restore international peace and security, a coalition bearing the standard of collective self-defence has to be forged in order to attain this purpose. Thus, notwithstanding the palpable changes in the world political landscape since the termination of the "cold war", the right of self-defence - individual and collective - remains the principal shield against armed attacks.

---

[5] Note by the President of the Security Council, 31 *I.L.M.* 759, 760 (1992).

[6] Secretary-General, An Agenda for Peace, 31 *I.L.M.* 956, 966 (1992).

[7] See H. Kelson, "Collective Security and Collective Self-Defense under the Charter of the United Nations", 42 *A.J.I.L.* 783, 785 (1948).

[8] N. Feinberg, *Studies in International Law* 70 (1979).

INDEX OF PERSONS

INDEX OF SUBJECTS